The Impact of World War I

A note for the general reader

Total War and Social Change: Europe 1914–1955 is an honours-level history course produced by the Open University. War and Society has always been a subject of special interest and expertise in the Open University's History Department. The appeal for the general reader is that the five books in the series, taken together or singly, consist of authoritative, up-to-date discussions of the various aspects of war and society in the twentieth century.

The books provide insights into the modes of teaching and communication, including the use of audio-visual material, which have been pioneered at the Open University. Readers will find that they are encouraged to participate in a series of 'tutorials in print', an effective way to achieve a complete command of the material. As in any serious study of a historical topic, there are many suggestions for further reading, including references to a Course Reader, set book and to two collections of primary sources which accompany the series. It is possible to grasp the basic outlines of the topics discussed without turning to these books, but obviously serious students will wish to follow up what is, in effect a very carefully designed course of guided reading, and discussion and analysis of that reading. The first unit in Book 1 sets out the aims and scope of the course.

Open University students are provided with supplementary material, including a *Course Guide* which gives information on student assignments, summer school, the use of video cassettes, and so on.

Total War and Social Change: Europe 1914–1955

Book 1 *Europe in 1914*
Book 2 *The Impact of World War I*
Book 3 *Between Two Wars*
Book 4 *The Impact of World War II*
Book 5 *Retrospect: War and Change in Europe 1914–1955*

Other material associated with the course

Primary Sources 1: World War I, eds Arthur Marwick and Wendy Simpson, Open University, 2000

Primary Sources 2: Interwar and World War II, eds Arthur Marwick and Wendy Simpson, Open University, 2000

Secondary Sources, eds Arthur Marwick and Wendy Simpson, Open University, 2000

Total War and Historical Change: Europe 1914–1955, eds. Clive Emsley, Arthur Marwick and Wendy Simpson, Open University Press, 2000 (Course Reader)

J. M. Roberts, *Europe 1880–1945,* Longman, 2001 (third edition) (Set Book)

The Open University

book 2

The Impact of World War I

Bernard Waites, Arthur Marwick, Bill Purdue, James Chapman, Clive Emsley, David Englander and Mark Pittaway

Total War and Social Change: Europe 1914–1955

This publication forms part of an Open University course: AA312 *Total War And Social Change: Europe 1914–1955.* Details of this and other Open University courses can be obtained from the Course Reservations Centre, PO Box 724, The Open University, Milton Keynes MK7 6ZS, United Kingdom: tel. +44 (0)1908 653231, e-mail ces-gen@open.ac.uk

Alternatively, you may visit the Open University website at http://www.open.ac.uk where you can learn more about the wide range of courses and packs offered at all levels by the Open University.

For availability of this or other components, contact Open University Worldwide Ltd, The Berrill Building, Walton Hall, Milton Keynes MK7 6AA, United Kingdom: tel. +44 (0)1908 858785; fax +44 (0)1908 858787; e-mail ouwenq@open.ac.uk; website http://www.ouw.co.uk

The Open University, Walton Hall, Milton Keynes, MK7 6AA

First published 2001 by The Open University. Reprinted 2002, 2006.

Edited, designed and typeset by The Open University

Printed and bound in Malta by Gutenberg Press.

ISBN 978 0 7492 1694 8

Cover illustration: Luciano Archille Mauzan, *For Liberation, Subscribe* (1917), 139.2 x 96.5 cm. Imperial War Museum, London.

2.1

385860B/aa312b2i2.1

CONTENTS

Acknowledgements

Grateful acknowledgement is made to the following sources for permission to use material in this book:

Text

Usborne, C. (1992) *The Politics of the Body in Weimar Germany: Women's Reproductive Rights and Duties,* Macmillan Press Ltd.

Tables

Table 11–13.1: Vernadsky, G. *et.al.* (eds) (1972) *A Source Book for Russian History from Early Times to 191,* vol. 3, Yale University Press; *Tables 11–13.2, 13.3, 13.4:* Koenker, D. (1976) 'Moscow workers in 1917', *unpublished PhD Thesis,* © D. Koenker, 1976; *Tables 11–13.5, 13.6, 13.7:* Ferro, M. (1972) *The Russian Revolution of February 1917,* Routledge and Kegan Paul; Table *11–13.10:* Bessel, R. (1993) *Germany After the First World War,* Oxford University Press; *Table 11–13.11:* Tobin, E. H. (1985) 'War and the working class: the case of Düsseldorf 1914–1918', *Central European History,* vol. 23, American Historical Association, Emory University; *Table 11–13.12:* Hardach, G. (1977) *The First World War 1914–1918,* Penguin; *Table 11–13.13:* Wall, R. and Winter, J. M. (eds) (1988) *The Upheaval of War,* Cambridge University Press; *Table 11–13.14:* Wegs, R. J. (1970) 'Austrian economic mobilization during World War I, with particular emphasis on heavy industry', unpublished PhD thesis, University of Illinois; *Table 11–13.15:* Wegs, J. R. (1976/7) 'The marshalling of copper: an index of Austro-Hungarian economic mobilization during World War I', *Austrian History Yearbook,* vol. 12–13, Rice University, Texas; *Table 11–13.16:* Spence, R. B. (1981) 'Yugoslavia, the Austro-Hungarian army and the First World War', unpublished PhD thesis, University of California.

Every effort has been made to trace all the copyright owners, but if any has been inadvertently overlooked, the publishers will be pleased to make the necessary arrangements at the first opportunity.

Unit 6 THE NATURE OF THE FIRST WORLD WAR

BERNARD WAITES

Open University students of this unit will need to refer to:

Set book: J. M. Roberts, *Europe 1880–1945*, Longman, 2001

Primary Sources 1: World War I, eds Arthur Marwick and Wendy Simpson, Open University, 2000

Social + economic factors & | political factors: each countries' objectives

Nature of the warfare led to consequences: nobody willing to compromise

1. "Resource denial" (p.4)   eg nitrates for explosives (p.5)

2. "Modern manufacturing" (p.4)

3. No treaties governing conduct of war (p.6)   <u>Beckett (p.27)</u>
   — only ratified war blockades (Dec. Treaty of London - 1909)
   — conduct had consequences — ie. U-boats (p.6)

4. Professional commanders lost in opening months of war (p.11)
   — replacements less knowledgeable/professional

5. Couldn't win the war w/conventional technology available to them.

(Total War) Strachan + Beckett
            (p.256 onwards)

A. Germans, under Ludendorff, looked to machinery + equipment
   to solve the ~~█████~~ deadlock. (p.13)

Britain didn't! (p.14)

1   SETTING THE GLOBAL SCENE

Introduction

The aim of this unit is to answer three deceptively simple questions: why did the European war that began in August 1914 last as long as it did? why did it become a 'world' war? in what ways was it a 'total' war? By answering them, you will, I hope, grasp the technological, military, political and economic conditions that made the war '*the* seminal catastrophe' of the twentieth century. But a word of caution: the war was not a homogeneous experience and we should not suppose that it had a unitary 'nature'. In Trevor Wilson's phrase, this was a war with 'myriad faces'. The most culturally familiar, and the one memorialized in every town and village, is the western front. This face is 'familiar' almost in the sense of being 'part of the family'. My father's father, a private in the Shropshire Light Infantry, was killed there in August 1918, and if – as is quite likely – you too grew up in a family that had lost men to the war, they almost certainly died in France and Flanders where the techniques of mechanized and depersonalized warfare came of age. Three out of five casualties were due to artillery shell fire, killed or wounded by an enemy who had never seen them; relatively few were invalided out by the infectious diseases that had plagued armies in the past. But the 'face' of war in its other theatres was very different. Those combatants with comparatively backward economies and infrastructures, and with largely illiterate forces, lost far more men to disease and desertion than they did to combat: in the Ottoman armies, seven times as many men died of illness as died of wounds during the war. Serbia had the highest mortality rate in 1914–18 partly because of the typhus epidemic of 1915 that devastated her retreating army and killed at least 300,000 civilians.

There were stark contrasts not only at the front but also in the civilian experience of war, especially between occupied and unoccupied zones and between 'Atlantic' and Central Europe. The German authorities imposed a brutal regime on occupied Belgium and ten *départements* of northern France: undernourished men were compelled to dig trenches for the German army, hostages were shot without trial, businesses were virtually confiscated. The Belgians had to pay the costs of their own occupation and, in late 1916, large numbers of unemployed men were deported to work in German factories. In Central Europe, especially in the big cities that were chronically short of food from 1916, civilian health deteriorated and living standards declined for the vast majority. Destitute Viennese with no relatives in the country starved to death in 1918. The British Home Front seems almost rosy by comparison: civilian health and living standards improved during the war: with full employment for men from early 1915, and the more frequent employment of women and adolescents, family income rose. Infants and schoolchildren became better fed and clothed; men of 45 found they were no longer too old for work.

There is a further question worth asking before we proceed: was 1914–18 the *first* 'world' war? I think not. Since the late sixteenth century, Europe's maritime and colonial expansion had carried the organized violence of the European states to all quarters of the globe. By the mid eighteenth century, coalition wars involving the maritime powers automatically had extra-European dimensions: the great battlefields were in Europe, but colonies and colonial commerce were major stakes in the conflicts, and the naval powers waged economic warfare by interdicting their enemies' overseas trade. A blockade strategy denied access to strategic raw materials and markets for manufactures (as well as cutting off state revenues from import duties) but had the inherent tendency to extend the scope of European wars by infringing neutrals' rights to trade. In 1812, during the last and longest of the pre-industrial world wars, Britain's blockade of Napoleonic Europe embroiled her in conflict with the United States of America.

A European war in a global economy

1914–18 bore some resemblance to previous world wars: the military outcome was decided in Europe but with 'satellite' campaigns – fought mainly by colonial troops – in Gallipoli, Salonika, Mesopotamia, Palestine and East Africa; neutrals were drawn into the conflict by the waging of economic warfare; the victors (Britain and France) extended their empires by stripping the vanquished (Germany and Turkey) of colonies and dependencies. So, what was unprecedented about 1914–18 and its settlement? Clearly, it was the first coalition war between great industrial powers. But I would add it was the first coalition war waged in the global economy created by industrialization and by the complex international division of labour that emerged after Britain became a specialist manufacturer and provider of services. Modern manufacturing enabled the belligerents to expend shells, poison gas, artillery and other industrial products on a prodigious scale, and industrialized warfare became a struggle between rival munitions industries. But only a continental economy, such as the USA, can be both industrialized and self-sufficient, and the war also became a struggle to supply these industries and feed the belligerent populations. Though not the first 'world war', it was the first to be fought at the world's industrialized heartland in which extra-European resources of food, *matériel* and manpower were indispensable for victory, and resource denial was a central part of wartime strategy.

To grasp why this was so we must remind ourselves that, in the two generations before 1914, Europe's advanced industrialized powers had relied increasingly on imports of food and raw materials, and on exports overseas to dispose of part of their manufactured output. Through the expansion of foreign trade and investment, the adoption of the Gold Standard and the free movement of labour and capital, the world's major economies had reached a degree of interdependence not matched again until about 1970. Britain was the most import-dependent economy: about a quarter of national income was spent on imports in 1913 and considerably more than half its food came from abroad. But Germany had also become a large consumer of imported primary products and raw materials (such as chilled meat, vegetable fats, textile fibres and non-ferrous ores). Her merchant marine was the second largest in the world and her industries were increasingly finding their markets abroad. The import dependence of the major European powers was complemented by the specialization of certain overseas economies on primary exports. The British Dominions, the temperate South American countries and, to a lesser degree, India and the tropical dependencies greatly increased their agricultural and mineral exports to Europe from the mid-1890s when trading patterns were established which ignored imperial frontiers. In 1913, to give one example, three quarters of the palm kernels from Britain's Nigerian Protectorate and 44 per cent of total exports went to Germany where they were an essential input for the margarine and soap industries.

What bearing – you might ask – would this have on the 'nature' of the First World War? In blockaded Germany, soap was rationed to as little as one small bar a month. Clothing and bed linen could not be properly washed, adding a ubiquitous shabbiness to the chronic discomfort of food shortages. All kinds of substitutes were tried for West African vegetable fats, just as substitutes were sought for coffee, rubber, cotton, and many other scarce commodities. One critical shortage, given the type of war in which Germany was engaged, was nitrates, which are a basic constituent of artificial fertilizers and explosives. About half Germany's peacetime requirement came from saltpetre imports from Chile, a source immediately denied by Britain's blockade. In a short war, this would have been of no consequence, but by the Spring of 1915 the demand from the munitions industry far outstripped the supply. The German chemicals industry solved the problem of nitrates for explosives by the industrial application of a laboratory process for 'fixing' atmospheric nitrogen, but there was still insufficient nitrates for fertilizers, and without them the productivity per acre of Germany's fields inexorably declined.

The global financial crisis of 1914

International economic integration was such that the outbreak of war in Europe had an immediate impact on cities as distant as Calcutta and Buenos Aires. The financial and commercial infrastructure which underpinned world trade seized up. The North American business community was made painfully aware of its dependence on foreign (especially British) investment and financial and shipping services. In the week ending 1 August, $45 million was lost on the New York stock market because of panic selling by foreign investors. On 14 August, the authorities closed the stock exchange for four months, so freezing billions of dollars of usually liquid assets. The US merchant marine carried less than 10 per cent of the goods in world trade before 1914, and with the diversion of foreign shipping there was insufficient capacity to move bulk crops, such as cotton. American merchants depended on British finance houses for short-term credit which was suddenly denied them. In October, the Secretary of the Treasury had to ask the British Government for aid in resolving the financial crisis caused by the outbreak of war; it was the last time Britain acted as the dominant partner in financial relations with the Americans.

The 'lopsided' recovery of world trade in the winter of 1914–15 was highly advantageous to the Entente powers, for no goods could cross the Atlantic directly to Germany and the quantities arriving via neutral Holland were much reduced. Britain and France became near monopoly purchasers of 'New World' primary exports. In December, following a poor harvest, the French authorities purchased 300,000 quintals of oats in Buenos Aires to feed the army's 600,000 horses.[1] In April 1915, French orders were placed in New York for 75,000 tonnes

[1] (1 quintal = 100 kilos)

of oats, 45,000 tonnes of wheat and 30,000 tonnes of flour. The French army alone required 20,000 fresh horses a month throughout the war: half were purchased in Argentina and the USA (Miquel, *La Grande Guerre*, 1983, pp.240–2). By 1916 30 per cent of France's total imports came from the USA and loans worth 3.4 milliard francs[2] had been raised to pay for them.

Rival blockades

Even without the British navy's total command of the sea, the Entente powers would have been favourably placed in the competition for world resources. They possessed nearly three fifths of the world's merchant shipping in 1914, and the proportion quickly rose as the Central Powers' ships were destroyed or interned. Germany could use neutral (especially Dutch) services but Britain controlled the approach routes along which imports reached the Netherlands, and pressured the Dutch government into restricting the re-export of 'war contraband' to the Central Powers. This was a category of goods narrowly defined by an international convention regulating wartime blockades (the Declaration of London, 1909) but Britain had not ratified it. The Foreign Office and Admiralty insisted on a wide definition of contraband and declared the North Sea 'a military area' in November, which entitled cruisers to divert neutral vessels to British ports to be searched. German goods not considered contraband under international law were seized from neutral ships and, in response, Germany made its first declaration of submarine warfare in February 1915. Allied merchant men around the British and French coasts were liable to be attacked without warning; neutral ships were also exposed to danger if and when U-boat captains suspected neutral flags were being abused. The tonnage sunk in the whole of 1915 was less than the monthly totals in mid-1917, and strategically insignificant. But it was diplomatically highly consequential because American opinion was outraged when the passenger liners, *Lusitania* and *Arabic*, were torpedoed by submerged submarines in May and August, and many civilians (including some Americans) drowned. U-boats usually attacked unarmed vessels on the surface which gave passengers and crew time to take to the boats. Underwater attacks minimized the chances of survival and, to contemporaries, represented a barbaric escalation of warfare. Under intense US diplomatic pressure, the German government revised the rules of engagement in the approaches to the British Isles (though not other waters) in October, thereby restricting the submarines' effectiveness. Nevertheless, it was evident that waging economic warfare had the inbuilt tendency to extend the conflict internationally and intensify it.

[2] Milliard = 1,000 million.

2   THE DURATION OF THE WAR

The failure of the war plans

All General Staffs had anticipated a short war, so why did it last for over four years? One answer is that, without exception, their plans for a short war failed. The Schlieffen Plan for the envelopment of the French armies by a great wheeling movement through Belgium broke down when the German army on the far right exposed its flank to a Franco-British counter-attack on the Marne. This immense setback made the perennial nightmare of German strategic thinking – a war on two fronts – a reality. But the French Plan XVII for a massive offensive through Lorraine fared even more disastrously: the best of the French forces, including irreplaceable professional officers, were squandered in fruitless assaults on defensive positions. Russia's Plan A for an invasion of East Prussia at first went smoothly: initial Russian successes so alarmed the German Supreme Command (*Oberste Heeres Leitung* – OHL) that it transferred two corps from the west to re-inforce the army in the east. (This was a serious blunder: the German armies on the Marne were weakened just before the French counter-attack, and troops sent east arrived too late to participate in the battles.) The two Russian armies in East Prussia enjoyed overall superiority in numbers, but were incompetently led and their intelligence was appalling. They became so out of touch that the Germans were able, by switching their troops by rail, to defeat them individually. The southern army under Samsonov was surrounded and annihilated at the battle of Tannenberg – the only victory of encirclement during the course of the war in Europe. The northern army under Rennenkampf was mauled at the battle of the Masurian Lakes but retired over the frontier in good order.

Austria-Hungary's main planned offensive was an invasion of Russian Poland from Galicia, but Conrad von Hötzendorf, the Chief of Staff, gravely weakened his forces there by deploying a reserve contingent against Serbia. The Balkan Wars ought to have alerted the Austrians to Serbia's formidable military capacity: it mobilized a higher proportion of the male population than any other European country and its first-line units were equipped with modern artillery and machine guns. By early December, the Serbs had repulsed two Habsburg invasions and temporarily occupied eastern Bosnia. Meanwhile, the main Habsburg forces had been heavily defeated in western Galicia. The Russian commanders in this theatre were more competent and brought to bear a crushing superiority in men and artillery in a series of engagements around Lemberg. A general retreat was ordered which led to the surrender of Habsburg territory to the depth of 150 miles and the investment of the great fortress of Przemysl. The Habsburgs lost 400,000 men out of 1,800,000 mobilized, including 300,000 prisoners (many of them Czechs and Slovaks who surrendered *en masse* to the Russians). In what was to become part of the pattern of the war in the east, Conrad was compelled to appeal to the Germans for assistance, and they opened an offensive in Poland to ease the pressure against Austria-Hungary.

In the west, the Germans attempted to salvage something from the wreckage of the Schlieffen Plan by outflanking the Franco-British armies in the so-called 'race to the sea'. This too failed. By the end of October, the opposing armies

50 miles

HOLLAND

GERMANY

Antwerp

Belgian
Army

1st
Army

Ostend

Ghent

Maastricht

Rhine

Cologne

Schelde

Aachen

Ypres

Lys

BRUSSELS

Liége

Coblenz

BELGIUM

Ancre

2nd
Army

Meuse

Namur

Moselle

Lille

Mons

Charleroi

Douai

3rd
Army

LUXEM-
BOURG

Cambrai

Maubeuge

Ancre

Le Cateau

Oise

Sedan

4th
Army

LUXEMBOURG

GERMANY

Somme

St Quentin

Mézières

Aisne

5th
Army

Diedenhofen
(Thionville)

LORRAINE

La Fère

Laon

1st
Army

2nd
Army

3rd
Army

4th
Army

Verdun

Metz

Morhange

Montdidier

Rheims

3rd Army

St Mihiel

6th
Army

Saarburg

Oise

Soissons

6th Army

Coulommiers

Marsh of
St Gond

Chalons-sur-
Marne

4th Army

2nd
Army

Toul

Luneville

7th
Army

PARIS

British
Expeditionary
Force

9th
Army

Provins

5th Army

Marne

Meuse

Moselle

FRANCE

Épinal

1st
Army

Mülhausen

Seine

Langres

Saône

Belfort

Dijon

Montbeliard

Besançon

Legend:

German advance

17 Aug 1914 ⎤ German
5 Sept 1914 ⎦ positions

French ⎤ Allied
British ⎥ positions,
⎥ 5 Sept
Belgian ⎦ 1914

Fortified town/
military fortress

The German advance, 1914
(Source: J. Keegan , *The First World War,* Hutchinson, London, 1998, p.124)

The Eastern front in outline, 1914–18

(Source: J. Keegan , *The First World War*, Hutchinson, London, 1998, p.156)

'*defensive war*'

were entrenched in a continuous front from the Swiss frontier to the Channel and, up to March 1918, no attack or series of attacks was able to move the line as much as ten miles in either direction. Why had a war of movement degenerate so quickly into a war of position? In what ways was the subsequent course of the war determined by the failure of the 'short war' strategies in 1914?

Exercise   Before answering those questions, I want to you to look carefully at the statistics of war-related deaths reproduced below and say what was the most lethal *period* of the war. How might these statistics help dispel popular misconceptions about trench warfare? Do they afford any insight into the way the failures of the opening campaigns influenced the subsequent course of the war?■

Table 6.1   French war-related deaths amongst men aged 16–60

1914	1915	1916	1917	1918	Total
306,585	334,836	217,502	121,545	225,733	1,206,203

('5 months')

Table 6.2   German war-related deaths amongst men aged 15–59

1914	1915	1916	1917	1918	Total
240,805	424,123	332,774	310,876	445,776	1,754,354

(5 months)

(Source: Wall and Winter, *The Upheaval of War*, 1988, Tables 1.3 and 1.12)

Specimen answers   The statistics demonstrate that the period of open warfare *at the beginning of the*
and discussion   *war* was, proportionately, the most lethal of the whole war. Twenty-five per cent of all war-related deaths amongst Frenchmen occurred in those five months when France lost far more men than throughout the whole of 1916 – the year of Verdun. The opening months were not quite so lethal for the German forces, for 14 per cent of all their losses took place in 1914; but had their rate of loss during these five months prevailed over a whole year it would have resulted in 580,000 deaths. Armies entrenched to save lives and to exploit the superiority of the defensive – a superiority much enhanced by the use of barbed wire and the deployment of machine guns in ever greater numbers. The statistics actually mask just how horrendous the initial battles were, for the French casualties were heavily concentrated in August and September. The figures should dispel once and for all the misconception that casualty rates were highest during the 'classic' confrontations at Verdun, on the Somme and Passchendaele. □

The professional officer corps of every army suffered disproportionally in the bloodletting of 1914, so one longer-term consequence was to be a shortage of trained officers as the armies expanded. This was less of a handicap in the German army, thanks to a system of recruiting well-educated, middle-class NCOs who performed many functions undertaken by junior officers in other armies. A *Feldwebel* (sergeant) on the reserve list was quite likely to be a manager, lawyer or schoolteacher in civilian life. The German army was tactically more innovative than others because it could delegate authority 'forward' to the NCOs who led small groups in battle. All Germany's opponents were handicapped by the lack of an NCO class with comparable qualities, but none more so than Russia. Casualty figures for the eastern front are unreliable, but it is certain that there, too, the opening campaigns were the most lethal. General Brusilov, Russia's most successful commander, underlined the consequences for the Tsarist army:

> After hardly three months of war the greater part of our regular, professional officers and trained men had vanished, leaving only skeleton forces which had to be hastily filled with men wretchedly instructed who were sent to me from the depots ... From this period onwards the professional character of our forces disappeared, and the army became more and more like a sort of badly trained militia ... The men sent to replace casualties knew nothing except how to march ... many could not even load their rifles ...
>
> (Quoted in Figes, *A People's Tragedy*, 1996, p.257)

Deadlock on the technological battlefield

Many reasons have been advanced for deadlock on the western front, but boneheaded generals, brilliant to the top of their cavalry boots, have always taken a lion's share of blame. The damning judgement of the historian, Llewellyn Woodward, who served throughout the war (and never doubted that Britain was morally justified in resisting Germany) fairly represents what many men thought of their military leaders:

> From Kitchener downwards these commanders just did not know how to set about their task of winning the war ... If the cavalrymen who cluttered up the high places in the military command had been as eager and co-operative in experiment as the pilots and designers of aeroplanes, the waste of life in futile attacks on the Western Front could have been avoided ... [T]he victorious generals nearly destroyed European civilization by the methods which they employed to save it. Fortunately for the Allies the enemy generals were equally obtuse.
>
> (Woodward, *Great Britain and the War of 1914–1918*, 1967, p.xiii–ix)

The British army, he added in a withering aside, was 'run by pass men'.[3]

Some generals fully merited this scorn: General Allenby's career as an army commander on the western front was described by the official military historian as one of 'gross stupidity from first to last'. His order to Third Army troops not to carry or wear greatcoats during the Battle of Arras – despite a freezing blizzard – typified his cretinously 'bullish' style of command. General Nivelle was a disaster as the French commander-in-chief in early 1917: he had not grasped the nature of industrialized warfare and, against all reason, expected victory to come through a crude return to the insensate spirit of all-out offensive of August 1914. The attacks he ordered were amongst the most sanguinary and senseless of the conflict, and their failure led to the military strike that paralysed the French army between April and June. Haig's reputation as a strategist has been somewhat redeemed by John Terraine and other military historians. But even his admirers recognize that prolonging the battle of Passchendaele in October-November 1917 was a woeful error of judgement. Haig may have been 'wearing down' the enemy – though that is debatable – but he was certainly sapping the morale of

---

[3] i.e. men who had obtained a pass degree.

his own forces. One consequence of their demoralization was mass surrenders during the great German offensive of March 1918.

But the shortcomings of individual commanders are only a part of the explanation for prolongation of the war until November 1918. The military technology available to them, and the geographic confines of the western front, made a war-winning strategy extraordinarily elusive. One difficulty was that instantaneous communication between the commanders at the rear and their attacking units broke down in battle when buried field-telephone lines were invariably severed. The portable two-way radio sets that might have called down the artillery in 'real time' did not exist. Eight to ten hours were needed on average for a message to reach the front from divisional headquarters. But there was a more fundamental problem trapping the generals 'in the iron fetters of a technology all too adequate for destruction but which denied them flexibility and manoeuvre' (Keegan, *The First World War*, 1998, p. 342). Put at its simplest, the problem lay in the mismatch between the concentrated fire-power available to the generals and its immobility. A generation of technical development before 1914 had greatly increased the weight, accuracy and rapidity of fire by field guns and heavy artillery, but done nothing to improve its mobility on the battlefield. Once armies had left their rail-heads, artillery pieces were horse-drawn and manoeuvred by muscle. By early 1915, all the combatants had exhausted their existing shell stocks, but by instituting greater state control of their industrial economies they were able to augment munitions production to meet their artillery requirements. A key part of offensive strategy became the concentration of huge quantities of shell fire on chosen sectors of the enemy front in order to destroy barbed-wire obstacles and machine gun posts, silence opposing batteries and break the morale of defenders in preparation for infantry assaults. Twenty-three million shells were fired off by the opposing sides at Verdun between February and July 1916. The physical devastation of fire-power actually hindered its intended objective – the breakthrough beyond the enemy's lines – for it destroyed roads and churned ground into a morass of shell-holes, and made the movement forward of artillery in close support of advancing infantry extraordinarily difficult.

The war was a forcing house for military technology and technique. Guns and shells were improved, new designs adopted, and 'unsighted' fire became much more accurate thanks to airborne observers and sound-ranging. Generals learned how to combine the artillery and infantry arms with 'creeping' barrages that protected assault troops. But the problem they never entirely solved was that of mobilizing the guns to catch up with foot-soldiers who had broken through the enemy defences, and without artillery cover these men were perilously exposed to counter-attack. The problem of sustaining an offensive was compounded because, with the exception of the assault on Verdun, the German army stood on the defensive in the west between late 1914 and March 1918 and adopted tactics of elastic defence-in-depth. The Supreme Command's initial response to the stalemate of late 1914 had been to order densely-packed and rigid defences and the re-taking of every foot of lost ground. Bitter experience was to show that allowing the enemy to sweep over a thinly held forward zone, and then subjecting him to counter-attack from a second or third line of defence, was far more effective. The western allies' strategic planning was ruined in 1917 because, in February-March, OHL conceived a superbly executed strategic retirement to the 'Hindenburg' defensive line. The retreating Germans poisoned the wells, cratered all cross-roads, felled the poplars and apple-orchards to make obstructions, and blew up practically every building. This ruthlessness gained them immense strategic advantage for they 'exchanged a bad, haphazard, bulging line for another well-sited, bristling with every device of the most up-to-date defensive art, and much shorter. It was calculated that thirteen fewer divisions were required as trench garrison' (Cruttwell, *A History of the Great War 1914–1918*, 1936, p.401).

Ludendorff's technocratic 'realism' – the Geyer thesis

The withdrawal to the 'Hindenburg' line was the brainchild of Erich Ludendorff, who was appointed Quartermaster General in August 1916 and is credited with bringing a new technocratic culture to high strategy. In an influential essay, Michael Geyer argued that Ludendorff appreciated more clearly than his predecessors that Germany's disparity in manpower and resources compelled her to follow a policy of 'scarcity' by which machines would be substituted for men and the functional organization of violence for heroism and the traditional military hierarchy. His staff advocated the full rationalization of machine war; soldiers were to be adapted to their weaponry, just as the industrial workers were adapted to machinery. To shorten the line and deploy men more efficiently, territory would if necessary be conceded (Geyer, 'German strategy in the age of machine warfare, 1914–1945', 1986).

Geyer's article has prompted military historians to ask whether the Entente generals made the same mental adjustment to the technological imperatives of the new warfare. One brute statistic indicates they did not: what is called the 'net body count' (i.e. the surplus of enemy killed or captured over one's own losses) strongly favoured the Central Powers. Just over 4 million of their soldiers were killed, compared with about 5.4 million Entente soldiers, so the Central Powers' superiority in killing was about 35 per cent (Ferguson, *The Pity of War*, 1998, p.294). As we shall see, they were extremely good at killing and capturing Russians, but even against highly motivated and well-equipped opponents on the western front the German army had a favourable net body count. From August 1914 to June 1918, there was not a single month in which the Germans failed to kill or capture more French and British soldiers than they themselves lost (ibid., p.300). The biggest Entente deficits were in August-September 1914, when the French expected victory to be achieved by the superiority of their troops' offensive spirit; though the price of courage might be high, the battle in which it was paid would be swift and decisive. British professional soldiers had similar misconceptions as to the nature of modern warfare, and similarly emphasized moral qualities of discipline and team-spirit over technical competence. The fear of 'national degeneration' (see Unit 2, p.70) that gripped military élites before 1914 led to their preoccupation with the infantry's moral fibre and their neglect of its co-ordination with the rapidly evolving artillery. To still be in deficit, in terms of the net body count, in mid-1918 suggests that the Entente generals never quite adjusted their 'mental set' to the technological battlefield. Whereas the Germans came to look to machinery and equipment to solve the deadlock, Haig's solutions to the problems of the western front remained mired in calculations about manpower. According to Tim Travers, the British high command was constantly struggling

> ... to come to mental grips with a war that had escaped its pre-ordained boundaries and structures. It was a war that had 'got away', so to speak, and the groping towards enlightenment of the 1914–18 period was a continuous attempt to overcome prewar conceptions of a simple and understood form of war, and to find new theories or structures to encompass the new technical warfare.
>
> (Travers, *The Killing Ground*, 1987, p.244)

Exercise Look carefully at the following tables. Do they confirm that the Germans' favourable 'net body count' was due to technological superiority? What problems do they raise for the Geyer thesis? Why do you think the Western powers had such a vast superiority in trucks by early 1918? (Think back to what I said earlier about the Entente blockade denying Germany global resources.) ■

Table 6.3 UK Munitions production, 1915–18

	1915	1916	1917	1918
Guns	3390	4314	5137	8039
Tanks	–	150	1110	1359
Aircraft (000s)	1.9	6.1	14.7	32
Shells (million)	6.0	45.7	76.2	67.3

Table 6.4 Military equipment of the rival armies on the western front, early 1918

	Germany	Western powers
Machine guns (per infantry division)	324	1,084
Artillery	c.14,000	c.18,500
Trucks	23,000	c.100,000
Tanks	10	800
Aircraft	c.3,670	c.4.500

(Source: Deist, 'The military collapse of the German Empire', 1996)

Specimen answer No, on the eve of the March 1918 offensive – Germany's most striking military successes in the west – the Entente forces were better equipped in every arm. Hardware does not explain why the German army killed and captured more efficiently than its opponents. The figures for tank production pose some problems for the Geyer thesis. This was the technological solution to the immobility of firepower, and had become a major item of Entente munitions production by 1917 but its development had evidently been ignored in Germany. There were two reasons for the Western powers' superiority in trucks:

with America's entry into the war, they had the world's largest automobile industry at their disposal but, equally important, Germany had no rubber for pneumatic tyres. This was the main constraint on vehicle construction.

Discussion   If hardware does not explain the German army's tactical superiority what does? I can only speculate that it was due to corporate professionalism: the better training of staff officers, delegated command systems, well-educated NCOs who could take decisions – these gave, it would seem, the German army a cutting edge over its enemies' inflexible line management. With respect to military technology as such, the Germans were not consistently more progressive than their enemies, as can be demonstrated by the attitudes of the opposing high commands to the tank. It is pure legend that the British high command thwarted its development: after his appointment as commander-in-chief, Haig took an immediate interest in the prototype machines and began incorporating them into his preparations for the Somme battle. If anything he was over-enthusiastic about their potential for they were prone to mechanical failure and required highly trained crews. The French general staff was equally eager to exploit what it called '*cuirassés terrestres*' (land cruisers), and ordered considerable quantities of heavy tanks from Schneider and Saint-Chamond as early as the spring of 1916. (At the same time, caterpillar tractors were being developed to haul the heavy artillery.) In March 1917 an order was placed with French industry for 2,500 tanks, the great majority being the Renault 'light' tank (the most successful machine developed during the war). In June, Pétain insisted on raising the Renault order to 3,500, though unfortunately very few were delivered before the spring of 1918. It is the Entente's opponent who appears blimpishly obtuse in spurning mechanized armour. German industry had the capacity to produce tanks, but Ludendorff saw no future in them. The German army's few operational tanks in 1918 were captured models. Admittedly, even in late 1918, the tank was still too slow and mechanically unreliable to be a war-winning weapon, but its deployment in ever greater numbers gave the Entente a considerable tactical and moral advantage over the dispirited Germans. □

The even balance of the rival coalitions: 1914–1917

If the war was to be decided on the balance of demographic and economic resources, then the signatories to the Pact of London (5 September, 1914) should have won hands down. France, Russia and Britain thereby agreed not to conclude a separate peace, and their combined manpower and *matériel* ought to have ground down the Central Powers in an attritional war. The Entente accounted for 28 per cent of the world's manufacturing output in 1913, as against the Central Powers' 19 per cent, and its demographic preponderance was far greater. But what is often overlooked in calculating the balance of resources is *time*, and if we take this factor into account the balance was more even than it appears on paper. At the outset Britain had no mass army and could not assume a major role on the western front until mid-1916. The British Expeditionary Force's (BEF) first reinforcements came from India, not Britain. Systems had to be improvised to train and equip the 'Kitchener' volunteers who spent months in camp before they crossed the Channel. It was quite different where mass armies already existed. In Germany, only six weeks was needed to turn an unpreposessing volunteer into a front-line soldier: Adolf Hitler was

war prolonged

inducted into the Bavarian army on 16 August 1914 and his battalion came under fire near Ypres in late October. In Britain, it took eight months or more: George Coppard enlisted on 27 August but did not arrive in France until early June 1915 (Coppard, *With a Machine Gun to Cambrai*, 1969). British armaments policy in 1914 was premised on an expeditionary force of six divisions: munitions output simply could not keep pace with the expansion of the army for the first sixteen months of the war. France had to be both blood-bank and arsenal of the alliance – this despite the enemy's occupation of regions producing two thirds of the country's pig iron, 58 per cent of its steel and 40 per cent of its coal. Two fifths of the heavy industrial staples needed for the French armaments industry were imported, which makes its achievements all the more impressive.

Russia – the weakest link

While Britain needed time to become a land power, time worked against Russia where the state was demonstrably vulnerable to the social stresses of attritional war. The regime had almost foundered in the 1905 Revolution, following defeat in the war with Japan. Though its army had since been impressively modernized, the administrative structures needed to mobilize the economy and society for a European war remained glaringly inadequate. After August 1914, the army authorities directly administered the large part of the Empire within the 'military zone' (including Petrograd) and behaved with astonishing ineptitude. During the retreat from Russian Poland in the spring of 1915, Tsarist Headquarters ordered a 'scorched earth' policy and forced huge numbers to flee before the German invaders. Cattle and food were requisitioned, so refugee children and the infirm starved to death on the clogged roads. Jews were deported *en masse* to the interior on suspicion of pro-German sympathies, which outraged liberal opinion at home and abroad, alienated Jewish bankers who were important in financing the war, and prompted anti-Semitic outbursts in reception areas. The civil bureaucracy was a helpless spectator to these calamities. The Minutes of the Council of Ministers noted on 30 July 1915:

> The devastation of a score of provinces and the expulsion of their population into the interior is equivalent to the condemnation of Russia to terrible sufferings. But common sense and the requirements of national interest meet little favour at Headquarters. The arguments of civilians are silenced before 'military necessity' whatever may be the horror covered by this term.
>
> (Quoted in Florinsky, *The End of the Russian Empire*, 1931, p.198)

[handwritten margin note: euphemism for "barbarity"]

The military authorities tried to extend the army's draconian discipline to industrial workers: behaviour considered subversive of the war effort was met with courts martial, armed force, and the suspension of exemptions from military service; the slightest signs of militancy were magnified into revolutionary threats. Officers administering the transport and supply system became notorious for their corruption. When retreating troops prepared to make a stand on the San River in May 1915 they found that officers had sold all the spades, barbed wire and timber needed for trenches (Figes, *A People's Tragedy*, 1996, p.266). One Minister described military rule behind the front as 'a revolting picture of anarchy, lawlessness and the paralysis of power' (Florinsky, *The End of the Russian Empire*, 1931, p.76). The dynasty gambled desperately on its prestige when the Tsar assumed personal command of the army, against the advice of nearly all civilian ministers. The Minister of the Interior considered it a 'fatal' decision, and resigned. The government lost all credibility with patriotic Russians who had organized themselves into voluntary committees to support the war effort. The civil bureaucracy had virtually disintegrated by 1917.

As a military power, Russia was not the slow-moving but unstoppable 'steamroller' imagined by French pre-war planners. Nearly half the men of military age were exempt from service as only sons or the sole adult male workers in their family, or else on account of their ethnic background (Muslims, Finns and, in practice, Jews were not required to serve). Whereas 12 per cent of the German population and 16 per cent of the French were mobilized for active military service, the figure for Russia was only 5 per cent (Pipes, *The Russian Revolution 1899–1919*, 1990, p.203). A low priority had been given to the periodic retraining of the reserves, who were divided into levies according to age. Only those in the First Levy were immediately fit for combat duties. Men in their thirties and forties, many years out of uniform, were no better than raw recruits. Russia fielded 6.5 million men in the first six months of the war: 1.4 million on active duty, 4.4 million trained reservists from the First Levy, and 700,000 fresh recruits. Between January and September 1915, a further 1.4 million reservists were inducted. This exhausted the pool of trained manpower. By the 'net body count' measure, the army's performance was appalling: there was little fighting on the eastern front after January 1917, so the vast majority of Russian casualties must have occurred in thirty months' campaigning. In this comparatively short war, 1.8 million Tsarist soldiers died and a staggering 3.5 million surrendered. (Russian PoWs became an important source of agricultural labour for the Central Powers.) Unsurprisingly, the army was short of men by 1916.

From late 1914 through to the autumn of 1915, Russian military effectiveness was cruelly impaired by shortages of weapons, shells, boots and uniforms. Russia traditionally relied on government factories to produce military equipment, and their output was quite insufficient to supply all the men under arms. They could produce only about a fifth of the monthly requirement of rifles in late 1914. Their total monthly output of artillery shells was only 9,000 rounds – far below the quantity needed. All combatants were facing munitions crises by the end of 1914, but Russia's was especially acute because Turkey's entry into the war in November closed the best route for imports from the Entente. Until the late summer of 1915, the government had no faith in the capacity of Russian private industry and looked to foreign suppliers to make good the army's needs, but only a fraction of orders placed abroad at this time were actually delivered. In August, about 30 per cent of front-line soldiers were still without arms. A censored soldier's letter written about this time records: 'Our position is bad, we are still retreating and the main reason is the lack of shells. This is what we've fought for! And it is the war ministers who did it. And now we have to use up men instead of shells' (Davidian, 'The Russian soldier's morale from the evidence of Tsarist military censorship', 1996, p.429). The sense of betrayal was universal.

When the state did move to mobilize domestic industry, huge increases in shell, artillery and rifle output resulted, but they were never sufficient to equip the 15.8 million men mobilized between 1914 and 1917. The army depended on foreign suppliers for 38 per cent of its cartridges, 40 per cent of its rifles, and

60 per cent of machine guns, aircraft, and aero-engines (Gatrell and Harrison, 'The Russian and Soviet economies in two world wars', 1993, p.436). Russia was, clearly, handicapped by the backwardness of her industry, but the fundamental reason for chronic problems in munitions supply was that she committed few economic resources to the war by comparison with the other combatants. This is borne out by the following table which compares the munitions supplied by the major European combatants per year of fighting. (The 'standard gun units' referred to in the table are reckoned by weighting rifles 0.01, machine guns 0.05, guns 1.00, tanks 5.0 and aircraft 5.0. The calculations make allowance for Russia's early withdrawal from the war.) As you can see, Russia contributed little to the ground and air armament of the Entente: her industries supplied only about a quarter of the munitions produced in Britain and France, and less than one-quarter of Germany's munitions output.

Table 6.5   Annual rates of supply of ground and air munitions in World War I

	1 Standard gun units supplied per year (000s)	2 Ratio to 1913 GDP (% of Russia)
Russia	17	100
Germany	80	533
France	70	770
UK	72	465

(Source: Gatrell and Harrison, 'The Russian and Soviet economies in two world wars', 1993, pp.431)

The second column requires more explaining, but is in some ways more revealing. It shows the proportion of Gross Domestic Product (GDP) each combatant allocated to munitions by comparison with Russia's, and so allows us to gauge the national industrial 'effort' of each state (taking into account the different sizes of their economies). What it reveals is that France, which had the smallest economy in absolute terms, made the biggest industrial effort relatively speaking. It committed annually nearly eight times the Russian share of pre-war GDP to munitions, Britain and Germany about five times.

Despite the loss of the Polish textiles and food processing industries, production of civilian goods (including foodstuffs) in Russia was not seriously affected before late 1916. However, by this date there were gross inequalities in the *distribution* of basic necessities which the government was quite unable to correct. Peasants who stayed on the land did not fare badly but, because of the breakdown of internal trade, they faced a dearth of consumer goods on which to spend farm income. They were given a further disincentive to market their surplus because the policy of financing the war through borrowing and the printing press stoked monetary inflation. Rather than accumulate depreciating paper money, the peasantry lived better. This disruption of normal exchange between town and country was exacerbated by labour shortages on the large commercial estates and the army's monopolization of the transport network. In the swollen industrial cities, the consequences were recurrent food shortages and falling real wages. Price

Use this for tma 04

increases for food, rent, fuel and clothing far outstripped wage increases for most industrial workers. The plight of urban soldiers' families who relied on separation allowances was desperate. By October 1916, popular discontent in urban Russia had reached such intensity that the Police Department's confidential reports compared the situation to 1905 and warned that another revolution was in the offing. The Ministry of the Interior was alerted to 'the relentless approach of great turbulence brought about and explainable exclusively by economic factors: hunger, the unequal distribution of food and articles of prime necessity, and the monstrous rise in prices' (quoted in Pipes, *The Russian Revolution 1899–1919*, 1990, p.243).

Controversy surrounds the extent of disaffection in the army. Michael Florinsky, who wrote a well-documented account of the empire's collapse (and could draw upon his own experience as a Tsarist artillery officer) argued that the army was thoroughly demoralized by late 1916. A report of the Petrograd Police which he cited referred to 'much strained' relations between the men and their officers who were widely despised for corruption and inefficiency. The ranks were rife with rumours of famines in Petrograd and Moscow and the ejection of soldiers' wives from their lodgings by grasping 'merchants' (Florinsky, *The End of the Russian Empire*, 1931, pp.214–15).

"despair"

More recent scholars have argued that the crisis in morale amongst front-line units in late 1916 was broadly apolitical. It was rooted in the feeling of utter despair that the slaughter would never end and that anything resembling victory could be achieved. The ranks wanted peace above all, but also better food and they were alarmed by the wild inflation in the towns. The refusal to attack was behind a rash of mutinies in late 1916, some involving entire regiments. Politicized unrest, fomented by revolutionaries, began amongst the huge numbers of troops stationed in the rear (Wildman, *The End of the Russian Imperial Army*, 1980, pp.106–19). Scholars do not agree whether the army could have recovered from mass insubordination (as the French army did in July 1917) or whether it faced disintegration, but one piece of quantifiable evidence points to the latter: the number of desertions in early 1917 was officially estimated at a million or more (Pipes, *The Russian Revolution 1899–1919*, 1990, p.244). A major factor behind demoralization and indiscipline was the brutal incompetence of so many 'temporary' officers: they squandered lives and had reluctant soldiers flogged or sent into battle with their own side's artillery aimed at their backs. In other armies, the solidarity of fighting men softened class hostilities; in the Tsarist army, they were accentuated. 'The internal war between the officers and their men', writes Orlando Figes, 'began to overshadow the war itself.' In this sense, he adds, 'the war was the social architect of 1917 as the army gradually turned into one vast revolutionary mob' (Figes, *A People's Tragedy*, 1996, pp.263–6).

revolutions in the offing.

To sum up: over time, the triple Entente was like a see-saw pivoting on France, but while British land-power rose, Russia's declined. Only for a relatively brief period in mid-1916, when Brusilov's offensive was smashing through the Austrians in Galicia and the Kitchener armies were engaged on the Somme, did both ends of the see-saw co-ordinate their full military weight. Here, in large part, lies the Entente's failure to capitalize on its superior demographic and economic resources.

nature of the war: organisation.

Uncompromising war aims

In November 1916, Lord Lansdowne – a former Conservative foreign secretary and architect of the *Entente cordiale* – circulated his Cabinet colleagues with a pessimistic analysis of the Entente's military and political prospects. It was in neither Britain's nor its allies' interests, he wrote, that the war should be prolonged 'unless it can be shown that we can bring it to an effectual conclusion within a reasonable space of time.' Lansdowne appreciated, much more clearly than the government's military advisers, that the Entente could not. Russia was on the ropes; there was war weariness in Italy; Britain had come 'within an ace of grave complications with Sweden and the USA' over the enforcement of the blockade; 'the best of the male population' was slowly but surely being killed off; the future was being mortgaged to the financial burden of the war. If, at the end of a further year (or two or three) the Entente found itself still unable to dictate peace terms, 'the War with its nameless horrors will have been needlessly prolonged, and the responsibility of those who needlessly prolong such a war is not less than that of those who needlessly provoke it'. Though guardedly expressed, the import of Landsdowne's memorandum was clear: the government should consider negotiating a peace. It should not have rebuffed President Wilson's attempts to mediate between the belligerents, as Lloyd George (then Secretary for War) so evidently did in an interview with an American journalist in September.

In France, another senior politician, Joseph Caillaux, was also questioning the purpose of a war that threatened to destroy European civilization. Before 1914, Caillaux had advocated Franco-German conciliation and he retained a strong following in the Chamber. The majority of deputies (who had, of course, been elected *before* July 1914) were not *revanchiste* or extreme nationalists by inclination.[4] To a man, they supported the *Union sacrée* and virtually abdicated the governance of France to Joffre and GHQ in September 1914. But, as they recovered the political initiative, Caillaux became the focus of hopes for a negotiated peace. Outside parliament, influential figures also moved from total support for the war to its repudiation: Alain, the philosopher, had volunteered in August 1914, though already in his forties. By 1917, he judged that Europe was foundering in a futile conflict. Romain Rolland, a refugee from the war in Switzerland had published a clarion call for renewed internationalism, *Au-dessus de la mêlée* in 1915, and was awarded the Nobel Prize for literature that year. The Prix Goncourt went to Henri Barbusse, another August volunteer, for *Le Feu* (*Under Fire*) which sold 200,000 copies (you will find an extract in *Primary Sources 1: World War I*, Document II.13). Barbusse's message was painfully simple: '*Être vainqueur dans cette guerre, c'est pas un résultat*' – 'There can be no victors in this war'.

Why were these voices ignored? Why was the war not shortened by a negotiated peace? The brief answer is that the belligerents had, largely in the course of the fighting, formulated war aims on which it was difficult to compromise. The unexpected costs of the war deepened the incompatibility of the opposing coalitions' objectives because any compromise would have made the sacrifices seem pointless. When Asquith and Viviani, the British and French premiers, publicly stated their countries' objectives in December 1914, these appeared straightforward: Britain demanded the evacuation of occupied France and

---

[4] *Revanchiste* – the term used to describe those in French public life seeking revenge for the loss of Alsace-Lorraine in 1871 (see Roberts, p.118).

Belgium, the latter's return to full independence; and restitution for war damage. Asquith spoke, too, of ensuring that 'the military domination of Prussia is wholly and finally destroyed', a phrase echoed by Viviani. The French premier also called for the restoration of Alsace-Lorraine, a claim which the British government did not publicly support. What they presumably intended by destroying 'Prussianism' was inflicting a military defeat on Germany so crushing that its authoritarian power structure would not survive. But the Entente did not demand the removal of the Hohenzollern dynasty and German democratization, and its official war aims towards the principal enemy were ill-defined. 'Victory' – wrote A. J. P. Taylor – 'was expected to provide a policy; in fact victory was the policy' (Taylor, *The Struggle for Mastery in Europe 1848–1918*, 1954, p.535). In the coming months, the apparent simplicity of the western powers' position was to be complicated by the secret commitments made to Russia and Italy, but these involved promises of Habsburg and Ottoman territory to give the Russians something to fight for and the Italians an incentive to join in. Against Germany, France and Britain fought the war not to lose. They considered Germany guilty of premeditated aggression and of a cynical disdain for international undertakings. French public opinion was outraged by reports of atrocities in the occupied *départements* and this created a bedrock consensus behind seeing the war through to the end. The neutrals' attempts to mediate between the belligerents were much resented in France where – for the great majority – the onus was always on Germany to open negotiations by suing for peace. This was the predominant attitude in Britain, though advocates of a compromise peace become much more publicly outspoken after March 1917. So what were Germany's war aims?

Exercise   I now want you to read the 'Programme' of 9 September (*Primary Sources 1: World War I*, Document II.1), written by Kurt Riezler, Bethmann Hollweg's political secretary, but which is generally thought to represent the Chancellor's own views. It was addressed to the Vice-Chancellor and Minister of the Interior, Delbrück. Summarize this document; say what it *presupposed* and describe the kind of peace settlement envisaged in it. Which country is *not* mentioned in the document? Does the document help you understand why there was no compromise peace? ∎

Specimen answer   In summary, German war aims were to reduce France to a second rate power for all time and confine Russia to the periphery of Europe. Russian domination of the Poles and other subject peoples was to be ended. The French iron-ore field of Briey was to be annexed, and very possibly Belfort and the western slopes of the Vosges, along with the coastal strip from Dunkirk to Boulogne. France was to pay a war indemnity that would prohibit defence expenditure for 15 to 20 years. France would also be tied economically to Germany by an unequal commercial treaty that would secure the French market for German exports and exclude British commerce. Belgium was to be reduced to a vassal state. Liège and Verviers were to be annexed and, very possibly, Antwerp. The Belgian coast would be under German military control and the country reduced economically to a German province. French Flanders would be attached to this vassal state. Luxembourg would become a German federal state. The document envisaged a large European economic association, under Germany's leadership, that would stabilize her economic dominance over *Mitteleuropa* (Central Europe). It also alludes to the creation of a continuous African empire (i.e. from the Atlantic to the Indian Ocean) so it would seem that Bethmann Hollweg envisaged taking over the Belgian Congo and, possibly, Portuguese Mozambique. Neutral Holland would be brought into a closer relationship with Germany.

The document presupposed the imminent defeat of France and – by implication – a permanent check to the Russian military threat. It envisaged an 'imperialist' peace but, although there would be some annexations in Europe, German hegemony would be secured mainly by informal, economic means.

implies that these thoughts originated in July 1914 when Britain was assumed to be wanting no part of any 'Continental' war.

The document makes no mention of Britain (though it alludes to British commerce) which is puzzling. Did Bethmann Hollweg propose welding Europe into an economic bloc partly as a prelude to a long struggle – as much commercial as military – with the British Empire? It is difficult to judge. What should be clear is that, if these represented the German government's settled objectives, there was no serious prospect of a compromise between British, French and German war aims.

Discussion

The precise status of the September Programme has been contested ever since its publication by Fritz Fischer in *Germany's Aims in the First World War.* (Unit 5, p.164). Some have seen it as confirmation of the government's complicity with the annexationism of the Pan-German, ultra nationalist pressure groups. Others as highly provisional jottings, inspired by the ephemeral euphoria of expected victory, which did not reflect the government's collective view. The balance of the evidence suggests that Bethmann moderated his views on the war's outcome for Germany according to the military situation. From the minutes of a discussion he had with Falkenhayn, the Chief of Staff, in mid-November 1914, it is evident that both men had concluded that Germany could no longer defeat the Entente by military means. They now identified Britain as the main enemy, and various strategies were proposed to isolate her from her Allies. Their objectives became a separate peace with Russia, as a preliminary to victory in western Europe, and a relatively lenient peace towards France. The Eastern Command (*OberOst*), under Hindenburg and Ludendorff, dissented: for them, Russia was the main enemy whom they hoped to defeat comprehensively. But for the moment Bethmann and Falkenhayn carried more weight in determining German war aims. Exactly what settlement Bethmann hoped to reach with France is not clear: some argue that he was seeking a peace without annexations (though with an indemnity), but according to Fischer he 'held to the demand for the annexation of Longwy-Briey almost until he left office in July 1917' (Fischer, *World Power or Decline*, 1975, p.36). It is clear, though, that the government would not contemplate relinquishing control of Belgium. Furthermore, Bethmann informed a group of industrialists that any treaty with France should seek to incorporate her in a central European customs union. Thus, though German policy remained expansionist, there was a willingness to moderate expansionism in order to split the enemy (Stevenson, *The First World War and International Politics*, 1988, pp.87–106). □

Britain as main enemy as Aug 1, 1914

The war aims of any power reflected the complex inter-play of public and private interests. Though Bethmann Hollweg tried to censor discussion of war aims, Germany's authoritarian government was no more insulated from domestic pressure groups than the parliamentary democracies. In May 1915, six interest groups – ranging from the Peasants' League to the Central Union of

Social pressures

Industrialists – petitioned Bethmann to settle for no less than a peace of 'exploitation' in the west and east. The annexations they demanded in Belgium and eastern France had a total area of 50,000 square miles and a population of *c*.11 million, but they also wanted territory in eastern Europe on which to settle agricultural colonists. A War Aims Movement (*Kriegszielbewegung*) was formed by the industrialist, Alfred Hugenberg, and the Pan-Germanist, Heinrich Class, to publicise demands so ambitious that they anticipated German conquests in the next world war. Intellectual support for an annexationist victory came from German academics, not least internationally renowned historians. Over 350 university professors signed a petition demanding 'the most ruthless humiliation of England' through an indemnity and the acquisition of overseas naval bases. A far smaller number signed a rival, anti-annexationist petition. The Reichstag 'war-aims majority' insisted that any peace terms would have to be commensurate with German sacrifices.

The government's attitude to the formidable unofficial movement in favour of sweeping annexations and opposed to a compromise peace was ambiguous. Bethmann and other ministers were constrained by the political truce or *Burgfrieden*[5] and avoided public pronouncements that would have jeopardized the SPD's support for a supposedly defensive war. Privately, they sympathized with much of what the nationalist right was demanding, though they preferred to consolidate German power through informal control of client states rather than outright annexations. Ambiguity also arose from the tensions within German government between its civilian and military wings. As is evident from the September Programme, ministers were prepared to defer to the military over key political decisions, such as the cession of Belfort, from the outset of the war. During 1915 and 1916, the power and authority of Germany's most successful military partnership, Hindenburg and Ludendorff, who were close to the extremist War Aims Movement, grew at the expense of civilian ministers. Unlike Falkenhayn (who was dismissed as Chief of Staff in August 1916) they still believed the war could be won by a decisive battle and therefore saw no reason to adjust German war aims to the military deadlock. Somewhat paradoxically, their successes on the eastern front wrecked the strategy of separating Russia from the Entente. The heavy defeats inflicted on the Tsarist army in Poland encouraged extremist proposals for expansion (including the forcible resettlement of 16 million Poles to make way for German colonists) but did not compel the Tsarist Empire to withdraw from the war. A separate negotiated peace would have entailed a compromise with Russian interests on her western borders. The policy eventually agreed by the Central Powers was the proclamation of an autonomous Poland (November 1916) tied militarily and economically to Germany on the Belgian model: a vassal in the east to complement that in the west. At the same time, it was decided to separate Courland and Lithuania from Russia and to establish a total border of German and Polish territory against Russia according to strategic considerations. This territorial expansion of German power precluded a separate peace with Russia based on anything but force.

[5] *Burgfrieden*: in the Middle Ages this meant the social peace within the besieged castle or fortified town; for Germany in 1914, it had the connotations of a unified nation under siege.

Exercise   In early December 1916, German forces achieved one of their most spectacular victories with the defeat of Romania and the occupation of Bucharest. The Central Powers' military prospects had appeared quite bleak in August (which tempted Romania to enter the war) but Germany had stabilized both fronts and now controlled Romania's agricultural and mineral resources. Hindenburg and Ludendorff could claim credit for these successes (though in Romania they were actually due to Falkenhayn) and were in a position to block any moderation of Germany's war aims. They had a new hard-line ally amongst the civilian ministers in Arthur Zimmermann, who had taken over the Foreign Office. By a huge majority, the Reichstag had voted the Auxiliary Service Law (5 December) conscripting male labour for the war effort. It was in these circumstances that Bethmann addressed his peace proposals to the US Chargé d'Affaires. Please read his note (*Primary Sources 1: World War I*, Document II.2), describe its tone and say what Bethmann proposed to bring the war to a negotiated conclusion. Does it strike you as a serious bid for a compromise peace? ■

12/12/1916

Specimen answer   The tone strikes me as belligerently self-confident. Bethmann referred to recent
and discussion   victories in the Balkans and anticipated 'fresh successes'. He proposed to do no more than enter into negotiations from what he evidently believed was a militarily impregnable position. There is no reference to Belgium or occupied France. In its context, the Peace Note could scarcely be construed as anything more than an invitation to end the war on the Central Powers' terms, and was contemptuously rejected by the Entente. Lloyd George told the House of Commons, on his first appearance as Prime Minister:

> There has been some talk about proposals of peace. What are the proposals? There are none. To enter, upon the invitation of Germany proclaiming herself victorious, into a conference is to put our heads in a noose with the rope end in the hands of Germany.

The German government – or, at least, its hard-liners – almost certainly anticipated and welcomed this rebuff, for they intended the Note as a 'public relations' exercise that would shift the blame for the continuation of the war onto the Entente. Its rejection could serve to justify the resumption of unrestricted submarine warfare. □

Bethmann wrote this to seem "belligerent", to appear on the side of the generals. 7 months later he was gone, replaced by von Hertling.

The most sustained efforts to secure a negotiated peace occurred between March and November 1917. The first was a piece of secret diplomacy initiated in December 1916 by the new Emperor Karl of Austria-Hungary who wanted to take his country out of the war before its disintegration became irreversible. Through his brother-in-law, Prince Sixte de Bourbon, an officer in the Belgian Army, Karl informed France and Britain that Austria-Hungary would enter negotiations for a separate peace provided satisfactory guarantees were given as to the empire's territorial integrity. Germany was kept in ignorance of these proceedings. What scuppered this initiative was the promises the Entente had made to Italy of Habsburg territory: Britain and France had to calculate whether Italy's continued participation in the war was of more value than Austria-Hungary's departure. By a fine margin, they decided it was, and the episode petered out in June. Whether Karl could have 'delivered' on a separate peace is a moot point, since once the Germans got wind of negotiations for an Austrian armistice they would probably have intervened militarily in Vienna.

Meanwhile, organized public opinion – especially social democratic opinion – had rediscovered its voice. In Germany, the *Burgfrieden* came under great strain in the winter of 1916–17 because of food and fuel shortages, price inflation and the immense anxieties caused by mounting losses and the absence of loved ones. The dissident minority in the SPD who refused to support the war grew larger each time the Reichstag was asked to vote war credits. When an emergency budget had been discussed in the spring of 1916 about thirty anti-war deputies defied party discipline to form a separate parliamentary faction (and what proved to be the nucleus of the Independent Social Democrat Party or USPD set up in the following April). At Frankfurt, in October 1916, a meeting attended by about 30,000 people demanded peace on the basis of the status quo. Apart from arresting the most prominent dissidents, the government did surprisingly little to suppress the public discussion of war aims which overlapped with renewed demands for suffrage reform in Prussia and an end to the Kaiser's prerogatives in ministerial appointments. Democratization and a compromise peace became inseparable for an opposition that was still, in the mass, patriotic but no longer mute. The Reichstag asserted its right to discuss foreign politics by creating a Main Committee (*Hauptausschuss*) that sat almost continuously and provided a key forum for criticising the highest direction of the war. What remained of the political truce collapsed in March with the news of the revolution in Russia. Even the staunchest patriots amongst the SPD leadership could no longer contain the clamour for political reform and a peace without annexations and indemnities now that the liberal democrats had taken power in Russia. The 'logic' of military participation made the Prussian three-class franchise[6] morally indefensible: Bethmann himself pointed to the injustice of a well-heeled shirker enjoying political rights denied to a private with the Iron Cross. To the consternation of the military hierarchy, the Kaiser bowed to popular pressure: William II's Easter message anticipated the abolition of the three-class franchise after the war's victorious conclusion.

For the Supreme Command, annexationist war aims and Prussia's Junker-dominated constitution were equally non-negotiable, and inseparable in much the same way as reform and a compromise peace were for the opposition. At Ludendorff's insistence, Germany's leadership restated the Central Powers' war aims at a meeting at Kreuznach in April 1917. The resulting memorandum envisaged a harsh settlement in the east where German confidence in victory had been boosted by the February Revolution.[7] In the west, some slight moderation of the terms of the September Programme was contemplated: 'In the most extreme case', the memorandum recorded, 'France may receive a few corners of the border ... in order not to let a peace fail.' Britain was not mentioned in the Kreuznach memorandum which tersely concluded: 'Any armistice is to be limited to the war on land; the war at sea continues.' At that time, the submarine campaign was expected to starve Britain into submission.

[6] The franchise for the Prussian parliament (Lantdag) involved a property qualification which divided voters into three classes according to their wealth. This was a key factor in the persistence of the social and political power of the Junkers.

[7] As far as Germany, and most of the world was concerned, the Revolution occurred in March, but Russia still used the Julian calendar which was 13 days behind the Gregorian calendar used in the west.

[handwritten margin note:] politicians actively seeking peace, whilst military generals sought one 'final' victory.

Though Bethmann signed the document, he did so only to protect himself against the machinations of Ludendorff who was attempting to discredit the Chancellor as a proponent of a 'soft' peace. Bethmann saw no possibility of imminent peace negotiations and, in a note placed in the files, made it clear that he considered the whole discussion futile: 'I have co-signed the protocol because it would be laughable to depart over phantasies', he wrote. 'Naturally I will in no way allow myself to be bound by [it].' (If you need to refer to these quoted documents for a double assignment they are reproduced in Feldman, 1972.)

That Bethmann felt compelled to sign a document in which he did not believe is, of course, compelling testimony to his gravely weakened position. He was under attack, not only from the Supreme Command, but also from a parliamentary opposition that was increasingly willing to use the discussion of new credits (i.e. war credits that had to be voted in the Reichstag) to question the whole direction of the war. Remarkably, the most vociferous criticism came – not from the socialists – but from the Catholic Centre party leader, Matthias Erzberger, who until the previous autumn had been an ardent annexationist and advocate of unrestricted submarine warfare. He had almost certainly been briefed by the Chancellor's enemies in the Naval Office, for at sessions of the Main Committee on 5 and 6 July he used confidential information to demonstrate the failure of the submarine campaign. He had, too, recently visited Vienna and been warned of Austria-Hungary's dire prospects should the war last another winter. After bitterly attacking the highest direction of the war, Erzberger called on the Reichstag to reaffirm its belief in a peace of conciliation.

1917

A cross-party majority was found for the Peace Resolution passed by the Reichstag on 19 July which condemned forced territorial acquisitions and political, economic or financial oppressions as irreconcilable with 'a peace of understanding'. But it added that, as long as enemy governments refused to enter such a peace, 'the German nation will stand together as a man ... and fight until its own and its allies' right to life and development is secured.' Meanwhile, the Supreme Command had made Bethmann's position untenable by threatening to resign if he remained in office. To the Reichstag majority he was an obstacle to a moderate peace, but to the patriotic, nationalist right, he was a luke-warm annexationist who had caved in to political liberalism. His successor, Count von Hertling, was virtually appointed by the Supreme Command.

Ludendorff strove to recuperate popular support for an imperialist war by a programme of patriotic instruction amongst the troops and by sponsoring the German Fatherland Party. Schoolmasterly efforts to indoctrinate the ranks on the evils of parliamentary government and the need for territorial expansion were a dismal failure. The Fatherland Party, which campaigned for an annexationist peace and against suffrage reform and the Reichstag peace resolution, was a formidable success. It was lavishly funded by German industrialists and within six months of its founding boasted 1.25 million members, more than the SPD. Though party political activity was formally forbidden in the armed forces, the military authorities turned a blind eye to the Fatherland Party when it recruited amongst the ranks. But Ludendorff and his political allies could not avert the deepening polarization of German society into those seeking a 'Hindenburg peace' with vast annexations and huge indemnities, and those wanting a 'Scheidemann peace' of conciliation (so-called after the SPD leader). The nearest the nationalist right came to re-uniting German society behind its programme was with the signing of the Treaty of Brest-Litovsk with Soviet Russia. Only the USPD (Independent German Social Democrats) voted against its ratification and popular exultation greeted the huge extension of German power. Russia was deprived of 30 per cent of its population and half its industry, and forced to pay an indemnity of 6 billion marks. A cordon of satellite states was created on her western border, all policed by German forces. Under a separate Treaty, the Ukraine was expected to make huge grain deliveries to the Central Powers. In the event, Ludendorff's territorial megalomania brought its own nemesis. Over a million troops were needed to occupy Germany's gains in the east when manpower was desperately required for the offensives on the western front. Scarcely any of the resources promised by the Ukraine were actually delivered. Not least, when news of the harsh terms reached the west, popular support for the peace movement ebbed away. Brest-Litovsk was widely seen as a demonstration of what a victorious Germany would impose on the Entente. France and Britain faced the German onslaughts of the spring of 1918 with unified societies – certainly by comparison with the Central Powers. Militarily, they had their backs to the wall, but the resolve to fight the war to a victorious conclusion created a renewed consensus. There could be no compromise.

3   THE EXTENSION OF THE WAR

Why did the war extend so widely? Why was it not confinable within Europe? If we consider the period up to American entry (April 1917) we can identify two processes that simultaneously sucked in an array of belligerents. First, once the rival coalitions had an inkling of the war's likely duration, they began to search for allies who, it was hoped, would tilt the military balance in their favour.

The search for allies

The first peripheral state to be drawn in was Ottoman Turkey, which negotiated an alliance with Germany in late July 1914 and declared war on the Entente on 1 November. Whether Turkey was 'sought out' by Germany is a moot point. As Ulrich Trumpener demonstrated, far from being over-awed by its mighty ally, Turkey stood up to and even exploited Germany from the signing of their alliance to the end of the war (Trumpener, *Germany and the Ottoman Empire 1914–1918*, 1968). In July 1914, the empire was reeling under a string of recent defeats and was considered militarily worthless by Liman von Sanders, the head of the German military mission in Constantinople. The initiative in seeking the alliance came from a clique of 'Young Turk' ministers, led by Enver Pasha (War) and Talaat Bey (Interior), who saw an opportunity to end the empire's humiliating dependence on the west and to transform it into a modern national state. The only attraction for the Germans was a Turkish commitment to take action against Russia, but Bethmann doubted whether Turkey would be a useful ally since its leaders were reluctant to participate in any fighting. Nevertheless, the Turks extracted a secret German guarantee of the empire's territorial integrity in exchange for strict neutrality in the conflict between Austria-Hungary and Serbia and an equivocal promise to support Germany in a war against Russia. The treaty was so worded that the Turks were able to avoid the second commitment on a technicality. On 4 August, Turkey ordered a general mobilization but simultaneously declared its neutrality. Before the archives were opened, it was believed that the despatch of two German warships to the Dardanelles intimidated the Turks into the Central Powers' camp. In fact, the ships were given sanctuary from a Royal Navy squadron, and allowed to enter the Black Sea, only on stiff conditions that demonstrated Turkish determination to avoid German – and other European – domination. (One condition was the abolition of the juridical and commercial privileges, known as the Capitulations, which Europeans enjoyed in the Ottoman Empire.) Once the warships were in Turkish territorial waters, Germany's ambassador was informed that Turkey contemplated joining a neutrality pact with Greece and Bulgaria, and the status of belligerent vessels needed to be regularized. A fictitious purchase, and their incorporation in the Turkish navy, was proposed. Though the Germans objected strongly to this ruse, the Turkish government presented them with a *fait accompli* by unilaterally announcing it. Germany had little choice but to acquiesce in this extortion: had the ships been ordered into the Mediterranean, they would have been destroyed and relations with Turkey would have deteriorated. In the following weeks, the 'Young Turk' clique in the government decided that it was in the national interest to enter the war because they believed Russia faced imminent defeat. The moment was opportune, they thought, to reverse the empire's territorial disintegration and expand into Turkic-speaking Central Asia. The Grand Vizier and the majority of ministers favoured neutrality but Enver conspired with the Minister for Marine to open hostilities with Russia by authorising the newly acquired ships to attack Odessa and destroy Russian shipping in the Black Sea.

The Ottoman armies depended for their munitions on overland shipments from Germany, so Turkey's entry into the war greatly enhanced the strategic significance of the southern Balkans. Both sides began wooing and cajoling Bulgaria and Greece, either to enter the war or maintain a strict neutrality and cut off supplies to Turkey. In October 1915, Bulgaria was finally persuaded by the promise of Serbian territory to join the Central Powers in the third invasion of Serbia. France and Britain violated Greek neutrality by landing forces at Salonika in a fruitless attempt to relieve Serbia. They acted with the connivance of the Prime Minister, the pro-western Venizelos, but against the wishes of the pro-German King Constantine. For the rest of the war, Greece was a pawn of the Entente, which infringed its sovereign rights quite as blatantly as Germany had Belgium's. Romania declared war on Austria-Hungary in August 1916 when it appeared that a Russian victory was imminent.

The most important of the neutrals – and the most assiduously courted – was Italy. Most Italian newspapers and the great majority of deputies had welcomed Italy's declaration of neutrality on 3 August. This was not a repudiation of the Triple Alliance which required Italy to come to the aid of Austria-Hungary or Germany only in the event of a *defensive* war. Once Britain declared war on 4 August, the Central Powers appreciated that there was little possibility of Italy joining them because she depended on imported coal and wheat and was very exposed to British naval power. Nevertheless, they valued Italy's continuing neutrality highly, so when it became known that the Entente was tempting the Italians to intervene with promises of territory in Dalmatia, the Central Powers offered them territorial inducements to remain neutral. Both sides meddled in Italian politics to further their ends. France and Britain subsidized Italian newspapers and politicians who favoured intervention; the Central Powers funded the non-interventionist press. The Italian Foreign Minister, Sonnino, found himself ideally placed to pursue his country's claims to *Italia irredenta*.[8] The most coveted region was the South Tyrol – or Trentino (also known as Alto Adige). Austria-Hungary was willing to concede parts of Slovenia and Croatia (where Italian-speaking minorities lent a spurious nationalist legitimacy to Italy's crudely territorial imperialism). But it balked at handing over the South Tyrol, which had been part of the Habsburg patrimony for centuries and had a German-speaking majority. By March 1915, Sonnino had concluded that the Entente was better placed to satisfy Italy's territorial ambitions. In April, after much haggling, he signed the secret Treaty of London by which Italy promised to enter the war within a month in exchange for the recognition of its claims to the Tyrol, Istria, Dalmatia, and Albania (where Italy was demanding a protectorate). The Treaty was incompatible with Britain's and France's public declarations in support of Serbian territorial integrity – but they had exaggerated notions of Italian military capacity and few scruples about disposing of far-away Balkan peoples. Vaguer promises were made to support Italy's colonial aspirations and its designs on Ottoman Turkey, which the Entente was expecting to partition into spheres of influence after the war. Britain stumped up an immediate loan of £50 million. Russia's objections to Italian expansion into Slav territory were assuaged by France and Britain simultaneously recognizing its claim to Constantinople and the Straits.

   The Central Powers probably learned of the Treaty's terms and raised their offer in a last-ditch attempt to avert Italy's entry into the war. Under intense German pressure, the Habsburg Foreign Minister conceded the Tyrol, provided the cession was kept secret and took place after the war. Italian neutrality was to be handsomely rewarded, but only when the Central Powers had won. Sonnino naturally suspected this offer, and realistically appreciated that Italy could not grasp 'world power' status without participating in the defeat of Austria-Hungary. Even so, the courtship was not over. When the Italian government failed to reply, the German ambassador, Bülow, approached Giovanni Giolitti, the former premier and still Italy's most influential parliamentarian. Giolitti was a neutralist out of expediency rather than deep conviction. He knew the country was militarily ill-prepared and thought more was to be gained by staying on the sidelines and bidding up the price of Italy's alignment. The great majority of deputies publicly signalled their support for a policy of 'wait and see' by leaving their calling cards at his Rome address, and it appeared that Giolitti's following would bring down the government and form a neutralist ministry. But parliament was sidelined by an interventionist *coup d'état*. In Rome and other big cities, irredentist mobs were threatening prominent non-interventionists and, in an atmosphere of rising tension, the king used his large residual powers

---

[8] 'Unredeemed Italy', i.e. those Italian speaking enclaves that had been 'left out' when the state was unified in 1861–70.

under the constitution to declare war on Austria-Hungary. (Declaration of war against Germany was delayed until August 1916.) The cowed deputies then endorsed this decision which damaged the country's political institutions and discredited its governing class. The Italian state was levered into its 'final war of unification'.

The manner in which Italy entered the war palpably conditioned its impact on Italian society and politics. Most Italians simply acquiesced in a squalid gamble that had been wished upon them by a violent minority. The peasants felt the war was nothing to do with them. The great majority of the Socialist Party adopted the equivocal formula: '*non aderire né sabotare*' (neither support for, nor sabotage of the war effort), which contrasted sharply with the full-blooded commitment of patriotic Labour in France, Britain and Germany. A French officer reported on public opinion in Rome:

> You simply would not believe here that Italy is at war ... The population does not seem to have the slightest interest in events ... The war is scarcely talked about. When it is spoken of, it is with blithe confidence. The Italians do not seem to have our feeling that the nation's life and indpendence is at stake in this war. They seem to think of it as a Libyan war on a larger scale.
>
> (Cited in Melograni, *Storia Politica della Grande Guerra 1915–1918*, 1969, p.7)

The army was ill-prepared for modern warfare, and its badly-led soldiers were soon demoralized by heavy losses in the Isonzo offensive. Indiscipline was rife by the winter of 1915–16, particularly amongst units resting out of the line. When an Alpine unit left its barracks for the front on 26 December, the men began yelling: '*Abbasso Salandra*! [the prime minister] *Viva Giolitti!*' They refused to entrain, cut the telegraph wire, and incited another unit to disobey orders. For this insubordination, a military tribunal condemned 31 men to prison terms ranging from 5 to 15 years. In a letter to Salandra of 14 January, the field commander, General Cadorna, deplored the leniency of the sentences. He insisted that the most effective measure of dealing with collective insubordination and safeguarding discipline was decimation – the shooting of every tenth man. From the spring of 1916, Italy's reluctant soldiers were subject to the most rigorous military justice administered in the war: decimation was applied on a vast scale. Panicking men were shot out of hand after the rout at Caporetto (October 1917). Because the Home Front was less cohesive and united than that of the other belligerents, it too had to be dragooned behind the war effort. The army took direct charge of industrial mobilization, and compelled war workers to wear uniforms, sleep in barracks, and labour under military discipline (Tomassini, 'The home front in Italy', 1996).

[handwritten margin note: barbarity as a result of politicians taking a country into a war nobody voted for.]

The Armenian tragedy

The Ottoman Empire remained in late 1914 a huge state embracing nearly all the Middle East, so the war's geographic limits were vastly extended by its participation. But the moral frontiers of war were also pushed back in a horrendous fashion because Ottoman belligerency occasioned the twentieth century's first genocide. Ethnic Turks constituted only about 40 per cent of the empire's population, of which about a fifth were highly visible non-Muslim communities of Jews, Greeks and Armenians. Arabs and Kurds were the other main ethnic groups. Communal tensions were rising before the autumn of

1914 because of a huge influx of Muslim refugees from the Balkan Wars, many victims of ethnic cleansing. The nationalist ideology of the Young Turk movement led to a spate of war-time legislation designed to foster Turkish national identity: a Language Law, for example, made Turkish the compulsory language of commerce. Though the Young Turks had originally espoused a cosmopolitan nationalism, under the impress of war they moved towards a policy of 'Turkification' that was immensely threatening to the empire's minority communities. Most non-Muslims could buy exemption from military service, and those who were recruited were used only in labour battalions. Arabs were considered inferior soldiers, so the burden of combat fell overwhelmingly on Turkish peasants from Anatolia. The war was thus 'nationalized'. It became a forcing house for violent ethnic nationalism to which Armenians, although generally loyal subjects of the Sultan, were the most exposed.

The Turkish army fought on four fronts, but always with more than half its forces committed to a savage campaign in the Caucasus where much of the local population was Armenian. Some openly sympathized with Russia, and at the outbreak of war the Armenian deputy for Erzerum in the Turkish parliament went over to the Russians with a large number of Armenian deserters. The facts have never been properly established but, according to a reputable Turkish account by Ahmed Emin, the deputy and an invading force of Armenian volunteers massacred the whole Muslim population in the plain of Passinlar, an area temporarily cut off from the rest of Turkey. 'These events created an unofficial state of war between the Armenians and the Turks' (Emin, *Turkey in the World War*, 1930, pp.218–19). Turkey's official representatives insist to this day that, with Russian support, Armenian insurgents were attempting to establish an Armenian state in a predominantly Turkish area. This was not a conclusion reached by the British historian, Arnold Toynbee, who gathered together a remarkable volume of testimony from refugees and American and German missionaries soon after reports of massacres of Armenians reached the west. He acknowledged that there had been Armenian sedition and anti-Muslim violence, but its scale was much exaggerated, and that the great majority of Armenians presented no threat to the empire. (Toynbee's research was embodied in the report by Viscount Bryce, *The Treatment of Armenians in the Ottoman Empire*, HMSO, 1916.) Nonetheless, the Young Turk leaders evidently *believed* in a vast Armenian conspiracy and ordered a terrible retribution. Emin himself conceded that 'certain influential Turkish politicians' were bent on 'the extermination of the Armenian minority ... with the idea of bringing about racial homogeneity in Asia Minor' (Emin, *Turkey in the World War*, 1930, p.220). Armenians throughout the empire were disarmed, their civic leaders and adult males near the fighting front were shot en masse, and civilian communities deported into the Syrian desert where huge numbers died of exposure and starvation. The Armenians were relatively wealthy, and their property was systematically pillaged by the gendarmes who perpetrated the massacres. Kurdish tribesmen, the Armenians' traditional enemies, were allowed to prey upon defenceless columns. The total number of deaths has never been accurately computed and estimates range from 500,000 to 1.5 million.

[handwritten margin notes:]

war gives politicians nationalists) the opportunity to 'ethnically cleanse' their country.

Germany 'believed' that Nürnberg had been bombed.

Communal victimization in the multi-ethnic Ottoman Empire was not a novel phenomenon: Armenians had been massacred in Turkey as recently as 1894–6 and 1909. But the scale and persistence of the atrocities in 1915–17, the demonization and destruction of a whole community, the fact that victims suffered simply for their ethnic and cultural identity, the implication of key ministers in the central government, the heightened nationalism used to justify extreme measures – all pointed to a new form of social violence. Modern total war had created the material and cultural conditions for a quantum leap in state criminality. The genocide of the Armenians was symptomatic of that terrible degeneration which led to the industrialized murder of Jews and Gypsies and the starving to death of millions of Soviet prisoners of war.

For the peoples of the Ottoman Empire, the First World War was only part of a traumatic decade that began with the first Balkan war in October 1912 and ended with the defeat of the Greek invasion in 1922 and the deposition of the Sultan. Much of Anatolia was devastated by almost continuous warfare and depopulated by a loss of life proportionately far greater than in western and central Europe. Some 2.5 million Anatolian Muslims died, perhaps one million Armenians and 300,000 Greeks. The population of Anatolia declined by 17.7 per cent through war-related mortality, compared with 3.5 per cent in France (Zürcher, 'Little Mehmet in the desert', 1996, p.238). The war unleashed vicious circles of communal violence: when Tsarist authority collapsed in 1917, Armenians in areas under Russian occupation massacred thousands of Muslims; the invading Greeks razed Turkish villages to the ground; when the Kemalist forces repulsed the Greeks, they forced about 1.5 million Greek refugees gathered in Smyrna (now Izmir) into the sea, amid appalling carnage.

Imperial co-belligerency

The second process that extended the war beyond Europe and sucked in more combatants flowed from British intervention: the 'white' Dominions, India and the colonies were, without any consultation, made co-belligerents. Despite their loyalty being taken for granted, most colonial subjects who expressed an opinion supported Britain. Local committees and public meetings throughout India, for example, resoundingly cast in their lot with the Empire. Over a million Indian soldiers – all volunteers – were despatched overseas during the war. Canada, Australia and New Zealand mobilized 1.2 million men, almost one-fifth of the numbers enlisted in the British Isles. The 'satellite' campaigns in Gallipoli, the Middle East and East Africa could not have been fought without the colonial co-belligerents. The longer the war lasted, the more significant became their contribution in manpower and economic resources at the war's European epicentre. By 1918, Australians and Canadians were spearheading the Allied offensives on the western front; one third of the Royal Flying Corps' new pilots were coming from Canada alone. The 'imperial' contribution significantly lightened the impact of the war on Britain. Had it fought simply as a European nation-state, its military casualties would have been 31 per cent higher, the fiscal burden of the war much greater, and the state's long-term commitments to veterans, the disabled and war widows proportionately larger. France, too, fought as an empire, and drew upon the lives and labour of its imperial subjects: about 600,000 colonial soldiers were recruited during the war, and the empire also provided about 200,000 labour conscripts. But the British Empire differed from the French in scale and character. Notionally, it brought a quarter of the world's population into the war, but as a coalition within the Entente coalition. The 'white' Dominions were virtually independent and self-interested states; by late 1916 their leaders were influencing the direction and aims of the war. Lloyd George, who succeeded Asquith as prime minister on 6 December, felt compelled to create an Imperial War Cabinet as a sounding board for Dominion opinion, and to appoint the South African general, Jan Christian Smuts, to his government in 1917. By the end of the war, South Africa and Australia were internationally recognized as regional powers in their own right: they became the Mandate authorities under the League of Nations of the former colonies in South West Africa and New Guinea.

Britain's participation also influenced the decisions of two allies, Japan and Portugal, to enter the war. Though not required by the terms of the Anglo-Japanese Alliance (1902), the Japanese Cabinet calculated that belligerency was in the national interest, and declared war on Germany on 23 August 1914. Japanese troops then occupied the German bases on leased territory in Shantung, on the Chinese coast, and later seized all German-held Pacific islands north of the Equator. The outbreak of war amongst the major imperialist powers had created a power vacuum in the Far East which Japan hoped to fill by establishing a protectorate over China. In the New Year, Japan presented a list of twenty-one demands to the Chinese government which were intended to consolidate its own informal imperialism in China while weakening the influence of all other Treaty Port powers.[9] In the event, American and British opposition led the Japanese to moderate their demands. The hapless Chinese government later declared war on Germany in the belief that its status as a western ally would afford some protection against Japan. Portugal offered to enter the war as an ancient ally of Britain, though the real motive was to ensure the continuation of its bankrupt African empire. Germany and Britain had very nearly agreed on a partition of Portuguese Africa in 1913, and it was well known that a victorious Germany would extend its colonial domain at Portugal's expense. Participating on Britain's side seemed the best insurance against the dissolution of Greater Portugal.

American participation

American belligerency in April 1917 marked the true globalization of the conflict, not in strictly military terms, but in the mobilization of a crushing weight of world economic resources against the Central Powers. The process by which the USA was drawn into the war, despite the avowed neutralism of all political leaders during the 1916 elections, arose out of the interlocking of the major economies discussed in part 1 of this unit. Long before America became a military and political Associate of the Entente, it was its principal economically. There was no reason, in principle, why the Central Powers should not have purchased American food and *matériel* but the British blockade was an effective deterrent. A German diplomatic note (4 April, 1915) bitterly reproached the US

---

[9] 'Treaty ports' – the term given to ports on the Chinese coasts in which the European powers and the USA were granted commercial and other privileges under the unequal treaties imposed on Imperial China during the nineteenth century.

government: 'In point of fact the United States is delivering goods only to the enemies of Germany. The theoretical willingness to supply Germany also, if shipments thither were possible, does not alter the case.' Subsequent attempts to break the blockade by using neutral carriers and merchant submarines did little to alter the Entente's huge advantage in access to American resources.

From late 1914, it was evident to many American businessmen and merchants that they could profit from neutrality and that their best customer would be Britain. Britain was in a better position than any other combatant to continue reciprocal trade, it commanded the sea and (what became crucially important as the war went on) British subjects owned huge portfolios of dollar-denominated assets which HM Treasury was empowered to purchase compulsorily for sale in New York. (British investors were given Treasury bonds for their US stocks and shares.) Wall Street was not interested in French investments in Tsarist and Ottoman bonds. Only the British government could draw upon a great reserve of dollars with which to purchase food and *matériel*, not only for its own war effort but for its allies'. From September 1915, Britain guaranteed the purchases of Russia and Italy in America, and from May 1916 those of France. Up to April 1917, some $14,000 million in foreign-held American securities had been repatriated to finance Entente purchasing. Vast though this sum was, it fell far short of the need. Within two years of the outbreak of war, British war expenditure alone in the USA totalled $20,000 million dollars. By February 1916, the orders of the British Ministry of Munitions required the movement of 90,000 tons of freight each month out of American ports. By November of that year, two fifths of British war expenditure was devoted to American supplies. Responsibility for placing contracts and ensuring that deliveries were fulfilled lay with a team of British civil servants (mostly businessmen temporarily recruited by Lloyd George) stationed in the USA. By April 1917, its 1,600 members were overseeing the expenditure of $83 million a week on behalf of the Entente.

Vital though American supplies were, it is essential to note that the USA was *not* the arsenal of democracy it became in 1940. The United States was not a great military power and had only a limited munitions industry. It produced very little artillery during the First World War; even in late 1918, the US army depended on the French munitions industry for heavy weaponry. American manufacturers mainly provided uncomplicated mass-produced goods (rifles, ammunition, uniforms, boots) and in-puts (such as steel) for the Entente munitions industries. The main 'high technology' exports were machine tools (indispensable for the expansion of the Entente munitions industries) and vehicle components, which were assembled under licence in Britain and France. Oils, petrol, preserved meat and other foodstuffs, and industrial raw materials were also exported in vast quantities.

By late 1916, Britain had exhausted its dollar assets and accumulated enormous debts to American financial institutions. Under American neutrality law, no public loans could be made to any belligerent and, initially, the Wilson administration had frowned on private loans. However, after the sinking of the *Lusitania*, it allowed the Anglo-French Loan Mission (September 1915) to reach an agreement with an American banking syndicate whereby Entente bonds issued in the USA would be underwritten. The bonds were a flop with the American public, but the Loan Mission convinced the bankers of Britain's credit-worthiness, and a series of loans at ever higher rates of interest were raised in New York. These loans were the indispensable financial lubricant of the Entente's purchasing; if they were not forthcoming, the highest strategic direction of the war was jeopardized. The deterioration in British-US relations during 1916 and the British government's declining credit-worthiness were having alarming consequences for its financial operations. The US merchant marine was expanding rapidly, and exporters – along with their Congressional representatives – were increasingly angered by the Royal Navy's blockade. Britain's moral standing had been lowered by the suppression of the Easter Rising and the execution of Sir Roger Casement. The British government's publication, in July 1916, of a blacklist of 87 US and 350 Latin American firms who were accused of trading with Central Powers greatly angered Wilson. He told his confidant, Colonel House:

> I am ... about at the end of my patience with Great Britain and the Allies. This blacklist business is the last straw ... I am seriously considering asking Congress to authorize me to prohibit loans and restrict exportations to the Allies.

> (Burk, *Britain, America and the Sinews of War,* 1985, p.80)

The declining value of the pound weakened Britain in its negotiations with Wall Street. In October, the Chancellor of the Exchequer warned the Cabinet:

> We ought never to be so placed that only a public issue in America within a fortnight stands between us and insolvency ... [B]y next June or earlier, the [US] President will be in a position, if he wishes, to dictate his own terms to us.

> (Ibid, p.81))

In the following month, an Interdepartmental Committee warned the Cabinet that the USA was 'an absolutely irreplaceable source of supply' (ibid.). At this time, J.P. Morgan – Britain's financial agent on Wall Street – was planning to issue $1 billion in British Treasury bills.[10] When he notified the Federal Reserve Board (as he was legally bound to) the Board warned banks and private investors in late November of the undesirability of investing too heavily in short-term foreign securities. The market for Allied bonds collapsed and the sterling exchange rate plummeted. Britain's credit in the USA was destroyed, and there were no more American securities to sell. Apart from purely financial considerations, the Federal Reserve's action had been closely linked to President Wilson's launching of a peace initiative and his determination to end the war by mediation. Except for isolated individuals (such as Lansdowne) most opinion leaders in the Entente deeply resented Wilson's initiative for they recognized that this was an unfavourable moment to open negotiations.

The crisis in British-US financial and political relations in the winter of 1916–17 was, perhaps, the most serious of the war. Its continued prosecution by the Entente depended on the goodwill of American bankers yet Britain was unable to meet its obligations and faced bankruptcy on Wall Street. Relief came from a quite unexpected quarter: the German government. On 31 January, the US administration was told that all shipping, including neutral vessels, would be liable to be sunk without warning in the seas around Britain, France and Italy. On 3 February, the USA broke off diplomatic relations. America's entry into the war did not inevitably follow, but with the sinking of American vessels public

[10] Treasury bill: the government's normal instrument for raising short-term credit.

sympathy swung back towards the Entente. New lines of credit were opened to ease the financing of the Entente's purchases. What brought the decision for war closer was one of German diplomacy's most spectacular 'own goals': on 19 January, Zimmermann had telegraphed the German minister in Mexico to advise him that Germany was about to resume unrestricted submarine warfare and to instruct him to seek out an offensive alliance with Mexico if the USA abandoned its neutrality. With German support, Mexico was to recover lost territory in Texas, New Mexico and Arizona. Germany also hoped to persuade Japan to change sides and wanted the Mexican President to act as intermediary. British Naval Intelligence intercepted and deciphered the message (as in the Second World War, British intelligence was brilliantly served by academics on loan from universities). When Wilson was informed, he was outraged. With the telegram's publication on 1 March, German-American opinion and the Hearst press (which had been hostile to the Entente) were silenced. There was now a popular demand for hostilities against Germany.

In the 1920s and 30s, it was often asserted that the munitions traffic and the financial operations that supported it were the decisive influence on America's ultimate participation in the war. Cynics claimed that the American financial oligarchy had lent so much to the Entente that Germany simply could not be allowed to win. The bankers had ignored the people's real interests and levered the country into a war. All the evidence shows that the alleged conspiracy to save J.P. Morgan's millions was a fantasy. But in one critical sense, the munitions traffic *was* decisive: it was such an overwhelming advantage to the Entente that the German government concluded the USA's formal declaration of war would make very little difference. It gambled on a course of action – which Bethmann described as 'a second declaration of war' – in the belief that it had nothing to lose: a belligerent USA would be no worse than a neutral USA.

[handwritten margin note: Why the war lasted so long]

Towards a peoples' war

The Central Powers precipitated a 'Cabinet war' in late July 1914: a short conflict with the limited objectives. They were defeated by a global coalition whose leading spokesman, President Wilson, insisted in October 1918 that it was no longer a 'statesmen's war' but a 'peoples' war', in which 'statesmen must follow the clarified common thought or be broken' (quoted in Mayer, *Political Origins of the New Diplomacy*, 1959, p.329). The extension of the war had, evidently, changed its ideological character. Wilson was little concerned as to which states or individuals were responsible for the war; he believed that its basic causes were irresponsible government *as such* and a lack of transparency in international relations. Consequently, he regarded the entrenchment of popular democracy and open diplomacy as necessary conditions for a just and lasting peace. Unlike the political leaders of Britain and France, Wilson was prepared to subvert the authority of enemy governments by appealing directly to the German people or the subject nationalities of the Habsburg empire. By the spring of 1918, his diplomacy had added a revolutionary dimension to the western powers' war aims, a dimension which Lloyd George and Clemenceau had resisted right up to January. Later commentators were to claim that, while they were 'realists', Wilson was an impractical doctrinaire. The truth was more complex. From early in the war, Wilson had appreciated that the balance of world power had been irrevocably altered by the self-destruction of the Concert of Europe. He brought the USA into the war determined to remould the international order in a way which would register the accretion of American political, economic and military power. He was as uncompromising in the pursuit of total victory as any western leader, but perceived more clearly than most that the political and social settlement imposed by the victors would be as significant for a lasting peace as the international arrangements. With considerable perspicacity, he recognized before the war was won that Lenin and the Bolsheviks would be as much a threat to the post-war order as German militarism. There were many reasons why Wilson failed to establish a 'New World Order', but excessive idealism was not one of them.

4   TOWARDS TOTAL WAR

The three dimensions of total war

The expression 'total war' can mean rather different things in different contexts. When Georges Clemenceau became French premier in November 1917, he told the Chamber of Deputies: 'we present ourselves to you with one thought – total war'. The forceful rhetoric was intended to dispel the defeatism associated with Caillaux and the mutinies. The premier went on: 'No more pacifist campaigns, no more German intrigues, no treason, no semi-treason. Just war, war, and nothing but war' (quoted in Bernard and Dubief, *The Decline of the Third Republic 1914–1938*, 1988, p.59). In Germany, Ludendorff also spoke of waging 'total war' but intended something more than an unwavering will to victory: he was referring to a military *doctrine* or a set of basic strategic precepts. Nineteenth-century military theorists had argued that the principal objectives in war were to destroy the enemy's armed forces and take possession of his material capacities for armed aggression. International conventions had embodied this doctrine in the laws of war by making the weakening of the enemy's military forces the only lawful procedure for a combatant state.[11] Civilian life and property had a protected status. Ludendorff contended that twentieth-century warfare between industrialized nation-states had to be guided by a different doctrine: 'War, far from being the concern of the military forces alone, [now] directly touches the life and soul of every single member of the belligerent nations. Total war is thus directed not only against the fighting forces, but indirectly against the nations themselves' (quoted in Falls, *The Nature of Modern Warfare*, 1941, p.8). The precept that modern warfare had to be waged without distinction as to armed forces and civilians had an obvious corollary: the pursuit of victory entailed the 'total' mobilization of the demographic and economic resources available to the combatant state.

I will use the term 'total war' to refer not to a doctrine but to a process. The more grammatically correct term would be 'totalization', and it is really more appropriate because 'total war' did not break out in August 1914. The

[11] The most important were the conventions humanizing and codifying the rules of warfare adopted at the first Hague Peace Conference in 1899 (discussed in Roberts, p.201).

Ludendorff's + quote

combatants 'totalized' the conflict only as they saw it becoming a protracted struggle between finely balanced coalitions. The process involved simultaneous 'widening' and 'deepening': the conflict was extended geographically, but also deepened its impact on populations and social institutions as states dug into their manpower reserves and more economic resources were diverted to war production. In thinking about the nature of the war, I have found it useful to envisage the process of 'totalization' in terms of a three dimensional, dynamic model. You may find this excessively abstract, but I hope it will help you answer such as questions as 'Was 1914–18 a 'total' war?' or 'How did the conflict that broke out in August 1914 become a 'total' war?' Unless we have a *concept* of total war, answering questions like these can involve fruitless semantic disputes in which historians disagree about the meaning of words rather than the events they are trying to explain. There is another question the model can help us address: 'Was 1914–18 the first 'total' war?' If 'total' just means long, very widespread, bitterly ideological, and hugely destructive of civilian life and property, then the Thirty Years War (1618–48) was 'total'. We could cite numerous examples of 'total' conquest from the destruction of Persia's irrigation-based civilization by the Mongol war-lord, Timur, to Sherman's march through the Confederacy in the American Civil War. Nobody would argue that 'totalization' of war after August 1914 was unprecedented in every respect, and our model should identify what features of the process were specific to the twentieth century's economic infrastructures and technologies (and its politics and culture), and what were generic to large-scale wars throughout the modern period.

We can start putting together the model with the banal observation that international wars in the modern world are fought by states in a system of states. One process of 'totalization' is the spread of a conflict throughout the *system*. Its theoretic limit is globalization – the world at war. The first box represents that dimension schematically.

The second dimension I call the *'enemy-oriented'* dimension of 'total' war, and it is one in which we can gauge the *intensity* of the conflict. In wars of low intensity (or limited nature) the enemy is the opposing armed forces. Civilians have recognized non-combatant status and are accorded rights of passage; the opposing forces might follow a convention of not attacking unfortified towns; truces might be observed to ensure that vital economic functions (such as harvesting) continue or to celebrate religious rituals in common. The intensification of the conflict in this dimension involves the ever closer identification of the enemy state with the society and people 'contained' within that state. Certain political and ideological factors would encourage this identification: where and when *nationalism* is the legitimating principle of the state, there is an inherent tendency to identify the enemy with a nation. The cultural conditions necessary for popular nationalism (widespread literacy, a mass press) facilitate the identification of the enemy state with the enemy nation in wartime. The theoretic limits of this dimension are (i) the obliteration of any distinction between combatants and non-combatants within the enemy nation and (ii) genocide. We are constructing a model, and it might be wondered whether any state has been so barbaric as to ignore the distinction between babies and enemy adults when waging war. In practice, even democratic states waging just wars have: the RAF's strategic bombing campaign in the Second World War was intended to 'de-house' a large proportion of Germany's civilian population. It killed Germans

The international dimension of 'total war'
Pre-war **coalition building**: the Triple Alliance [Austria-Hungary, Germany, Italy] (1882, re-negotiated 1887, 1891) → the Dual Alliance [France, Russia]; Entente Cordiale [France, Britain] (1904, followed by Anglo-French staff talks)
    outbreak of coalition war → military stalemate →
    search for allies [November 1914, Turkey enters war; May 1915, Italy declares war on Austria; September 1915, Bulgaria concludes convention with Central Powers and attacks Serbia; August 1916, Romania declares war on Austria] →
    blockade warfare → infringement of neutral rights → worsening relations between Britain and USA →
    unrestricted submarine warfare [February, 1917, Germany resumes attacks on neutral shipping] →
    widening of the anti-German coalition [April, USA declares war on Germany; the Central American states – except Mexico – follow suit, as does Brazil. By 1918, 38 of the world's states were at war with Germany]
'Globalizing' factors:

1   alliance building in the international system

2   international division of labour between industrialized powers and primary producers

3   new military technology (submarine + radio communication)

The 'enemy-oriented' dimension of 'total war'
violation of neutral and civilian rights → atrocities against Belgian, French and other civilians →
    'demonization' of the enemy → xenophobia → spy mania → internment of enemy aliens → Royal family changes its name to Windsor, Battenbergs become Mountbattens
    economic warfare waged against enemy economies resource denial → unrestricted submarine warfare → hunger blockade
    war waged on enemy morale → Zeppelin and Gotha raids to terrify civilians → strategic air offensive against Germany planned by the RAF in the autumn of 1918 but not executed
'Intensifying' factors:

1   nationalist ideology + the mobilization of public opinion

2   strategic imperatives of mass mobilization

3   new military technologies (submarine, Zeppelin, bomber)

without distinction. In 1918, the 'hunger blockade' contributed to the lowering of food supplies in the Central Powers by over 50 per cent; by October/November, famine conditions prevailed in many German cities and industrial regions. The continuation of the blockade until March contributed to an excess mortality of about a quarter of a million. In February 1919, women in childbirth were dying on a terrible scale in Berlin (Howard, 'The social and political consequences of the allied food blockade of Germany, 1918–19', 1993, pp.161–88).

Ideally, a schematic representation of this dimension would incorporate the 'national' perspectives of all major combatants. To simplify matters, I have illustrated the 'totalization' of war in this dimension only by reference to the German-British conflict.

The *society-oriented dimension* refers to the exploitation by the combatant state of the resources of the society *it* 'contains' when waging war. Such resources are demographic, economic, cultural and intellectual: they range from unskilled labour to theoretical physics. All states command resources in the normal course of events, and we can gauge the intensity of the conflict in this dimension by the extension of the 'command economy' and 'command society'. The theoretic limit of this dimension is *totalitarianism*: the fusion of state and society in every sphere, the political, the economic, and the cultural.[12] Arguably, the origins of 'totalitarian war' lay in the mass conscription, economic mobilization and orchestrated state propaganda of the Revolutionary and Napoleonic wars. But the conjunction of mass armies with advanced (and increasingly science-based) industrialism brought a qualitative shift towards twentieth-century totalitarianism. The technologies of warfare and armaments production were transformed by a cluster of innovations, known collectively as the Second Industrial Revolution, that were first exploited economically from *c.*1890: the internal combustion engine; precision manufacture and assembly line production; electrical power and motors; organic chemistry and synthetics; wireless telegraphy and telephony. The capacity of states to mobilize populations was, at the same time, being enhanced by mass schooling, near universal literacy amongst young men, and the thickening network of symbolic communication.

Before 1914, the war planners had little inkling of how durable 'advanced' societies would prove under the stress of total war. Industrialized economies were thought to be too import-dependent and too financially vulnerable to withstand a long war: if a quick victory was not secured, economic paralysis would force the combatants to negotiate. The reality was, of course, quite different: industrialized economies proved tough and resilient. France lost one fifth of its manufacturing labour force when its most industrialized regions were invaded, and the mobilization of 2,887,000 reservists and the collapse of the credit market brought commerce and industry to a virtual standstill for four months. During the course of the war, 62.7 per cent of active male workers were conscripted. Yet French industry recovered from the near paralysis of the autumn of 1914 to produce more munitions per head of population than any other combatant. How was this achieved? By importing industrial raw materials to compensate for the catastrophic fall in coal, iron and steel output; by the government advancing interest-free credit to businessmen so they could equip their factories for

[12] Totalitarianism is more fully defined and discussed in Units 15–17 on Fascist Italy, the Soviet Union and Nazi Germany.

munitions production; and by a massive re-allocation of labour from non-essential occupations. Women's industrial employment rose; refugees and foreign and colonial workers were recruited for the factories; prisoners of war were drafted into the labour force; skilled men were released from the trenches to work in munitions; disabled soldiers were retrained; factory work was intensified by the introduction of the 'Taylor' system of scientific management.[13] Only the state could co-ordinate this industrial effort, but it worked through the capitalist system. War factories were not nationalized and profit remained an essential incentive for munitions entrepreneurs. Surprisingly, perhaps, French war-time governments never felt the need to conscript civilian labour. Rather than bureaucrats running war industries, official powers were vested in industrialists. The organization of raw material imports, for example, was undertaken by business consortia that were given official status, but run as private companies. This arrangement afforded businessmen undreamt of opportunities for profiteering.

The command economies of the main combatants had a common structure which contemporaries referred to as 'war collectivism' or 'war socialism', though a more appropriate term, in my view, is *warfare state capitalism.* In general terms, it resulted in the co-option of the capitalist system to the state apparatus. State capitalism was nowhere a conspiracy and varied considerably amongst the combatants. But basically it expressed a conviction that the war could not be won without the capitalist, the wage earner and the private investor. Businessmen became bureaucrats 'for the duration'; labour representatives (such as Arthur Henderson in Britain, Albert Thomas in France) were recruited to government; collective bargaining was recognized and facilitated by the state; governing functions were delegated to cartels of private economic corporations and organized labour. It was capitalist because the productive apparatus was not socialized (though there was public control of the railways and mines in Britain) and most *matériel* was produced by private companies for profit. The publicly-owned arsenals could not meet the demands of attritional warfare and the state had to relinquish its monopoly on armaments production. The combatants were prepared to pay a high price for victory, and everywhere company profits rose. The costs of the war were covered basically by the state borrowing from its own citizens and resorting to the printing press. Britain was alone in entering the war with a progressive income tax and a sophisticated fiscal system. It was the only combatant to cover a substantial part of war expenditure by taxing current income and excess profits. But even Britain had to borrow from its wealthier citizens at ever high rates of fixed interest, and for them the war proved to be a sound investment. The real income from war bonds rose substantially in the 1920s and 1930s when prices and commercial interest rates fell. The French Senate, after decades of squabbling, had approved an income tax in July 1914, but it was promptly suspended until the conclusion of hostilities. France could prolong the war only by accumulating massive financial obligations to its citizens.

For geopolitical reasons, Germany was compelled to go much further towards the 'totalization' of war in the society-oriented dimension; indeed, when 'totalitarianism' was first analysed systematically in the 1930s, war-time Germany

[13] F. W. Taylor (1856–1915) American pioneer of time-and-motion study as an aid to efficient management and author of *The Principles of Scientific Management and Shop Management* (1903).

was considered the progenitor of the phenomenon. It had a narrower resource base than the western allies, fought on two fronts, and had to be the arsenal of the Central Powers. Austria-Hungary was the only one of Germany's allies with a domestic armaments industry, and its output was insufficient to equip the Habsburg armies adequately. The schematic representation shows stages of the 'totalizing' process that were only implemented in Germany. What it cannot show is the tension – experienced more sharply in Germany than Britain and France – between adopting 'totalitarian' measures to command the economy (and society at large) and maintaining the minimal economic freedoms necessary for the efficient functioning of the market. In the abstract, it is not difficult to see that totalitarianism could be self-defeating for a state depending on the capitalist system to furnish its weapons of war. The accumulating inefficiencies that come from suspending the price mechanism and allocating labour and capital according to military rather than economic critera will begin to sap the state's capacity to wage industrialized war. The dilemma is particularly acute where the governing regime does not enjoy democratic legitimacy – as we shall see when considering warfare state capitalism in Wilhelmine Germany.

The 'society-oriented' dimension of total war
mass mobilization + disruption of normal trade flows + collapse of the credit market → many businesses close → **widespread unemployment**, especially amongst women;   government control of credit and rationing of raw materials
    shortages of skilled labour → release of skilled men from the army; 'dilution' of labour food and fuel shortages →
    rationing of necessities; price and rent control
    mobilization of **morale** on the 'Home Front'
    general **labour scarcity** → closing of non-essential industries trade union and employers associations co-opted to the '**corporate**' management of labour
conscription of male labour for war industries
    conscription of women (contemplated but not implemented in 1914–18)

State capitalism in Germany, 1914–18

Germany's leaders appreciated by the late autumn of 1914 that they faced a long war on two fronts and swiftly co-opted its powerful corporate economy for the war effort. The business structure of German heavy industry facilitated co-operation between capitalism, the military machine and civilian government. Giant firms accounted for a large proportion of production in key sectors (especially chemicals, and electrical and heavy mechanical engineering) and many firms were organized into cartels that regulated output and restricted competition. Some cartel agreements covered the allocation of industrial inputs, so it is not surprising that the proposal to control access to raw materials came from organized capitalism. In August 1914 the disruption of trade had led to acute shortages of inputs, and a senior executive of AEG (*Allgemeine Elektrizitätsgesellschaft* or General Electricity Company – one of Germany's biggest industrial combines) suggested that a special body be created to regulate their supply. His boss, Walther Rathenau, persuaded the Prussian War Ministry to set up the *Kriegsrohstoffabteilung* (KRA) – War Raw Materials Department – to control materials supply throughout Germany. Rathenau was its effective head until March 1915, by when he and his colleagues (nearly all industrialists) had set up corporations to purchase metals, chemicals, and other materials in short supply, store them centrally and resell them according to wartime priorities. These were private undertakings, owned or controlled by the big firms, but acting in an official capacity for the KRA and with the power to requisition supplies. They did not seek to restrict profits. To Rathenau, it was 'self-evident that trade and industry had a well-established right to make money and to enjoy the greatest possible freedom of movement'. A KRA official wrote in a confidential memorandum: 'The exploitation of the national emergency to promote private interests does not mean that capitalism is decadent; rather it is a logical outcome of capitalism's basic views and a fruitful field for the employment of capitalist expertise' (quoted in Hardach, *The First World War 1914–1918*, 1977, p.61). The state subsidized the building of new plant to produce nitrates and other key inputs. The net profits of the Krupps steel works had, by 1917, increased two and half times over the pre-war average; allowing for inflation, dividends paid out by metallurgical and chemicals companies rose by between 175 per cent and 200 per cent.

Production of munitions was co-ordinated by the Prussian War Ministry in consultation with the War Committee for German Industry. One of the first problems it had to deal with was the return from the army of skilled men. As the war progressed, every combatant found the manpower requirements of attritional war conflicted with need for skilled and tractable industrial labour. Union leaders were consulted on what categories of men ought to be released from the army and became regular visitors to the War Ministry. Its officials encouraged the trade unions to organize in the war industries and even on the railways where unions had long been proscribed. Under the Ministry's auspices, arbitration committees were established to resolve grievances between employers and employed.

In the late summer of 1916, the new Supreme Command moved to solve Germany's inherent deficiency in manpower *vis-à-vis* the Entente by huge increases in munitions production: shell output was to be doubled, the supply of artillery and machine guns tripled – all by May 1917. The military's demands were known collectively as the Hindenburg programme, and involved an array of fundamental structural changes calculated to bring about the full-scale mobilization and militarization of the economy. Non-essential industries were to be shut down; capital investment, raw materials and labour were to be directed to firms producing war *matériel*. They were to receive an additional three million workers. Germany was to be driven along the society-oriented dimension of total war towards totalitarianism. The Prussian War Ministry was sidelined by a new mammoth organization, the War Office, that was given wide powers over the economy and in which organized labour was represented. Leaders of heavy industry, such as Carl Duisberg and Gustav Krupp, influenced the programme's targets and their firms profited handsomely from Ludendorff's insistence that financial considerations could be ignored in its implementation.

The Supreme Command promised to release thousands of skilled workers from the army, but it was also persuaded that the programme could not be fulfilled without the conscription of civilian labour, including women's labour. The Imperial government was initially opposed to labour compulsion and pointed out that more women were looking for work than there were jobs available. But from late October, Bethmann lent his support to OHL's (the German High Command) main demands. Measures to compel unemployed Belgians to work in German industry were instituted.

The government could have introduced labour conscription under the Enabling Act of August 1914, but preferred to carry a Reichstag majority behind the Auxiliary Service Law (6 December). This empowered the authorities to direct all males between 17 and 60 (below and beyond the age of conscription) from inessential occupations to war work. Certain categories of workers were exempted, the largest being in agriculture. Most decisions on exemptions were left to local arbitration committees chaired by military officers, but with two representatives each from the employers and the employees. In order to wage total war, the state was compelled to make significant concessions to organized labour: under paragraph 11 of the Auxiliary Service Law, workers' committees were instituted in firms of over 50 employees, with responsibility for settling disputes over wages and conditions of employment. Unions won the right to organize in war industries, and collective bargaining agreements were given the force of law. This was the price the government and OHL had to pay the trade unions and majority socialists before they agreed to the Law and to restrictions on the movement of labour. Industrialists who had for decades been trying to keep labour organizations at arm's length were loath to give trade union secretaries an official platform. Their objections were overridden by a new breed of technocratic soldier who recognized that organized labour had to be conciliated if the war was to be won and the regime preserved. As General Groener, the War Office Chief, told a Bundesrat delegation: 'We can never win this war by fighting against the workers ... reservations of an internal political nature must be put aside ... '.

Exercise   The success (or otherwise) of the Hindenburg programme and the impact of labour conscription on the German war economy can be gauged from the record Rathenau made of his conversation with Ludendorff in February 1917 (*Primary Sources 1: World War I*, Document II.3). On the basis of that document, I would like you to form your own impression of how the programme worked in practice. ∎

Specimen answer   The document makes clear that the programme was extremely ill conceived. Output targets, demanding much new factory construction, had been set without any consideration of how this would feed back into the wider economy. The transport requirements had not been anticipated. The Auxiliary Service Law had turned into a 'legislative monster' and required a huge bureaucracy to work efficiently. The proliferation of committees, and the need to consult interest groups, were clogging up the process of labour allocation. One gets a sense of totalitarian measures being self-defeating because they undermined the efficiency of the market.

Other evidence confirms that the Hindenburg programme greatly disappointed its progenitors. Steel production actually declined in late 1916, early 1917. The Auxiliary Service Law failed to mobilize much additional labour, for there simply were not the men to be mobilized. The return of skilled workers from the army weakened the field forces. In pursuing an ill-conceived total mobilization, Ludendorff promoted economic instability and bureaucratic chaos. Though production rose, there were no effective controls over costs. The reckless financing of the programme was a major element in spiralling inflation. Germany was shifted beyond the point at which 'totalitarian' measures became dysfunctional because they obliterated the price signals that prompt rational economic decision-making. There was no effective central government to substitute for the social rationality of the market by, for example, soaking up excess money through taxation. Germany had a command economy without the democratic legitimacy of the British government in the Second World War and without the ruthless efficiency of the Stalinist police state during Russia's Great Patriotic War. Despite this, the achievements of the German munitions industry were pretty extraordinary. The German army did not run out of guns and ammunition, and the Bulgarian and Turkish armies were supplied with all their modern weaponry by Germany up to the autumn of 1918. □

5   HOW WAS GERMANY DEFEATED?

Is there any mystery about the defeat of the Central Powers, and of Germany in particular? On 8 August, General Rawlinson's 4th British Army demonstrated its painfully acquired professionalism with a model attack to the east of Amiens. Four hundred and fifty tanks had been assembled, and 2,000 guns. The western forces had achieved complete mastery of the air: 38,000 air photographs were issued to the attacking troops. The Dominion divisions tore into the weak German defences, punching a hole from seven to nine miles deep, capturing 13,000 prisoners and 400 guns. It was, Ludendorff wrote in his *Memoirs*, 'a black day for the German army'. Units surrendered wholesale and reinforcements were jeered at as 'Black Legs' and 'War Prolongers'. In the following weeks the western powers inflicted a continuous series of similar reverses on the retreating Germans. The French army recovered its fighting spirit; the Americans, who were pouring into France at the rate of 250,000 a month, undertook their first independent attack at Saint-Mihiel. After agonizing indecision, Ludendorff informed the German government that an armistice had to be requested at the end of September. Behind this decision, according to military historians, lay the demoralization and disintegration of the German army. It had suffered heavy losses in the Spring offensives and the deterioration of its discipline was evident when advancing troops had stopped to loot British dumps of food and drink. The desertion rate was rising, particularly amongst soldiers being transferred from the eastern to the western front. Approaching a million men were 'shirking' at the rear in the last months of the war. Officers were losing their authority; covertly, the ranks were striking against the war. The situation was aggravated by the first wave of the influenza pandemic which incapacitated about half a million men in June-July. Ludendorff was forced to admit on 29 September that 'OHL and the German army have reached the end ... The troops can no longer be relied on' (Deist, 'The military collapse of the German Empire', 1996, p.205). On the same day, Bulgaria asked for an armistice on the Salonika front, which cut off Turkey from its German supplies and hastened the rout of the Ottoman army in Palestine.

What is odd about the supposed disintegration of the German army is that nobody told the other side. On 14 October, Haig met the War Cabinet and gave a pessimistic appreciation of the military situation and the prospects of a satisfactory armistice. He attached little weight to the abandonment of Germany by her allies: Lloyd George had been wont to refer to the Balkan and Italian campaigns as 'knocking out the props', but Bulgaria, Turkey and even Austria-Hungary had been military liabilities rather than assets. In Haig's opinion, the German Army was capable of retiring to its own frontiers and holding the line against equal or even superior forces. In a few weeks, it had reduced the length of its line from 400 miles to about 235 miles. The net body count was once again in its favour. The French army seemed greatly worn out to Haig, and he thought many disinclined to risk their lives. The US Army was 'disorganized, ill-equipped and ill-trained'; it would take at least a year before it became a serious fighting force. The British infantry was seriously under strength, and not sufficiently fresh or strong to force a decision by itself. The Allies, Haig asserted, 'were not in a position to prevent the enemy from doing an immense amount of material damage ... [W]e must conclude that the enemy will be able to hold the line which he selects for defence for some time after the campaign of 1919 commences' (cited in Lloyd George, *War Memoirs*, p.1,970).

Haig surely knew what he was talking about, and his evidence suggests that Germany was far from defeated in strictly military terms. As the army withdrew towards the frontier, it regained the advantages of the defensive while the western forces experienced ever greater logistical problems and suffered heavy casualties. Germany's eventual defeat was inevitable but it had yet to come on the battlefield. Does this imply that the German Army was 'stabbed in the back', as Ludendorff and the nationalists were to claim in the 1920s? Emphatically no, the decision to seek an armistice was entirely OHL's and was made after an agonizing analysis of the military situation. Haig's pessimism was partly that of a reformed optimist, but stemmed too from his narrowly professional view of the war. For him, it was a matter of defeating an enemy army. Historians can form a synoptic view of events, and to them it is increasingly evident that the western powers defeated the German nation as whole. Once news of the proposed armistice became public, the cumulative grievances of the home front could no longer be contained. The confidential reports on public morale furnished by the military governors became deeply pessimistic in the late summer of 1918: the evident failure of the great offensives of March to July produced utter dejection; finding enough food was a source of chronic anxiety for the great majority of housewives; traders and shop-keepers dealing in the black market (and their affluent customers) were loathed by the poorer consumers. Prostitutes selling sex for food were a prominent symptom of the general deprivation. An Englishwoman stranded in wartime Berlin noted:

> Women are realizing the enormous burden imposed upon them ... Naturally they begin more than ever to say, 'Why should we work, starve, send our men out to fight? What is it all going to bring us? More work, more poverty,

"demoralised", according to Ludendorff

"total war" required to defeat Germany.

our men cripples, our homes ruined. What is it for? ... The State which called upon us to fight cannot even give us decent food.'

(Quoted in Bonzon and Davis, 'Feeding the cities', 1997, p.338)

The situation of small-scale farmers was just as grim as that of the great majority of the working class: their horses had been requisitioned and they lacked labour and fertilizers. Basic foodstuffs had been rationed since 1915 and price ceilings imposed; tens of thousands of regulations had been issued at every administrative level concerning the production, distribution, and consumption of food. This frenetic interventionism had signally failed to achieve anything like an equitable distribution of the necessities of life. The creation of a War Food Office (*Kriegsernährungsamt* – KEA) had merely added to bureaucratic confusion because jurisdiction in matters of food supply was divided between civil and military authorities, and between imperial, state, and local levels of government. It was another instance of the dysfunctionality of totalitarian measures.

The home front and the fighting front were not insulated from each other. Declining civilian morale affected military morale; 'shirking' and desertion meant that the brutalized cynicism of the soldiers permeated everyday life. As Scheidemann told Ludendorff on the 17 October:

The lengthy war has ... broken the spirit of the people, and to that [add] their disillusionment. They have been disillusioned by the submarine war, by the technical superiority of our opponent, by the defection of our allies ... and, in addition, by the increasing distress at home. Now the reaction is coming. Men on leave come from the Army with unpleasant stories; and they return to the Army bringing unpleasant news from home. This traffic in ideas depresses the morale. ... Workers are coming nearer and nearer to the point of view, 'An end with horror is better than horror without end'.

(Quoted in Offer, *The First World War*, 1989, p.76)

In a total war, German society had gone down to total defeat.

CONCLUSIONS

This unit has endeavoured to capture the 'nature' of the First World War in all its complexity. If the material has been daunting, then that is, I fear, a reflection of the historical reality I have tried to describe and explain. The war was not a singular event, but a dense intermeshing of processes operating at different levels: the level of the battlefield, of the individual belligerent states, of the coalitions in which they participated, of the economies and societies that furnished the men, the labour, the munitions, and the money with which to wage industrialized warfare. How we sum up the 'nature' of the First World War will be partly a matter of historical interest. A military historian would have written a different unit. To me, it was the first coalition conflict between industrialized states in a truly global capitalist economy and, as such, a great turning point in world history. When thinking about the material covered in this unit for your assignments and your exam revision, bear in mind those simple questions with which we started: why did the war last as long as it did? Why did it suck in so many belligerents? Why did it become a 'total' war, for Germany at least?

CHRONOLOGY

Table of principal events

1914	Western Front	Eastern Front (including Serbia)	Turkish Front	Naval	Political
Aug. 1		War declared by Germany on Russia.			
2	War declared by Germany on France. Luxemburg invaded.				
4	Belgium invaded. War between Great Britain and Germany.				
10				*Goeben* and *Breslau* enter Dardanelles.	
14	Battle of the Frontiers begins.				
17	Last fort of Liége surrenders.				
23	Mons.				Japan declares war on Germany.
26	Le Cateau.				
28				Heligoland.	
29	Guise.				
30		Tannenberg. 1st Austrian invasion of Serbia defeated.			
Sept. 3		Lemberg.			
6–11	Marne.				
13–25	Aisne.				
Oct. 9–19		1st battle of Warsaw.			Entente Treaty to make only a common peace.

1915	Western Front	Italian Front	Eastern Front (including Serbia)	Turkish Front	Naval	Political
10	Fall of Antwerp.					
19	1st battle of Ypres begins.					
Nov. 1			2nd invasion of Serbia begins.	War with Turkey.	Coronel.	
9					*Emden* destroyed.	
11			2nd battle of Warsaw begins.			
18–25			Lodz.			
Dec. 6			Austrian rout in Serbia.			
8					Falkland Islands.	
Jan. 2				Turkish defeat in Armenia.		
19						1st Zeppelin raid on England.
Feb. 4			Winter battle in Masuria.			
18					1st German submarine campaign opens.	
March 1					British blockade of Germany begins.	
10	Neuve Chapelle.					
18					Failure of attempt to force Dardanelles.	
22			Fall of Przemysl			
April 22	2nd battle of Ypres begins. First German gas attack.					

25	Treaty of London signed.
25	Landing on Gallipoli.
May 1	Gorlice and Russian retreat.
9	Franco-British offensive in Flanders and Artois
23	Italy declares war on Austria.
26	British Coalition Ministry formed.
June 22	Lemberg retaken by Austrians
Aug. 4	Fall of Warsaw.
6	Landing at Suvla.
Sept. 25	Franco-British offensive.
25	Champagne and Loos.
28	Battle of Kut.
Oct. 2	Russian retreat ended.
5	Allied landing at Salonika.
7	3rd Austrian invasion of Serbia.
12	Bulgaria delares war on Serbia.
Nov. 24	Ctesiphon.
28	Serbia conquered.
Dec. 19	Haig appointed Commander-in-Chief.

		Western Front	Italian Front	Eastern Front (including Romania)	Turkish Front	Naval	Political
					Suvla and Anzac evacuated.		
1916							
Jan.	8				Helles evacuated.		
	16				Fall of Erzerum.		
Feb	21	Battle of Verdun begins.					
March	18			Lake Narotch.			
April	29				Fall of Kut.		
May	14		Austrian attack in Trentino.				
	31					Battle of Jutland.	
June	4			Brusilov's offensive in Galicia begins.			
	5						Death of Kitchener
July	1	Battle of Somme begins.					
Aug.	8		Italians take Gorizia.				
	27			Romania declares war on Austria.			Hindenburg and Ludendorff become head of the German Staff.
Sept.	15	First use of tanks.					
	24						Venizelos forms provisional government in Salonika.
Oct.	24	Recapture of Dousamont.					
Nov.	13	Battle of Ancre.					

Date		Political	Naval	Turkish Front	Eastern Front (including Romania)	Italian Front	Western Front
Dec.	6	Lloyd George forms War Cabinet.			Fall of Bucharest.		
	12	German Peace note.					
	18	American Peace note.					
1917							
Feb.	1	USA breaks off diplomatic relationship with Germany.	Unrestricted submarine warfare begins.				
March	11			Fall of Baghdad.			
	12	Russian Revolution begins.					
	14						German retreat to Hindenburg line.
	26			1st battle of Gaza.			
April	6	USA declares war on Germany.					
	9						Arras.
	16						French attack on Chemin des Dames defeated.
June	7						Messines.
	11	Deposition of Constantine.					
July	1				Last Russian offensive in Galicia.		
	19	Peace Resolution in Reichstag.					
	31						3rd battle of Ypres begins.

	Western Front	*Italian Front*	*Eastern Front*	*Turkish Front*	*Naval*	*Political*
Aug. 1						Papal Peace note.
17		Last Italian offensive on Isonzo.				
Sept. 3			Fall of Riga			
Oct. 24		Italians routed at Caporetto.				
Nov. 7		Italian stand on Piave.				Bolsheviks seize power.
9						Clemenceau becomes Premier.
20	Cambrai. First massed tank attack.					
29						Lansdowne Peace letter.
Dec. 9				Capture of Jerusalem.		
17			Armistice between Central Powers and Russia.			
1918	*Western Front*	*Italian Front*	*Eastern Front*	*Turkish Front*	*Naval*	*Political*
March 3						Peace of Brest Litovsk.
21	1st German attack against British in Picardy.					
26						Foch appointed Commander-in-Chief of Allied Armies.
April 9	2nd German attack in Flanders.					
23					Zeebrugge.	
May 9					Ostend.	

Date	Western Front	Southern / Eastern Fronts	Political
27	3rd German attack on Chemin des Dames.		
June 15		Last Austrian attack against Italy defeated.	
July 15	Last German attack on Marne.		
18	Foch's counterstroke on the Ourcq.		
Aug. 8	Battle of Amiens begins.		
14			German Crown Council at Spa.
Sept. 2	Drocourt-Quéant line broken.		
12	American Victory at St. Mihiel.		
14		General attack on Bulgaria begins.	
15			Austrian Peace move.
18		Battle of Megiddo begins.	
26	General Allied attack.		Bulgarian Armistice.
29	Hindenburg line broken.		
Oct. 3			Prince Max of Baden Chancellor. 1st German Peace note.
23		Final advance in Mesopotamia begins.	

24	Italian attack begins.		
29		German mutiny begins.	
30	Last General attack begins.		Turkish Armistice.
Nov. 2	Austrians routed and dispersed.		
3			Austrian Armistice.
4			Revolution in Germany begins.
9	British reach Mons.		Abdication of Kaiser. Republic proclaimed in Berlin.
11			German Armistice.
21		Surrender of German Battle Fleet.	

References

Bernard, P. and Dubief, H. (1988) *The Decline of the Third Republic 1914–1938*, Cambridge University Press.

Bonzon, T., and Davis, B. (1997) 'Feeding the cities' in Winter and Robert.

Burk, K. (1985) *Britain, America and the Sinews of War, 1914–1918*, Allen and Unwin.

Cecil, H. and Liddle, P. (eds) (1996) *Facing Armageddon: the First World War Experienced*, Leo Cooper.

Coppard, G. (1969) *With a Machine Gun to Cambrai*, HMSO.

Cruttwell, C. (1936) *A History of the Great War 1914–1918*, second edition, Clarendon Press.

Davidian, I. (1996) 'The Russian soldier's morale from the evidence of Tsarist military censorship' in Cecil and Liddle (eds).

Deist, W. (1996) 'The military collapse of the German Empire: the reality behind the stab-in-the-back myth', *War in History*, vol.3, no.2, pp.186–207.

Emin, A. (1930) *Turkey in the World War*, Yale.

Falls, C. (1941) *The Nature of Modern Warfare*, Methuen.

Ferguson, N. (1998) *The Pity of War*, Allen Lane/Penguin.

Figes, O. (1996) *A People's Tragedy: The Russian Revolution 1891–1924*, Jonathan Cape.

Fischer, F. (1975) *World Power or Decline*, Weidenfeld.

Florinsky, M. T. (1931) *The End of the Russian Empire*, Carnegie, Collier reprint, 1961.

Gattrell, P. and Harrison, M. (1993) 'The Russian and Soviet economies in two world wars: a comparative view', *Economic History Review*, vol.46, no.3 pp.425–52.

Geyer, M. (1986) 'German strategy in the age of machine warfare, 1914–1945' in P. Paret (ed.) *Makers of Modern Strategy from Machiavelli to the Nuclear Age*, Oxford.

Hardach, G. (1977) *The First World War 1914–1918*, Allen Lane.

Howard, N. P. (1993) 'The social and political consequences of the allied food blockade of Germany, 1918–19', *German History*, vol.11, no.2, pp.161–88.

Keegan, J. (1998) *The First World War*, Random House.

Lloyd George, D. (1938) *War Memoirs*, Odhams, two volume edition.

Mayer, A.J. (1959) *Political Origins of the New Diplomacy*, Yale University Press.

Melograni, P. (1969) *Storia Politica della Grande Guerra 1915–1918*, Mondadori.

Miquel, P. (1983) *La Grande Guerre*, Fayard.

Offer, A. (1989) *The First World War: An Agrarian Interpretation*, Clarendon Press.

Pipes, R. (1990) *The Russian Revolution 1899–1919*, HarperCollins.

Stevenson, D. (1988) *The First World War and International Politics*, Oxford University Press.

Taylor, A. J. P. (1954) *The Struggle for Mastery in Europe 1848–1918*, Clarendon.

Travers, T. (1987) *The Killing Ground: The British Army, the Western Front and the Emergence of Modern Warfare, 1914–1918*, Allen and Unwin.

Tomassini, L. (1996) 'The home front in Italy' in Cecil and Liddle (eds).

Trumpener, U. (1968) *Germany and the Ottoman Empire 1914–1918*, Princeton.

Wall, R., and Winter, J. M. (eds) (1988) *The Upheaval of War: Family, Work and Welfare in Europe, 1914–1918*, Cambridge University Press.

Wildman, A. K. (1980) *The End of the Russian Imperial Army*, Vol.1, *The Old Army and the Soldiers' Revolt*, Princeton.

Winter, J. M. and Robert, J.-L. (1997) *Capital Cities at War: Paris, London, Berlin 1914–1919*, Cambridge University Press.

Woodward, L. (1967) *Great Britain and the War of 1914–1918*, Methuen.

Zürcher, E. (1996) 'Little Mehmet in the desert: the Ottoman soldier's experience' in Cecil and Liddle (eds).

Further reading

Becker, J.-J. (1985) *The Great War and French People*, Berg.

Bourne, J. M. (1989) *Britain and the Great War 1914–1918*, Arnold.

Chambers, F. P. (1939) *The War behind the War 1914–1918: A History of the Political and Civilian Fronts*, Faber.

Chickering, R. (1998) *Imperial Germany and the Great War, 1914–1918*, Cambridge University Press.

Feldman, G. D. (ed.) (1972) *German Imperialism, 1914–18: The Development of a Historical Debate*, John Wiley.

Feldman, G. D. (1966) *Army, Industry and Labor in Germany 1914–1918*, Princeton.

Ferro, M. (1973) *The Great War 1914–1918*, Routledge and Kegan Paul.

Fischer, F. (1967) *Germany's Aims in the First World War*, Norton.

Fridenson, P. (ed.) (1992) *The French Home Front: 1914–1918*, Berg.

Godfrey, J. F. (1987) *Capitalism at War: Industrial Policy and Bureaucracy in France 1914–1918*, Berg.

Herwig, H. H. (1997) *The First World War: Germany and Austria-Hungary 1914–1918*, Arnold.

Hovannisian, R. G. (ed.) (1992) *The Armenian Genocide: History, Politics and Ethics*, Macmillan.

Pogge von Strandmann, H. (ed.) (1985) *Walther Rathenau: Notes and Diaries 1907–1992*, Clarendon Press.

Sheffield, G.D. (2001) *Forgotten Victory: The First World War, Myths and Realities*, Headline.

Stone, N. (1975) *The Eastern Front 1914–1917*, Hodder and Stoughton.

Strachan, H. (2001) *The First World War, Vol. 1: To Arms*, Oxford University Press.

Strachan, H. (ed.) (1998) *The Oxford History of the First World War*, Oxford University Press.

Strachan, H. (1996) 'The morale of the German army, 1917–18' in Cecil and Liddle (eds).

Wilson, T. (1988) *The Myriad Faces of War: Britain and the Great War, 1914–1918*, Polity Press.

Winter, J. M. (1985) *The Great War and the British People*, Macmillan.

Winter, J., Parker, G. and Habeck, M.R. (2001) *The Great War and the Twentieth Century*, Yale University Press.

Units 7–10 THE GEOPOLITICAL AND SOCIAL EFFECTS OF THE WAR

ARTHUR MARWICK, BILL PURDUE AND JAMES CHAPMAN

(Introduction and 'Social reform and welfare policies' to 'Institutions and values' by Arthur Marwick; sections 1 and 'Social geography' to 'National cohesion' by Bill Purdue; section 3 by James Chapman)

Please note that Units 7-10 are not divided into four discrete units, although they do, of course, represent four weeks' work. For the purposes of your study time, therefore, you should note that Unit 7 covers the 'Introduction' to 'Social geography', Unit 8 covers 'Economic performance and theory' to 'National cohesion', Unit 9 covers 'Social reform and welfare policies' to 'Role and status of women' and Unit 10 is from 'High and popular culture' to the end.

Open University students of these units will need to refer to:
Set book: J. M. Roberts, *Europe 1880–1945*, Longman, 2001
Course Reader: *Total War and Historical Change: Europe 1914–1955*, eds Clive Emsley, Arthur Marwick and Wendy Simpson, Open University Press, 2000
Primary Sources 1: World War I, eds Arthur Marwick and Wendy Simpson, Open University, 2000
Secondary Sources, eds Arthur Marwick and Wendy Simpson, Open University, 2000
Maps Booklet
Video 1
Audio 1

INTRODUCTION

From what you have learned about the nature of World War I from Unit 6 you will appreciate why those who lived through the war felt, as far as can be established from such sources as we have, that it had had a profound impact on their lives. Many of those who left diaries, autobiographies or collections of letters (a very tiny minority, of course) stated clearly that they felt their world had been changed by the war. Historians, subsequently, have not always been so certain. In fact, it would probably be true to say that the main fashion in writing about war towards the end of last century was to argue that neither World War I nor World War II had any significant or long-lasting effects in the realms of social change. We saw in Book 1, Unit 4 that changes were already taking place in most European countries before the war. Writers in the 1980s and 1990s tended to stress long-term structural and ideological trends, seeing the war as of little real significance compared with them, but rather as, perhaps, a temporary distortion of, or even an interruption to, long-term change. A substantial proportion of those writers had strong socialist or feminist sympathies and argued (perfectly correctly) that the war experience certainly did not result in an era either of socialism or of complete equality between the sexes. They pointed to the deprivation, misery and horrific slaughter involved in the war and suggested that these are more compatible with regression than with beneficial change. Some stressed – and this is a particularly important point – that even if there were changes during the upheavals of war, what one must examine is societies as they settled down in the post-war years to see whether these changes really did last. It has also been pointed out that governments at the time, for propaganda and political reasons, greatly exaggerated the changes that were taking place and *would* take place once victory was won. Ordinary people, it has been argued, too readily fell victim to the idea that because the war was so horrific it must result in beneficial change.

Those historians who stress structural factors, it could be said, tend to play down the significance of war. However, one relatively recent development is that historians are beginning to put renewed emphasis on the significance of events, including wars. It would certainly be quite wrong to say that attempts to identify the effects of war have in any way become unfashionable. The distinguished French scholar, Patrick Fridenson, called his introduction to the collection of essays, *The French Home Front 1914–1918* (1992), 'A new view of France at war', writing:

> There is a conventional wisdom on the French home front during World War I. It says that for the French economy and society this war is both a parenthesis – the major trends at work in pre-war France are suspended, all the more as industrial regions like the North and the East are soon occupied by German troops – and a catastrophe ...
>
> On the contrary, the aim of this book is to show that not only most major changes already taking place in the French economy and most conflicts dividing French society continued during the war, but also that the war was the theatre of deep transformations, some of them still having consequences on today's France. To be sure, this book duly takes into account the destruction and disruption caused by what was the first war of attrition. But it

argues, in keeping with recent works by British historians, the war is a contradictory phenomenon, whereby short-term and long-term damages may co-exist with a pursuit of growth by unusual means.

The notion of total war as 'a contradictory phenomenon' (and indeed a complex one) is useful in suggesting that we should not envisage a simplistic debate, with historians on one side insisting that total war must always, and inevitably, bring change, and historians on the other arguing that wars have no significant effects at all. All that this course argues is that war is such a frequently recurring phenomenon that it bears close analysis to see whether indeed it does have significant effects. It argues that even if broader forces would have brought certain changes anyway, it is still worth trying to pin down why certain precise developments took place *when* and *in the way* that they did. What is required is to establish the balance between the effects of the long-term forces which we studied in Book 1, and the particular circumstances of war in bringing about certain clearly identifiable changes. It is a mistake to think of war as something external acting upon society. Societies are themselves involved in war. If there are changes, even temporary, those changes come not from war acting as an external force upon society, but from society's being involved in war, experiencing war. My own contribution to the debate has not been, as is sometimes suggested, to insist that there is always and inevitably a correlation between war and social change, but rather to suggest that it can be helpful to make a distinction between 'society not at war' and 'society at war', going on then to try to isolate what happens in 'society at war' that does not happen in 'society not at war' to see whether these new happenings can be related to any change that is apparent after the war. The way in which I have tried to define and systematize the new mechanisms operating in 'society at war' need not concern us here, though one key concept is that of *participation* (derived from the over-elaborate original formulation of the sociologist Stanislav Andreski, *military participation ratio*). The basic idea of this is that in 'society at war' those whose participation in the war effort is vital (for example, certain skilled workers, or women replacing men in certain jobs) will tend to make gains in wages, social benefits, etc., other things being equal – which, of course, they are not, the very destructiveness of war always being a countervailing negative force.

However, as we have seen in Book 1, the societies of 'Europe not at war' were by no means all identical to each other.

Exercise   What broad lines of distinction can be drawn between the different European societies as they were on the eve of World War I? ■

Specimen answer   1   We have the broad distinction made by Roberts (set book) between
and discussion   constitutional states and autocratic states.

2   We have the differences between 'developed', industrial states, and 'underdeveloped', predominantly agricultural states.

3   There is the distinction between relatively nationally homogeneous states (like Britain and France), and multinational ones like Austria-Hungary, the Ottoman Empire, and, indeed, Russia. □

Exercise   Why might these differences affect the possible consequences of involvement in war? ■

Specimen answer and discussion   Agricultural, underdeveloped countries might find it more difficult to support the enormous costs of total war, and might therefore suffer much greater negative effects and perhaps nothing in the way of desirable social change. Autocratic countries might be able to control the repercussions of war more effectively than constitutional countries. Multinational states might be more prone to falling apart under the pressure of war than nationally homogeneous ones. □

Exercise   Two other broad lines of distinction might be made with regard to establishing the effects of war on particular countries, the first to do with the society's attitudes towards involvement in the war, and the second to do with its actual experience of the war. What are these? ■

Specimen answer and discussion   Some societies, e.g. Britain, France and Germany, entered wholeheartedly and unitedly into the war, some much less so, particularly Italy, and probably Russia. With regard to experience of the war it might seem likely that in assessing the consequences of the war there would be a difference between whether a country was on the victorious or the defeated side; more particularly, there would be differences depending upon how much direct destruction a country suffered, whether it was invaded, fought over, occupied, etc. □

Exercise   Reflecting on some of the main points made about the nature of the war in Unit 6, what arguments could be made to support the view that to look for major social reforms and higher living standards as consequences of the war would be quite absurd? ■

Specimen answer and discussion   The main argument concerns the enormous destructiveness and cost of the war. Roberts estimates that the war cost the equivalent of eight years' peacetime accumulation of wealth. This doesn't clinch the argument, however. Apart from anything else, some countries suffered much more than others, as I have already hinted. But certainly this major point bears careful thinking about. □

In these three units we shall look in turn at the ten areas of social change introduced in Book 1, Unit 1, and discussed in Book 1, Unit 4. We start, however, with the question of international, geopolitical and strategic change, and we end with a study of a special aspect of popular culture, film. In each section it will be necessary to make a distinction between changes taking place during the war, and the long-term consequences which are the major source of contention in the general debate.

1   INTERNATIONAL, GEOPOLITICAL AND STRATEGIC CHANGE

Geopolitical changes

The First World War was one of the great cataclysms of Europe which divided one epoch from another. Yet this was not quite so, for the change in public opinion of Europe was a more important dividing point. The First World War completed a process started much earlier ...

(George L. Mosse, *The Culture of Western Europe*, 1988)

In the above, somewhat contradictory, sentences Professor Mosse combines two of the well-established views regarding the impact and consequences of World War I: that the war was a great watershed in history, with effects which created a divide between the pre- and post-war worlds; and that the war completed, perhaps speeded up, and, in some versions, was a culmination of pre-existing processes and tendencies.

The test of the 'watershed' may well depend upon the sort of factors we are considering. Professor Mosse was primarily concerned with cultural change, and there is room for considerable debate as to the war's effect upon cultural and, indeed, social developments. When it comes to the physical boundaries of states and to their very existence, it is difficult to question the decisive impact of the war. Whatever other effects World War I may have had, it is certain that the period of the war and its immediate aftermath saw a radical change in the political map of Europe. The war was more than just the catalyst for such change, for its outcome did much to shape it. Yet, notwithstanding the overriding impact of the war, there are other factors we must consider in assessing the geopolitical changes. They include:

1   the effects of nationalism, particularly the nationalisms of 'those people without history', as Marx dismissed the hitherto largely subject nationalities of east central Europe who had been busy discovering or inventing their histories before 1914;

2   the ideals and aims of the statesmen of the victorious states who gathered at Paris to make the peace settlement;

3   the effect of the ideological dimension inserted by the Bolshevik Revolution;

4   the changes to the map that were dependent on the outcome of the chaotic struggles and wars which continued in eastern Europe between 1914 and 1923, a period during which that map can be said to have altered continually.

Exercise   What changes to the map of Europe occurred during World War I itself? Consult Maps 4 and 5 in Roberts, pp.xvii and xviii. ■

Specimen answer and discussion   We can distinguish here between the *de facto* map, as areas and regions changed hands with the advances and retreats of armies, and changes to the map which were given some legal form by treaties – even if, as with the provisions of the Treaty of Bucharest (May 1918), which gave territory to

Bulgaria and Hungary at the expense of Romania, they were overturned after the war was over.

On the western front only the opening and closing stages of the war saw a war of movement. The result of the virtual stalemate, which began in November 1914 and lasted, despite major offensives, until 1918, was that both sides faced each other along a 400-mile line from the Channel to the Swiss frontier. This left Germany in control of most of Belgium and part of Northern France, areas rich in industry which were useful to the German war effort.

The Italian front, which opened with Italy's entry into the war on the Allied side in May 1915, saw another stalemate and no significant territorial gains for either side as the Italians failed to break the Austrian front along the river Isonzo.

On the eastern front the war was much more mobile, and both sides made sweeping advances at different times; by October 1917, however, the Central Powers had made enormous gains. Serbia, Montenegro, Albania and Romania had been overrun. With the 'October' Revolution and Lenin's decision to accept peace at almost any price, the Central Powers were able to dictate the terms of the Treaties of Brest-Litovsk (March 1918) and Bucharest. German troops and Austrian troops occupied vast tracts of what had been Russian territory, and Germany was in a position to encourage the creation of semi-independent client states – Finland, the Ukrainian Republic and the Baltic States – and to reward her allies, Bulgaria and Austria-Hungary. □

Of course, most of the territorial changes that took place during the course of the war were ephemeral (although, as we shall see, the Treaty of Brest-Litovsk left its mark) and were to be overturned by the final outcome of the war, the defeat of Germany in the west. We need now to take a longer view and consider the redrawing of the map of Europe that took place between 1914 and 1923. This is not just a matter of considering the Versailles Settlement, for much of eastern Europe was not directly affected by Versailles, and not all the provisions of that settlement were ever put into effect.

You should note here my use of the term 'Versailles Settlement' to refer to the five treaties which together made up the Paris Peace Settlement. The Treaty of Versailles (28 June 1919) was the treaty between the victorious Allies and Germany and there were treaties, as we shall see, between the Allies and the other defeated powers, Austria (the Treaty of St Germain, 10 September 1919), Bulgaria (the Treaty of Neuilly, 27 November 1919), Turkey (the Treaty of Sevres, 20 April 1920) and Hungary (the Treaty of Trianon, 4 June 1920). Technically, the term the Paris Peace Settlement is the correct way to refer to the treaties as a whole but many historians refer, as I do, to the Versailles Settlement. The important thing is to distinguish between the *Treaty* of Versailles and the wider *Settlement*.

Exercise   Look at your *Maps Booklet* and summarize the major differences between Europe in 1914 and in 1923. ■

Specimen answer and discussion   The greatest changes have taken place in east central and eastern Europe; the changes in western Europe are comparatively minor.

The old framework of east central Europe has disappeared with the erosion of the eastern frontiers of Germany and the western frontiers of Russia, and with the disintegration of the Austro-Hungarian Empire. Austria and Hungary are now separate states and much attenuated. Bulgaria is reduced in size, while Romania has acquired new territory and Serbia has become the nucleus of the new state of Yugoslavia, incorporating territory previously belonging to the Austro-Hungarian Empire together with Montenegro. Much of the non-Russian periphery of the Russian Empire is independent of the Soviet Union. In the wake of the old empires, 'successor' states have appeared: Poland, Czechoslovakia, Finland, Estonia, Latvia and Lithuania. Italy has acquired a modest amount of territory from the old Austro-Hungarian Empire, while Greece has extended its frontier at Bulgaria's expense and, like Italy, gained islands from Turkey. The Ottoman Empire has been replaced by a Turkish Republic, but Turkey retains a toe-hold in Europe. In western Europe France has regained Alsace and Lorraine, Belgium has made small gains, and Germany has ceded North Schleswig to Denmark.

Such radical changes amounted to a redrawing of the map of Europe rivalled only by the transformation at the end of the Napoleonic Wars. □

This great reconstruction of Europe was not synonymous with the Versailles Settlement, for the Treaties of Versailles, St Germain, Neuilly, Trianon and Sèvres did not cover all the areas where territory changed hands, and Sèvres (the treaty with Turkey) was never ratified or fully implemented and was replaced by the Treaty of Lausanne of 1923. Russia and the frontiers of Russia and her neighbours were excluded from Versailles. In much of eastern Europe the boundaries and the very existence of states were decided not by gentlemen in tail-coats at Paris but by the outcome of often confused and little recorded fighting on the ground.

Exercise How does Roberts (p.254–5) distinguish between the different processes which made for the general reconstruction of Europe? ∎

Specimen answer and discussion He separates the reconstruction into three processes:

1   a series of treaties with defeated nations;

2   the cancellation of Brest-Litovsk and the stabilization of Russia's relations with its neighbours;

3   the settlement of the eastern Mediterranean and Aegean. □

I shall follow Roberts's categories, but it is worth noting at this stage the tremendous difference that the Bolshevik Revolution, the Treaty of Brest-Litovsk and the severance of relations between Russia and her erstwhile allies made to both the dispensations and the scope of a post-war peace settlement. A peace settlement in which Russia ranked among the victorious powers at Paris would undoubtedly have provided for areas in eastern Europe not covered by the Versailles Settlement, might have made very different provision for areas that were covered by it, and would have been in a better position to enforce its decisions on Turkey.

The Versailles Settlement

World War I and World War II (in the European sphere) can be seen as the hot phases in Europe's Thirty Years' War of the twentieth century, which was fought to decide whether or not Germany was to become the dominant power in

Europe. Such a reading not only relegates the characters of particular regimes and the immediate causes of both wars to a secondary importance, but contrasts sharply with the official war aims of the powers. The pursuit of power and natural self-interest were, however, unsuitable motives for public consumption while states were engaged in a mode of warfare which demanded mass participation and major sacrifices from their populations. Loftier aims had to be found. Thus, although for the Allies World War I was no more a 'war for civilization' than World War II was, in its essential motivation, a 'war against fascism', states became the victims of their own propaganda and were hamstrung both when it came to war short of total victory and to making a rational peace settlement.

The expectations aroused by the feverish propaganda of the Allies in the minds of their electorates were both unrealistic and contradictory: if, on the one hand, the central powers and particularly Germany were peculiarly wicked and culpable, then any settlement should be punitive; but if, on the other hand, the victorious powers were peculiarly virtuous, then a settlement should create a better, more peaceful world that reflected the principles which made those powers so worthy. The actual peace settlement was an unhappy compromise between the pursuit of the interests of the Allied powers, a desire to punish the vanquished, and the furtherance of notions of internationalism, democracy and national self-determination. Such notions gained increased importance with America's entry into the war and were enshrined in President Wilson's Fourteen Points, which is included in *Primary Sources 1: World War I* as Document II.3 (a); this document saddled the Allies with a written manifesto of a highly idealistic nature which contrasted with the secret treaties concluded by the European Allies during the course of the war. 'Fourteen Points', exclaimed the French Prime Minister Clemenceau, 'it's a bit much. The Good Lord had only ten!'

Given the underlying purpose of the war, the ideal peace settlement from the viewpoint of the Allies, as they were constituted early in 1917, would have been one which modified the map of Europe as it existed in the mid-nineteenth century. Such a settlement would have expanded the frontiers of Russia and her Balkan allies, retained a weakened and federal Austro-Hungarian Empire, and partially dismembered the German Empire, giving France control of the Rhineland. A secret treaty between France and Russia in March 1917 had been a move in this direction, underwriting Russian control of Poland and providing for French domination of the Rhineland. By 1919 the Russian Revolution, Russia's defeat by Germany, the disintegration of Austria-Hungary and America's entry into the war had radically changed the situation, leaving Clemenceau to press for more limited aims with a weaker hand.

Exercise   1   How does Roberts describe France's aims in 1918?

2   To what extent does Roberts think France succeeded in achieving those aims at the Peace Conference? ■

Specimen answers   1   Roberts sees security as the French goal and, following from this, a
and discussion   'determination to wound Germany as deeply and permanently as possible'.

2   He considers the final terms of the Versailles Settlement as a diplomatic
         defeat for France. □

At first sight the terms which Germany was forced to accept seem harsh enough.
The Germans certainly thought so, and liberal opinion in Britain and the United
States soon came to feel remorseful about the supposed harshness of the terms.
Germany was labelled the guilty party, was forced to pay reparations, and
suffered limitations on the size and nature of its armed forces. Germany also lost
territory, including all its colonies; Alsace-Lorraine was returned to France; a
small amount of territory went to Belgium; part of Schleswig went to Denmark;
and in the east, a large tract of territory went to the new Polish state.

   But France gained little security. Germany remained substantially intact and
potentially strong. As Roberts points out, France had hoped to detach the left
bank of the Rhine from Germany, but obtained only the demilitarization of the
Rhineland and its occupation by Allied troops for fifteen years as well as the
occupation under the League of Nations of the Saar coalfield. The French would
also have liked control of the Ruhr. It soon became clear that to enforce the
Treaty of Versailles France could depend on no one but itself. An Anglo-
American guarantee of assistance in the event of an attack by Germany was
abandoned by the Americans, and Britain made it clear that it would not bind
itself to observe the guarantee unilaterally.

   My colleague, Professor Tony Lentin, has commented on the Treaty of
Versailles as follows:

> It was a wise precept of Machiavelli that the victor should either conciliate his
> enemy or destroy him. The Treaty of Versailles did neither. It did not pacify
> Germany, still less permanently weaken her, appearances notwithstanding,
> but left her scourged, humiliated and resentful. It was neither a Wilson peace
> nor a Clemenceau peace, but a witches' brew concocted of the least palatable
> ingredients of each, which though highly distasteful to Germany, were by no
> means fatal.
>
> (A. Lentin, *Lloyd George, Woodrow Wilson and the Guilt of Germany*, 1985,
> p.132)

France lacked even the comfort it had enjoyed prior to 1917 of an ally to the east
of Germany. Instead of its erstwhile Russian ally, France would be forced to rely
upon alliance with the new states of east central Europe to contain Germany.
These states were a poor substitute; they all shared some commitment to their
midwife the Paris Peace Settlement, but had many quarrels and rivalries among
themselves.

   As we observed at the beginning of this section, the major changes to the map
of Europe were in central and eastern Europe. Even if the Allies had wished to
preserve the Austro-Hungarian Empire, as perhaps they were still prepared to
do in 1917 if the Emperor Charles had been able to break free from Germany
and make a separate peace, it was certainly too late by 1919. At the same time as
German armies had been winning the shooting war in the east, nationalist exiles,
with western historians as their fuglemen, had been winning the propaganda
war. In the last month of the war the Habsburg government came out in
desperation with a federalist manifesto, but the Empire was being torn apart.
The efforts of the exiles and of liberal academics and journalists in the western

capitals inclined western opinion towards the break-up of the Empire, but, by November 1918, its disintegration was already well advanced.

The Allied statesmen were thus already sympathetic to the idea of national self-determination and the setting up of new states in east central Europe at a time when, as the old order disintegrated, national councils were seeking to pre-empt their decisions. In addition to the principle of self-determination, two other guidelines influenced Versailles, modifying and cutting across it: the desire to punish Germany and its allies, and the need to create buffer states on Germany's eastern frontier after the collapse of Tsarist Russia. All three guidelines can be detected in the Treaty of Versailles itself, the Treaty of St Germain with Austria, the Treaty of Trianon with Hungary, and the Treaty of Neuilly with Bulgaria.

The attempt to make state boundaries correspond to divisions between nationalities was, of course, unrealistic in east central Europe, where there was not even a patchwork of nationalities. Nationalities overlapped each other, so that towns might be primarily German and Jewish with a Slavonic hinterland, or one village might be Magyar and the next Croat. The re-establishment of the Habsburg Empire was probably not an option but its many advantages for the stability of east central Europe are retrospectively apparent. Nationalism had not been, nor was it to be, either a rational or a civilizing influence in the region. That the Allies permitted their enthusiasm for national self-determination to be modified by their desire to punish the vanquished central powers and to make the successor states as strong as possible only compounded the problem and ensured that more, not fewer, minorities were created.

Exercise Can you find examples of where the settlement departed from the principle of self-determination? ■

Specimen answer and discussion A notable example is the treatment accorded to Germans. The new and much reduced Austria was forbidden to unite with Germany, regardless of the wishes of its German population. The Sudetenland Germans were incorporated into Czechoslovakia, and the South Tyrol passed to Italy without benefit of plebiscite.

Romania, Czechoslovakia and Yugoslavia swallowed up 1.75 million, 0.75 million and 0.5 million Magyars respectively.

Even the small adjustments to the German-Belgian frontier arguably contravened the national principle as both Eupen and Malmédy which were ceded by Germany to Belgium were German-speaking areas. □

How were all these territorial changes decided? Who decided on which side of a border a particular area or town would go? Here is an extract from the diary of Harold Nicolson, a British diplomat:

March 2, Sunday

... At 5.00 to Quai d'Orsay for sub-committee of Slovak frontiers. We put Lerond in the chair, which is a great help. We begin with Pressburg and secure agreement. Then we get to Grosse Schlutt. French want to give it to the Czechs. The US want to give it to the Magyars. I reserve judgement, saying it depends on whether German Hungary is given to Austria. Then examine frontier from Komorn to Jung. The very devil. The Yanks want to go north along the ethnical line, thus cutting all the railways. We want to go south, keeping the Kassa-Komorn lateral communications, in spite of the fact that this will mean putting some 80,000 Magyars under Czech rule. Eventually a compromise.

The Yanks give way as regards Eipel and we as regards Miskolcz. As for the rest we decide to wait and hear Benes. Dine with Princess Soutzo at the Ritz – a swell affair. Painlevé, Klotz, Bratianu there. Also Marcel Proust and Abel Bonnard. Proust is white, unshaven, grubby, slip-faced.

(Nicolson, *Peacemaking 1919*, 1944, p.275)

Exercise   1   What do you suppose was the real basis of the disagreements in this sub-committee?

2   What factor that I haven't mentioned so far does Nicolson note as having to be taken account of?

3   What term comes to mind to describe these sort of compromises? ∎

Specimen answers   1   The Americans were in this instance the most persistent in wanting to
and discussion   pursue national self-determination, while the French put their influence on the side of making the new Czechoslovakia as big as possible with the most defensible frontiers. The British were more flexible and pragmatic though others might have considered them cynical.

2   Communications: roads and railways cut through ethnic boundary lines.

3   'Horse trading' or 'give and take' are the terms that occur to me. The future of Eipel and Miskolcz are decided fairly casually on a 'one for you and one for us' basis. It is striking that the future of Pressburg doesn't seem to have caused any disagreement and yet the decision to give it to Czechoslovakia ignored the fact that the town, with its mixed racial composition, stood amidst a region containing 700,000 Magyars and had been the capital of Hungary during the Turkish occupation of Buda. ☐

It was over the question of the Polish-German frontiers that the Versailles treaty-makers disagreed most strongly among themselves; it was also one of the most flagrant departures from their principle of national self-determination. No one (save General Smuts) doubted the wisdom of re-establishing a state of Poland after well over a century of division, but France and the United States on the one hand and Britain on the other disagreed over the extent of the territory to be awarded to it. The report of a commission on the Polish frontiers proposed that many areas which were predominantly German should be given to Poland. France and the USA both supported the most extreme Polish claims. Lloyd George extravagantly argued that it was folly to place 2,132,000 Germans 'under the control of a people which is of a different religion and which has never proved its capacity for stable self government throughout its history' (quoted by W. N. Medlicott in *British Foreign Policy since Versailles,* 1940). The exact number of Germans in inter-war Poland is a matter of contention. A. J. P. Taylor has estimated that the German minority was one and a half million *(The Origins of the Second World War,* 1961) but P. Wandycz argues that, *excluding* Danzig, the German population was 585,000 (*'Origins of the Second World War' Reconsidered,* ed. G. Martel, 1986). It was decided that there should be a plebiscite in the disputed region of Upper Silesia and that Danzig should be made a free city, instead of going outright to Poland.

By the time the plebiscite was held in March 1921, France and Poland had concluded a military alliance (in February 1921) and France was determined to strengthen her ally as much as possible. To the chagrin of the French and the Poles, the plebiscite in Upper Silesia resulted in a clear majority for those wishing to be part of Germany. The Polish plebiscite commissioner then resorted to force and, at the head of an irregular army, took over a large part of the region. British troops had been withdrawn and French troops took the Polish side. The Germans organized themselves for resistance and British troops were sent back to Silesia. The French government went so far as to issue a solemn warning to Britain that its attitude threatened a definite rupture between the two countries, which elicited a firm response from the British Foreign Secretary, Lord Curzon. The Silesian question was eventually referred by the Conference of Paris, August 1921, to the League of Nations, and a committee of four – a Brazilian, a Chinese, a Belgian and a Spaniard – arrived at a decision. Poland received about one-third of the territory but about half of the inhabitants and the greater part of the industrial resources.

This crisis illustrates some of the salient features of the Versailles Settlement and the immediate diplomatic aftermath:

1 It demonstrates the enormous difficulty of securing frontiers in east central Europe which would correspond with national self-determination. Upper Silesia was a classic case of German towns and villages surrounded by a Slav countryside.

2 It illustrates the way in which the powers, in this instance France and the United States, were prepared to subordinate self-determination to other factors: the desire to punish Germany and keep her weak and the aim of creating strong states to the east of Germany.

3 It shows how Anglo-French relations had deteriorated within a few years of victory. The French, insecure in the absence of British and American guarantees for the settlement, were seeking to build up allies on Germany's eastern frontiers. Britain now favoured a 'normalization' for Germany which would have been made easier if the important industrial areas of Upper Silesia had been returned to Germany. To the French such a move appeared senseless as it would have strengthened the already considerable industrial potential of Germany.

4 The episode illustrates the difficulties of Poland's position and also the dangers that its position held for the future stability of east central Europe. Sandwiched between two powerful states, Germany and Russia, Poland was able to gain more at Germany's expense than Germany, once resurgent, was likely to accept. The Silesian industrial resources would obviously strengthen Poland but not enough to make her the economic or military equal of Germany. Poland was threatened by Russia but her victory against the latter in the 1918–21 war resulted in such territorial gains as Russia was not in the long term going to accept. Perhaps Poland was too successful for its own good and that success fuelled great power pretensions which made the Poles unwilling to come to terms with either of the powerful neighbours.

always a buffer between : Russia and Prussia/Germany

5   The outcome could be seen as an example of the smooth working of the
     League of Nations system, but the League was called in only as a result of
     Anglo-French compromise, and its decision was only accepted by Germany
     because of the latter's weak position at the time.

The historian H. A. L. Fisher, who was a member of the Lloyd George coalition
government, later defended the territorial provisions of the settlement. Despite
problems and anomalies he argued (and he was writing in 1935): 'the political
map of Europe is drawn more closely than ever before in accordance with the
views of the populations concerned' (*A History of Europe,* Vol. III). He did admit
that the treaty had 'left sore places'. He could have said that again!

Eastern Europe

The provision of the Versailles Settlement and of the statesmen who met in Paris
did not extend to the greater part of eastern Europe. Here the post-war map of
Europe as it was established by 1923 was the outcome of a series of struggles
which were often complex and confused but always bloody. As we have seen,
Poles and Germans skirmished in Upper Silesia to decide Poland's western
frontier, but its eastern frontiers were decided by a full-scale war with the Soviet
Union.

Like Austria-Hungary to the west, two great multinational empires, the
Russian and Ottoman Empires, tottered and fell apart in eastern Europe during
1917 and 1918. Their subject nationalities made their bids for independence, and
the successor regimes to the old central authorities, the Soviet Union and the
Turkish Republic, rallied and fought back. We will deal first with Russia, the
establishment of new national states on its periphery, and the reconquest by
Soviet Russia of other states that had won a short-lived independence.

The Soviet Union and eastern Europe

Germany had won the war on the eastern front only months before being forced
to concede victory to the western powers. The Treaty of Brest-Litovsk, signed on
3 March 1918, was testimony to Germany's overwhelming victory. Roberts refers
to Brest-Litovsk as 'an imposed peace – a diktat – in a far truer sense than
Versailles', but if this was so, it was largely because Russia was in a far weaker
position in March 1918 than Germany was at the time of the armistice.

Brest-Litovsk has the paradoxical quality of a treaty that was formally
abrogated within a matter of months: one of the conditions of the Allies'
armistice on 11 November 1918 was the abandonment of Brest-Litovsk, and yet
it was of lasting importance in doing much to shape the eastern Europe of the
post-war years.

From early in the war the Germans had encouraged nationalism as a weapon
against Tsarist Russia, and indeed attached greater hopes to the effects of such
nationalisms than to that 'plague bacillus', Lenin, whose return to Russia they
facilitated in April 1917. The Russian state began to disintegrate with the
February Revolution, and this disintegration accelerated after the October
Revolution. By March 1918, Finland, Estonia, Russian Poland, Lithuania, Latvia,
the Ukraine and Moldavia were all claiming independence from Russia, most of
them encouraged by Germany. Their chance of success depended upon the
continued weakness of Russia and the support of Germany. Brest-Litovsk and its

immediate aftermath saw a German hegemony in eastern Europe under which many of these movements for national independence, but not all, were able to establish themselves securely enough to retain their independence into the 1920s and 1930s.

If Brest-Litovsk can be seen as a German 'diktat', it also represented the revolt of the non-Russian peoples of the Tsarist empire in the context of Russia's defeat. In the late twentieth century, after the demise of the Soviet Union, it was apparent that the map of eastern Europe bore some resemblance to that of 1918 with the exception of the division of one multi-ethnic state, Czechoslovakia, then being created, and the disintegration of another, Yugoslavia.

Exercise   Read Roberts, pp.242–4, and answer the following questions:

1   The acceptance of the terms of Brest-Litovsk was a victory for whose view among the Bolshevik leaders?

2   Which national independence movements had their claims underwritten by the treaty? ∎

Specimen answers and discussion

1   It was a victory for the view of Lenin, who was prepared to accept peace at almost any price in order to use time to consolidate power. It is not clear in fact whether there was a realistic alternative. To have waged a revolutionary war as Bukharin advocated would have required a revolutionary army capable of standing up to the Germans.

2   Roberts mentions that Russia gave up Poland, Lithuania, the Ukraine, the Baltic Provinces and Transcaucasia. It was also agreed that Finland would immediately be cleared of Russian troops. ☐

As Roberts argues, the Treaties of Brest-Litovsk and Bucharest together brought Germany close to the realization of a *Mitteleuropa*. Despite the recognition of the Ukraine as an independent state, German and Austro-Hungarian armies remained in occupation of the border territories from the Baltic to the Caucasus and occupied the Ukraine, defeating the advancing Bolsheviks.

[margin handwritten note: Germany's war was partially redeemed, in their own eyes, by the treaty of Brest-Litovsk.]

The events of 1918, prior to the defeat of Germany in the west, seemed to foreshadow the dissolution of Greater Russia. If all the areas which declared themselves independent had succeeded, Russia would indeed have been diminished; as it was, the eventual success of the Bolsheviks in Russia's civil war (1918–20) enabled them to re-establish control over White Russia, the Ukraine, Georgia and Azerbaijan and Armenia (the Allies sponsored the formation of a single Armenian state out of Russian and Turkish Armenia, a scheme which foundered in 1921 with Turkish recovery under Mustafa Kemal – later Kemal Ataturk – with the aid of a Soviet-Turkish treaty).

The states which did emerge independent from the confused fighting of the years 1918 to 1922 owed their independence in the first place to Germany's triumph in the east. But an independence within a German-dominated *Mitteleuropa,* though no doubt preferable to being part of the Soviet Union, would have been a very qualified independence, and Germany's attitude towards the independence of Poland and the Baltic states was equivocal. Such genuine independence as the smaller states and peoples of eastern Europe could ever hope to enjoy was dependent, at best, on both their great neighbours being weak and, at second best, on the ability to play one off against the other.

Their inter-war independence was a lucky break, depending as it did on Germany's defeat of Russia, the subsequent defeat of Germany by the western Allies and then on the weakening of Russia by civil war and Poland's victory over Russia in 1920. From the viewpoint of the early twenty-first century we can see how the demise of the Soviet Union in 1989–91 gave the Baltic States and those, like Ukraine, whose bids for independence were crushed in 1919–22 a new opportunity for national self-rule.

The Russo-Polish war of 1920 came at a time when the Bolsheviks were decisively gaining the upper hand in the civil war. Intervention by the Allies had largely ceased and, save for Wrangel in the Crimea, there was little left of White Russian resistance. At this point, the Poles, led by Marshal Joseph Pilsudski, negotiated an agreement with the Ukrainians, who were losing their bid for independence, and advanced into Russia. The Poles got as far as Kiev and were then beaten back by a Russian counter-attack which came close to Warsaw in August 1920. Pilsudski then counter-attacked in turn, pushing the Red Army back into Russia. The Treaty of Riga, 18 March 1921, set the Russian-Polish frontier until 1939, placing it much further east than had been suggested by Lord Curzon in 1920. Poland's victory did much to force the Soviet Union to accept the independence of Finland and the Baltic states of Estonia, Latvia and Lithuania, and treaties recognizing their independence were signed in 1921.

Thus was concluded a wonderfully confused period of constant warfare on Russia's borders, a period of topsyturvydom which witnessed British sailors fighting in Latvian trenches alongside German soldiers and the offer by a German Social Democratic government to provide Ludendorff to serve under Foch at the head of a combined Allied-German army which would have aided the Poles.

Turkey in Europe

The demise of the Ottoman Empire had been long anticipated, and Turkey's entry into World War I led to a number of secret agreements among the Allies over the final dismemberment of the empire. The ambitions of France and Britain to gain control of large tracts of the Ottoman Empire in the Middle East were to be largely satisfied, but a resurgent Turkish national movement led by Mustafa Kemal (Ataturk) proved capable of defying the diktat of Sèvres, the territorial ambitions of Greece and Italy and an Armenian separatist movement, and was able to preserve not only Anatolia but its last territory in Europe, Eastern Thrace including Constantinople.

In 1915 the Ottoman Government had begun the forcible deportation of the Armenian population of eastern Anatolia. The Armenians were suspected of sympathizing with Russia. This exercise in 'ethnic cleansing' has been seen as the first modern incidence of genocide and possibly as a model for the Nazi 'final solution' to the 'Jewish problem'. As many as 2 million Armenians may have perished while another million survived deportation.

By August 1920 an Allied force was occupying the Straits and Constantinople, Greek and Italian troops had landed on Turkish soil, and an independent Armenian Republic had been proclaimed. The Treaty of Sèvres of that month provided for a small and much weakened Turkish state which would have been an insignificant power: as well as losing the Middle Eastern provinces of the Empire and most of the Aegean islands together with the Dodecanese, Turkey

War becoming ? more 'barbaric'!

was to lose Armenia, which was to be independent, and Eastern Thrace was to go to Greece, while Smyrna and the surrounding area in eastern Anatolia were to be administered by Greece for five years followed by a plebiscite; what remained of Turkey was to enjoy only a qualified independence subject to a commission of representatives of France, Britain and Italy.

The treaty, however, was signed by the discredited government of the Sultan, which was now challenged by the national government of Kemal in Ankara. By a combination of successful generalship and skilful diplomacy, Kemal was able to overturn the least acceptable features of Sèvres. Armenian independence and Greek invasion were smashed by force of arms. A succession of treaties with the Soviet Union, Italy and France settled frontiers and isolated Britain as the only power determined to uphold Sèvres. Although Britain and Turkey came close to war in the Chanak crisis in 1922, this crisis was settled by negotiation, and the Treaty of Lausanne of July 1923 considerably revised the provisions of Sèvres.

By the Treaty of Lausanne, Turkey became the only ex-enemy state not required to pay reparations. Turkey regained full control of Smyrna and surrounding Western Anatolia, and of Armenia; the Straits, although demilitarized, were returned to its sovereignty; and with its re-acquisition of Eastern Thrace, Turkey remained in Europe.

Roberts comments that Lausanne was the only 'negotiated, rather than imposed, peace treaty, and it has lasted longer than any of the other post-war settlements'. One reason for this may well have been that the compulsory exchange of Greek and Turkish minorities that accompanied the settlement meant that populations were ruthlessly made to fit frontiers, and the removal of the Greek minorities on the Turkish mainland signalled the end of Greek ambitions for an Aegean empire.

Lausanne settled effectively two questions that had been central to European diplomacy for a century: the question of the control of the Straits, and the question as to whether Turkey would remain in Europe. The demilitarization of the Straits was amended by the Montreux Convention of 1936, when Turkish sovereignty was restored subject to certain restrictions, the most important of which was the closure of the Straits to warships of belligerents in time of war. Turkey remained, albeit marginally, a European power through its possession of Eastern Thrace. This was to be important psychologically to a country undergoing rapid westernization under Ataturk, and was to buttress Turkey's self-image as a secular European state.

Conclusion

The geopolitical changes that took place in Europe between 1918 and 1923 were, indeed, overwhelming, and their strategic implications incalculable, but to what extent were they attributable to World War I?

Exercise To what extent do you consider that the war was responsible for these great changes to the map of Europe? List other factors which influenced such changes. ∎

Specimen answer and discussion It is undeniable that the war was responsible for both the sweeping nature of change and for many, but not all, of its specific features. The war was responsible for the disintegration of great states and for the changed balance between victorious and defeated nations. The Versailles Settlement was, obviously, the direct outcome of the war.

Other factors are closely associated with the results and effects of the war. There were many national movements in Europe prior to 1914, but the nature of the war gave some of them their opportunity. The Russian Empire had problems and weaknesses, but a successful Bolshevik revolution was an unlikely outcome in 1914. Even the predilection of Versailles for self-determination can in large part be attributed to the course of the war and America's entry into it. □

Nevertheless, the effect of the war on the political geography of much of eastern Europe can be seen as essentially contextual. It destroyed the old framework, but what replaced it was often due to the success or failure of national movements and armies in that confused period of sporadic warfare which continued up to 1923. Perhaps we should properly conclude, if we suspend our west European viewpoint, that the wars that took place in eastern Europe until that date were in fact part of World War I, or at least of Europe's 'Thirty Years' War'.

2   SOCIAL CHANGE

Social geography

In any consideration of historical change there can be no more basic a variable than population change. The impact of World War I and of events in the years immediately after the war on the numbers, composition and geographical distribution of the European population was considerable.

Wars, inevitably, result in people being killed, but do not necessarily result in a decline in the population. The Great War saw enormous loss of life but no overall decline in Europe's population. The war rather cut back the rate of growth of the European population, cut across long-term patterns of growth, and altered the balance between the sexes and between different age groups.

How many people were killed by the war? The answer is that we don't know precisely. We have to choose between informed estimates and rough guesses whereby we 'give or take' a few million. You should recall our attempt to provide some 'precise' figures in Unit 6.

Exercise   Read Roberts, p.292, on the 'biological cost' of the war, and answer the following question: Why is it so difficult to estimate precisely the biological cost of the war? ■

Specimen answers   1   Because accurate figures for the numbers killed in the fighting do not
and discussion   exist for all states.

2   Much depends on whether November 1918 is taken as the end of the war or whether we also consider the aftermath in the east.

3   We have to take into account births which would have taken place had it not been for the war, as pre-war demographic trends were interrupted by it.

4   We have to take account of deaths that occurred after the fighting ended, in so far as many died earlier than they would normally have done due to the effects of wounds, malnutrition and diseases which flourished in conditions of social and administrative disarray and famine. □

The inclusion under war losses or costs of deaths due to the Spanish influenza pandemic is somewhat contentious. The Spanish 'flu spread throughout the world, affecting combatant and neutral nations alike. Its impact can only properly be considered part of the war's toll in so far as it may have had a greater effect because of widespread malnutrition in the last year of the war.

One estimate by B. C. Urlanis puts European losses due to the war (including Russian but excluding Turkish losses) at 8,260,000 (quoted in L. A. Kosinsky, *The Population of Europe*, 1970, p.11). This estimate of deaths differs from that of Roberts (p.292), which is taken from W. S. and E. S. Woytinsky's *World Population and Production* (1953). This puts death directly caused by the fighting at nearly 10 million. The difference may be accounted for by the fact that Urlanis did not include Turkish deaths, but it also bears out the point made by Roberts as to the difficulty of precision. The experts disagree, in part because of what they include or don't include as European war deaths and in part because for many countries accurate figures simply do not exist.

Total losses are obviously greater if we consider the fighting which raged before and after World War I itself and look at a longer period, say 1912–23. The First Balkan War began in 1912, and Urlanis estimates the losses of the Balkan Wars as 142,000, including Turkish deaths. The warfare which continued in Eastern Europe until 1923 resulted in hundreds of thousands of deaths. Urlanis estimates deaths due to the fighting in the civil war and the foreign intervention in Russia as some 800,000, but this figure pales beside the figure of twenty million given by Nicholas V. Riasanovsky in his *History of Russia* (1984) as his estimate of total losses due to 'epidemics, starvation, fighting, executions and the general breakdown of the economy' (p.488) between the October Revolution and the end of the civil war.

Roberts goes on to quote 13 million deaths due to fighting for the period 1914-20 (he takes the figure from M. R. Reinhard and others, *Histoire-générale de la population mondiale,* 1968). He concludes that, if we include the losses of potential births in the calculation, we have to think in terms of a 'demographic cost' of between 20 and 24 million people due to World War I. Seeing that his higher figure is only 4 million above that given by Riasanovsky for Russia in the period 1917–21, we have to reconcile ourselves to the fact that even well informed historians can differ widely in their estimates.

The war interrupted a rapid increase in the European population which had been taking place since the eighteenth century. The population had increased from 152 million in 1800 to 296 million in 1900. A glance at Roberts's table (Appendix 1, p.488) will show you how rapid the increase in population was in the first decade of the twentieth century.

You will see from the table, and should remember from the discussion of population in Book 1, Unit 4, that the long-term trends in population growth that the war cut across were by no means uniform throughout Europe. The European population was certainly increasing in the late nineteenth and early twentieth centuries, but it was increasing at different rates in different countries.

Roberts doesn't claim more for his table than that the figures give a general picture of comparative population movement. We shall see that the difficulties with it are greater than he implies, but for the moment let us take it at face value and consider what it tells us about population increase *before* 1914.

Exercise	1	Which countries stand out from the table as having particularly high rates of population increase and which as having particularly low rates before World War I?
	2	Can you see any broad distinction between categories of European nations? ■
Specimen answers and discussion	1	Romania has a phenomenal rate of increase, trebling its population between 1880 and 1910. Bulgaria and Russia register an increase of around 50 per cent in the same period, while Germany is just below 50 per cent. The British increase is more modest at around 30 per cent, while France is positively sluggish, expanding by only 5.5 per cent in thirty years.
	2	The sharpest increases are in eastern Europe and the lowest in western Europe. □

A valid generalization about European population growth up until 1914 is that, although a historically unique surge in population growth was continuing, population growth in the richer northern and western countries was beginning to decrease, while it was accelerating in the poorer eastern and southern countries (see Unit 4). It is often argued that, by the late nineteenth century and early twentieth century, countries that were industrialized and urbanized were exhibiting decreasing birth rates, although the continued decline in the death rate made up for this; largely agricultural societies in eastern and southern Europe, on the other hand, had soaring birth rates and an accelerating population increase. Those of you who analysed Roberts's table very closely may have noticed a flaw in this argument. France had a very low rate of population increase and remained a largely rural society – agriculture remained its largest industry and, as late as 1935, more than 55 per cent of the French population lived in villages or very small towns – yet France's birth rate was notoriously low. Norway, too, was a largely rural society with a modest rate of population increase. Rural areas were exhibiting some of the lowest as well as the highest rates of population growth.

The equations of agricultural/rural equals high and industrial/urban equals low birth rates do seem far too simplistic. Historical demographers have pointed out that differences between the birth rates of western and eastern Europe (and indeed the rest of the world) go back a long way, with western Europeans having a late age at marriage and a propensity to match population to resources by adjustment of both the age at marriage and the numbers getting married (H. J. Hajnal, 'European marriage patterns in perspective', 1965). Some west European agricultural societies adopted birth control as a means of reducing marital fertility as an alternative to and in part a substitute for delayed marriages.

Industrialization and urbanization led at first to an initial increase in the birth rate, which was slackening in the industrialized areas of western Europe by the end of the nineteenth century. It was in agricultural eastern Europe when there were peasant economies based upon the extended family, within which marriage traditionally had taken place at an early age and children had been seen as a source of wealth, that population increase was accelerating in the early twentieth century. The evaluation of the effects of World War I on the population figures of individual countries is beset with considerable difficulty and numerous complications. You should, I think, be able to work out what the problems are.

Exercise Identify the major problems in estimating population increase or decrease due to the war in specific countries. ■

Specimen answer and discussion

1 The redrawing of the map of Europe in the years immediately after the war makes estimation very difficult. States disappeared or were broken up and new states appeared; frontiers changed.

2 There was a series of large migrations, referred to by Roberts, p.293, which redistributed population and changed the pattern of racial and national groups in some areas of Europe.

The United Kingdom was one of the few European combatant countries whose frontiers did not change at the end of World War I, although they suffered a contraction in 1921 when the Irish Free State was given separate Dominion status. Frontier changes in western Europe were modest in comparison to those in eastern Europe, but France's acquisition of Alsace-Lorraine brought 1.8 million new citizens, and for all continental states the difference between the population figures for 1910 and 1920 in Roberts's Appendix 1 reflect, as well as the birth rates and mortality rates, losses or gains in territory and the exodus or influx of migrants or refugees. □

Exercise From Roberts's table, which countries appear to have had an absolute decrease in population as a result of World War I? ■

Specimen answer Only France registers a decline in population in this table for the period 1910–1920. So far so good, but remember the warnings about the difficulty of obtaining accurate figures and the question of the basis of calculation of any figures used. It may well be that Roberts's table rather underestimates the effect of the war. The American demographer, D. Kirk, calculated that Poland, Yugoslavia, Czechoslovakia, Belgium and Romania all had a decrease in population *within the boundaries as they were during the interwar period (Europe's Population in the Interwar Years,* 1946). □

Let us consider the cases of some individual countries.

Germany

Here are two sets of figures for German population (in millions):

1880	1890	1900	1910	1920	1925
40.2	44.2	50.6	58.5	61.8	
45.2	49.4	56.3	64.9		63.1
			58.4		

The first row of figures are Roberts's, while the second row is taken from B. R. Mitchell's *European Historical Statistics 1750-1970* (1975), p.20. Clearly we have a problem. Mitchell's figures are taken directly from the census returns, and although these are by no means always entirely reliable, the difference between his figures and Roberts's are too great to be accounted for by any exaggeration in the returns, especially as the German Empire was a state noted for its bureaucratic efficiency. The clue to the differences is in the two figures given by Mitchell for 1910, the higher figure being that for the German Empire and the lower figure that for the *post-war* boundaries of Germany with the population they contained in 1910. Thus, although you may be forgiven for having thought that Germany's population had gone up by 1920, despite war casualties (estimated by Roberts at three million, although other sources suggest lower figures around two million), you were in fact comparing figures for the German population within Weimar's boundaries. The three million rise in population is accounted for by the arrival of refugees from Germany's lost eastern territories mitigating the effect of war losses.

Russia

Roberts remarks that even Russia's great losses during the war were not sufficient to prevent the continued growth of its population but it would appear that the Russian Empire lost a lower percentage of its population due to death at the hands of the enemy than most other combatant nations. One estimate of the numbers of the Russian armed forces killed in the war is 1,650,000 (N. Golovin, *The Russian Army in the World War,* 1931), but of course the number of civilians who died from war-related causes was enormous. As we have seen, the war itself was followed by the death toll of the civil war and the droughts and famines of 1920 and 1921. We have also to take into account the loss of territory, for the USSR lost territory that had been part of the Russian Empire, territory that had contained nearly 28 million people in 1897. Roberts's figure of 153.8 million for 1920 can be compared with the census figure for 1926 of 147 million.

Romania

Romania's apparent increase in population over the period 1910–20 in Roberts's table is entirely due to its acquisition of large tracts of territory after the Balkan Wars and as a result of the Versailles Settlement (the Treaties of St Germain and Trianon). This extra population disguises a probable absolute decrease in population within the pre-war frontiers. Romania's losses during World War I have been estimated at 250,000 or 3.3 per cent of the population (Urlanis, *The Population of Europe,* 1970) and, using wider criteria, as 1,088 or 14 per cent by D. H. Aldcroft *(From Versailles to Wall Street 1919–1929,* 1977).

Yugoslavia

The Kingdom of the Serbs, Croats and Slovenes, as Yugoslavia was called until 1929, had perhaps the highest war losses of any country. Serbia and Montenegro, which had been overrun during the war, ended up with a population deficit estimated at 31.3 per cent by Aldcroft. The 11.9 million population in 1920 shown in Roberts's table is, of course, the population of the new kingdom, made up not only of Serbia and Montenegro but of Bosnia, Herzegovina, Slovenia, Dalmatia, Croatia and other territory acquired at the end of the war.

France

World War I inevitably had a greater impact on France with its low birth rate than on almost any other European country. Paul Gagnon has succinctly summarized its effects:

> A quarter of all Frenchmen between the ages of 18 and 30 were dead. Six hundred thousand were disabled in body or mind or both. Counting civilian deaths and those unborn because of war, France lost 3 million people. Only the return of Alsace-Lorraine (1.8 million) and immigration enabled her to return to 40 million by 1930.
>
> (Paul Gagnon, *France since 1789,* 1972, p.329)

By 1930 there were over 1.5 million foreign wage-earners in France, mainly Poles, Spaniards, Belgians and Italians.

Britain

Roberts estimates the numbers of British dead at 0.75 million, but as you can see from the illustration overleaf from a rather grisly book of photographs, *Covenants with Death,* published by the *Daily Express* in 1934, there have been higher estimates. War losses were not sufficient to prevent the slow growth of the population, which increased by over a million and a half during the decade 1910–20. As with other countries, the fact that emigration ceased during the war years helped to balance war losses.

Greece

Greece is not shown on Roberts's table, but the increase in its population between 1907 (2.3 million) and 1920 (5.0 million) was spectacular and was due to its acquisition of new territory in the period. By 1928 the population had expanded to 6.2 million, reflecting not only changes in birth and mortality rates, but also the arrival of more than one million Greek refugees from Turkey and Thrace after 1922, and the exodus of some 350,000 Muslims (Roberts, p.293).

Clearly there are special difficulties with the successor states of the Austro-Hungarian Empire (the Empire's war dead have been estimated by B. C. Urlanis at 1.1 million or 1.8 per cent of the population) and with the newly created states of east and central Europe. The lack of continuity, the boundary changes and the migration and exchanges of population make any attempt at estimating the effects of war on the population difficult in the extreme, although, as we have seen, three of them – Poland, Czechoslovakia and Yugoslavia – are among those estimated by D. Kirk as having had an absolute decrease in population.

Exercise   Two further effects of the war, evident in the population structure of every combatant country after the war, can be detected in Table 7–10.1 below. What are they? ■

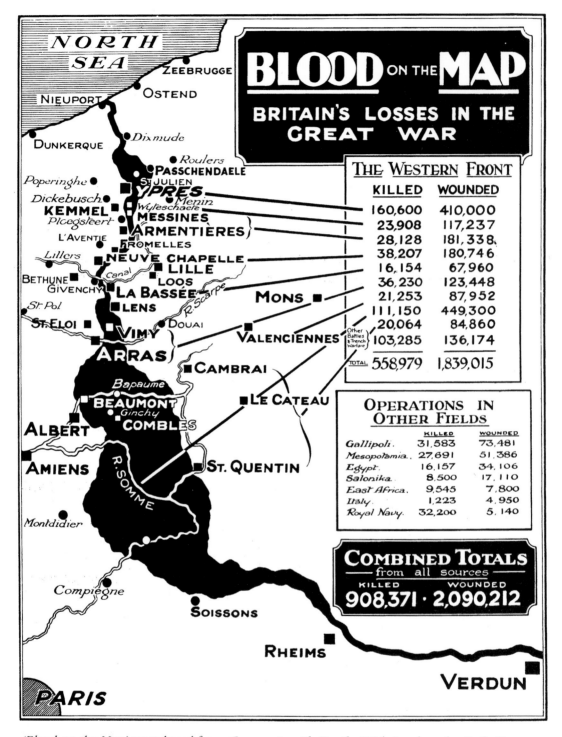

'*Blood on the Map*' reproduced from *Covenants with Death*, 1934, London, the Daily Express.

Table 7–10.1 Population of countries by sex and age groups (in thousands)

Age Group	Germany 1925		France 1921		United Kingdom 1921		Bulgaria 1920	
	M	F	M	F	M	F	M	F
0–4	2,984	2,887	1,148	1,121	1,632	1,640	253	243
5–9	2,023	1,963	1,507	1,501	1,767	1,752	315	303
10–14	3,134	3,079	1,714	1,699	1,837	1,823	330	312
15–19	3,285	3,258	1,734	1,721	1,728	1,775	271	268
20–24	3,065	3,086	1,410	1,643	1,448	1,703	213	221
25–29	2,468	2,839	1,235	1,556	1,340	1,620	165	178
30–34	2,027	2,553	1,256	1,516	1,281	1,520	138	163
35–39	1,965	2,319	1,227	1,501	1,273	1,472	151	160
40–44	1,853	2,054	1,320	1,444	1,223	1,378	108	117
45–49	1,860	1,936	1,275	1,335	1,162	1,244	95	96
50–54	1,588	1,645	1,137	1,209	971	1,043	87	92
55–59	1,327	1,401	1,021	1,107	782	849	83	71
60–64	1,029	1,137	852	966	601	681	67	70
65–69	740	876	651	774	449	537	51	45
70–74	467	591	736	984	281	376	41	41
75–79	246	338			159	234	21	18
80 and over	135	200	160	265	92	129	28	28

(Source: B. R. Mitchell, *European Historical Statistics*, 1750–1970, 1975)

Specimen answer and discussion   World War I resulted in the deaths of far greater numbers of men of fighting age than of any other groups it may have been responsible for. This resulted in (a) an imbalance between the sexes, and (b) a skewing of the age-group profile by the shortfall of men in the age groups who had fought in the war. These imbalances had a continuing impact during the inter-war years. There was a disproportionate number of old people in the population and a large number of unmarried women. At the 1925 German census there were 100 men to every 113 women in the 20–44 age group, while in 1911 the comparable ratio had been 100 to 101. Roberts notes that in 1933 Germany had nearly one million more women than men aged 40–54, while the 1931 census in France revealed a 'surplus' of 728,000 women aged 35–49. Despite high birth rates in the immediate post-war years, the low birth rates of the war years and the shortage of husbands, combined with a trend towards small families in the inter-war years as a whole, meant that the proportion of children in the population of west European countries was disproportionately low. In 1925 the birth rate per 1,000 of the population in European countries varied as follows: Germany 20.8; Italy 28.4; France 19.0; United Kingdom 20.3 (England and Wales 18.3; N. Ireland 22.0; Scotland 21.4); Russia 44.7; Poland 35.4; Romania 35.2; Hungary 28.3; Bulgaria 36.9; Austria 20.6. The pattern of much higher birth rates in Eastern than in western Europe had become even more pronounced. The overall fall in European emigration and the ending of what Roberts calls the 'Great Resettlement' partially counteracted the effects of falling birth rates in many west European countries (the French indeed came to rely on immigrants to offset a shortage of labour) but added to the problems caused by high birth rates in countries whose economies were in little shape to absorb rapidly rising populations. □

Exercise   What do you think the implications of these demographic changes were for international politics (see Roberts, pp.294–6)? ■

Specimen answer   Size of population is an important though by no means the only factor in determining the military strength of a great power. The enormous population of Russia had always been its great asset and it maintained Russia's great power status even when its cumbersome bureaucracy and backward economy had made it a less 'modern' state than the other great powers of Europe. The French had been conscious throughout the nineteenth century that their low birth rate imperilled the country's military potential and its great power status. Britain, because of its island situation and reliance on naval rather than land-based military might, had been able to adopt a more insouciant attitude towards its birth rate. Germany had enjoyed the best of all worlds since 1870, with the second largest population and an industrialized economy, together with an efficient bureaucracy. As regards the two most populous powers, Russia and Germany (see Roberts, p.371), the effects of the war and the demographic trends of the early twenties were to increase Russia's preponderance in population though leaving Germany superior in terms of its economic infrastructure and the education and skills of its labour force. The gap between the military potential of France and Germany had actually increased to France's disadvantage, despite France's victorious position achieved with the aid of formidable allies, in 1918. □

Exercise   You should read Roberts, pp.295–6, and then answer the following question: What were the reactions of states to the decline or increase in their populations? ■

Specimen answer   Given the implications for military potential, no government, save perhaps the British, could remain unconcerned at the relative decline of its population as against possible rivals. The French were, vainly, to attempt to encourage larger families, to forbid abortion and to discourage birth control. During the inter-war period the totalitarian states were to enjoy some success in encouraging larger families (the Italians hardly needed to, nor did the Russians). It seems doubtful, however, whether such policies had much effect in comparison to the long-term trend for eastern European populations to speed ahead of their western counterparts. □

During the nineteenth and early twentieth centuries there had been considerable movement of population. Emigration outside Europe had been the most spectacular example of this, but there had also been movements from country to expanding towns and from backward rural regions to thriving centres of industry and commerce. Such latter movements had affected the balance between regions in individual countries, for example the shift of population to the north in nineteenth-century Britain, and a massive migration from the rural provinces of eastern Germany to Berlin and the industrial regions of the west. After the great shake-up of populations in eastern and central Europe in the years immediately after World War 1, movement tended to be much more restricted within often smaller national boundaries, although the movement of Italian and Spanish workers into France was an exception to this.

Exercise   Read Roberts, pp.296–8, and summarize his conclusions on changes in the distribution of population in the post-war period. ■

Specimen answer   1   Urbanization continued to increase, but along lines that had already been laid down. It was a matter of the growth of existing cities rather than the creation of new ones. Cities spread out into sprawling conurbations with extensive suburbs. The old industrial area 'running from Manchester across northern France and Belgium, and on across north Germany from the Rhine to Upper Silesia' consolidated its position, and the countries in its swathe became even more different, as regards the balance and the relations between town and country, to southern and eastern Europe.

2   In central, southern and eastern Europe large populations in the countryside grew even larger. There was considerable movement into towns, but into relatively small towns with populations of between 20,000 and 100,000. □

Economic performance and theory

The effects of World War I on the European economy were almost all disagreeable. It is possible to find compensatory developments: scientific and technological advances; 'spin-offs' from the wartime production of weapons and armaments which would be utilized by other manufacturers; and the diversification of industries within some national economies. The value of these spin-offs is very much a matter of interpretation. Arthur Marwick, for example, has argued, from his seminal work *The Deluge* (1991) to his recent *A History of the Modern British Isles* (2000), for the significance of developments in medicine (DDT), medical psychology ('shell shock'), motorized transport, aircraft, radio valves (in war, for communication with aircraft), electricity as a power source, and new heavy metal industries in Paris (see Marwick, *War and Social Change*, 1974). Nevertheless, the fact remains that Europe was, both absolutely and relatively, a poorer place in 1919 than it had been in 1914. The accumulation of debts and the liquidation of assets to pay for the war together with the need to pay war pensions to the bereaved and injured all played a part.

To the majority of contemporaries in 1919, the most obvious effects of the war must have been the enormous loss of population and the tremendous physical damage. We have already considered the loss of population due to the war, though not its economic dimension, but the years of warfare had also resulted in the destruction of factories, houses, ships, railway lines, bridges and machinery, while millions of acres of agricultural land were put out of use.

'total war'? →

Exercise   Which areas of Europe and which countries do you suppose suffered the most extensive physical devastation? ■

Specimen answer and discussion   Naturally, the theatres of war received damage from the actual fighting, while some areas that were occupied found their resources pillaged by the occupying power. In many cases the same regions were fought over and then occupied. France and Belgium suffered most in the West, while extensive areas of east and central Europe were devastated as the eastern front was more mobile. The physical damage to Russia was considerable, exacerbated as it was by policies of 'evacuate and destroy' in front of advancing enemy armies, though such damage was to be exceeded by that caused to many areas of the country during the civil war. In relation to its size, however, Serbia probably came off worst. The relative size factor is important, since, though in absolute terms the destruction suffered by countries like Romania and Poland was modest, it involved the loss of a large proportion of their net assets. Those countries which were not fought over (Britain, Germany, Austria and Bulgaria) escaped relatively unscathed in respect of physical damage. □

A few cases will suffice to exemplify the amount of physical damage suffered by the worst hit countries.

Belgium

Nearly all of Belgium was invaded and occupied. D. H. Aldcroft details the damage as follows:

> Some 100,000 houses, equivalent to 6 per cent of the 1914 stock, were destroyed or damaged beyond repair; three-quarters of the railway rolling stock and one-quarter of the fixed stock were destroyed, and by the Armistice only eighty locomotives were in reasonable working order; about half the steel mills were smashed completely and most of the remainder were badly damaged. The position was little better on the land. Over 240,000 acres . . . of land were rendered unfit for cultivation by shelling while the animal population was decimated. One-half of the horned beasts, two-thirds of the swine, one-half of the horses, 1,500 million fowl and 35,000 goats perished or were seized during the course of hostilities.
>
>   (D. H. Aldcroft, *From Versailles to Wall Street 1919–1929*, 1977, p.19)

Poland

According to Antony Polonsky,

> By 1920 when operations came to an end, 90 per cent of the country had been touched directly by war and 20 per cent the scene of heavy fighting. In consequence 55 per cent of bridges, 63 per cent of railway stations, 48 per cent of locomotives and 18 per cent of buildings had been destroyed. Polish industry had been seriously affected by the requisitioning by the occupying powers. The metallurgical industry of the Kingdom of Poland had ceased production. As late as 1922 only 7 out of the 11 furnaces working in 1914 were in operation.
>
>   (R. F. Leslie (ed.) *The History of Poland Since 1863*, 1987, p.140)

Poland was primarily an agricultural country. Nearly 11 million acres of land were made unfit for agricultural use, 6 million acres of forest were destroyed, and a vast amount of timber was removed by occupying armies.

The situation in Belgium, France (where the regions laid waste were both important agriculturally and also major industrial centres) and in Serbia (where the economy lay in ruins after the Austro-Hungarian retreat) has to be borne in mind before we join in any criticisms of the demands for reparations as vengeful and short-sighted. Such physical damage was far more economically debilitating than was population loss, despite the fact that the majority of those killed were men between 18 and 45 and that many of them were highly skilled; the interwar period was to see large-scale industrial unemployment and a surplus of agricultural labour.

Great as the loss of property was, the financial cost of the war to the belligerents was far greater and was spread more evenly, as it fell both upon those countries like Britain and Germany whose territory was not fought over and on those like France and Belgium who were invaded. D. H. Aldcroft has estimated the financial cost as follows:

> The direct cost of the war to all the belligerents amounted to some $260 billion, of which the Allied share accounted for $176 billion. The largest expenditures were incurred by the UK, the United States, Germany, France, Austro-Hungary and Italy in that order. Some idea of the magnitude of the total outlay can be gained from the fact that it represented 6.5 times the sum of all the national debt accumulated in the world from the end of the eighteenth century up to the outbreak of the First World War.
>
> (Aldcroft, *From Versailles to Wall Street*, p.30)

Just how were such vast sums found? In the stress and urgency of war, financial orthodoxy and peacetime common-sense were thrown to the wind. as governments embraced deficit financing (called debt when individuals do it). Even though taxation was increased in every country, no country financed more than 25 per cent of its wartime expenditure (the figure for Britain) from taxation, with the balance being raised from credit of one sort or another. The gold standard was an early victim of the war, the money supply was rapidly expanded with inevitable inflationary consequences, while the respective trade values of currencies altered rapidly.

Germany kept going by relying almost entirely on internal borrowing; France utilized a mixture of internal borrowing, sales of foreign assets and loans from its allies (more than 30 billion francs, mostly from the United States); Britain, although raising far more from taxation than the other European powers, sold some £207 million of dollar investments and another £54 million of sterling, in addition to borrowing £1,027 million from the United States. The British and French financed the Russian war effort to a considerable degree, the British government lending Russia £568 million (Britain lent a total of £1,741 million to its allies). Such loans, together with the 12 billion francs of French investments, were to be a virtual write-off after the Bolshevik Revolution.

Exercise   1   What do you think were the long-term consequences of the financial and monetary policies followed by the European powers for their economic positions in the post-war world?

2   Can you think of any other way in which the war and the economic effort involved in fighting would affect the economic position of the European powers after the war? ■

Specimen answers   1   The main result of the war as regards Europe's economic importance *vis-*
and discussion   *à-vis* the rest of the world was that it suffered a considerable decline.
                           Britain in particular was to feel the effect of the loss of a considerable
                           proportion of its foreign investments and the burden of its debt to the
                           United States; the impact on the position of sterling and the influence of
                           the City of London was to be considerable.

                     2   The effect of the war-time economies was to direct production towards
                           the war effort and away from manufacturing for civilian use and for
                           exports. Combined with the physical damage experienced by many
                           countries, this meant that output and exports suffered a reversal during
                           the war. Imports from other parts of the world of both raw materials and
                           manufactured goods increased, and markets for exports were lost. □

The European economy was thus in a mess, even if the position of individual
countries varied greatly: its financial and trading pre-eminence was gone and its
productivity had fallen alarmingly. Inflation was widespread, the relative values
of currencies veered drunkenly, while the issue of war loans compounded by
the renegation of the Soviet Union was to bedevil international relations. The
powers that gained most from all this were the USA and Japan.

   It was not, of course, the war alone that affected the European economy and
the performance and future prospects of European status at the end of it. We
must take account of the post-war settlement and the aftermath of the war,
especially in eastern Europe.

Exercise   From your reading of Roberts, pp.285–8, what aspects of the post-war settlement
                 do you think adversely affected the European economy and the economies of
                 the European states? ■

Specimen answer   1   The dismemberment of the multinational empires, the founding of new
and discussion   states, and the pursuit of the principle of national self-determination all
                           had economic implications. Economic factors and the economic viability
                           of the new states were not, however, uppermost in the minds of the
                           statesmen at Versailles when they made their decisions. Roberts has
                           noted that 'None of the new states except Czechoslovakia had a balanced
                           economic structure.'

                     2   The reparation terms, which Roberts calls 'the heaviest and most unwise
                           penalties inflicted on Germany.' □

Certainly the new states of eastern Europe lacked balanced economic structures.
The most viable economy was that of Czechoslovakia, the exception mentioned
by Roberts; part of the reason for that viability was that the principle of national
self-determination was imperfectly applied in the instance of Czechoslovakia.
The new political map of east central Europe cut across trading patterns,
communications systems and mutually dependent branches of industries which
had grown up in the context of empires which now no longer existed. The new
states were poor and heavily dependent on agriculture, while their pasts lay
heavily upon them – Poland, for instance, was composed of three parts
possessing different systems of law, different customs units and, to begin with,
three different currencies; Yugoslavia inherited five different railway systems
with four different gauges (Aldcroft, p.28). The co-proprietors of the old Dual

Monarchy, Austria and Hungary, were left an undesirable legacy, Austria inheriting a capital city with industrial suburbs along with a largely agricultural country, and Hungary denuded of most of its valuable resources.

In attacking reparations Roberts has a great weight of historical opinion on his side. One is tempted to assert that the only aspects of the Versailles Settlement to have stood the test of time are the criticisms of it. But in respect of reparations one has to ask whether the error is supposed to lie in the idea of reparations, in the size of the amount Germany was supposed to pay, or in the size of the payments Germany did in fact make. There was nothing new or surprising in the notion of making the losing powers pay indemnities. Certainly the sum fixed by the Reparations Commission of $33 billion was, to say the least, dauntingly large, even if compared with Allied war debts of $26.5 billion. Whether the crisis that arose in 1923 over repayments was the result of Germany's not being able to afford to pay or was provoked by Germany to show that it could not afford to pay, is a moot point, but the Dawes Plan set up a much more feasible system of payments. The initial mistake was probably to consider Allied debt repayments and German reparation separately. France, Britain and Italy could hardly be expected both to repay their wartime loans and forgo reparation. Russia owed France and Britain but refused to pay; France, Britain, Italy and Belgium owed the United States and were reluctantly prepared to pay; and each felt that they had the right to expect payment from Germany. David Aldcroft has suggested *(From Versailles to Wall Street)* that it might have been easier to cut out the middle men and make Germany settle with the USA, offsetting the debts and credits to the other Allied powers. The Dawes Plan was succeeded in 1929 by the Young Plan by which Germany would have continued to pay reparations until 1988. In the end a large part of the Allied war debts was never repaid, with America and Britain coming off worst. The Americans recovered only about one-sixth of their loans, while the bulk of German reparation payments were made with American loans which were also never recovered. Britain was the only country to continue debt repayments on a large scale though it too defaulted eventually.

The problems that beset the economies of the European states at the beginning of the 1920s were many and varied. We should perhaps start by looking at the victorious western Allies, as one might expect the economies of the victors to be in the best shape.

Britain

Britain had emerged from the war without serious damage to its manufacturing capacity. By 1920 its productivity level was approaching that of 1913, though it did not fully regain that level until 1923. The war and its effects had two deleterious consequences for the British economy, one serious and the other deeply damaging. There had already been signs before 1914 that Britain was dangerously dependent on a number of heavy and long-established industries such as coal, steel, shipbuilding and cotton textiles. The demand for these products, although high in the immediate post-war years, was to be affected by the lost markets and new competition due to the war, and in the case of coal by the increased use of oil. Of far greater consequence was the shattering of the old international economy in which Britain had performed so well and of which it had been the financial and trading centre.

France

At the end of the war, France appeared to be in a much worse position than Britain. Part of its territory had been fought over and occupied – 289,000 houses had been destroyed, and three million acres of land rendered unfit for cultivation. France also had enormous debts, both international and internal, and was particularly affected by the loss of all the capital which French governments and individuals had invested in Russia. France had lost 50 per cent of its pre-war purchasing power. The recovery of Alsace and Lorraine with their mineral and industrial assets was, however, an advantage and, of course, much was hoped for as regards reparation.

By the early 1920s France was on the way to a good recovery. In its case the depreciation of its currency may have been a positive benefit, encouraging exports and tourism. The agricultural sector may have been both large and old-fashioned, but it did mean that France had a more balanced economy than other Western European powers and wasn't very dependent on imports. The patchy nature of its industrialization before 1914 meant that it was able to concentrate on developing modern metallurgical and chemical industries. By 1924 production had climbed back to pre-war levels and French gold reserves were high.

Belgium

We have already mentioned the devastation suffered by Belgium. Recovery was remarkably swift. By 1924 most of the spoilt agricultural land was back in use, and agricultural production stood at about the 1913 level. The destruction of war provided an opportunity for a complete rebuilding along modern lines of the iron and steel industry, and by the mid 1920s industrial production was above the pre-war level.

Italy

Of all the European allied powers Italy appeared to have emerged from the war with its economy in the best shape, if its performance in the immediate post-war years is anything to go by. Italy was to experience continuous industrial expansion up to 1926, and by 1922 industrial production was some 13 per cent above 1913. Progress was especially marked in iron and steel products, the manufacture of rayon and the expansion of the merchant fleet. This period of comparative prosperity was, however, based upon a number of short-lived favourable factors, among them the temporary weakness of its neighbours France and Germany.

Germany

Magnanimity in victory may be both an elevated virtue and often of long-term utility to the victors, but it is not particularly common. The victorious powers of 1918 were not notably magnanimous, though it is possible to argue that if they had wanted to prevent Germany's revival, they should have been a great deal harsher than they were. Certainly Germany, its economy and therefore its population, suffered in the immediate post-war world.

As measures of the damage wrought by the war upon the Germany economy, one can cite the figures that in 1919 the general level of industrial production was about 38 per cent of what it had been in 1913, and that agriculture was also badly affected, with grain production some 30 per cent below pre-war levels in 1920. The latter fall in production was partly due to the loss of territory to the east, which had been largely rural, but Germany remained a country with a large proportion of its workforce engaged in agriculture – nearly 10 million or 30 per cent in 1925.

Some of Germany's post-war economic problems were self-inflicted: the roots of its massive post-war inflation were to be found in the way it had financed the war by internal borrowing, while industrial production was handicapped by the way the maintenance of machinery had been neglected during the war years. Revolution, strikes, the loss of territory, the problems of demobilization and reparations were all to exacerbate the problems of the economy, as were the optimistic plans for expansion and the wildly generous social welfare arrangements of the early Weimar governments. With other central and east European economies in as bad or a worse state, export potential was limited.

Historians, given time, will find advantages in almost every disaster, as they will detect the seeds of ruin in every success, and many historians have recently pointed to the benefits of the post-war German inflation. There were indeed some advantages in inflation: not only did it permit the painless (for the government) repayment of war debts, but it also helped exports and employment and may well have aided the socially egalitarian aims of governments. It was, however, the disadvantages – the destruction of savings and capital, together with the general loss of faith in currency – which were seared on the collective German memory.

Central and eastern Europe

The destruction wrought by the war in an area which had seen mobile warfare and the effects of a territorial settlement which had paid little attention to economic considerations, left east and central Europe in a state of chaos and poverty. As we have seen, Austria was left as a small, largely agricultural economy, with a capital city out of all proportion to the country's size. The bulk of the industry of the old Empire had been located in what became Czechoslovakia, while Hungary, to a lesser extent, inherited an industrialized economy. The economy of the empire was parcelled out between the successor states in a way which left industries separated from their raw materials and which severed trading and communication links. Austria, Hungary and Poland all endured the inflation of their currencies, and economic pride led almost all east European states to attempt to maintain the value of their currencies at a higher rate than their economic position warranted.

Perhaps the main problem for all east and central Europe was agriculture. Even in Czechoslovakia agriculture was backward, while everywhere the rural population was increasing rapidly. Land reform was called for in all states of the region, but the type of reform instituted (taking land away from large estates and giving it to peasant proprietors) was a reform for political and social, rather than economic, goals. The large estates had not on the whole been efficient, but the smaller holdings which resulted from reform were often less so.

As in the case of Germany, one can see some advantages in the widespread inflation of the immediate post-war years. It aided the initial industrial recovery of Austria, Hungary and Poland, but it was a feverish and weakly based expansion which in the longer term resulted in excess capacity.

A general tendency in central and eastern Europe was towards economic nationalism and protectionism, which were later to become characteristic of the world economy in the interwar period.

'The Great Crash'

Russia

Roberts comments that 'Russia has, for our purpose, an almost independent economic history during these years.' Beset by civil war, national rebellions, war with Poland, and foreign intervention on top of the devastation of World War I, that history was inevitably one of chaos, falling production and widespread famine. One estimate is that the total output of mines and factories fell in 1921 to 20 per cent of the pre-war level, and that cultivated land had fallen to 67 per cent of the pre-war acreage, with a harvest yield 37 per cent of that of 1913 (Riasanovsky, *History of Russia,* 1984, p.488). Recovery only began with the end of the fighting and the inauguration of Lenin's New Economic Policy in place of war communism.

Corporatism and the challenge to the market economy

The widespread dismay in business circles at the outbreak of war in 1914 (see Book 1, Unit 2) was justified by events. Not only had the war destroyed factories, disrupted trade and distorted patterns of production, but it had dealt body blows to the old world economy and to previous assumptions as to the limitations of the state's role in economic as well as in social life. If the all-powerful state is best symbolized by the industrial-military complex headed by Ludendorff in Germany during 1917 and much of 1918, it is also discernible in the war economy headed by Lloyd George.

The new pretensions of the state were not to be easily blown away by peace. If one reaction in 1918 was to return to normal and re-establish the ground rules of 1914, another was to use the power of the state for national directives in peace, as it had been used in war. The social and economic problems and divisions of the post-war societies could be dissolved or ameliorated by the buttressing of the power and role of the state and its attendant ministries, commissions and experts in a number of ways: as planner, as conciliator, and as umpire. The 'common sense' of a contemporary 'progressivism' that ranged over Left and Right invested enormous capital in the role of the state. Collectivism might be the *raison d'être* of the Soviet Union, and corporatism was soon to become the official philosophy of Mussolini's Italy, but in Britain, France and Germany a collectivist or corporatist tendency can be detected.

In Britain the Lloyd George coalition began with an enthusiasm for 'reconstruction' that gained support from liberal and conservative members alike and was seen as involving the government in economic planning, in such social initiatives as house-building and the co-ordination of the insurance and medical services, and in intervention in employer-employee relations via Joint Industrial Councils. If the damage wrought by the war to the economy and society was one reason for this corporatist tendency, another was the new power of the trades unions, which had been given greater stature by their involvement in wartime government. Keith Middlemas has argued in *Politics in*

Industrial Society (1979) that influential politicians came to believe that tripartite arrangements between the state, organized labour and employers' organizations were necessary in order to deal with or head off industrial conflict. What had merely been interest groups (the Trades Union Congress and the National Conference of Employers' Organizations) 'crossed the political threshold and became part of the extended state'. Middlemas is careful to distinguish this development as leading to a system with a 'corporate bias' rather than a corporate state.

The more statist initiatives of the Lloyd George coalition lost popularity as the fortunes of the coalition waned, and with the fall of the coalition one can see the end of a period of flirtation with corporatism. The peak of this corporate tendency had come with the National Industrial Conference in 1919, which had made sweeping proposals regarding wages, working hours, the state development of new industry and a permanent National Industry Council. What remained, apart from Whitley Councils, local wage boards and a penchant for Royal Commissions, were a considerable widening of the perceived responsibility of government in matters industrial, a tendency to treat organized labour and organized employers as estates of the realm, and an influential but oppositional view, shared by such diverse politicians as Lloyd George, Sir Oswald Mosley, John Strachey and Harold Macmillan, that government, in partnership with industry, should plan and direct the economy.

The liberal market economy, like liberal democracy, had never been so firmly established in Imperial Germany as in Britain, and the series of compromises between Right and Left, between civil authority and the army, and between employers and unions which characterized Weimar Germany, moved the German economy and society a long way towards corporatism. In November 1918 an agreement was reached between leading German employers headed by Hugo Stinnes and trades union leaders led by Carl Legien, which, as well as giving workers an eight-hour day and other concessions, recognized the unions as the legitimate bargaining representatives of the workers and provided workers' committees in industry to supervise collective bargaining agreements. In a sense Weimar had a tacit economic and social constitution, as well as a political constitution, and the Stinnes-Legien agreement can be seen as a cornerstone of the former. Germany in the early 1920s was a society in which the state figured very prominently in social and economic affairs and in which not only were employers and workers highly organized, but they came together in the *Zentralarbeitsgemeinschaft* (ZAG, the Central Association of Employers and Employees).

Exercise I would now like you to read Document II.4 in *Primary Sources 1: World War I,* the 'Programme of the Union of Economic Interests' adopted on 7 April 1919. What does this programme of an employers' organization tell us of the attitudes of French employers towards such questions as the role of the state in economic life and co-operation with trades unions? ■

Specimen answer The document begins with what seems a trenchant defence of property and private enterprise and opposition to state control of industries and services. Further points, however, suggest that the employers do see a considerable role for the state and foresee industry co-operating with various interest groups and

'interventionism'

workers' organizations. There are calls for harmonization, co-operation and organization rather than for economic freedom. Training and education should be organized (presumably to suit industry's needs); the state should play a major social role, taking account of the needs of different regions and their economies.

Discussion The tone of the document does not exude confidence. One does not feel that here is a group of employers confident that they can flourish and make profits in a world of market forces. Rather this is a call for the co-ordination of a national effort.

The immediate socio-economic background to the document was of widespread social unrest. Early in 1919 the Chamber and Senate had passed laws on the eight-hour day and on official recognition of collective bargaining, but strikes and demonstrations continued during the spring, and both the Socialist Party and the unions were split between reformers and revolutionaries. The document is not, however, representative of the attitudes of French employers as a whole. Many, among them the most powerful, were far from ready to accommodate the demands of unions or to accept limitations on their freedom of action.

There *was* a challenge to the principles of the market economy in most post-war western societies – a challenge based on the growth of government powers during the war, the problems of reconstruction and demobilization, and the increased strength of socialist parties and trades unions. Greater governmental responsibility for economic and social matters and a more influential position for trades unions were to remain features of most western societies during the 1920s, but within a few years of the war Britain, France and even Germany were demonstrably once more free market economies. □

We will conclude this section by returning to the wider picture of the European economy as a whole and, indeed, to the world economy of which Europe had been the centre before 1914 and of which it continued to be an important part.

Exercise I would like you to read D. H. Aldcroft's introduction to his book *From Versailles to Wall Street* (1987 edition) in the *Secondary Sources*. In this introduction he discusses two alternative interpretations of the main effect of World War I on the international economy. What are they? ■

Specimen answer 1 The war had a decisive impact and effectively destroyed the old
and discussion   international economy which had developed during the nineteenth
                       century. Without the war the world economy would have continued on
                       much the same lines as formerly.

                    2 The war did knock the world economy off course, but, after a period of
                       recovery and readjustment, economies reverted to their previous practice
                       and direction. Aldcroft is, of course, looking ahead, beyond the period of
                       painful post-war recovery we have been concerned with, to the
                       depression that began in 1929. □

What cannot be denied is that the European economy and the individual economies of the European states emerged much weakened from the war. Extra European markets were lost, some never to be regained; the United States and Japan improved their productivity and their trading position; and Europe's, and particularly Britain's, position as the financial and trading centre of the world economy was never to be recovered. The balance of economic power swung away from Europe.

Social structure

Assessment of the effects of World War I upon European society and the social structure is complicated, to say the least, by sweeping and widely differing views as to the nature of the pre-war society. The titles of two books, extracts from which are in your Reader, point to one controversy: Arno J. Mayer's *The Persistence of the Old Regime* (1981) and Charles S. Maier's *Recasting Bourgeois Europe* (1975). Clearly, if an aristocratic *ancien régime* persisted up until 1914, then a 'bourgeois' Europe could not have been *recast* after the war. (You have already been introduced to *The Persistence of the Old Regime* in earlier units, and *Recasting Bourgeois Europe* will be discussed in Book 3, Unit 14. For the moment it is sufficient to say that Maier's central argument is that after a post-war crisis in which socialist and revolutionary elements threatened the existing order of 'bourgeois' Europe, governments and establishments rallied and adopted policies which skilfully maintained the essential features of pre-war society.)

Considering the ubiquity of monarchies, the prevalence of great landed estates, and the wealth and prestige of great aristocratic families in Edwardian Europe, it may seem to you a trifle odd that Arno J. Mayer's thesis – that monarchies, aristocracies and landed wealth retained the greater part of political power and social influence – should be seen as startling and even 'revisionist'. As Arthur Marwick has already pointed out in Book 1 (Unit 4), F. M. L. Thompson *(English Landed Society in the Nineteenth Century,* 1963) described the influential position of the landed aristocracy in pre-1914 Britain some time ago, and that thesis has recently been reinforced by J. V. Beckett *(The Aristocracy in England 1660–1914,* 1988). Both Thompson and Beckett have challenged the historical timetable that comes from the penchant of Whiggish or Marxist historians for the 'new' and from their discounting of continuity. Such 'progressive' historians have tended to find the dissolution of *ancien régimes* and the emergence of modernizing or revolutionary forces in almost every century and have perceived in the nineteenth century industrializing or modernizing waves sweeping all before them.

We should remember from Unit 4 that Mayer's book lies within a sectarian historiographical tradition and, indeed, the Mayer-Maier controversy is within that tradition. It is a tradition at once materialistic, teleological and loosely Marxist, which starts with a theory of historical development that finds 'meaning' in history via economic change and class conflict; their divergence is about the timescale of a scenario rather than about the scenario itself. Maier is, of course, much closer to Marx's view that aristocratic society was finished as early as 1848, while Mayer attempts to account for the 'failure' of the 'bourgeoisie' to do its 'historic duty'. For both these historians, whether a society can be termed 'bourgeois' or aristocratic/old regime is the most vital of all questions, for almost all else follows from it, as if to have the name was to possess the essence. Those who take a more empirical view of class terminology, such as Arthur Marwick (see Unit 3) and myself, and who see class structure as an aspect, rather than a definition, of a society may, nevertheless, still accept the importance of the question as to how far it was changed by World War I, along with the other delineating characteristics of and divisions within European society. Such other characteristics and divisions – religious, national and cultural – could, confusingly, both cut across and contribute to social stratification.

Whether we can generalize to much effect about a European society or social structure is questionable. Albania, at the end of World War I, consisted of a million or so inhabitants who were divided between the tribal Ghegs in the north and the semi-feudally organized southern Tosks. Things were, obviously, very different in Surrey! If we take any general list of social groups or classes, such as Arthur Marwick's list in Book 1, Unit 3 (p.107), and look for those groups in every European state, it becomes apparent that, in the social structure of individual states, there are gaps. We find, for instance, that there is no peasantry in Britain (save perhaps in the north of Scotland), no aristocracy in Serbia or Bulgaria, and little in the way of industrial working classes in much of eastern Europe. It is usually, therefore, considered necessary to classify European societies in subgroups, and the usual divides are between east and west, wealthy and poor, industrialized and largely agricultural, or rural and urbanized societies. There is only a rough and ready correlation between these divides, and one may question whether, for instance, the religious division is not as important as any of them; the vitality of Catholicism in contrast to Greater Russian Orthodoxy as a sociopolitical force is difficult to explain in economic or class terms.

One important division, which makes it difficult to disentangle this section from the section on 'National cohesion', is between those, mainly western, societies where we can consider social structure as separate from racial or national composition, and those where national identity and social position remained inextricably intertwined. Thus in Latvia the nobility was German, merchants were Germans or Jews, and the peasantry was Latvian, while in Slovakia the nobility was Magyar, the merchants usually Germans or Jews (or Jewish-German) and the peasantry Slovak. The importance of the Jews in the social structure of many European societies, as indeed in the cultural and economic life of these societies, cannot be underestimated. In Romania, for instance, Jews were, by themselves, almost what Marxists call the bourgeoisie: they were the merchants, the manufacturers, the agents of landowners who were mortgaged to them, the professionals and, to a great extent, the intelligentsia. Norman Stone, in *Europe Transformed 1878–1919* (1983), has argued that in secularized Calvinism and secularized Judaism we find the roots of modernity in both its economic and cultural forms.

Thus there were considerable variations both before and after the war between the social structures of different European societies (Unit 4 discussed in some detail the pre-1914 social structures). Such differences could be found within states as well as between them. Unit 4 emphasized the disparity between north and south Italy, while the Austro-Hungarian Empire encompassed a number of diverse societies. The Italian north-south divide was still apparent in 1920, as indeed it still is today, while even the successor states to Austria-Hungary exhibited internal variations (Czechoslovakia, for instance, had in Bohemia one of the most industrialized areas of central Europe and contained not only a large number of industrial workers but considerable middle-class sectors, while in the province of Ruthenia, the peasantry made up the great proportion of society).

As with other aspects of the question of the impact of the war, in dealing with social structure we have not only to decide whether change took place at all between 1914 and, say, 1921, but, if there was change, whether that change was due to the war. An ancillary question, even if we accept that change took place in a particular society and it was due to the war, is whether it was due to the nature of warfare as experienced between 1914 and 1918 (or 1921) or to the special outcome of the war for that particular society, i.e. was it on the winning or the losing side?

Exercise   Can you think of reasons why World War I *could* have affected the social structures of European societies? ■

Specimen answer   1   In the first place, the social and economic pressures of the war on the
and discussion   societies which engaged in it were enormous. Vast numbers volunteered
                            or were conscripted for the armies of the combatant states and, as we
                            have seen, the death toll was considerable. The economies of the states
                            lost their peacetime direction as they were abruptly harnessed to the war
                            effort; wartime needs and shortages altered patterns of supply and
                            demand. Such developments could affect the relative positions and
                            advantages of different sections of society.

2   The impact of defeat in war would have a destabilizing effect on the
     political structures of the defeated states and, in so far as political and
     social leadership were intertwined, a destabilizing social result. It could
     (as it did) lead to the break-up of states, with immense social
     implications, and to revolutions with overt social aims.

As you will have realized, the specimen answer above corresponds to my previous distinction between changes due to the nature of the war which could affect all participants, and changes due to the losing of the war. In their attempt to enlist mass support, governments gave their war aims a quasi-ideological dimension and invested more in the necessity of victory than would have been wise if defeat had ever been considered possible. The implications of defeat were momentous. □

But *did* the war have much of a long-term effect upon social structures? As Arthur Marwick has pointed out in the introduction to these units, many recent studies by historians have tended to deny that the war had any significant long-term effects in the way of social change. Such a denial appears more credible for western than for eastern and central Europe (the massive transfer of population between Greece and Turkey seems, for instance, to be a fundamental type of social change), but we need, in any case, to be clear what we mean by change to the social structure. Do we mean that whole sectors of society disappeared or that sectors changed place in the pecking order? Do we, more modestly, mean that although the social order remained similar in its gradations, the relative power and influence of different social groups changed? While recognizing the distinction, I shall assume that both sorts of change may be counted as changes to the social structure.

Exercise   Can you think of a particular social group, structure or class (I'm not too worried about which terms you prefer, although I'll probably slip into class terminology as it is most current in everyday language) that appears to have lost ground as a result of the war? ■

Specimen answer   Aristocracies do seem to stand out as the social groups which suffered a
and discussion   diminution in political influence, economic position and social standing across Europe.

I suppose that, if we thought of royalty as a class – and if not a class it is certainly something of a caste – we could have even more definitely plumped for it. The kings certainly departed, if only because so many of the most powerful monarchs were on the losing side (one can, of course, see the Tsar of Russia as a ruler whose country lost the war, even if his allies subsequently won it). But if we define aristocrats as those whose families own great landed estates and who are usually, but not always, titled, then it does seem clear that to a greater or lesser extent, and whether in countries that won the war or lost it, World War I was a disaster for aristocrats.

The demise of aristocracy was most obvious in Russia, where the war ended in revolution, and death or exile was the fate of so many aristocrats. It was obvious, too, in parts of central and eastern Europe, where many aristocrats, especially if their nationalities were different from those dominant in the new states, lost all or the greater part of their estates. Prince Lichnowsky (German ambassador in 1914) found that with the new frontiers his estates were now just inside the Czech borders. He thought, wrongly, that the Allies had arranged this deliberately. Even in Britain a case can be made for a major decline in aristocratic wealth and influence as a result of the war. □

Exercise   What factors do you think may have contributed to a weakening of the position of aristocracies? ■

Specimen answer   1   The position of many aristocracies was intimately bound up with that of
and discussion   the monarchies and governments that had gone to war in 1914. When under the impact of defeat monarchies and governments fell, the position and influence of aristocracies declined.

2   In many areas of east and central Europe aristocracies were of a different nationality from the peasantry, and with the creation of new national states, they lost their land and position.

3   Demand for land reform grew among the peasantries of east and central Europe, encouraged by promises made by governments and national movements. Such a development threatened the economic position of aristocrats.

As regards point 1, it is clear that the German aristocracy lost ground in 1918. It has been argued that, as the aristocracy depended for its wealth upon agriculture, it was in any case in a long-term decline, a decline that would have been accelerated by the agricultural depression after 1870 had it not been checked:

by the ossification of Wilhelmine society – partly due to military influence – and by the constant political, economic and ideological support which the landed gentry received from the Wilhelmine state. The collapse of the state in the revolution of 1918–19 did not remove altogether the gentry's influence, but rather restricted it to certain areas – to Westphalia, Pomerania and East Prussia – and narrowed its focus even more than before the war to the representation of sectorial economic interests.

(Michael Geyer, 'Professionals and Junkers: German re-armament and politics in the Weimar Republic', 1981).

According to Roberts (p.298), land reform in east and central Europe resulted in the redistribution of some 60 million acres from great estates to the peasantry. In Russia, of course, a more drastic change took place by which peasants gained or seized the land of the great estates only to lose it again when the collectivization policy was imposed some years later. Outside Russia, by far the greatest absolute amount of land was redistributed in Romania, and the greatest percentage of land in the Baltic states. It is noteworthy that in Latvia and Estonia the landowners were German and in Lithuania Polish. In general the confiscation of land was highest in the areas where the aristocracy was not of the nationality of the new state. Thus in Romania landowners were allowed to retain most land in the *Regat*, where they were Romanian, and least in Transylvania and Bukovina, where they were respectively Magyar and Russian. In Czechoslovakia, too, landowners from the national minorities such as the Magyar landlords in Slovakia were discriminated against.

The number of aristocrats killed in battle was relatively higher than the proportion for other sections of the population. The following quotation from Trevor Wilson is instructive for British death rates:

> That numbers of the officer class were drawn disproportionately from the upper ranks of society may be inferred from statistics comparing the death rate for mobilised men as a whole with that for men from various élite institutions. For mobilised men in *toto*, the death rate was 12 per cent. For students from Oxford and Cambridge who served in the war it was, respectively, 19 and 18 per cent. For members of the peerage it was 19 per cent.

> (Wilson, *The Myriad Faces of War*, 1986)

It seems likely that the disproportion would have been true for other European armies, and would have had an effect on the vitality of aristocracies in the post-war years. In a country like Britain, which had death duties, it could also have profound economic consequences for aristocratic families. □

So far so good (and so Mayer); a picture seems to be emerging of a definite decline in the position of the upper echelon of the social structure, but there are important *caveats*. So far as western Europe is concerned it is debatable whether we can see the aristocracy and those possessed of great industrial and financial fortunes as distinct before or after 1914. The pristine images of aristocratic and 'capitalist' may seem clear enough, but theories of an 'embourgeoised aristocracy', an 'aristocraticized bourgeoisie' or a general symbiosis between aristocracy and upper middle class suggest all is not quite so distinct after all. We probably need to distinguish between lesser landowners or gentry who, entirely dependent upon incomes from land or salaries as army officers, had for long been in straitened circumstances, and those great landowners whose incomes were supplemented by mineral royalties or who, like the Dukes of Westminster, owned urban land. A word commonly used to describe the wealthiest sections of society in Edwardian Europe is plutocracy, and plutocracy and aristocracy had in many instances become intertwined. American heiresses had married into the European aristocracies; the Krupps, von Thyssens, Devonports and Northcliffs acquired titles, as did Bismarck's Jewish banker, Bleichröder; Lord Rosebery married a Rothschild, while Sir Ernest Cassel's grand-daughter was to marry the future Earl Mountbatten. Perhaps we should conclude that so far as aristocracy dependent purely upon birth and land ownership was concerned, the Great War dealt it, as it did monarchy, a severe blow, and that certain symbols of aristocratic life, like the great London town houses, disappeared soon after its end. The decline of European agriculture had arguably been eroding its position for long enough, but the war precipitated a more rapid decline. The wealthiest strata of European society, however, continued to have aristocratic connections, titles and aspirations. In Poland, where large and medium landowners continued to occupy a strong position in agriculture, leading industrialists sought country estates for the prestige they gained from them; however impoverished the individual, a claim to belong to the lesser gentry still conferred social status.

If the war hastened the decline of those sections of the upper classes who most closely fitted the profile of aristocrats and gentry, it may well have increased mobility into the upper classes. Certainly, fortunes were made by those who manufactured and organized supplies for the war effort. The notion of 'hardfaced men who had done well out of the war' is, of course, something of a caricature: no doubt most profits were honestly earned out of the provision of services necessary to the war effort, and if it is true that few failed to take advantage of war-time opportunities, then manufacturers behaved little differently from other sectors such as trade unionists in key industries. Nevertheless, a philanthropic gesture, such as that of Stanley Baldwin, who gave a substantial part of his fortune to the nation in recognition that much of it came from war profits, was rare, while there are many well publicized examples of those who emerged from the war with fortunes made by questionable means. In Britain, Italy and France and even in defeated Germany, financial and manufacturing wealth not only survived the war but was often increased by it. Wartime corporatism also brought manufacturers closer to and often into governments, increasing influence and prestige as well as wealth. There were both winners and losers. Smaller manufacturers and businessmen whose affairs were not related to the war effort found their position diminished by restrictions, labour shortages and increased taxation, while the war was disastrous for those who lived on fixed incomes or relied upon rents. Many, especially French, investors lost heavily from the collapse of Tsarist Russia and the Austro-Hungarian monarchy. If the wartime and post-war inflation in Germany and other central European states can be seen as benefiting the working classes (see the section on 'Economic performance and theory'), then it also worked to the advantage of landowners who were able to pay off their mortgages and industrialists who paid off their loans and turned inflated profits into new factories.

It is especially difficult to generalize about the effects of the war upon the middle classes. As you know from Unit 4, this group can be broken down into numerous sub-sections, with little in common save that they were in the middle. The profile of this middle group, and indeed its wealth, also changes considerably as we go across Europe. The steady expansion of the middle classes is a feature of modern European history, but in eastern Europe they were less numerous and, as we have seen, often consisted of nationalities different from the majority nationality of the new states.

Overall, however, it would appear that the war had a deleterious effect on most members of the middle classes, though the effect was for the most part shortlived. Like the aristocracy, the middle classes suffered disproportionate losses from war deaths, not just because the proportion killed was greater than for the working classes or peasantries, but because many of the middle classes had tended to have smaller families than other social groups, so that the number of middle-class families who lost their only or both of their sons was particularly high. There was no clear divide between upper middle class and upper class, so that the effects we noted above of increased taxation and a decline in rental income and fixed income penetrated well down into the middle classes. The salaried middle classes found that salaries tended to lag behind wages and prices in the wartime and immediate post-war economies. Wartime and post-war inflation, especially in central Europe, destroyed middle-class savings. Craftsmen and shopkeepers suffered from the general decline in middle-class spending power, though where, as in Britain, working-class spending power increased, manufacturers and retailers were able to find new customers among those who could now afford to buy better clothes and food and modest luxuries.

As we move towards eastern Europe it becomes apparent that west European generalizations about social structure and the war's effect upon it are difficult to substantiate. I would like you to read the following extract from a chapter by Antony Polonsky in *The History of Poland since 1863*, edited by R. F. Leslie, which describes the social structure of the urban areas of the new Poland:

> Industrialists and capitalists, who with their dependants numbered about 260,000 persons, did not play an important part in social life. Industry was not highly developed. Indeed, industry and commerce gave employment to a larger number of Germans and Jews which excited prejudice against them, but industrialists were able to exert pressure on the government through the Central Union of Polish Industry, Mining, Trade and Finance, commonly known as 'Leviathan'. The absence of a strong native bourgeoisie explains the role of the intelligentsia, which embraced a far wider group than it did in western Europe and totalled 1.4 million persons in urban society. *Swiat pojec*, a popular pre-war encyclopaedia, defined the intelligentsia as follows: 'The intelligentsia in the sociological sense of the term is a social stratum made up of those possessing academic higher education. Typical representatives of the intelligentsia ... are professors, doctors, literary figures, etc. The social position of the intelligentsia does not mean that its members have a rigidly defined social or ideological position. Members of the intelligentsia can identify with the most varied social and political trends. In fact, they occupy the leading role in all political groupings.' Membership of the intelligentsia was not in fact to be identified strictly with the possession of a high school diploma. It was more important that a man's manners should be those of the

educated classes and that he should have some familiarity with the humanities. In spite of many differences of income and status the intelligentsia had a markedly strong feeling of solidarity and responsibility. Descended from *szlachta* [minor gentry] who had migrated to the towns in the 1870s and 1880s, they saw their careers as an alternative to a way of life which had collapsed. The intelligentsia saw themselves as representatives of the nation, the keepers of its conscience and its directing force. A post in the service of the state enjoyed great prestige, while a certain disdain for trade and industry led some to develop pretensions to wide cultural interests. Respect for culture and knowledge was often that of the dilettante and not of the specialist. An overproduction of 'literary intellectuals' had much to do with the right-wing radicalism prevalent in the universities.

There were other significant urban groups, 1.3 million people deriving their livelihood from trade. Petty trade was primitive, but it was adapted to existing conditions of economic development. The government tried without much success to replace private tradesmen with peasant co-operatives. Trade was concentrated in Jewish hands. In 1921 62.9 per cent of persons employed in trade and industry were Jews, but of those 88.9 per cent were engaged in retail trades. It is difficult to estimate the number of people owning handicraft workshops, because many were not registered with the authorities. The figure of 1.1 million for such workers and their families is therefore hypothetical. Most workshops were small, often employing only members of the owner's family. Many were owned by Jews, especially in tailoring, leather work, baking and bookbinding. Jews were correspondingly not numerous in heavy industry. Industrial workers and their families amounted to 4.6 million. Of these 1.8 million were employed in handicrafts or cottage industries, while 2.8 million worked in heavy industry and mining. Standards of living varied widely among the working class. Workers in government monopolies were among the better-off enjoying higher wages and relative security. Unskilled workers were often very poor as were those employed in cottage industries, especially in and around Lodz, Bialystok and Bielsko-Biala. The majority of industrial workers were Poles, but many skilled workmen in Upper Silesia and Lodz were German. In common with other underdeveloped countries, industrial workers in Poland were better-off than the peasantry.

Antony Polonsky, in R.F. Leslie (ed.) *This History of Poland since 1863*, 1983, pp.143–4)

Exercise   Which features of the social structure of urban society in Poland strike you as being markedly different from most west European societies? ■

Specimen answer   1   The degree to which nationality and occupation are intertwined and the
and discussion   degree to which so many of the social groups we would put within the
                         middle classes are not made up of Poles. Germans and Jews are
                         prominent in industry and commerce, while trade is concentrated in
                         Jewish hands.

2   The concept of an 'intelligentsia' and the size of this group. The intelligentsia is unknown in Britain, and while the French and Italians are

fond of the notion of 'intellectuals', they confine this to a fairly small group, including academics, writers, etc.

What was true of Poland was also true for much of east and central Europe. Several factors accounted for the lack of commercial and industrial middle classes of the national majorities. The diversity of races and nationalities and the history of conquests, partitions and alien regimes had contributed to a class-ethnic or occupation-ethnic correlation. Racial or religious cohesion and the laws against Jews engaging in many occupations had resulted in a high degree of specialization for the Jewish community, while the urban world of eastern and central Europe had experienced something of a German hegemony. Industrialization had usually come from a conscious state initiative and from outside local society rather than in response to local conditions and demands. □

A feature of eastern Europe after the war was the existence of a larger number of arts and, to some extent, law graduates than state jobs or the private sector could properly absorb. This chronically dissatisfied sector was to be a source of political instability.

In much of east and central Europe the main effect of the war so far as middle-class groups who did not belong to the national minorities were concerned was discrimination, if not disappropriation. In many instances the ambitions of those members of the national majorities who via the educational system rose out of the peasantries were directed towards the state bureaucracies or to becoming army officers, rather than towards industry or commerce. The lack of substantial middle classes involved in manufacturing and trade was to be a major handicap to many central and east European countries in the inter-war years; it was a problem that had been made worse by the formation of new national states, with the consequent diminution of the security of the minority middle-class sectors and the disinclination of the national minorities to take their place.

Exercise   Which sectors of European society do you think might have gained most from the war? ■

Specimen answer and discussion   The industrial working classes in western Europe and the peasantry of east and parts of central Europe did appear in the immediate post-war period to have made gains.

So far as the industrial working classes are concerned, it has been argued (Arthur Marwick, *The Deluge*, 1991) that one effect of total war is that groups whose support for the war effort is crucial will achieve gains in influence and in standards of living. For Britain, there is considerable evidence of an increase in working-class living standards. Trevor Wilson (*The Myriad Faces of War*) quotes A. L. Bowley to the effect that 'the proportion in poverty in 1924 was little more than half that in 1913', and concludes that although the size of the cake was not greater in 1924 than in 1913, the better-off were getting marginally less of it at the later date and the worse-off marginally more'.

Trades unions representing workers in key industries were able to ensure that their members did better than most of the population in keeping their wages in step with inflation, while wartime corporations saw labour leaders consulted by government and participating in government. Bernard Waites (an Open

University colleague) has argued that distinctions between skilled and unskilled working men were eroded by the wartime experience ('The effect of the First World War on class and status in England 1910–20', 1976).

In both Italy and France there were pointers towards greater trades union influences and working-class militancy at the end of the war. Socialism flourished in the major Italian industrial centres, namely Milan, Turin and Genoa, which had grown rapidly during the war. By 1919 large groups of industrial workers had gained the eight-hour day, while the membership of the Socialist Party had grown fourfold since 1914 to 200,000 members. In France the action of the Chamber of Deputies and the Senate in passing laws for the eight-hour day and giving recognition to the results of collective bargaining failed to stem a wave of strikes and demonstrations. French workers made few of the strides of their British counterparts in increasing their standard of living: the dislocation to industry caused by occupation and the fighting (the areas occupied and fought over included some of the most industrialized regions of France) ensured a general lowering of living standards; taxes were not, as in Britain, increased; and the short-lived post-war inflation brought French workers no advantages.

In Germany there appeared to be major advances for the industrial working classes. The early years of the Weimar Republic saw increased co-operation between industry and the trade unions, the establishment of the eight-hour day, increased welfare provision, and an increase in taxation with distributive effects. As we have seen, it has been claimed that the inflation which began during the war and reached its zenith in 1923 had positive advantages for urban workers.

As regards the peasantry, Norman Stone has argued that, 'By 1906, a movement that had nothing at all to do with traditional politics was under way: the mobilisation of backward peasant Europe' *(Europe Transformed,* p.127). The war may have accelerated such a mobilization, as wartime service in armies brought more of the peasantry into contact with the world of the towns, with their superior living standards and raised new ambitions. The emergence of new national states gave the peasants of the national majorities opportunities to press their demands for land reform and for greater influence in government. Within existing states like Bulgaria or Romania, peasant parties were to be a major feature of inter-war politics. In countries with little in the way of aristocracies and where the peasantry constituted the mass of the population, as in Yugoslavia and Bulgaria, it appeared that the potential for the social and political dominance of the peasantry and peasant/agrarian parties was strong.

In Russia the fall in living standards for almost everyone that resulted from famine, drought, revolution and civil war makes it difficult to argue that any class had improved its position in an absolute sense. The industrial working classes now had a government that was in theory their dictatorship, while, prior to collectivization, the peasantry could hope to retain their increased holdings and in better times reap some benefit from them. The strata above proletariat and peasantry had largely been removed and replaced by a new party bureaucracy, though the New Economic Policy marked a temporary retardation of the process.

The effects of the war upon the European social structure looked less considerable when viewed from the mid rather than the early 1920s. While the European economy and largely the individual economies were depressed, stagnant or had not returned to the production levels of 1914, the early twenties do appear to have seen a turbulent political situation in which working-class, socialist or peasant parties were able to maximize their influence, and this was a time in which diminished economic rewards were distributed in a more egalitarian fashion By the mid 1920s, in a more successful economic environment, the erosion of different standards of living between middle classes and working classes appears to have been halted and perhaps reversed: the effects of unemployment were felt more severely by workers, while deflation favoured those on salaries and fixed incomes rather than wage-earners. It was not that workers started to get poorer; indeed, all in work were getting richer, and in many countries the unemployed were better provided for than they had been in 1914. However, the better-off began once more to get richer faster. At the same time the threat from millenarian socialist parties largely receded, and reformist socialist parties found themselves with an often enhanced (compared to 1914) but rarely dominant place in refashioned political systems. The German economy, for instance, can be seen as going back to normal in late 1923 with the end of inflation due to the revalued currency, the Rentenmark, and the abrogation of the eight-hour day in December. □

A 'recasting of a bourgeois Europe' or a return to normal economic and social life according to taste – had taken place. So far as western Europe was concerned, the effects of the war, its dislocating effects, the shortages and its emergencies, had resulted in the classes being temporarily squeezed together in a concertina effect, but in the longer term, perhaps because what Arthur Marwick has called 'structural factors' triumphed over the cataclysm of war, the social structure of west European society reasserted the social pattern and the process of change discernible before 1914. This is not to deny that the war may have speeded up changes to the social structure discernible before 1914, nor that there were distinct differences between the pre-war and post-war societies. If the development of what has been called 'mass society' had been discernible before the war, the conflict had speeded this process. The 'common man's' appetites had become more important and politicians and businessmen alike had to cater for them or exploit them as never before.

In eastern Europe it can be argued that the changes were greater, but they owed more to the force of nationalism and to the national/political, geopolitical changes consequent upon the post-war settlement than to social forces. The relative position of the east European peasantry was enhanced by the removal of minority aristocracies and the political control over towns, merchants and bureaucracies that resulted from national rather than social revolution. Yet even where land reform was greatest, and it was rarely sweeping, the position of the peasantries of eastern Europe in the context of increasing populations and declining agricultural incomes, represented an empty inheritance, although a less invidious one than that of their Russian equivalent.

National cohesion

It is significant that it was the League of *Nations* that was established by the Treaty of Versailles and not a League of *States*. Although 'nation' can be defined as a people under the same government and inhabiting the same country, our use of the word tends to be coloured by its other meaning of a people belonging to the same ethnological family and speaking the same language. The word 'state' sits rather more happily on a multinational empire like Austria-Hungary than does 'nation'; a subject could be loyal to and even patriotic about the Empire, but he or she could not be a nationalistic Austro-Hungarian, though they could be a Hungarian, a German or a Czech nationalist. The term League of Nations was thus in harmony with the importance attached by the Versailles Settlement to nationalism and the principle of national self-determination.

Nationalism, whether regarded as a 'natural' force or a conscious political and social philosophy (see Units 3 and 4), is the joker in the pack of modern history. It has cohabited with every other 'ism', with socialism, liberalism, conservatism and even monarchism, yet it cuts across all of them.

For long, historians of twentieth-century European history, mesmerised by the supposed dominance of ideology as a determinant of historical development, played down the importance of nationalism or conceived of it as a residual force. Today, when the map of eastern Europe resembles more that of 1919 than that of 1945, the importance of nationalism in shaping the century's history cannot be denied.

Historians, as those of you who took A221 will know, differ as to the nature of nationalism and as to whether it is a modern phenomenon, born in the context of industrialization, secularization, romanticism and the erosion of hierarchical society, or has a longer history as an inevitable corollary of ethnicity. A common ethnic origin is not the only criterion of national identity. Language, common traditions, a shared history, common interests and religion can both buttress ethnic considerations and override them. Thus new senses of national identity can develop which are composites of other identities: Thus British identity grew from the mid-eighteenth century; a Belgian identity survives uneasily despite language/national divisions; similarly, but with greater longevity, there is the linguistic, ethnic and religious patchwork that is Switzerland. Conversely, Pan-Slavism foundered on the rocks of diverse national traditions, religions and alphabets. Whatever the factors that contribute to a sense of national identity, it can be said that from the late eighteenth century the 'nation state' embodying it has become progressively the most common and cohesive form of state.

Nationalism became an ever more important force from the beginning of the nineteenth century and its growth was powerfully stimulated by the spread of literacy, the increase in the numbers of books and newspapers and improvements in physical communications. Various distinctions have been made between different kinds of nationalism. One is the distinction between state nationalism, as opposed to popular or ethnic nationalism; the former, in which national cohesion was encouraged by the state, can be exemplified in the cases of Britain, France, Spain or, most markedly, the USA, while popular nationalism came from a growing sense of the importance of ethnic bonds and made a strong appeal to peoples living in societies where government and governors came from different ethnic backgrounds to the lower orders. State nationalism tended also to be 'civic' in that being a citizen, a status granted by the state, was equated with nationality, while ethnic nationalism saw nationality as a matter of blood and birth.

The two great success stories of nationalism in the nineteenth century were the creation of the German and Italian states. Both cases were something of a halfway house between states made by national feeling and nationalism encouraged by the state as, if national feeling based on culture, language and history can be said to have been the driving force, it was effectively harnessed by two existing states, Prussia and Piedmont. The development of Italian and German unity was widely seen, especially in its early stages, as liberating and unifying, while the new states did have borders encompassing largely homogeneous populations.

Two developments made late nineteenth-century and early twentieth-century nationalism appear a less liberal force and a threat to European stability. A blood and soil nationalism came increasingly to the fore and opposed an exclusive view of nationality to the essentially legal concept of civic nationality, while nationalisms within the great multinational empires found themselves thwarted not just by dynastic rule but other peoples with whom they rarely shared neat frontiers. The Balkans demonstrated, as the Ottoman Empire retreated, that successor nation states were not to co-exist harmoniously. World War I brought about the final disintegration of that empire and the demise of two other multinational empires, though one of these in the guise of Soviet Russia was to claw back most of its Tsarist inheritance.

It can be argued that the war's most fundamental consequence was that national identity became paramount as the basis for the existence of states and that increasingly the basis of national identity was ethnicity. Of the new states that emerged at the end of the war only two can properly be considered multinational. One was Czechoslovakia in which, although Czechs were dominant, there were, in addition to the Slovaks, several minorities. Norman Davies has commented that: 'Czechoslovakia had a reputation for democracy that was stronger abroad than among the country's own German, Slovak, Hungarian, Polish and Ruthenian minorities' (Norman Davies, *Europe, A History*, 1996, pp.978–9). Yugoslavia (until 1929 the Kingdom of Serbs, Croats and Slovenes) was not meant to be a multinational state but rather a union of south Slavs; as elsewhere, however, Slavs were divided by religion, alphabet and history and the Croats were soon agitating for independence from Serbian hegemony. It is a significant pointer to the strength and endurance of nationalism that Czechoslovakia and Yugoslavia, divided in 1938–9 and 1941, but re-emergent in 1945, fell apart once more in the 1990s. Even those states with a secure national identity like Poland and Hungary had minorities and ambitions to incorporate their fellow nationals who were minorities within neighbouring states.

Exercise   What factors other than ethnic identity do you consider bound together the peoples of the states of Europe in 1914? ■

Specimen answer and discussion

1   As above, national identity did not have to be ethnic. Switzerland was a linguistic and religious patchwork but had a secure national ethos, while citizens and subjects of France and Britain could identify with the political and cultural values their states appeared to embody and with the past achievements and histories of their states.

2   The subjects of monarchies could feel loyalty to monarchy and dynasty.

3   States were economic as well as political units, and economic self-interest could be a cohesive force. □

Such factors could merge with a pride in ethnic identity to create national identities, but they could also be separate from it and an alternative to it.

Of the forces making for cohesion within states in the world before the war, the national and the monarchical principles were by far the most important; the former had increased in importance during the nineteenth century while the latter had waned. Monarchism nevertheless remained an important force for stability in *ancien régime* Europe. Nationalism and monarchism could appear opposed, with monarchical legitimacy seeming cosmopolitan in contrast to nationalism; thus in Austria-Hungary, for example, it provided a focus for unity above competing nationalities. The blood relationship of the royal families of Europe made them supra-national; as Queen Victoria wrote, 'a freedom from all national prejudices ... is very important in Princes' (H. Nicolson, *King George V,* 1952, p.14). In practice the relationship between nationalism and monarchism had been somewhat confused: the self-consciously national states that had emerged in the Balkans had, with the exception of Serbia and Montenegro, chosen to be ruled by German kings, while the Emperors of Germany and Russia synthesized legitimism with nationalism.

Exercise   From the knowledge you have acquired in the course so far, say what effect you think the outbreak of hostilities had upon the cohesion of the European states. ■

Specimen answer and discussion   The war fanned nationalism in nation states and was, in the long run, to give national movements in multinational states their opportunity. In the short run, however, the multinational empires – Austria-Hungary, Russia and the Ottoman Empire – stood up better to the strain of war than an emphasis upon their pre-war national problems might have led us to expect. The effect of the war upon Austria-Hungary confirms Arthur Marwick's comment in Book 1, Unit 4 that in 1914 'the monarchy was managing to hold together its disparate nationalities'. Austro-Hungarian armies remained loyal until the last months of the war.

If the war gave national movements in east and central Europe their opportunities, it was not immediately apparent what those opportunities were, for they depended upon whether the Allied or the central powers would eventually win the war. Should, for instance, Polish nationalists support the war effort of the central powers and hope for an Austro-Polish or German solution to their national aspirations, or should they support Russia, hoping for a better deal from that quarter? The war was, of course, ultimately fatal to the Austro-Hungarian Empire, and it detached western regions from Russia – developments which were to the benefit of Polish, Czech, Serbian, Lithuanian, Latvian, Finnish and Estonian national ambitions. □

Exercise   Going beyond the war itself and also considering the effects of the Versailles Settlement and the continuing warfare in eastern Europe until 1921, what do you see as the overall effect of the war upon national or state cohesion? ■

Specimen answer and discussion
1   It increased the number of European states, giving Europe many more miles of frontiers.

2   National or ethnic identity became more than ever before the main basis for the existence of states.

3   It dealt a mortal blow to the principle of monarchical legitimacy.

Roberts comments that Versailles saw 'the end of a century-long struggle between legitimacy and nationalism, which won its greatest triumph at Versailles'. Legitimacy had, of course, been the underlying principle of the last great European settlement in 1815. □

It is perhaps paradoxical that Woodrow Wilson, the President of a state engaged in an unremitting effort to weld a new sense of national identity binding diverse ethnic groups, should have supported so unswervingly the notion of national self-determination. The concept can, of course, be seen as a democratic one and, indeed, plebiscites were held in many areas, but democracy, whatever admirable features it may have, does not by itself provide for the rights of minorities, and if Versailles turned minorities into nations, it created new minorities. Far from each national group cosily nestling in its own national box, the post-war settlement created as many new minorities as it satisfied old ones, and all the guarantees for the linguistic, cultural and religious rights of minorities that were to be provided by the League of Nations were to prove worthless. In east and central Europe the new nationalism penetrated deeper down the social scale than in the past; nationalism became a matter for peasants as well as professors, and in doing so became far less tolerant of minorities.

Exercise What do you think were the main threats to the national cohesion of the European states in the post-war period? ■

Specimen answer and discussion

1 Even though most states were now national states, the main threat to their national cohesion came from nationalism – the nationalisms of their minorities and of their neighbours. Most states in east and central Europe had hostile minorities to contend with and frontier disputes with neighbouring states.

2 A further threat to national cohesion was ideology. Socialism was ostensibly international and claimed that class divisions ran across natural frontiers, though, as we have seen, in 1914 most socialists and the great majority of the working classes rallied to national banners. The Soviet Union was from the beginning equivocal on the issue of international revolution: on the one hand it sought to export it, setting up the Comintern or Third (Communist) International to this end, but, on the other hand, it sought to retain control of as much of Tsarist Russia as possible, maintaining, after the adoption of the policy of 'socialism in one country', near normal relationships with other states. Fascism was a nationalist ideology, seeing the nation rather than class as the dynamic historical force, so it presented in principle less of a threat to the cohesion of states, though in practice fascist parties could be divisive and gain support from fascists in other countries.

3 Religion could be a divisive factor, particularly in those parts of eastern and central Europe where the divide between the Orthodox and the Catholic Churches ran within a new state. Croatian and to some extent Slovenian separatism was fanned by Catholicism within the new Yugoslavia. That this phenomenon was not confined to east and central Europe is, of course, demonstrated by the religious dimensions of the Irish problem. Bavarian separatism in Germany had much to do with the Catholic south's suspicion of a Protestant Prussian hegemony. Even

Islam, the majority religion in Albania, was a potential problem in Yugoslavia and eastern Russia. □

Religion

The potential of religion to influence cohesion and disunity and, indeed, its political and social influence deserves a closer look. There has been a tendency for historians of twentieth-century Europe to see the influence of religion as residual; important enough because of its past influence in shaping societies and cultures and significant in its lingering pervasiveness, but condemned to give way in the face of the dynamic thrust of modernization of which secularization was such an important strand. As with much else, developments in the last decades of the century have necessitated a reassessment of the importance of religion. The centrality of Poland's Catholicism to Polish identity and opposition to Communist rule together with the enduring nature of religious divides in the Balkans remind us of the continuing force of religion. It is not just these present-day concerns which suggest that the religious factor should be taken into account in an evaluation of the consequences of World War I for there is ample evidence that religion played an important part, not only as a force for unity or disunity at the end of the war, helping form or dislocating national identity in new as in established states, but in providing the impetus for significant political movements. It can also be argued that, although Catholic movements were often nationalistic, the concept of 'Christendom' and of the rebirth of a European Christian empire that would sweep away the national boundaries that had led to the war, became influential in Catholic political thought as a result of the war.

Sixteenth, seventeenth and eighteenth-century monarchs had generally regarded religious unity and conformity within their realms as of great importance, not only on theological grounds, but because religious diversity presented a challenge to political authority. Their perception was substantially correct. Secularism had, for much of the nineteenth century, seemed to go hand in hand with liberalism in attacking the confessional state, and in religiously unified states, like Spain or France or the emergent Italy, the divide had been between church and secular or anti-religious forces. Liberalism to some extent produced its own nemesis in that it favoured the extension of democracy, yet, in much of Europe, extensions of the franchise brought socialist or popular Catholic parties into being. Catholic parties were, in general, anti-liberal. They tended to get support from the lower middle class in the towns, from artisans and tradesmen and, as the political mobilization of the European peasantry began, from the countryside. Catholic parties became important in Germany, Austria, Italy, Holland and Belgium. Norman Stone has said of the fall of the Protestant landowner, Charles Parnell, from his position as leader of the Irish Home Rule Party that it was 'symptomatic, not only of changes in Ireland, but of changes all over Europe. 'Christian democracy' had been born. It offered bureaucracy, social reform and "peasantism"' (Stone, *Europe Transformed 1878–1919*, 1983, p.57). The higher birth rate of Catholics assisted the growing importance of political Catholicism in countries with religious divisions such as Germany and Holland, which was, by 1914, ceasing to have a protestant majority. Protestants, by and large (Ireland is a significant exception), tended not to form denominational parties, in part because Protestantism in its internalization of religion represents a stage of secularization.

Throughout pre-1914 Europe religion mattered politically. Even in Britain it was an indicator of political loyalty. Look around any area of England and note whether the schools built in the late nineteenth century were Board schools or Church of England schools and you will probably find that the answer correlates with a liberal or conservative voting pattern. Throughout Catholic Europe the church was involved in politics and Catholic parties such as the German Centre Party, the second largest party in the *Reichstag,* and the Austrian Christian Social Party were highly successful. Catholicism in politics could, to a degree, run across the political spectrum and there were conservative and radical elements within it. On the whole, however, what liberal elements there were in Catholic political parties tended to be edged out in the later 1880s.

The simplicities involved in the use of the terms left and right do little to help us describe the nature of politicized Catholicism. It opposed secularizing tendencies and sought to protect religious education which could bring it into opposition with the state. In France and Italy this could find archetypical expression in the hostility between mayor and priest in the small town or village. In Italy, where the Pope had retreated into the Vatican in 1870, the Church did not even recognize the existence of the state. Socially and economically Catholic parties tended to be conservative in the sense that they opposed economic liberalism and the changes that it, in conjunction with industrialization and urbanization, were creating. They, thus, tended to be protectionist, seeking to shield producers, whether peasants, craftsmen or shopkeepers, against the effects of the free market. In this they were not anti-state but rather looked to the protectionist or even the corporatist state. In places they were landowner led, whilst in others they represented the interests of peasants and small producers. In industrial regions, worker priests, as in industrialized northern Italy or Barcelona, embraced the proletariat and were close to syndicalism. They constituted a very broad movement and found difficulty in satisfying the demands of both their richer and poorer supporters. Anti-socialist, Catholic parties also tended to be anti-capitalist and conservative. The church had, after all, a long history of opposition to usury. The central thrust was for a 'third way' that sought to protect the social structure from the consequences of the dynamic but frightening forces of economic change and to make economic life the servant of a socio-religious view of social justice.

Surveying the Europe that emerged from World War I and its aftermath, it would seem a truism that religion was a force for national cohesion in states where there was only one important religion or denomination and a potential force for disunity where there were religious divides. There are, however, important caveats. If a common religious tradition was an enormous asset to the unity of the new Poland, it was no bar to the deep divide in Belgium, where Flemish identity began to assert itself against the hegemony of French speaking Walloons, nor in Czechoslovakia was it a bar to Slovak separatism. Even within Catholic countries, Christian democratic parties could range themselves, not against other religions, but against secular forces, whether socialist or liberal.

It is often argued that one effect of World War I was an erosion of religious belief and a further impetus to moves towards a secularized society and politics. There is therefore a certain irony in the fact that the two new states to emerge during the inter-war period, as the historian Norman Davies points out, had, to say the least, a pronounced religious identity. One, Eire, was a national republic but with confessional clauses in its constitution, and the other, all 100 acres of it, was the Vatican. Davies, rather teasingly, comments that, 'The Vatican State was almost as papist as Eire' (Norman Davies, *Europe, A History*, 1996, p.945). Concentration on conflict between socialists and communists on the one hand and fascism on the other can easily obscure the continued importance of Catholic political parties and religion as a force in European society. Germany and Italy were the only western European states where totalitarian movements came to power and both Hitler and Mussolini found it necessary to come to terms with the Catholic Church (the Concordat 1923 and the Lateran Treaty 1929), while prior to the Nazi rise to power, the Centre Party provided the main opposition to socialism in Germany. The importance of the religious-secular divide in inter-war Spain and Portugal and in pre-*Anschluss* Austria can scarcely be exaggerated, while in France and Belgium Catholic movements and parties remained important and, though they veered between nationalism and 'Europeanism' (as with the influential Belgian-based Ordre Nouveau), continued to provide a distinctive Catholic voice opposed to both socialism and 'Anglo-Saxon economics'.

Western Europe

The major powers of western Europe were, on the whole, nationally cohesive, and their cohesion had been strengthened by the experience of war, even though Germany and Italy had only short histories as national states.

France

France had a long history as a national state, was a highly centralized state, had a cohesive common culture, and no major separatist problems. It was, therefore, a nationally cohesive country, and its eventual victory after four years of war in which a portion of its territory had been fought over and occupied, further cemented such cohesion. French nationalism had always been as much cultural as racial and, as an imperial power, France had tended to have Roman aspirations, feeling that colonies could be assimilated and become truly French. Thus Algeria was part of metropolitan France.

However, the reintegration of Alsace and Lorraine, part of the German Empire since 1871, proved surprisingly difficult. Although the great majority in the provinces welcomed their reunification with France, the effects of nearly half a century of German rule were not to be swept away. The re-incorporation of the provinces was accompanied by friction between French officials and the local population, and the desire of the radical government of Herriot to extend all the anti-clerical legislation passed in France between 1871 and 1914 provoked strong resistance among the large number of devout Catholics, who under German rule had had close associations with the German Catholic Central Party. Herriot was forced to withdraw his proposals, but the incident left a legacy of discontent and unrest.

Britain

Britain also emerged from the war with the strong sense of British identity that had developed in the nineteenth century having been heightened. One effect of the wartime experience was that, as a result of the war effort of the dominions,

British public opinion was extremely conscious of the empire and felt little empathy with Europe. It is a measure of wartime patriotic fervour that the royal family was forced to sever its German links. In the atmosphere of 1917 the German connections of the ruling dynasty were, increasingly, an embarrassment. Told of H. G. Wells's charge that the court was 'uninspiring and alien', George V retorted: 'I may be uninspiring but I'll be damned if I'm an alien.' The inauguration of the House of Windsor and the dropping of their German titles by the junior members of the royal family completed the family's anglicization and was a blow to the cosmopolitan traditions of royalty. As Count Albrecht von Montgelas commented, 'The true royal tradition died on that day in 1917 when, for a mere war, King George changed his name' (Kenneth Rose, *King George V*, 1983, p.174).

Ireland

The great exception to the cohesiveness of the United Kingdom was, of course, Ireland, where the outbreak of war had interrupted a crisis over Home Rule that had seen unionists and nationalists facing each other in armed intransigence and a Liberal government faced with the refusal of both northern unionists and the Conservative and Unionist Party to accept the passage of the Home Rule Bill. The Act of Union of 1801 had not been accompanied by the removal of the civil and political disabilities of Catholics and even when these were removed throughout the United Kingdom, the discontent of much of the Irish catholic population had been manifest throughout the nineteenth century. Disraeli summarized the many facets of the Irish question brilliantly as early as 1843:

> One says it is a physical question, another, a spiritual. Now it is the absence of aristocracy, then the absence of railways. It is the Pope one day, potatoes the next.

T.P. O'Connor, *Lord Beaconsfield*, 1884, p.254

Perhaps, however, he was wrong and these were only different aspects of what was termed a 'national demand' for separation from England. He was correct, however, in discerning a discontinuity in the character of Irish nationalism. The 'national demand' waxed and waned but always had support among the three quarters of the population who were Catholic but throughout the nineteenth century its appeal to Protestants decreased. Britain failed to integrate catholic Ireland into the United Kingdom but Irish national movements, especially as their cultural dimension became more pronounced, failed to integrate protestant Ireland. Nationalism and unionism became in the course of the century roughly synonymous with Catholicism and Protestantism (the 1900 census revealed that Catholics made up 73.9 per cent of the population).

By the end of the century many of the elements of the Irish question Disraeli cited had been redressed or ameliorated but from those areas of Ireland with a majority of Catholics a solid body of Nationalist MPs was being returned to parliament. It is also significant that he didn't mention that other aspect of the <u>Irish question, the Protestant population of Ulster.</u> Largely composed of the descendants of Scots and English who had settled there in the seventeenth century, their importance was not appreciated until Gladstone's Home Rule Bill of 1886 revealed their determined loyalty to the union. There were, of course, unionists throughout Ireland, but only in Ulster, as Protestantism and unionism became increasingly synonymous, was there a sufficient concentration of Protestants to form a successful political movement.

Irish Nationalist MPs in the late nineteenth and early twentieth century were content with the prospect of an Irish parliament combined with continued representation at Westminster. Essentially they demanded a limited independence for a state they did not conceive as culturally distinct from Britain. The growth of cultural nationalism was to harden political nationalism and make it much more of a 'blood and soil' movement. One of the paradoxes of nationalism is that, although many historians see it as a child of modernity, it received a considerable impetus from the rediscovery of 'pasts', national musical and literary movements that drew upon past cultures, and the revival of languages and folk cultures. Almost inevitably, the leading proponents of cultural nationalism were not those born or educated within the cultures they rediscovered and sought to revive. Cultural revival came late to Ireland but had by 1905 enjoyed modest success in its mission to de-anglicize Ireland, though the association between English influence and modernity limited its impact. It had also inspired a then moderate political party, Sinn Fein, whose aim was an Irish-British relationship along the Austro-Hungarian Dual Monarchy model.

The importance of the cultural revival, and of Sinn Fein and the Irish Republican Brotherhood (IRB) to Edwardian Ireland has been exaggerated in the light of subsequent history. Sinn Fein's solitary candidature in a by-election was unsuccessful and it didn't even contest the general elections of 1910. The IRB, as the Fenian movement of the mid-nineteenth century was now called, was a secret organization dedicated to revolution but lacked the popular support to initiate one. Majority Irish opinion remained satisfied with the limited independence promised by Home Rule. A succession of events was to transform the situation.

The result of the elections of 1910 meant that Asquith's Liberal government was dependent on the votes of the Irish Nationalist MPs and had to bring in a new Home Rule Bill. The refusal of Ulster unionists and the Conservative and Unionist Party to accept the passage of the bill led to the growth of extremism amongst both unionists and nationalists. The drilling of volunteers, gun-running and outrages and reprisals by both sides, combined with fears that the British army could not be relied upon to support the government, led to constitutional crisis in Britain as well as Ireland. By August 1914 the outlines of a settlement by which a northern Ireland would remain within the Union were already discernible and with Irish Nationalist MPs pledging their support for the war effort, the Home Rule Bill was passed, though its operation was suspended until the end of the war.

Volunteers for the army came in great numbers from Ireland (about 150,000) but the IRB remembered the principle that England's difficulty is Ireland's opportunity and contacts were made with Germany by several of its leaders. The Easter Rising of 1916 in Dublin was an effective fiasco. It was a fiasco because it was badly planned, poorly supported and unpopular with Dubliners; nevertheless, it resulted in several hundred army and police casualties. It was effective because the government's response in having fourteen of the ring-leaders shot was widely seen as draconian. Whether it actually was, is debatable (after all this was a rebellion which had been promised German support) but irrelevant for the executions made 'martyrs'. Martyrs, however, are not made without widespread latent sympathy.

In an excellent and fair-minded study of the Easter Rising, Brian Barton and Michael Foy link the rising with the enormous casualties sustained by the Ulster Volunteer Force, which has formed the 36th Division and fought gallantly at the Somme:

> At Easter 1916 the republican tradition was rejuvenated by the rising and some weeks later the pride of northern Unionists was strengthened by the UVF's sacrifice at the Somme. More than any other, these two political movements were to shape Ireland's political destiny in the decades to come.
>
> (Brian Barton and Michael Foy, *The Easter Rising*, 1999, p.244)

The Easter Rising and the response to it were largely responsible for the rapid transformation of Irish politics but plans to extend conscription to Ireland and the arrest of Sinn Fein leaders on the grounds of a supposed German plot in 1918 played their part. In the general election of 1918, Sinn Fein, now dedicated to a republic, won a sweeping victory, though this was assisted by IRB pressure, and the old Nationalist Party was reduced to six seats as against Sinn Fein's seventy-three. Twenty-six Unionists were elected in the north. The Sinn Fein MPs refused to go to Westminster and, meeting in Dublin, declared independence.

Throughout 1919 and 1920 a bloody war was waged between British forces and Royal Irish constabulary on the one hand and the Irish Republican forces on the other. The settlement of 1921 provided for an Irish Free State with dominion status and kept the six northern counties within the union. It was followed by an even bloodier civil war in 1922–3 between anti-Treaty and pro-Treaty factions of Sinn Fein and the IRA, which resulted in some 4,000 deaths and ended in victory for the pro-Treaty forces.

Exercise   To what extent do you think that World War I altered the course of Irish history? ■

Specimen answer   Although the outlines of a settlement instituting Home Rule and excluding most of Ulster were discernible until 1914 and, indeed, the Home Rule Bill was put in the statute book in September 1914, the post-war outcome was different in several ways:

(a)   there were to be no southern Irish MPs at Westminster, while dominion status marked a greater degree of separation than Home Rule and gave the new state virtual independence.

(b)   the political complexion of the new dominion was very different from that of pre-war Ireland. The experience of the war had exacerbated relations between Britain and catholic Ireland and taken support away from the Nationalist MPs. The war may be seen as having given violent and revolutionary elements an opportunity and from the war and the 'Troubles' that followed, there emerged a much more ethnic nationalism more conscious of its cultural distinctiveness. □

Historians of Russia have debated whether the effects of World War I were to derail moderate constitutional and economic development and recreate an older context in which revolutionary elements found their opportunity. With caution, we can ask a similar question of Ireland.

Germany

A unified German state was less than fifty years old at the end of World War I. In fact, the German Empire had not been a full unitary state, for the old Bismarckian structure had recognized the existence of individual states within it which had retained their identity as kingdoms or duchies. The particularism of individual states had remained a force, albeit overlaid by a strong and fervent German nationalism. The possibility of breaking up Germany and replacing it with a number of smaller states was one that occurred to the Allied powers during both the First and Second World Wars.

The Weimar Republic was more of a unitary state than the Empire had been. Many of the prerogatives of the old states were abolished: they had to have republican governments, the *Reich* government assumed the power of direct taxation over all citizens, and central government controlled the army. But the *Länder,* as the states became, continued to have considerable powers: they controlled education, the police and the process of law. The existence of the *Länder* gave a weapon to separatists or to those who simply wished to defy the will of the *Reich* government.

In 1923 the French gave support to separatists in the Rhineland who were encouraged to declare an independent Rhineland Republic (there was an earlier attempt at this in 1919), and supported a Palatinate Republic which was recognized by the Rhineland Commission in January 1924. Neither of these Republics lasted for more than a few months, as there was little real support for them. The events in Bavaria in 1923 were more serious and drew on a more significant vein of separatist sentiment. In fact, two elements came together: national right-wing movements under the leadership of Hitler's National Socialist Party, and conservative Bavarian separatists who wished to regain Bavaria's previous more independent status. One must not, however, exaggerate threats to the national cohesion of Germany. Regional pride, a suspicion of Prussia and Berlin, and a nostalgia for separate cultural and political traditions coexisted with German national feeling while Weimar Germany was more nationally homogeneous having lost alien minorities, Danes, French and Poles, formerly within the empire.

Italy

Italy, too, was politically a recent creation and economically and socially a less homogeneous entity than Germany, but, despite the continuing disparity between north and south, Italian cohesion can be said to have increased during the war years. Italian territorial ambitions, if fully satisfied, would have impaired such cohesion; even as it was, the more modest gains made by Italy in 1919 (the frontier on the Brenner and Istria) and the later seizure of Fiume brought into the Italian state discontented German and Slav areas on its periphery.

Central and eastern Europe

It was clearly in central and eastern Europe where there was such a multiplicity of overlapping national and ethnic groups that threats to national cohesion were greatest. As we have seen, Versailles attempted to provide for the principle of national self-determination but vitiated this by its parallel preoccupations with rewarding victors and providing against a German revival. Further east, frontiers were settled and states established after years of continued warfare. It was something of a paradox that the more national aspirations were satisfied, the greater were the problems of national cohesion for the expanded nation states. For a state to fulfil its national ambitions was to be saddled with greater numbers of hostile minorities. After 1918 Bulgaria and Hungary were cohesive states largely because they came out of the war and the peace settlement diminished in size (and bursting with a desire for revenge), while Czechoslovakia had endemic racial problems largely because the most grandiose plans of Czech patriots had been fulfilled. The diplomatic success of Romania and the diplomatic and military success of the new Poland had extended frontiers well beyond areas that were homogeneously Romanian or Polish. As we have seen in the section on 'Social structure', almost all east and central European states inherited from pasts characterized by successive conquests, important social elements that were not of the majority nationality. Thus in Finland the aristocracy was Swedish, and in Slovakia, Magyar, while the divide between town and country in many states was characterized by German and/or Jewish predominance in towns which were surrounded by a Slav (or Latvian or Lithuanian) countryside.

A specific example will have to suffice to illustrate the ethnic and social mix that existed especially in frontier areas. We have already come across Bratislava in section 1, where we saw how it was given to Czechoslovakia by the peace settlement. Here are some passages from a traveller's account of it in 1933, although the account was not written until many decades later. Patrick Leigh Fermor walked across Europe to Constantinople, and in his book A *Time of Gifts* (1977) described his experiences. His companion on this stage of his travels was Austrian:

> His family lived in Prague and, like many Austrians at the break-up of the Empire, they had found themselves citizens of the new-born Republic, tied there beyond uprooting by old commitments; in this case a family bank. Hans helped to run the branch of an associate establishment in Bratislava – or Pressburg, as he still firmly called it, just as ex-Hungarians stubbornly clung to Pozony ...

Fermor describes three different drinking places:

> a lively drinking hell with the Magyar word VENDEGLÖ printed in large letters across the frontpane and [I] bumped into a trio of Hungarian farmers ... rigorous, angular-faced, dark-clad and dark-glanced men with black moustaches tipped down at the corners of their mouths. Their white shirts were buttoned at the throat. They wore low-crowned black hats with narrow brims and high boots of shiny black leather with a Hessian notch at the knee ... My next call, only a few doors away, was a similar haunt of sawdust and spilt liquor and spit, but this time, KRCMA was daubed over the window. All was Slav within. The tow-haired Slovaks drinking there were dressed in conical fleece hats and patched sheepskin jerkins with the matted wool turned inwards ... I singled out one of the many Jewish coffee houses ... conversing and arguing and contracting business round an archipelago of tables, the dark-clad customers thronged the place to bursting point. (These marble squares did duty as improvised offices in thousands of cafes all

through central Europe and the Balkans and the Levant). The minor hubbub of Magyar and Slovak was outnumbered by voices speaking German, pronounced in the Austrian way ... But quite often the talk was in Yiddish.

(Fermor, *A Time of Gifts,* 1977, pp.213–20)

These extracts from Fermor's account of his impressions of Bratislava bring out several important facets of life not only in Bratislava but in much of central Europe: the legacy of Austria-Hungary was to be found in the importance of Germans in banking and trade; the Jews were similarly important in all branches of finance and commerce; the different nationalities not only lived separate social lives but they dressed differently; and different languages were to be encountered at every turn. These were formidable obstacles in the way of national cohesion.

The constitution of the Czechoslovakian state declared the Republic to be a 'Czechoslovak national state', recognizing only Czechoslovaks and, in Ruthenia, Ruthenes as *Staatsvölker,* which made the other inhabitants Germans, Magyars and Jews – not peoples of the state, but minorities. The concept of Czechoslovaks, as opposed to Czechs and Slovaks, was itself denied by many Slovaks, who saw it as a device to submerge Slovak identity.

In the new Kingdom of the Serbs, Croats and Slovenes (Yugoslavia in 1929) from the beginning there was antipathy from the Croats towards Serbian hegemony, and Croatian separatism was fuelled by Croatia's different religion and distinct traditions, as well as by Serbian arrogance. Was the new state a union or a Greater Serbia? It was fractured not just by Serbo-Croat rivalry but by numerous other divisions and its peoples had no common history. Some had been part of the Ottoman Empire, others part of Austria-Hungary. Religion divided Catholic Croats and Slovaks from orthodox Serbs and Montenegrins and both from Bosnian and Albanian muslims. Bosnian muslims had been relatively content under Austrian rule (1878–1918) and had looted Serbian property in Sarajevo while Archduke Franz Ferdinand was assassinated; while Kosovo, with its majority of Albanian muslims, had been seized by Serbia in 1912 and reconquered in 1918. From west to east Yugoslavia demonstrated a very uneven pattern of economic development with Slovenia having by far the most advanced economic structure and Macedonia the least. The new state had many minorities: 'some half-million each of Germans, Magyars and Albanians, a quarter of a million Romanians and the half-million Macedonian Slavs, many of them strongly Bulgarophile' (Macartney and Palmer, *Independent Eastern Europe,* 1962, p.172).

By contrast, the rump of a great empire that was Austria was now fairly homogeneous nationally – a German state that was forbidden to unite with Germany – but divided socially and economically between the former capital of the Empire, Vienna, and the largely rural provinces. Vienna, which possessed about a third of the population of the new state, was dominated politically by the Social Democratic Party, while provincial Austria tended to be conservative and Catholic.

Along with Czechoslovakia and Yugoslavia, Romania and Poland were the great winners of the post-war settlements. Poland was a far from nationally homogeneous state. The census of 1921, which almost certainly exaggerated the number of Poles, counted some nine million non-Polish citizens out of a population of 27 million: four million Ukrainians, over two million Jews, a million White Russians, a million Germans, and a quarter of a million 'others', chiefly Czechs and Lithuanians. In fact there may well have been over three million Jews and over five million Ukrainians. Nor were the Poles themselves completely united, as ex-Russian, ex-German and ex-Austrian Poles had different outlooks and traditions. Romania's new territories diluted its homogeneity, for in the ex-Hungarian provinces there was a bare majority of Romanians over Hungarians and Germans, while in Bukovina the north was purely Ukrainian; in Bessarabia the Romanians, although the largest single national group, made up less than half the population, and in Southern Dobruja the population was largely Bulgarian (figures taken from Macartney and Palmer).

Soviet Russia, after December 1922 the Soviet Union, remained, like the Tsarist Empire it succeeded, a multiracial and multinational state dominated by Greater Russia. The Finns, the Latvians, the Lithuanians, the Estonians and the Poles had made good their bids for national independence, while others like the Ukrainians had failed. The history of Soviet Russia was not just one of revolution and civil war but also of a war by which the Bolsheviks reconquered the Ukraine and the Caucasus. The constitutional arrangement of a union of republics could be seen as a recognition of national diversity, but real power lay in the central control of the Communist Party; that firm control would disguise and hold down separatist tendencies as firmly as the Tsarist governments had done.

Not only were the states of east and central Europe not nationally homogeneous or cohesive, but territorial disputes and conflicting ambitions between neighbours ensured that national minorities and their treatment would become the pawns of national rivalries. Sandwiched between the great powers of Germany and the USSR and faced with the revisionist ambitions of Bulgaria and Hungary, the powers that had benefited from Versailles and the aftermath of World War I were almost universally divided against each other by territorial disputes. The only exceptions were Finland and the Baltic states, who had no differences with each other, although Lithuania and Poland had a bitter dispute over Vilna. Czechoslovakia, Romania and Yugoslavia had minor differences with each other, although these paled when set beside the ambitions of Bulgaria and Hungary to reclaim their *irredenta* or lost territories. But in the hostility between Poland and Czechoslovakia over Teschen, two of the new powers of central Europe had a major dispute. People did not, unfortunately, fit frontiers.

Social reform and welfare policies

Table 7–10.2 Major welfare legislation in Europe from c.1870 to c.1930

Country	19th century	1900–1914	1914–18	1919–24	After 1924
Austria	Workmen's compensation 1887–94 Compulsory health insurance 1888	Compulsory old-age insurance for white-collar workers 1906	General Commissariat for war and transition economics March 1917 Improvements in adult education 1916–17 Workmen's compensation extended December 1917 Unemployment assistance 1918	Education reforms embodied in new constitution 1919 Holidays with pay (workers) 1919 Compulsory unemployment insurance 1920 Poor relief written into Austrian constitution 1920 Housing Act (state subsidies) 1921 Holidays with pay (white-collar workers) 1920–23 Unemployment assistance extended 1922	Unemployment assistance further extended 1926 Compulsory Social Insurance Act 1926 Education Act 1927 Workmen's compensation extended 1928
Belgium	Cheap mortgage loans for workers' housing 1889	Compulsory workers' old-age and widows' and orphans' insurance 1900 Workmen's compensation 1903 Voluntary unemployment insurance 1907		National Society for Cheap Houses (with government subsidies and loans) 1919 Employers' equalisation funds for family allowances 1919 Extended voluntary unemployment insurance 1920 Compulsory old-age and widows' and orphans' insurance extended 1924	
Bulgaria			Voluntary social insurance for workers in transport and public works 1915 New medical provisions in conjunction with Red Cross 1915	Compulsory Social Insurance Act (accident, sickness, maternity, invalidity, and old-age insurance) 1924	

Country	19th century	1900–1914	1914–18	1919–24	After 1924
Czecho-slovakia	Workmen's compensation 1887–94 Compulsory health insurance 1888	Compulsory old-age insurance for white-collar workers 1906	Improvements in adult education 1916–17 Workmen's compensation extended December 1917 Unemployment assistance 1918	Workmen's compensation extended 1919–21 Holidays with pay (miners) 1921 Cheap dwellings legislation 1921–24 Compulsory social insurance (sickness, invalidity, old-age, and widows' and orphans' insurance) 1924 Family allowances (state officials and teachers) 1924	Holidays with pay (employees in general) 1925
France	Free elementary education 1881 Compulsory elementary education (age 6–13) 1882 Government tax concessions for purchase of cheap dwellings 1894 Workmen's compensation 1898	Voluntary unemployment insurance 1905 Local Authority subsidies to builders of low-rent houses 1906, 1908, 1912 Compulsory old-age and widows' and orphans' insurance 1910 Assistance for large families 1913 Unemployment assistance 1914	Workmen's compensation extended July 1914 Separation allowances and free meals August 1914 National unemployment fund to provide unemployment assistance 20 August 1914 New factory regulations 1915–16 Compulsory arbitration and conciliation schemes January 1917 Employers' equalization funds for family allowances 1918	Workmen's compensation extended 1919, 1922, 1923 48-hour week, 1919–20 Central committee for family allowances 1921 Housing Act (subsidies for cheap dwellings) 1922	General compulsory social insurance 1928 Housing Act sets targets and provides low-cost loans 1928

Country	19th century	1900–1914	1914–18	1919–24	After 1924
Germany	State inspection of all schools 1871 Compulsory Sickness Insurance Act 1883 Workmen's compensation 1884 Compulsory workers' invalidity and old-age insurance 1889 Legal framework established for housing co-operation 1889	All existing insurance schemes consolidated and extended in one National Insurance Code 1911 Widows' and orphans' insurance 1911	Laws protecting dependants of soldiers from eviction, 4 August 1914 and 14 January 1915 Stinnes-Legien Agreement on reduced working week 1918 Unemployment assistance 1918 Measures to 'protect tenants' and work 'against the housing shortage' 23 September 1918 Decree providing national subsidies for house-building October 1918	New Weimar constitution guarantees education for all (articles 143–6, human dignity (article 151), and healthy housing (article 155) and the Weimar state assumed responsibility for the health and welfare of the family and of the total population 1919 Prussian government fixes rents December 1919 Pensions Act for military persons and dependants 1920 Rent control and anti-eviction laws 1920–23 Requisitioning of empty property and subsidies for house-building 1920–23 Health clinics founded throughout Germany 1919–21 Prussian Health Council established 1921 Family allowances (at employers' expense) 1921–4 Public assistance 1924	Youth welfare programmes 1927 Workmens' compensation (occupational diseases) 1925
Italy	Casati education law, theoretically making two years' elementary education compulsory, but poorly enforced 1859 Voluntary sickness insurance 1886 Workmen's compensation 1898 Voluntary insurance for incapacity or old age 1898	Housing Act (subsidies for cheap housing) 1903 School attendance (theoretically) compulsory from ages 6–12 1904	Workmen's compensation for agricultural workers 1917 Unemployment assistance 1917–19	Compulsory insurance for incapacity or old age 1919 Compulsory unemployment insurance 1919 School attendance compulsory ages 6–14 1923	

Country	19th century	1900–1914	1914–18	1919–24	After 1924
Russia	Free medical treatment for factory workers 1866 Labour Code (generally harsh and restrictive but some protection for workers) 1886	Workmen's compensation 1903, 1912 Act calling for compulsory elementary education to be introduced within 10 years 1908	Declaration of Soldiers' Rights May 1917 Unemployment insurance 11 December 1917 Sickness benefits and free medical care 29 December 1917 Maternity and welfare services 30 April 1918 Social security 31 October 1918	Social insurance 1922 Labour Code (includes holidays with pay) 1922	Compulsory insurance for old-age 1925
United Kingdom	State elementary schools established 1870 Elementary education compulsory 1881 Elementary education free 1891 Workmen's compensation 1897	Education Act establishes state secondary schools 1902 School meals 1906 Old-age pensions 1908 Compulsory health insurance 1911 Compulsory unemployment insurance (selected trades only) 1911	Maternity and Child Welfare Acts 1915, 1918 Unemployment insurance extended to cover all persons employed in trades related to the war effort December 1916 New war disablement and widowhood pensions February 1917 Education Act 1918	Ministry of Health established 1919 Housing Act (state subsidies) 1919 Compulsory unemployment insurance for entire working class 1920 Extended to white-collar workers 1924	
Serbia/ Yugoslavia					Compulsory social insurance (accident, sickness, maternity) 1922
Denmark	State loans for cheap rented housing 1887 Voluntary sickness insurance 1892 Workmen's compensation 1898	Voluntary unemployment insurance 1907	Compulsory industrial accident insurance 1916	Grants and loans to housing co-operators 1919 Unemployment assistance 1921 Extended old-age pensions 1922	Semi-compulsory health insurance 1933 Compulsory old-age and invalidity insurance 1933

Country	19th century	1900–1914	1914–18	1919–24	After 1924
Sweden	Voluntary sickness insurance 1891	Workmen's compensation 1901 Loans to workers for home building 1904 Voluntary sickness insurance extended 1910 Old-age pensions 1913	Compulsory industrial accident insurance 1916 Unemployment assistance 1916 Rent control and subsidies for house-building 1917		Voluntary unemployment insurance 1934
Netherlands		Compulsory accident insurance 1901 Loans and subsidies for house-building 1901 Compulsory sickness insurance 1913 Compulsory old-age insurance 1913	Voluntary unemployment insurance 1916 Increased subsidies for house-building 1918	Extended compulsory accident insurance 1921	Compulsory sickness insurance extended 1929
Switzerland		Compulsory industrial accident insurance 1911 Voluntary sickness insurance 1911	Unemployment assistance 1917	Voluntary unemployment insurance 1924 Extended unemployment assistance 1924	

Note: Insurance means that individuals have to make regular contributions in order to receive benefits when they need them. Assistance is simply handed out by the government without a requirement for previous insurance payments. Compulsory schemes usually indicate a more full-blooded commitment to welfare than voluntary ones.

Cherish that table!

It contains a unique compendium of information vital to any discussion of the social effects of World War I, compiled from specialist studies of housing, education, social insurance, etc. in Europe, as well as detailed studies of individual countries. Read through it a couple of times now, reflecting on what it tells you (and perhaps also on what it does not tell you). But before we discuss the table I want you to read carefully the last part of the extracts from the Treaty of Versailles (I.13 in *Primary Sources 1: World War I*), the extracts from Article 427 on 'Labour'. Just as the Covenant of the League of Nations incorporated in the Treaty was unprecedented in an international treaty, so was this section entirely devoted to the welfare of labour and the setting up of an International Labour Office.

Exercise   1   Does Table 7–10.2 taken in conjunction with these clauses from Article 427 *prove* that the experience of World War I brought about substantial advances in social welfare? ■

Specimen answer and discussion   No, they don't *prove* anything. The clauses of the Versailles Treaty express good intentions, but they are not in themselves evidence of social reform actually taking place. In the table, the quantity of legislation during, and perhaps more important, after the war, is impressive, but we must beware of what is often referred to as the *post hoc propter hoc* argument (that because something happens *after* something else, it happened *because* of that something else). There is a strong suggestion of a link between the horror of the war experience and the *idea* of social justice in the Versailles Treaty. Thus if we take the quantitative evidence in the table, together with the phrasing of the clauses in the Versailles Treaty, we do at least have a strong case that there is some connection between the war and the outburst of social legislation. At the same time the table does also show us that a considerable amount of legislation had been enacted before the war, so we still have to satisfy ourselves that the wartime and post-war legislation, though quite impressive in its bulk, isn't really just a natural continuation of what had gone before. ☐

this?

or this?

The table does show that a number of important social reforms were enacted during the war. But it also indicates very clearly that if we are to have a serious discussion of war and social reform we do have to consider the reforms enacted after the war. Nonetheless, I want now to look at what happened during the war.

Exercise   On a common-sense basis, in the light of what you already know about the nature of the war, it would be possible to argue:

1   that certain aspects of the war made certain forms of social welfare action essential; and

2   that, on the contrary, certain other aspects of the war made social welfare policies extremely unlikely, if not impossible.

Write down the main points in support of both arguments. ■

Specimen answer and discussion   1   The mobilization of large numbers of husbands and fathers, the disruptions to family and business life, sometimes leading to unemployment, the loss of income for dependants at home and the threat of increased rents, and the very high risk of injury and death on the various fronts, created a pressing need for separation allowances, pensions, disability payments, unemployment assistance, rent control, family allowances, etc. From one point of view these can simply be seen as governments merely meeting their barest obligations (often in an extremely stingy way) rather than real advances in social welfare; from another point of view they can be seen as precedents leading to more comprehensive developments as the war progressed and in the post-war period.

2   The very destructiveness of the war, the immense stress it placed on resources, particularly of the less developed countries, very much ran against the setting aside of funds for social welfare.

With regard to the likelihood of social reform, other arguments have been advanced, and you have my heartiest congratulations if you thought of throwing them in here. These arguments (which are closely interrelated), based on the notion of *participation* which you encountered in Book 1, Unit 1, are:

(a)   that in this total war, this war of entire peoples, governments needed to buy the support of their people, or keep their morale up, by granting social reforms; and

(b)   that because they were so necessary to a successful war effort, ordinary people, and particularly those organized in trades unions, were able to force governments to make concessions in the realm of welfare. □

governments need people

It is arguments such as these which help us to *connect* social reform to the war experience, getting beyond the unsatisfactory *post hoc propter hoc* non-argument.

Given the contrast between the amount of legislation enacted after the war, compared with that enacted during the war, one might feel that the really important factor was not the war itself but the revolutionary changes in government taking place at the end of the war, that is to say, one might argue that it is not the war experience which brings social reform, but revolution.

Exercise   Actually, the table, taken as a whole, does not really support this argument. Why not? ■

Specimen answer   Social reform is just as evident in the countries which did not go through
and discussion   revolutions. Belgium, France, Italy – not immediately anyway, and the UK did not go through revolutions, yet substantial social reform does take place in each of these countries. □

Once or twice, I have suggested that it can be useful to categorize forces, circumstances, changes as structural, ideological, or institutional.

Exercise   In the clauses of Article 427 of the Versailles Treaty, what sort of change is being signalled? ■

Specimen answer   I'd say 'ideological'. There is not just a new concern for labour, but almost a
and discussion   prioritization of the needs of labour. Let us not for a moment believe that this

was a universal, unchallenged, change in prevailing ideas. Many of the Acts listed in the table were hotly contested, and sometimes there was heavy resistance to their implementation. All the same, a new public orthodoxy had been enunciated, an orthodoxy which claimed a special concern for the ordinary person, for the ordinary men who had fought in the war and their families. This, one could say, is the ideology of the common man and of 'mass society': whether democratic or totalitarian, societies in the inter-war years *claimed* to be concerned for the welfare of all of their people, hence the reforms listed in the table. Where there were revolutions, notably in Austria-Hungary, Germany, and Russia, the new orthodoxy becomes embedded in the new constitutions of these countries. If we do wish to give special weight to the setting up of new states with new constitutions, we will, of course, have to tease out how far the revolutions were themselves products of circumstances brought about by the war.

evolution lead to war?

Links can, I think, be persuasively established between war and social reform. All governments, whether revolutionary or not, were infected by the new ideology. During the war and after, governments had to respond to the new challenges and crises. The demands and stresses of war exposed the inadequacies of existing social provision. Participation by workers (particularly where there were strong trade unions), peasants, subject nationalities, women did all make rewards *possible*, even if subsequent developments prevented these rewards from being fully realized. What I have referred to as the ideological change was reinforced by a general feeling that such a horrific war must result in a better world, and that social reforms were a concrete expression of that feeling. □

Rather a heavy load of abstract generalizations! In a moment I'll take each of the countries in turn, in the hope of adding some of that detail which is crucial to historical study.

Meantime, one more question.

Exercise   At the end of my table I list four of the main neutral countries (the most noteworthy omission is Spain which, frankly, enacted practically no social legislation during the period under review). What do you think the evidence from Denmark, Sweden, the Netherlands and Switzerland contributes to the general arguments unfolded above? ■

Specimen answer and discussion   You *could* argue that since there are reforms in all of these countries during and after the war, this invalidates the argument that the war experience had anything to do with bringing about social reforms in the other countries. Alternatively, you could argue that it was as a result of the war experience that the new ideology emerged and new international standards were set, as in the Treaty of Versailles, and that the neutral countries, though not themselves involved in the war, were simply responding to these new standards. Or, you could point out that, in respect of reforms which had already taken place before 1914, there is less of a sharp change in these countries with, indeed, some of the most important legislation coming quite a long time after the war. It is for you to work out these various puzzles to your own satisfaction, but my own position is that there is nothing striking enough about the experience of the neutral countries to invalidate the general arguments I have been unfolding. Let us now turn to specific instances. □

Bulgaria

Bulgaria, for the war period, was in effect a kind of client state of the Germans, and thus was protected from the devastation and economic deprivation which affected surrounding countries. Prior to the war, as we saw in Unit 4, Bulgarian politicians and publicists, as part of the attempt to bring Bulgaria within the ambit of European civilization, were advocating social reforms of the type to be found, for example, in Italy. Georges T. Danaïllow, in his standard work *Les effets de la guerre en Bulgarie* (1932) follows the argument that the pressures and sacrifices of war, the desire to reward soldiers and their families, led to these pre-war aspirations being turned into practice, though not, it has to be said, on a very substantial scale. The main piece of legislation was the introduction in March 1915 of social insurance, but this was limited to workers in transport and public works. Largely as a direct development from the need to treat wounded soldiers, there was an improvement in medical provision, partly in association with the Red Cross, which was greatly assisted by the presence in Bulgaria of German doctors.

At the end of the war, after King Ferdinand had abdicated in favour of his son Boris, the Bulgarian parliament was dominated by Alexander Stamboliski, leader of the peasant party, BANU, who had been imprisoned during the war. Stamboliski pursued reform policies, but it was actually after he had been overthrown by a coup in the summer of 1923, that the comprehensive social insurance measure listed in Table 7–10.2 was enacted.

Russia

Given the nature of the regime, the backwardness and inefficiencies of Russian society, and, from the very start, the direct impingement of military events, such minimal legislation as already existed, for instance protecting women and children from night work, was rescinded. Even if it had had the will, the state did not have the means to persevere with anything effective in the way of price controls, rent controls, rationing, or the procurement and distribution of food and fuel. Sporadic and entirely counter-productive rationing schemes were introduced, but a project for the procurement of coal at fixed prices, together with planned distribution, was abandoned in the face of the opposition of mine owners and industrialists who declared it an unwarranted infringement of freedom of enterprise. Out of sheer necessity, the autocracy did, reluctantly, have to allow a place in the organization of the home front to what are usually referred to as 'voluntary organizations', that is to say the unions of town councils and unions of village councils (*zemstvos*) which were established by patriotically minded middle-class citizens, and also the War Industries Committees, likewise mainly the product of voluntary action by middle-class individuals; through this *participation*, such groups were in a position to press for egalitarian social reforms. In the *Duma* the Progressive bloc called in particular for reforms which would give the peasants civic rights on a par with those of other classes. Workers' representatives on the War Industries Committees put forward claims for comprehensive social legislation, including the eight-hour day and land for the peasants. All such initiatives failed.

The interrelationship between the needs and pressures of war and the first Russian Revolution of February 1917 is discussed in Units 10–12. One implication of this revolution was that the claims just discussed were, in theory at least, recognized. The new government enacted the eight-hour day, a minimum wage, and nominal pay rises averaging 50 per cent. On 11 May, Kerensky, as Minister of War, produced his Declaration of Soldiers' Rights, which met some of the major grievances that had been rumbling throughout the war. The Provisional Government's last Agrarian Bill aimed to set aside reserves of land for the peasants, though with all kinds of qualifications and exceptions. The Tsarist regime had been unable to meet the levels of organization and efficiency required in 'society at war' and had collapsed. The Provisional Government did enact significant measures of social legislation, but in face of the continuing high costs of war and continuing inefficiencies within Russian society, they were largely a dead letter. What happened was the second revolution and the conclusion of peace, as we shall see later.

Integral to the new Bolshevik Russia were the social insurance and health care measures detailed in Table 7–10.2.

Austria-Hungary

As you learned in the discussion of national cohesion, not only did the experience of war offer opportunities for the minority nationalities to express their disaffection from the Empire, but the pressures and demands of war provoked an increasing split between Austria and Hungary themselves. In addition, then, to the autocratic nature of the regime, these developments have to be taken into account in any discussion of the possibilities of social policy. Austria-Hungary provides, in virulent form, a classic mix of the following:

1   existing welfare legislation being forced into abeyance because of the demands and destructiveness of war;

2   new legislation, which might be described as 'dire straits legislation', being introduced to try to mitigate some of the worst privations brought on by the circumstances of war, but which was decreasingly effective, and which scarcely brought standards back to what they had been before the war; and

3   legislation, generally more theoretical than practical, related to the general need to reorganize society in order to meet the exigencies of war, and even plans for social reconstruction after the war.

The first point is exemplified by the legislation governing the employment of women and children, which was largely ignored. As a consequence, and for other reasons as well, children were deprived of schooling, their teachers having been conscripted and their schools having been taken over for use as hospitals and for other military uses (by 1918 nearly two hundred had been thus taken over). With regard to the second point, both price controls and rent controls were introduced, but proved increasingly ineffective: in fact, because of desperate food shortages people had to shop on the black market, where prices were grossly inflated. By the War Service Act of 1913, within the Austro-Hungarian autocracy everything, if deemed necessary, could be put at the disposal of the military apparatus. Thus, throughout the war, factories and mines were placed under military supervision, and everywhere workers were subject to military regimentation: 'the discipline of the barracks was transplanted to the factory' (A. J. May, *The Passing of the Hapsburg Monarchy 1914–18*, 1966). Thus the opportunities for labour to exploit the need which their country had for them were greatly curtailed; the need for the authorities to buy their support was scarcely felt. The third point is best illustrated by the setting up in March 1917 of a Commission for War and Transition Economics, which included representatives of commerce and distribution, delegates from the Chambers of Commerce and labour, and representatives of the workers' organizations. The secretariat to this Commission was called the General Commissariat for War and Transition Economics, headed by a general Commissary. 'Because', in the words of David Mitrany in *The Effect of the War in South-Eastern Europe* (1936), 'of the great importance which questions of social policy were bound to acquire, especially in connection with unemployment, the chief of the social section in the Ministry of Trade acted as assistant to the General Commissary.' In other words, the organization and the personnel for social planning were there: because of the actual destructiveness and privations of war, not a lot was actually accomplished. Governmental initiatives apart, we do find that in the hectic, but sometimes stimulating, new circumstances of 'society at war', various other initiatives develop – people, for instance, are brought together in new ways, they become interested for the first time in national and international problems. At any rate, A. J. May, in his *The Passing of the Hapsburg Monarchy*, singles out adult education as a flourishing development in wartime Austria. (I have cited May's rather elderly book here and earlier in the course because he does make some useful points, but a much more up-to-date book is Alan Sked, *The Habsburg Monarchy*, (1989)).

The events of the Austrian Revolution are fully discussed in Units 11–13. As in Germany, certain basic social rights were enshrined in the new constitution. However, while the Social Democrats were strong in Vienna, right-wing elements were very powerful in the rest of Austria, so that the new Republic of Austria is a classic instance of social welfare policies congruent with the new post-war ideology being bitterly contested by conservative and Catholic elements. A Catholic hierarchy opposed the educational reforms which made elementary schooling free, providing grants for poor children to go on to middle schools and even high schools which, in addition, were for the first time thrown open to girls. There was strong resistance to most of the other legislation listed in the table, and the Housing Act at first applied only to Vienna, which became famous for the model workers' flats built there. Only in 1927 was the Act applied to the whole of Austria.

Italy

In entering the war, Italy made a decisive break from its autocratic allies, Germany and Austria, and threw in its lot with the democratic *Entente*. In the excitements of war, and conflicts over whether or not Italy should have remained neutral, the always highly coloured rhetoric of Italian parliamentarianism became greatly inflated. Italian politicians and publicists liked to believe that their society was organized very differently from that of Austria-Hungary. Yet, in face of the exigencies of war, substantial areas of Italy, including many factories, were placed under military rule. Thus, as in Austria-

Hungary, there were severe limits on the extent to which labour could try to exploit the national need for its services. Italy was a poor country, desperately dependent, particularly for such basics as grain and coal, on imports. Thus there were no surpluses with which to fund welfare benefits. Nonetheless, the history of social welfare during the actual period of hostilities did differ significantly from the one we have just been looking at. Principally, Italian governments, to a greater extent than their Austrian counterparts, felt the need to impose collaboration between employers and employees in securing the materials of war, and also felt the need to preserve some show of democratic forms. Of the two major developments while the war was actually being waged, the first concerned one of the most traditional of all aspects of social legislation, and the other, arguably, worked very much to the disadvantage of working men. Compulsory workmen's compensation was essentially a late nineteenth-century idea. In Italy in August 1917 this provision was extended to agricultural labourers. The other main development was in the realm of compulsory arbitration for industrial disputes. Beginning with regulation 1377 of 22 August 1915, the new compulsory arbitration system started in factories and workshops designated as being subject to the rules governing industrial mobilization. Similar procedures were introduced in factories within the even more strictly governed 'war zones' – the term was an elastic one, and Turin, an important industrial centre but quite far from the war front, was declared a war zone in the autumn of 1917. For most of the war the regulations taken together generally served to limit the bargaining power which the workers otherwise might have had, though the comprehensive decree 1672 of 13 October 1918 which universalized the system of compulsory arbitration probably operated less unfairly towards the workers. To satisfy the demands of the munitions industries for labour there was a great influx of population into the cities of the northwest, producing all kinds of sanitary, health, housing and overcrowding problems. Remedies were called for, though not usually immediately implemented.

As in other countries, claims and plans for social reform were articulated in time of war more clearly than they had been in time of peace. Some sense of what the country owed to those who waged war on its behalf (and recognition too of the new assertiveness and confidence of peasants forced out of their traditional ways by the upheaval of war) is to be found in the promise made by Prime Minister Salandra in 1916 that peasant soldiers would be granted land of their own on their return from the war. During the war the Italian Socialist Party and the Italian trades unions were brought into much closer co-operation than ever before, and together, in the last stages of the war, they were making claims for the eight-hour day. Inclining more to the workers than the employers in this case, the government had advised the adoption of grievance committees, though stopping far short of legalizing these; there was considerable resistance from employers.

There was no immediate revolution in Italy (the fascist take-over came in 1922), but the two major insurance acts listed in the table embody both the new ideology and the consequences of the participation and new-found power of labour.

France

French workers were free of the kind of direct military control which obtained in Italy. On the whole, it seems that they benefited from the compulsory arbitration and conciliation schemes which the government introduced in January 1917. In the same month minimum wage rates were established in all of the industries involved in direct government contracts. From practically the start of the war (5 August 1914) the French, in a highly practical way, introduced a system of fairly generous separation allowances, so that soldiers' wives might maintain themselves and their children. Schemes of public assistance, mainly in the form of the distribution of free meals, were also instituted.

In August 1914, in a development similar to those we have noted in other countries, French labour inspectors were instructed to interpret existing factory regulations less stringently in order that production might be increased. But as it became clear that employers, under the plea of national interest, were grossly abusing their employees, overworking them and evading safety regulations, it became necessary for the government to take much stronger action. Thus, through the exigencies of war, new regulations which gave French employees greater protection than ever before were introduced in 1915 and 1916. Furthermore, the problem of unemployment in the early days, together with the influx of refugees, forced the government to increase its provision of pensions.

During the war Socialist and trade union figures (particularly Léon Jouhaux) became quite influential in French government. But at the end of the war a right-wing ministry was elected, and the social reform record immediately after the war is not outstandingly impressive. The war experience had directed attention towards the importance of technical education, so in 1919 it became compulsory for working-class children, between the ages of 14 and 18 who had left school, as practically all of them had, to attend four to eight hours of compulsory technical education a week. From 1920 there was to be an extra two years of 'advanced primary education' which, again, was technical education. Very advanced ideas of comprehensive schooling were developed during the war, but in the post-war atmosphere of retrenchment and restoration of old values, nothing was done. Likewise, demands for economy rather reduced the effects of the 1922 Housing Act. The two really major pieces of social legislation (social insurance and housing) did not come until 1928.

Germany

Our understanding of what happened inside Germany during the First World War was enormously advanced by the pioneering study, published over thirty years ago, by the American historian Gerald Feldman, entitled *Army, Industry and Labor in Germany 1914–1918* (1966). More recently the overall effects of the war have been brilliantly analysed in Richard Bessel, *Germany After the War,* 1993) from which there are excerpts in your Reader. Feldman pointed out that it was just at the time of apparently intensified military control of the domestic economy, the time of the regime of Hindenburg and Ludendorff and the introduction of the Hindenburg programme in 1916, that organized labour was able to insist on substantial concessions for itself. The Hindenburg programme, in the words of Professor Wolfgang Mommsen:

envisaged the total mobilisation of all human as well as material resources for war production regardless of the economic consequences or the social costs which this would bring, in order to maximise the production of war materials and raise the recruitment levels once again. But this programme could no longer be implemented without the cooperation of the trade unions. So the trade unions were now officially acknowledged as an equal partner of the government in implementing these new stringent regulations intended to push the German war effort up to hitherto unknown levels. The unions succeeded in having those stipulations in the new legislation eliminated which restricted the free choice of the employer, that is to say the exploitation of the opportunities of a favourable labour market on the part of the workforce. It had become a widespread practice to change employers frequently in order to enhance one's wages, in particular in the engineering industries. Certainly neither the employers' nor the military authorities' attitude to the trade unions changed in substance; the old distrust of working-class organisations continued to rule labour relations even now. But the first step toward social partnership had been achieved. Henceforth the trade unions had to be consulted and indeed were given substantial influence in all legislation affecting wage and price policies. This certainly must have had a positive effect on the material well-being of the industrial workforce.

(Wolfgang Mommsen, 'The social consequences of World War I: the case of Germany', 1988, pp.33–4)

Germany appears a classic case of the participation effect benefiting the workers. In that the reactionary Empire collapsed, and was replaced by a new democratic government led by the Social Democrats, it also seems a classic case of the progressive effects of war as challenge to and test of existing institutions. However, the German experience was also a classic of the destructive effects of war, causing appalling shortages during and immediately after the war, and contributing to the catastrophic inflation of the early 1920s (also caused by deliberate economic and political actions – for a sketch of events see Roberts, pp.367–73). So we get a complex picture of ups and downs, gains and losses (again, in a way, a 'classic' of the difficulties in assessing the overall consequences of the war everywhere). The most significant 'up' was the Stinnes-Legien' Agreement of 15 November 1918, which reduced the working day to eight hours without any reduction in wages.

The Weimar Constitution in its social clauses, perfectly expressed the aspirations towards looking after the interests of the common man and his family. The point to note, however, is that the actual implementation of these aspirations was left very much to the individual states (a reformed Prussia was a leader in social reform; the smaller states often, apart from anything else, did not have the resources to implement social reforms) and the municipal authorities. In education, the influence of the clergy was finally removed from the state system and schooling was made compulsory and free for a period of at least eight years, with free and compulsory continuation school till the age of 18. Grants were made for poor children to go to middle and higher schools. Wartime and post-war upheavals forced government intervention in housing, which before the war had been regarded as essentially a private matter between landlord and tenant. Hence the nation-wide legislation of 1914, 1915, and 1918,

[handwritten margin note: only because Germany lost.]

and the Prussian Act of December 1919, which was followed by other measures between 1920 and 1923. Government intervention affected middle-class housing as well as working-class housing, so that between 1919 and 1932 four fifths of all new housing in Germany was in some degree publicly subsidized. Yet scarcity of housing remained a terrible problem for ordinary Germans – rent controls, for instance, probably discouraged private house building. As Richard Bessel, in another important work, sums up:

> Thus the Weimar state got itself deeply involved in yet another thankless task involving the welfare of millions of Germans. Because of the problems created by war, demobilization and inflation, the Weimar governments could not ignore the housing problem; but because of the scale and the limited resources available to deal with it, the Weimar governments could not solve the problem either.
>
> (Richard Bessel, 'State and society in Germany in the aftermath of the First World War', 1997, p.223)

Paul Weindling, in the same book ('Eugenics and the Welfare State during the Weimar Republic', p.134) writes: 'The Weimar Constitution marked the birth of the German welfare state, which assumed responsibility for the health and welfare of the family.' However, the rest of Weindling's important chapter brings out that while this may just about have been so in theory, in practice implementation was weak, particularly outside of Prussia, where the Prussian Health Council was established in 1921. The most important development in Germany was the growth of health and welfare clinics, founded between 1919 and 1921, but again most notably in Prussia.

The disruptions, injuries and deaths of war, had made pensions a pressing issue. Bessel (*Germany After the War*, p.275) describes the national and Pension Law of 28 April 1920, providing pensions for military persons and their dependants, as 'among the most important pieces of legislation enacted during the Weimar Republic'.

Great Britain

With respect to legislation actually enacted and welfare plans taken to their advanced stage, more was achieved in Britain during the war than in any of the other countries studied. Britain already had the unemployment insurance and health insurance schemes established in the 1911 Act, which came into operation in the year before the outbreak of war. A number of piecemeal developments were enforced by the war emergency. Then, in late 1916, a new Act, concerned as much with the disruptions and flux in domestic employment as with the military situation, extended the 1911 unemployment insurance provisions to cover all persons employed in trades relating to the war effort. On 26 February 1917 a more generous schedule of war disablement and widowhood pensions was introduced. Throughout 1917 discussions proceeded on the issues of education reform, housing reform, and the establishment of health reforms through the creation of a new Ministry of Health (formed in part out of the old Local Government Board). The education proposals were put before the House of Commons in August 1917, and the Act passed into law in the summer of 1918, some months before the end of the war. A universal minimum leaving age of 14 was to be enforced, and there were to be compulsory day continuation schools for those aged between 14 and 18 not undergoing suitable alternative instruction. All fees in public elementary schools were to be abolished. In a particular expression of the general concern for health, a Maternity and Child Welfare Act was passed just before the war ended. Under its provisions local authorities were to establish Mothers' Welfare Clinics (see Document II.6 in *Primary Sources 1: World War I*).

Exercise Why was there more in the way of social reform and welfare planning in Britain than in the other countries we have discussed? ■

Specimen answer and discussion This was due to a combination of factors, I would suggest. Britain was both a wealthier country than France, or even Germany, and while Britain's human losses were horrific enough, the cost of waging war high, and times of desperate crisis far from unknown, it suffered nothing like the deprivation of basic foodstuffs of Germany, nor the direct destruction of France. Britain had the most developed labour movement of all of the European countries, and, despite censorship and other wartime restrictions, the most open society during the war period, when discussion of problems of social reconstruction could carry on quite freely. More than that, Britain was a very unified society, and there was both a genuine feeling among the powerful and the wealthy that those who were contributing to national survival deserved to benefit, and a relatively dispassionate atmosphere in which to discuss remedies. In short, the various factors which earlier I suggested could make for social reform were at their strongest in Britain, whereas the negative factors which I referred to at the same time were at their weakest. (For Britain see Arthur Marwick, *The Deluge: British Society and the First World War,* 1991, and the selection of essays, *The First World War in British History*, edited by Stephen Constantine, Maurice W. Kirkby and Mary R. Rose, 1995.) □

Material conditions

Exercise Given what you already know about World War I, would you expect living standards generally to rise or fall over the war period, or would you expect them to rise in some cases and fall in others? Write a few sentences elaborating and explaining your answer. ■

Specimen answer and discussion Given the destructiveness of war, one would expect living standards overall to go down, though once again this would be much more pronounced in countries which were directly devastated than in those which were not. As is well known, ordinary soldiers are not well paid (though, for the destitute, if they were fit enough to be considered for active service, the army might well have supplied a level of subsistence above what they previously enjoyed). Within that broad picture, however, one might well expect living standards for certain individuals and groups to go up. Certain industrial workers in Germany, as we saw, were considered essential to the national war effort, and one might expect this also to be true of other groups of workers in other countries. As food shortages developed, those who continued to work on the land might well have hoped to cash in (this effect could be completely cancelled out if governments simply requisitioned food supplies, or if all the able-bodied workers in a family were in fact conscripted into the army). Above all (I hope you thought of this one) there would be opportunities (as Bill Purdue has already pointed out in his section on 'Social structure') for munitions manufacturers, army suppliers, etc. to make vast profits. On the other hand, for the ordinary fee- and salary-earning middle class, high wartime taxation, as well as inflation, might well have deleterious effects. □

I hope you thought of at least some of these points. You see how, taking what you already know about the war and applying a little common sense, you can come up with some sensible general answers. Of course, that is not enough in historical study. We need to go on now and acquire some precise information so that we can see which countries and which groups did worst during the war and which did best, and to see, particularly, where there were long-term changes in living standards as a result of the war experience.

Look now at Document II.14 in *Primary Sources 2: Interwar and World War II*, 'Wages and cost of living in the United Kingdom, Germany, France, Italy and Serbia, *c.*1910–1955'. Information of this sort is absolutely vital if we are to have any really serious discussion of the effects of war on standards of living. Calculating it is very complicated, and as you will see the information is presented in slightly different ways for the different countries. In some cases wages or 'earnings' are given in percentages, with 1913 being taken as 100 per cent (United Kingdom and France). In other cases they are given in the local currency (Germany – marks per annum, Italy – lire per day). In the case of all countries except Serbia, cost of living figures have been given in percentages, with 1913 again in every case being taken as 100 per cent. This is just my selection from the variety of statistics compiled by P. Scholliers and V. Zamagni and while not accurate in detail (the compilers refer to them as 'nominal' wages and 'nominal' earnings) they give us as reliable a comparative picture of broad changes in earnings as one could get from a relative handful of tables.

Exercise   In the case of the United Kingdom we have the additional column of 'real earnings', given in percentages. For Serbia we simply have what has been termed the 'food wage', given in dinar per day. Explain the first of these terms and have an intelligent guess at explaining the second. ■

Specimen answer and discussion   Real earnings are earnings once cost of living has been taken into account. As you will see, from the war onwards money earnings are high, but, of course, if we are to establish what is happening to living standards we have to take into account what money can buy. Thus real earnings is a much better measure. The same principle applies with regard to the 'food wage' in Serbia, though in a much more simplistic way. The 'food wage' is the wage with respect to the amount of basic foodstuffs it can buy. The implication is that Serbian wage earners would not be expecting to purchase much in the way of basic household fixtures ('mod. cons') let alone luxuries. □

With regard to France, Germany, and Italy we will have to do little calculations of our own, using the cost of living indices to help us see what real wages were as distinct from the money wages listed. In Italy agricultural employment continued to be more important than industrial employment so it is particularly helpful to have two sets of figures.

Once again, we must beware of *post hoc ergo propter hoc* arguments. All the movements in real wages after the war, obviously, were not necessarily caused by the war. They might be due to the particular policies of particular governments. They might be due to the particular economic problems of particular countries. Above all, they are bound to be related to the unemployment, depression, and inflationary crises which followed the war. In so far as these can all be related to the disruptions and destructiveness of war, then of course changes in real wages *can* also be attributed to the war. These problems are very much a concern of Book 3 of our course. Here, I shall refer to these statistics as I look at the individual countries.

Exercise   We must obviously bear in mind the differential effects of invasion and direct devastation. Neither Germany nor Austria-Hungary suffered more than relatively minor incursions (by Russia) on their territories prior to the armistice in November 1918. Yet there is a general geopolitical and strategic factor which meant that Germany and Austria-Hungary, and all the central and east European countries, were at a disadvantage compared with France, Britain, and even Italy, in access to necessary foodstuffs and war materials. What is this factor? If you are puzzled, look briefly at Map 3 in the *Maps Booklet.* ∎

Specimen answer   The central and eastern powers were 'closed in' and thus fairly easily blockaded, *and discussion*   and so cut off from access to potential overseas suppliers. Above all (and, of course, this was also a political factor, since the United States supported the western powers and joined them in 1917) they did not have access to American supplies. □

Exercise   Which of the three western countries would you expect to be best off, and which worst off? Explain why. ∎

Specimen answer   Britain was best off, because it had the greatest overseas possessions and *and discussion*   connections, the biggest merchant fleet, and the biggest navy. Italy was worst off, as a poor country with few overseas possessions, no Atlantic ports, and no great merchant fleet or navy; supplies from its allies had to come through the Mediterranean, or over the Alps. □

Now, having set up some broad comparative principles, I am going to give quick sketches of living conditions during the war in the various major countries.

Russia

From very early on unskilled labour was brought into the burgeoning war industries, but workers were often forced to take pay lower than the previously going rates and to work compulsory overtime. While there was more work for women and children, restrictions on night work, for example, were lifted, as we have already noted. For a short time skilled workers generally did well, but from the beginning of 1915 inflation wiped out any gains they made: by the second half of 1916 prices were at three times the level of 1913. As happened in so many countries (for instance Italy) there was terrible overcrowding in the towns, rents were high, and there were long queues for food and fuel. Sporadic attempts at rationing in the autumn of 1916 did not bring any sugar into the shops, but simply drove up black market prices. The rationing of flour and bread, introduced in Moscow on 20 February 1917, caused panic buying and further shortages. Poor nutrition and the upheavals of war meant that many parts of the country were afflicted by epidemics of scurvy and typhus. By October 1917 the price of bread was nearly three times the pre-war price, and the real wage of the unskilled worker had fallen by 57 per cent. The Provisional Government deliberately doubled the fixed grain price in the hope of stimulating deliveries; the result was that the actual market price rose by a further 75 per cent on top of the official price. The question of living standards is of importance in itself, but, naturally, it also relates to more dramatic political developments. As Hans Rogger sums up, 'shortages, black markets, and speculation grew apace and with them class hatreds and cleavages' (*Russia in the Age of Modernisation and Revolution 1881–1917*, 1983, p.281). Revolution, civil war, and 'internal war' caused further problems as you will see in Units 11–13.

The Balkans

I am now going to give you an encapsulated account (published in 1929) of one of the Balkan countries, leaving out the name of the people and the country, in the hope that you may be able to fill these in for yourselves.

> The most vivid picture left by the War in the memory of the —— is not of a cemetery of a blood-stained battlefield, although —— had given a formidable number of victims and had been the scene of the fiercest fighting. The most clear-cut impression of the —— campaign is the motley, pitiful spectacle of the 'bejaniwa', the endless, disorderly flight of fugitives muffled to the eyes, old men, women, children, on foot or in wooden carts patiently drawn by emaciated and exhausted oxen, driving in front of them some cattle and carrying on their backs or under their arms some chattels, the number and importance of which grew less with every stage of this removal which was always beginning again and never coming to an end. In short, the outstanding event of the —— war is not a great battle such as Verdun, but the Great Retreat, that retreat which led the —— into exile through Albania – the last after so many others following on each advance of the enemy.

Exercise   Fill in the blanks in the above quotation. ■

Specimen answer and discussion   Serbs, Serbia, Serbian, Serbian, Serbs. Romania would not have been a bad guess (Bulgaria, remember, being on the German side, was not invaded), but I think you already have enough information, together with the reference to Albania, to make it clear that the country is Serbia. Whenever one is tempted to talk of the social gains resulting from the experience of the war (as one may very properly do in certain instances) it is important to remember such extremes of suffering and deprivation as this. (The quotation is from Dragolioub Yovanovitch, *Les effets économiques et sociaux de la guerre en Serbie*, Paris, 1929, p.28). □

As you can see from Document II.14 (*Primary Sources 2*), food wages in Serbia, once we have them again from 1926 onwards, were never as high as they had been immediately before the war, and they go into decline, being particularly low after the great international economic crisis of 1931.

Exercise From what you already know about the basic differences between Austria and Hungary (geography, natural resources), in which of the two kingdoms do you think suffering and deprivation were greatest during the war? ■

Specimen answer
and discussion The basic difference is that Austria was more industrialized and more densely populated, while Hungary was more agricultural. The implications are not necessarily straightforward. To begin with, people in Austria seemed to benefit from Austria's greater industrial power, but as the war wore on (and this is the basic answer I am looking for) the balance swung to Hungary (because it could produce basic foodstuffs, while Austria had increasing difficulty in importing them). When Hungary closed its frontiers to Austria (this development could be used in support of the argument that wars put great stress upon contrived or 'artificial' political arrangements), making the transfer of food impossible, the differences sharpened. □

I have suggested that in some respects war can be likened to natural disaster. The presence of war, of course, does not rule out the possibility of real natural disasters. In central Europe, the harvest of 1917 was a particularly poor one (the war probably had a marginal, though not determining, effect in so far as it created great shortages of fertilizers, etc.).

From Austria come some of the most striking statistics of the destruction of war, and some of the most telling tales of its deprivations. In 1917–18 total production was down to 67 per cent of that of 1910; national income was down to 69 per cent. For even the most prized workers, inflation far outstripped wages (even in Austria there were signs of the participation effect: to begin with men called up for military service, but continuing in their jobs, received only soldiers' pay; this had to be changed in July 1916 when they were again given the going civilian rate). By 1917–18 it was impossible for most people to light or heat their rooms, street lighting was totally inadequate, and the trams stopped in the early evening. For a brief time it was almost better to be in the army, because food rations were more adequate there. But by the summer of 1918 there was real hunger in the army, and uniforms were in rags. One unit possessed uniforms only for men in the front line, so that men in reserve wore only underclothes. To save clothing materials it was recommended to civilians that their dead should be buried naked. Attempts were made to extract fats from horse-chestnuts and rats. Iron tyres were substituted for rubber ones, with no great benefit to road surfaces.

Our understanding of the sufferings inflicted on civilians in Austria, Germany and Belgium has been greatly increased by the series of specialist essays published in *The Upheaval of War: Family, Work and Welfare in Europe, 1914–1918* (1989), edited by Richard Wall and Jay Winter. Reinhard Sieder, in his chapter on 'Working-class family life in Vienna', makes effective use of interviews with men and women who were children during the war. These children had to queue throughout the freezing winter nights for potatoes, dripping or horsemeat, had to go begging for bread and for milk, had to go miles foraging for branches to burn. The chapter by Peter Scholliers and Frank Daelemans on 'Standards of living and standards of health in wartime Belgium' indicates that (apart from Serbia and possibly other parts of eastern Europe) the people of Belgium underwent the most terrible of deprivations. They, of course, did not participate in the war effort: they were simply occupied, and brutally exploited, by the Germans.

Unfortunately we do not have reliable real wage statistics for Austria. Workers and peasants did strengthen their bargaining position; they were benefited by social reform. But, on the whole, any gains were wiped out by the destructive effects of war and the economic depression which followed (see Units 10–12 and Book 3).

Germany

Up to the armistice, conditions were never as bad in Germany as they were in Austria. They became substantially worse with the 'turnip winter' of 1917, when because of the shortage of potatoes and grain, turnips became a staple foodstuff. Deprivation was very serious by the summer of 1918. The salaried middle class probably suffered most. Relatively, skilled workers did quite well, though in absolute terms their living conditions probably declined from what they had been in pre-war days. Some industrialists made immense profits.

Exercise Turn to Document II.5 in *Primary Sources 1: World War I*, 'Memorandum of the Neukölln Municipal Council' (Neukölln is a suburb of Berlin), and read the entire document. You will find, I think, that it gives a graphic impression of chaos, discontent, near-starvation, and illegality. Concentrate now on the section beginning 'This panorama ...' to '... alleviating popular discontent', and answer the following questions:

1   The official system is clearly very inefficient. What phrase does the Neukölln Town Council use to describe it?

2   What crime are suppliers committing?

3   What illegality are town councils being led into? ■

Specimen answers 1   'A mixed system of regulated and unregulated trade'.
and discussion
2   Extortion.

3   Breaking the maximum prices laid down by the government in order to feed their own people. □

Exercise You should now read the extract from *Germany After the First World War* by Richard Bessel, in the Course Reader. Write a short paragraph teasing out what in the previous section are called the 'ups and downs', the gains and losses with respect to living standards in Germany. Do you get the impression that the industrial workforce as a whole made substantial gains? ■

Specimen answer During the war those in war-related industries did reasonably well, women
and discussion workers did relatively well, but generally real incomes fell. There was an equalizing effect in that differentials between industrial workers and middle-class employees were reduced. Food shortages had adverse effects on health as well as morale. However, demobilization, thanks largely to the threat of revolutionary action, was accompanied by a substantial rise in real wages ('bribery through wage concessions'); true to the 'ups and downs' pattern this was short-lived. Still, the inflationary boom stimulated employment and benefited skilled workers. There were even renewed job opportunities for

women workers. Then came the massive 'down': catastrophic inflation in the summer of 1923 wiped out such gains as had been made. Bessel concludes: 'When the demobilization period formally came to an end on 31 March 1924, the labour movement was in retreat, real wages were substantially below pre-war levels, and unemployment was at dizzying heights.' □

Italy

You have already acquired some understanding of the different positive and negative factors that affected Germany and Italy. Italy could import in a way that Germany could not, but on the other hand it had had, unlike Germany, a long-standing need to import both wheat and coal. The relatively greater deprivation suffered in Italy is, I think, well expressed in the cost of living indices. Taking 1913 as 100, prices in 1918 were at 228 in Germany, and 264 in Italy. Italy was subject to particularly severe disruption at the beginning of the war, when hundreds of thousands of workers who had followed the normal pattern of immigration returned in haste to the homeland, thus greatly swelling unemployment. At certain points in the war some districts were totally without bread for days on end. Real wages (1913 = 100) dropped steadily to 64.6 in 1918.

Yet if we look at the figures in Document II.14 (*Primary Sources 2*), and do some quick calculations, we can see that (as a result of labour's enhanced bargaining position, and perhaps even general good-will at the end of the war) they have crept slightly ahead of the cost of living in 1919, with occasional slight rises in real wages thereafter. And even in 1918, real agricultural wages are slightly higher than those of 1913.

France

For those in the occupied zones, conditions were about as bad as could be found anywhere else in Europe, but for France as a whole living conditions during the war were second only to those in Britain, and it is possible that in some rural areas standards of life, or at least of food consumption, were higher than anywhere among equivalent classes in Britain. Jean Jacques Becker, in an important study which is essentially built up from a series of local studies based on reports on the war situation deposited in local archives by leading local personalities, has written that, at the outset of war, 'The income of many rural families did not fall appreciably with the departure of the men; in the urban working-class, by contrast, it was enough for the breadwinner to be called up for the family income to disappear'. However, he then points out that separation allowances, a moratorium on the payment of rents, the fact that there was one mouth less to feed, all helped to keep living standards at least to acceptable levels (Jean Jacques Becker, *The Great War and the French People*, 1985; see p.21 in particular, and chapter 1 in general).

Documents II.7 and II.8 in *Primary Sources 1: World War I* provide further detail on living conditions in France during the war. However, quotations in Becker relating to various parts of France show that while there were upsets, truly serious deprivation of the Austrian type did not exist. The first quotations relate to Brittany:

Fresh food supplies did pose many problems in rural areas, as a few examples show: thus in August 1918, at Plouha, people had to queue for an hour to obtain 'a chunk of hard bread, black and indigestible not even fit for the beasts'. There was a bread shortage at the same time at Paimpol. 'People queue outside the bakers for hours on end.' At Ploubazalnec, bread was scarce in June 1918, and at times customers had to queue for half a day outside the baker's door, but potatoes never ran short. Some items such as sugar, paraffin or chocolate could be difficult to obtain at times, but most agreed that supplies of essential foodstuffs were almost normal. As one witness put it, no single product was ever totally unobtainable.

(p.119)

Does that mean that there were no more poor people? The records often make this claim, while not holding that everyone had become rich. To use an expression of the time, 'pauperism had disappeared'. Few or no families were in want, said one reporter; most of the poor had received relief. There were no truly indigent families left in the commune, no needy people during the war. The schoolmaster of Yvignac was not alone in thinking that while there was certainly adversity, there was, on the whole, little financial hardship.

(pp.122–3)

In rural areas, it might make a difference whether you were a peasant paying out wages, or a labourer receiving them. Sometimes the very rise in wages meant that casual labourers couldn't get jobs, because employers couldn't pay them.

... the shortage of hands had evidently increased the cost of labour. In one commune, domestics who had been paid 250 francs for six months received 400 francs at the beginning of 1916, while labourers were paid 2.50 to 3.00 francs a day, plus their keep. 'Agriculture, which had suffered little during the first year of the war, suffers a great deal now.' The number of uncultivated fields increased, in one commune by at least a quarter, and the harvest of 1916 was judged to be two-thirds of a good normal harvest, the yield having dropped even further for lack of fertilizer.

(p.126)

... some casual labourers did find it difficult to obtain work, not for lack of vacancies, but because of the very high wages that all hands now fetched. As for local government officials, they had to face inflation with salaries that scarcely altered.

(p.129)

The statistics in II.14 (*Primary Sources 2*) show industrial wages falling behind the cost of living throughout the war and right up to 1921. Thereafter, real wages improve from 1922 to 1925, when they again fall behind the cost of living, before making a recovery from 1929 right up to the outbreak of the Second World War. There is at least some evidence here of the enhanced power of labour brought about by the war experience having positive long-term effects.

United Kingdom

All three of the most authoritative commentators on the British experience during World War I, Jay Winter, Bernard Waites and Alastair Reid, are agreed that for the working class as a whole living standards rose during World War I, and that the rise was particularly significant for those at the bottom end – those who fell into the residuum of pre-war times (J. M. Winter, *The Great War and the British People*, 1986; Bernard Waites, *A Class Society at War: England 1914–18*, 1988; and Alastair Reid, 'World War I and the working class in Britain', 1988). Shortages of various commodities affected all classes in some degree, but as far as real income is concerned, no single class suffered seriously from the war. Older middle-class interests may have suffered marginally: there was a considerable expansion in white-collar jobs, which presumably meant that there was recruitment from the working class. Some landed families suffered severely from paying death duties several times as members of the family were killed at the front, and tenant farmers as a whole did relatively well compared with landowners.

The statistics in II.14 show us that overall real earnings (that is to say not reflecting the formerly worst-paid workers who were actually doing relatively well) fell during the war, but from 1918 onwards real wages show an almost continuous slight rise. The big problem, of course, was unemployment, but for those in work there is evidence to suggest that as a result of the war experience the bargaining position of British workers had greatly strengthened.

Conclusion

The equation is a complex one. Wartime participation played a part in strengthening the hands of workers and peasants, and in places wartime demand played a part in stimulating new industries. If we take social reforms into account there were gains for the working class (as long as they were not victims of long-term unemployment), but often, because of the severely damaged economies discussed by Bill Purdue in the section 'Economic performance and theory', actual wages were lower than they had been before the war, and where there was protracted unemployment, conditions of the severest deprivation existed. On the whole Bill Purdue, in his discussion on 'Social structure', suggests that in the long term the working class did not make gains. I would, however, refer you to what I said about the growth of mass society and the attempt to placate 'the common man'.

Customs and behaviour

Exercise   1   Is it reasonable to expect that there would be changes in customs and behaviour due to the war experience? Answer either way, and give reasons for your answer.

2   In which countries – relatively developed ones like Britain, France and Germany, or relatively undeveloped ones like the Balkan countries – do you think there was more possibility for change in customs and behaviour, whether brought about by the war or not? Give reasons for your answer. ■

Specimen answer   1   The argument for expecting change in customs and behaviour would be
and discussion   based on the upheavals of war, the disruptions to normal patterns of behaviour – the movement, for example, of women into new activities – all the features, in short, of 'society at war' not present in 'society not at

war'. The argument against would maintain that customs and behaviour are determined by long-term economic and industrial developments, by national traditions, etc.

2   This question could also very reasonably be answered in two opposite ways. If it is argued that customs and behaviour depend on economic, and particularly technological, development – as, for instance, the development of a mass consumer society, or of films, gramophone records and radio – then one would expect the most striking developments (whether related to the war or not) to take place in the more advanced countries. On the other hand, it could be argued that since the more advanced countries already had many of the aspects we associate with twentieth-century lifestyles, it would be in the backward countries that far more scope for extensive change ('catching-up', as it were) was to be found.

What I am going to suggest is that in both types of country there are, of course, long-term forces making for change in customs and behaviour, but that such forces are more apparent in the advanced countries; that within the context of long-term change, the war did indeed have identifiable effects in both sorts of country; that limited but important changes, which can be related to the war experience, are apparent in the developed countries, but that, given their relative level of backwardness, the really striking shake-up, as it were, comes in the less developed countries, where the cataclysmic effect of war was felt most strongly.

There is no absolute end to the argument as between the effects of war and the effects of longer-term trends. My argument with regard to the less-developed countries would essentially be that because of the disruptions of war, because of the way individuals were projected into new situations and brought into contact with foreign influences, predominantly peasant societies began to adopt some of the customs of urban societies. Now one could immediately argue that there was, in any case, a long-term trend towards urbanization, and that this would have happened at some time anyway. So we come back to the point that when talking about the influence of war we are talking about how things came about at the precise time and in the precise way that they did. To derive a general idea of the sorts of changes taking place in a peasant society over the war period, I want you to read Document II.9 (*Primary Sources 1*), which is an extract from a book written in the late 1920s by the Yugoslav historian we have already quoted, Yovanovitch, for the Carnegie series on the social and economic history of the war. □

Exercise   1   Putting together all the information you have on this document, assess its value, its strengths and weaknesses, and its reliability for the historian as a primary source for the effects of World War I on peasant society.

2   For your own use (I am giving no specimen answer for this one) note down the main changes identified in the document. ■

Specimen answer   You might well query first of all whether this can properly be described as a
and discussion   primary source. It is, as I have made clear, an account written by a historian ten

years after the war. However, it is written by a Serbian Yugoslav with direct, intimate knowledge of his own society. Much of the style of the book (though it might be difficult for you to determine that on the basis of this extract and the one I quoted earlier) is in the form of direct personal testimony. But the crucial point which I hope you got was the date, which shows that this is an account written up later. That, in one sense, is a weakness, yet on the other hand one could regard this favourably as the mature reflections of someone who has had time to see the changes of the war period working themselves out. Remember, though, that the author is a Yugoslav with direct experience of the society he is describing; but he is an academic, and therefore might be a little detached from the realities of peasant society. As a historian writing about the social and economic effects of the war he might be inclined to exaggerate. I think myself that his account is a little too precise and cut-and-dried, too eager to make an academic point. Nevertheless, I think we have to see this as a valuable, and on the whole reliable, account of someone who knows what he is talking about. It refers, of course, specifically to Serbia, and in that sense cannot be taken as an ideal source for other peasant societies. However, within the limits to which we have to work on this course, I think we could say that this source gives us a fair idea of the sorts of changes in east European peasant mentalities that were brought about by the cataclysmic upheavals of World War I. □

When it comes to questions of possible changes in customs and behaviour in the more developed countries we find that there are overlaps with three of our other headings: popular culture, the role and status of women, and, with respect to institutions and values, the family. Let me list here the main areas that I think would be worth exploring:

1   sexual attitudes and behaviour, the roles of women, and the nature and status of the family;

2   respect for authority, religious observance, etc.;

3   recreational activities: cinemas, public dance halls, radio, etc.;

4   fashion, dress, etc.

It is in this very subject area of customs and behaviour that film and other cultural artefacts have great importance as sources. In briefly developing these three points I am going to confine myself to a few further generalizations, and one exercise based on film material.

Sexual attitudes and behaviour, roles of women, position of the family

It is not unreasonable to postulate, and there is a fair amount of supporting evidence, that the frantic conditions of war, the disturbances to family life, the taking of young men out of the home environment, and the doom-laden partings of sweethearts, led to a loosening of traditional constraints upon sexual behaviour. A Royal Commission on Venereal Diseases had been set up in Britain just before the war; but in the general wartime atmosphere of national crisis, of the need to face realities, to call a spade a spade, the whole subject was discussed much more openly than it would have been in pre-war days when the Commission reported in 1916. There was also much frank discussion of the plight of unmarried girls, pregnant by soldier boyfriends serving at the front. From the later nineteenth century onwards, contraceptives had been quite widely used within respectable middle-class marriages; during the war working-class soldiers were issued with them as protection against venereal diseases. I think it would be reasonable to say that the upheavals of World War I brought quite a sudden and widespread diffusion of contraceptive methods throughout the main countries engaged in warfare. But we must not underestimate the continuing power of traditional delicacies and sensitivities: contraception was still a topic that could not be publicly talked about.

As I have had to keep stressing, it is very difficult to establish whether certain things which happened during, or at the end of, the war could only have happened because of the war, or would have happened anyway. My own view is that the new wartime frankness (relative, of course) helped to make possible the publication in March 1918 of *Married Love* (subtitled *A New Contribution to the Solution of Sex Difficulties*) by Marie Stopes, and definitely provided the circumstances in which the book was sold and circulated widely; indeed, it was a best-seller. Such was the response from readers that by November 1918 Stopes published another best-seller, *Wise Parenthood*, which concentrated on the question of birth control, only briefly discussed in *Married Love*.

During 1923 Marie Stopes achieved celebrity (and notoriety) when she brought a libel action against a Catholic doctor: sales of *Married Love* practically doubled, from 241,000 to 406,000. Now the new (relative) openness about sexuality joined hands with a significant new recreational activity of the time: the British film company, Samuelson's, invited Marie Stopes to collaborate in the making of a fairly traditional little romantic story which, however, was to be entitled *Married Love* and would contain elements of causes close to Marie Stopes's heart, the advocacy of eugenics (that is to say, creating a fitter race) and birth control. Not altogether surprisingly, the film ran into various censorship difficulties: some cuts were insisted upon, and the title had to be changed to *Maisie's Marriage*, but it did have a successful commercial distribution. *Maisie's Marriage* was, naturally, a silent film, so much of the message is carried in the printed captions or 'intertitles'. The opening caption reads:

> Not ours to preach nor yet to point a moral – yet if, in the unfolding of our story, the thought that comforts, helps or guides, then are our efforts doubly paid.

We start off in Maisie's horribly deprived family background.

> The Burrows family live in Slumland but their prototypes dwell in all our cities – wherever our artificial civilization has planted its weeds, where the struggle for existence is hard and ruthless and a narrow dogma of our disciplined beliefs turn life and the joys of living into meaningless phrases.

Maisie is courted by a fireman, Dick Reading, but, fearing the endless pregnancies which have destroyed her mother, Maisie rejects him, though he has brought to her 'dim tremulous thoughts of waking womanhood'. Maisie is thrown out of her slum home by her brutish father, attempts suicide by jumping into the River Thames, is rescued, but gaoled for the crime of attempted suicide (a law repealed only in 1961). She becomes a maidservant in the family of Mr Sterling, her rescuer. From Mrs Sterling, who has three lovely children, Maisie learns that she can enjoy married love without the fearful consequences which had driven her apart from Dick. Maisie, alone in the house with the Sterling children, is visited by her degenerate brother, seeking to extort money from her.

Fire breaks out, and Maisie is rescued by fireman Dick. Happily reunited, Maisie and Dick get married, with a guard of honour provided by Dick's colleagues.

Exercise   I want you now to watch item 8 on video-cassette 1, which is the sequence from *Maisie's Marriage* in which Mrs Sterling makes her revelation to Maisie. When you have viewed this clip, answer the following questions:

1   How clear do you find the explanation of contraception?

2   What conclusions do you draw about public attitudes towards contraception?

3   Apart from the fact that the sequence is perhaps as much about eugenics as contraception, what other, totally different message do you receive from this sequence?

4   What, finally, is the significance of the film with respect to changing customs and behaviour? ■

Specimen answers   1   The explanation is extremely obscure. One could scarcely be surprised
and discussion   that British people, or many of them, continued to be extremely muddled in their ideas about contraception. One wonders if young men went around dreading that young ladies might suddenly produce a pair of secateurs.

2   Obviously public standards demanded the utmost delicacy and restraint in the discussion of this topic to the point of complete obscurity.

3   The other message, surely, is of romantic love, but, in all the circumstances, particularly the association with Marie Stopes, it is romantic love in which sexuality is very strongly stressed.

4   The film is significant in that it is broaching the topic of birth control, and broaching it through film, itself a symbol of cultural change. Perhaps more importantly, it strongly, if obliquely, focuses on the physical aspect of romantic love. □

With regard to the roles of women, wartime necessity meant large numbers of women being projected into entirely new experiences. James McMillan, who is generally hostile to the idea that the war had any significant effects on the position of French women, does accept that unchaperoned young French women were subjected in hospital work and elsewhere to experiences from which they would have been completely shielded in pre-war years (James R. McMillan, *Housewife or Harlot*, 1981). Generally, in the new situation of war, the institution of the chaperone had to be dropped.

Respect for authority, religious observance, etc.

Traditional close-knit communities were disrupted by the war, with young men going out into the big, wide and often irreligious world. Pastors and clerics did their cause little good by enlisting God and religion in support of their own country's military effort. The very havoc of war made many doubt the existence of God. True, there was a long-term trend away from religion, yet the war was significant in bringing together in concentrated form a whole complex of reasons for rejecting religion. There was a tendency, too, to blame the very fact

of war, and its attendant horrors on the older generations in power on the eve of
the war.

Recreational activities

The era of the erection of huge custom-built cinemas was during the immediate
post-war years. During the war cinema had been exploited by governments for
patriotic purposes and thus tended to gain respectable middle-class, in addition
to the previous working-class, audiences. The immediate post-war years were
also the era of erecting large public dance halls. The notion of the public, as
distinct from the private, dance, gained respectability during the war when so
many young female war workers were, as never before, out in public on their
own. The new rhythms upon which the newly popular dances were based
originated in America before the war, but as with cinema and so many other
developments, it was the conditions of war which gave them wider currency in
Europe.

Here I have been speaking largely of cultural change. When it comes to radio,
the crucial development was a commercial and technological one – the
enormous expansion in the production of radio valves in order to meet the
needs of wartime aviation. This capacity having been created, there had to be an
outlet, and that outlet came in the form of general broadcasting of news and
entertainment.

Fashion and dress

Let's approach dress, etc. with an exercise.

Exercise   1   What would be the best source for seeing how dress changed between
                    the pre-war and the post-war years?

              2   What were the most striking changes (a) for women, and (b) for men? ■

Specimen answers   1   Fashion items in the press might be an obvious answer, but I think the
and discussion   best source would be film material, for that shows what people actually
                            wore, rather than what fashion writers said people ought to wear
                            (photographs could obviously be useful, if one had a range of them – the
                            trouble with individual photos is that one cannot always be sure how
                            representative they are).

              2 (a)   For women the most obvious change was the advent of the short skirt.
                       Now, once again it is true that fashion was changing, and dress lengths
                       were very slightly shortening in the period after 1905 (associated
                       particularly with the French designer Paul Poiret). Nonetheless both
                       shortage of materials and the need for freedom of movement among
                       women engaged in war work, were important developments during the
                       war. I believe also that post-war fashion can be seen very much as
                       representing the desire to make a break from the bad old restrictive stuffy
                       world, and to put a particular emphasis on youth as the only hope for the
                       future.

              2 (b)   For men there was a move towards informality (though, as with birth
                       control, this is not to be exaggerated). □

Role and status of women

In my view, the winning of political rights remains absolutely central to all other improvements in the role and status of women – that certainly was the view of feminists at the time. Actually, I believe, in face of a certain current orthodoxy that feminists won the vote through their own unaided efforts that two considerations deserve much more exploration by historians than they have recently received.

1 That political and military events have been important in the granting of votes to women (obviously World War I is the big example, but I have other events in mind too).

2 Often women have gained the vote as a product of a general democratic ideology which also brought the vote to *men* who had previously not had it.

If you look at Table 7–10.3 you'll see that only in Finland and Norway did *any* European women have the vote in 1914. But these countries were *political* oddities. Norway had only recently gained independence from Sweden, the hegemonic power in Scandinavia. Finland was a duchy within the Russian Empire, with a political class which spoke Swedish, not Finnish. The Russian revolution of 1906 swept through the duchy, and on a wave of democratic and nationalist sentiment a unicameral assembly was set up and the vote given to *all* Finns over 24 – the *political* reasoning was that the more voters there were the stronger the assembly would be against Russian tsarism. In Norway, one year later, the vote was given to all men and women over 25, possessed of a small property qualification (abolished in 1913). The political argument was that women voters would strengthen the nationalist cause against Sweden. You can already see the relevance of all this to my second consideration. More on that will emerge as we move on.

I want you to consider the following table very carefully; then I want you to look at Document I.13 'The Treaty of Versailles', carefully reading the following: Clause four of the annexe to article 88; Article 91, the first five sentences; Article 427, *seventh* clause.

Exercise   What information from the table *suggests* that women *may* have made gains due to the war?

What information suggests that they have not made gains? I say 'suggests': what are the arguments against the evidence here being regarded as conclusive? ■

Table 7-10.3 Votes for women (and men!)

Dates of introduction of votes for women, and of universal male suffrage.

	Pre-war (over 21 unless otherwise stated)		War and post-war (over 21 unless otherwise stated)	
	Women	Men	Women	Men
Finland	1906 (over 24)	1906 (over 24)	1919	1919
Norway	1907 (over 25)	1907 (over 25)	1919 (over 23)	1919 (over 23)
Denmark		*	1915 (over 25) 1920	1915 (over 25) 1920
Russia		*	1917	1917
UK		1884 (but had to fulfill residential qualification)	1918 (over 30)	1918
Austria		1907	1919	1919
Germany		1871	1919	1919
Czechoslovakia		† (1907)	1919	1919
Netherlands		*	1919	1917
Poland		†	1919	1919
Bulgaria		*	1920	1921
Sweden		1909 (over 24)	1921	1921
Spain		*	1931	
France		1848	1945	
Italy		*	1946	1919
Switzerland		*	1971	
Belgium		*	1948	1920

* limited male franchise based on property.

† part of one of pre-war empires.

Specimen answers and discussion   From the table we can see that in a large number of countries women did get the vote during or immediately after the war. The suggestion that there is a connection with the war experience is reinforced by the fact that in two of the most conspicuously neutral countries, Spain and Switzerland, women did not get the vote until much later. On the other hand: (a) the fact they got the vote in Finland and Norway well before the war, in the neutral country Denmark during the war, and the other neutral country Sweden soon after the war, might well suggest that the war was not a critical factor; an argument (b) reinforced by the fact that in Italy and France, both deeply involved in the war, women did not get the vote till after the Second World War. However – to put forward my own particular views – the argument does not have to be that war is essential before women get the vote, but rather that where there was strong resistance to women getting the vote (as in the major European countries) war could help to overcome that resistance. In both France and Italy the lower houses of parliament voted for women to get the franchise; it was the conservative upper houses which ultimately rejected the proposals. It is noteworthy that Sweden took longer than the other industrialized countries, and it *could* be argued that Sweden was simply conforming to an ideology which had already been established elsewhere by the belligerent countries.

The fact that universal male suffrage, in many cases, only came at around the same time fits in with my earlier arguments about the belief at the end of the war that the interests of the common man must be catered to. One can, I think, make a convincing argument that the *participation* of both the common man and the common woman in the national efforts resulted in women as a sex, and those men previously excluded from the franchise, all getting the vote.

We must beware (to come to my second question) of *post hoc propter hoc*: but I do think a pretty good case can be made on the basis of the close clustering of the enfranchisement of women at the end of the war, and the participation argument. But I'll look at things more closely shortly, with respect to certain individual countries.

With regard to the Versailles Treaty we see women getting equal voting rights with men (this was true in all of the various plebiscites). We also see the aspiration that women should get equal pay – important, I think, that this should be stated though of course it remained largely an aspiration (it was of most effect where women moved into professional jobs – in medicine say – hitherto almost totally monopolized by men). On the negative side, though, when it comes to choosing nationality women were to be governed by their husbands; and as was to remain the custom for another fifty years or more the pronoun 'he' is used when we would now feel it proper to say 'he/she'.

The role and status of women is the area in which the debates over the effects of war on society have raged most furiously. ☐

It is worth lingering a little longer on the case of France. In many countries, as we have just seen, votes for women came as integral parts of new democratic constitutions. And in Britain, the granting of votes to women (over the age of 30, and with a small property qualification – both limitations being removed in 1928 without any controversy at all) was an integral part of an act giving the vote to that two-fifths of the male population over 21 who had not previously had the vote – the reform of the male suffrage provided the *opportunity* for women to be included, but the arguments very definitely were that women had earned the vote by their contribution to the war effort.

Feminist historians have generally taken the line that women's position in society did not change very much anyway (remember 'the Double Helix' briefly mentioned when I discussed 'Gender' in Unit 3), and that where it did this was due either to long-term economic and technological trends, or to the militant activism of women themselves, or both. There are three points here of very great weight, which deserve your full consideration. I am going to make the case (which you are entirely free to reject, particularly if you do some more reading on your own) that there were some changes in the role and status of women, and that the particular way in which these changes came about, and the timing of them, can be attributed to the war experience.

What is not in doubt is that, while the war was being waged, the enlistment of large numbers of men in the various armies meant that women took on new kinds of employment, or entered into paid employment for the first time. Two questions pressed by those who argue that the war had no significant positive effects on the status of women, must be considered:

1   How permanent were these changes in employment? In general, the statistics show (see Table 7–10.4 and Figure 7–10.1, which apply to Britain) that while there was a considerable expansion in women's employment during the war years, once the war was over the figures were not very different from those of pre-war years (this is not universally true, since, as we shall see, there was permanent expansion in certain countries, France, for example). The general conclusion must therefore be that, as far as working-class employment was concerned, there were not (apart from the exceptions) significant changes for women. However, the figures do suggest that in certain important professional occupations, from which women had very largely been excluded before the war, there were long-term changes, particularly in the legal profession, accountancy, and medicine. The actual numbers involved, of course, are small, and it is very much a matter of personal assessment what weight one gives to them.

Table 7–10.4 Some broad census data (England and Wales only)

	Total population	Total females	Over 10 years	Total females occupied	Married	Widowed	Females per 1,000 males	Females per 1,000 males in age group 20–45
1901	32,527,843	16,799,230	13,189,585	4,171,751	917,509		1,068	
1911	36,070,492	18,624,884	14,357,113	4,830,734	680,191	411,011	1,068	1,095
			Over 12 years					
1921	37,886,699	19,811,460	15,699,805	5,065,332	693,034	425,981	1,096	1,172
			Over 14 years					
1931	39,952,377	20,819,367	16,419,894	5,606,043	896,702	389,187	1,088	

(Source: Arthur Marwick, *Women at War 1914–1918*, 1977, Table 1, p.166)

The Bessell extract in your Reader gives a clear impression of the ups and downs in the employment of German women during and after the war. No substantial gains it would appear (apart from the vote), but a certain amount of new experience.

2   The second question can be phrased in two rather different ways:

(a) How different was this employment of women in wartime? Those who argue against the war having any significance, point out that industrial drudgery had been the lot of many women since at least the onset of industrialization.

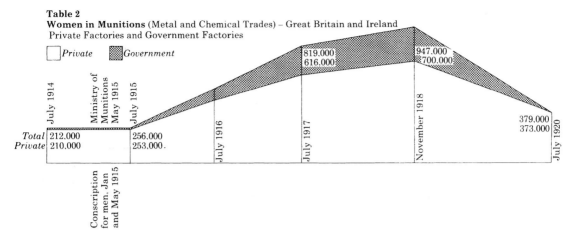

Table 2
Women in Munitions (Metal and Chemical Trades) – Great Britain and Ireland
Private Factories and Government Factories

Figure 7–10.1 Women in munitions (metal and chemical trades) Great Britain and Ireland, private and government factories
Source: Arthur Marwick, *Women at War 1914–1918,* 1977, Table 2, p.166.

(b) Economic and technological change was leading anyway to the employment of women: wasn't the war simply an exaggeration of this trend, and in so far as it did continue in the post-war years wasn't it just part of that trend, and unrelated to the war?

These are questions I want you to bear in mind in looking at some of the evidence.

More generally, the point is made that the basic relationships between men and women did not change, the family continued to be regarded as a fundamental institution, and woman's role as child-bearer and child-rearer continued to be stressed. This is undoubtedly true. The argument really centres on whether within that unchanging framework, women did also have a greater role outside the home, did expect some sharing of roles within the home, did value themselves more highly, and were prepared to speak up for themselves more than formerly. Some feminists have joined with historians such as myself in arguing that working in new situations and supporting the national effort in wartime did raise women's consciousness, and made them more prepared to speak up for themselves. This is a further point I would like you to keep in mind as you look at some of the primary and secondary sources.

Exercise   After completing the reading/viewing itemized below, and recalling also any points I have already made regarding changes in customs and behaviour relating to women, note down:

1   what the source is, how useful and reliable you take it to be, and what peculiar features it has;

2   how far the source supports the general view that the war did bring positive changes in the role and status of women, and how far it supports the opposite.

***Extract (a) by
historian Paul
Smith***

Suffragist-feminists looked forward to the end of hostilities with eager anticipation. The contribution of both feminist élites and the broad mass of women led them to feel that capturing the vote was a real possibility. As early as March 1917, the review *La Renaissance politique* published a series of articles edited by Suzanne Grinberg, which quoted the opinions of leading political and literary figures on the future role of women in French politics and society. All believed that the part played by women in the war effort not only merited some reward in itself, but demonstrated that women were as developed morally and intellectually as men ... Henri Robert [a leading barrister] ... went so far as to proclaim that the war would be 'the women's '89' [1789, date of the French Revolution]. Grinberg herself believed that the war had converted enough members of the Senate [the upper chamber in the French Parliament] to women's suffrage to ensure a success, despite warnings from '... prudent friends' ...

The political enfranchisement of women aged 30 and over in Britain gave a tremendous boost to morale amongst suffragists in France. Surely the Senate could not be more conservative than the House of Lords? ... The majority of the members of the French Senate had undergone their political education during the struggles between the Church and State ... These men were convinced that if women were given the vote they would use it to hand over power to the priest party, since the majority of women were still educated by the Church ...

The proposal on the table at the end of the war, the Dussaussoy bill, envisaged women voting and standing in municipal and *cantonal* [regional] elections ... Suffragists accepted this as a necessary first step towards full political equality, arguing that, after all, even in Britain, the franchise had not been extended to women in equal measure with men. (The equal status of women under the new Weimar German constitution was not regarded as an acceptable example.) ... The question seemed to have been resolved, however, by a shift in opinion in the Chamber of Deputies [the lower house in the French parliament] in May 1919.

In an act of patriotic self-denial, the suffragists had suspended their activities at the outbreak of war. It was male politicians who re-opened the issue from 1916, when Maurice Barrès suggested the introduction of 'le suffrage des morts' giving the votes of dead soldiers to their widows. Talk of rewarding women's war effort with the vote provoked Émile Magniez (Independent, Somme) to table a municipal suffrage bill in early 1917 ...

Unexpectedly [in May 1919], veteran Socialist Jean Bon proposed an amendment extending the bill to include legislative [i.e. parliamentary] elections. The Chamber accepted Bon's proposal, and adopted a measure 'which makes applicable to all French people, without distinction of sex, the laws and regulations regarding the vote and eligibility to stand'. The margin by which the vote passed was remarkable: 329 votes to 95, a ratio of nearly four to one. On the whole the opposition to the Bon bill was on the Center-Left, in the Radical Party, with some Republican Socialist also against the proposal.

Suffragist-feminists were in jubilant, if cautious, mood following the pleasantly unexpected turn of events in the Chamber. The Senate was an entirely different prospect and they knew it ...

Generally conservatives were in favour of the vote, believing the Radicals' propaganda that women would vote for them. On the other hand, many were in favour of the family vote [i.e. that the husband voted on behalf of himself and his wife and family] ...

The onset of legislative elections and the 1920 renewal of the Senate gave opponents a potential shield to hide behind. It should be understood that the Senate met infrequently: 3 times a week, and for only 6 months in a year, in the Spring and Autumn ... The backlog of legislation caused by the end of the war meant that it was not difficult to procrastinate over women's suffrage ...

In late 1921 the Senate had finally and unwillingly ratified the government's policy of re-establishing diplomatic links with the Vatican ... The Radicals who voted against the Vatican embassy in the Senate in December 1921 formed the core of the opponents of women's suffrage a year later. Of the 123 senators who voted against the embassy, 107 later opposed votes for women. This suggests that for over two-thirds of the anti-suffragist majority in November 1922 anti-clericalism was a decisive factor ...

The Senate never directly considered the women's suffrage bill. Under the Third Republic it was traditional to hold a debate of general principles before getting down to a specific proposal ... Suffice to say that the opponents of women's suffrage ... employed a mixture of anti-clericalism, social conservatism, insult, misogyny, and the 'France does not need to learn anything from the Anglo-Saxons' – kind of argument, to dissuade their colleagues ... On 21 November 1922 the Senate rejected discussion of the bill by twenty-two votes (156–134).

[The bill was returned to the Chamber, but then never discussed again. Smith explains the important institutional factor that it was customary for the Chamber of Deputies not to challenge decisions of the Senate.]

(Paul Smith, *Feminism and the Third Republic: Women's Political and Civil Rights in France 1918–1945*, 1996, pp.104–16)

Extract (b):
The article on 'Italian peasant women' by Anna Bravo, Chapter 5 in the Course Reader.

Extract (c):
Document II.10 in *Primary Sources 1: World War I*, extracts from the journal of Brand Whitlock.

Extract (d):
The extract from 'A day in the life of a munition worker', item 7 on video-cassette 1.

Extract (e):
Document II.11 in *Primary Sources 1: World War I*, the newspaper report on British servants, 1919. ■

Specimen answers and discussion Before giving answers with respect to the texts that I have asked you to look at, the point that I thought you might have picked up from earlier reading in these units is the one about changes in customs, dress, etc., with regard to peasant women in Serbia.

Extract (a)   This is from an authoritative secondary source, which, note, is much more recent than the book by James McMillan which I quoted from in Unit 1. It is clearly based on primary sources (note, for instance, the reference to *La Renaissance politique*). It also seems to be a very balanced and dispassionate account – it tells us what happened, without really entering into the debate over whether or not the war had significant effects.

The extracts from Smith's book certainly support the view that there was a great change round in opinion in favour of votes for women due to the war. At best, before the war, there was a proposal to give women the municipal vote; now the four-to-one majority in the Chamber of Deputies was prepared to give women the parliamentary vote. The fact that the British example was influential should be noted – this tends to support my point about there being, internationally, a change in ideology (represented above all in the Treaty of Versailles). Perhaps, though – Smith does not go into this – the example of the German enemy was an off-putting one.

Clearly, though, opposition to votes for women was stronger in France than in Britain, and clearly, in the end, the influence of the war was not as great in France as it was in Britain. The Radicals, whom one might have expected to be in favour of reform, were against because they feared that the influence of the Church would persuade women to vote against them. Thus, conservatives tended to support votes for women, but some were also influenced by the idea of the 'family vote', i.e. that the votes should be confined to men, who then voted on behalf of their wives and family. One might perhaps conclude: on the one hand, that the war did have a positive and clearly identifiable effect; but that, on the other hand, while the new ideology in favour of women's suffrage was strong, two contrasting countervailing ideologies, the anti-clerical one of the Radicals, and the family vote one of some conservatives, remained too strong to be overcome by the effects of the war. There was also the institutional factor of the Chamber's unwillingness to fight the Senate.

[handwritten marginal note:] ruling classes making decisions based on fear of losing their seat.

Extract (b)   This is a secondary source, a learned article, but almost entirely based on one type of primary material, oral interviews. I have to say that it did strike me as slightly peculiar that a researcher working in the 1970s should be able to interview people about experiences which took place sixty years earlier. I know from my own experience of collecting written testimony from British women who lived through the First World War that they often get things wrong (many actually believed that they were conscripted into the war effort, though in fact, as you know, there was no conscription of women then). Nevertheless, I find the evidence impressive, and it is in fact congruent with what we know (not a lot!) from other types of source material.

Overall, the article does give an impression of positive long-term changes being brought about in the lives of Italian peasant women by the war, though clearly there were losses as well as gains. The first point is the general one of the massive disruption to normal patterns of life brought about by the war (the massive call to arms, the material difficulties, the increased interference of the state in the fabric of daily life). There was a change in the work balance, and an ending to the traditional division of labour (much of this, of course, was temporary, but one does get the definite impression of some changes enduring). Women took work in factories, even as far afield as France, and ended the tradition where such work stopped at marriage. Here we have a crucial point, often ignored by those who deny that the war had any significant effects, and one which will come up again with respect to World War II: it is true that women did factory work before the First World War, but we have to look closely at what happens with respect to married women. Mothers worked in fields, while daughters looked after children, sometimes for several families; in part, of course, this may also be seen as reinforcing traditional roles. That comment might also apply to the instances of women making their own butter and bread, but the new 'managerial' tasks brought about by rationing certainly were of a new order. Even more critical in this 'managerial' development was the part women had to play in the new complicated relationships with the state authorities. Bravo's summing up is well worth full quotation:

> The women's lives, previously restricted to the house and community, were now filled with new tasks: going to government offices, discussing with local administrators and officials, travelling as far as provincial capitals to follow through these extended chores. Thus greater contact was established with the outside world, with new places, with a new environment of different experiences, with the public sphere of life. The women now had a direct relationship with the activities of a state authority which they also identified as responsible for the war.

Here we begin to go off into a slightly different point, that of women's part in a 'more general estrangement from the state' and 'peasant societies' opposition to the war'. We then come to a point which is being increasingly recognized in studies of war and women, the change in 'mentalities', the growth of 'self-realization' (as Bravo puts it), a new self-confidence, which I personally see as crucial in the changed role and status of women that I perceive in the post-war years. With regard to relations between the sexes, Bravo seems to identify one gain and one loss: women's sexuality was now, Bravo says, less restricted and less orthodox (echoes of my discussion of Marie Stopes), but on the other hand their productive and reproductive power, and their role as sexual objects was perhaps intensified. I have already broached the question of whether war brought changes in sexual morality: Bravo's evidence gives a very definite negative for this type of community. Bravo gives a very balanced conclusion:

> A venthole had been opened, which could not be wholly closed; and a good many wives continued to exercise their new-found expertise in dealing with state officials, now on behalf of their husbands. But, within the community, old roles were resumed, and the women forced back into traditional peasant silence, leaving the men to monopolise the claim to war honours.

Extract (c) This is a diary, usually a very valuable type of primary source. However, we have to note that though the subject is the behaviour of Belgian women, the author of the account is an American male. Nevertheless, I can't think of any reason as to why his testimony should be false, and there is indeed corroborating official and other material on the new roles and activities of Belgian women. There is the peculiarity that Belgium at this time was occupied by the Germans, but clearly the women, like other civilians, very sensibly believed that only through hard work would Belgian society be kept together, and the conditions of desperate deprivation be in any way mitigated.

This definitely is evidence of changed activities and attitudes of women during the war. It tells us nothing about activities after the war, but in so far as it refers to attitudes, that might indicate a more enduring change (that is how I would argue, anyway).

Extract (d)   This is a documentary silent film – in fact a propaganda film made by the Ministry of Information. The purpose of the film was to show what women were already doing, and to encourage more of them to do it. There may be some artificiality in having just one woman going through every process in the making of a shell, but I think in general the film does give an authentic sense of the kind of work women were undertaking.

The extract certainly tells us nothing about what happened to women after the war, but it is solid, if not wildly exciting, evidence of the sort of wartime tasks taken on by women.

Extract (e)   This is a newspaper report, a type of primary source often treated with great suspicion by historians. However, while editorial matter must be treated with great caution as an indication of that mysterious entity 'public opinion', straight reporting of this sort is extremely useful to the historian.

What the document convincingly demonstrates, I believe, is the new assertiveness and self-confidence which women showed in the *post-war* years, but which was derived from the new experiences of war. The document, of course, does not *prove* that connection, but in the light of other evidence (you'd have to consult some of the secondary authorities here), it does seem to me a reasonable deduction to make. □

It is in the nature of the textbook by Roberts that he doesn't single out very sharply the effects of the war on women. Rather buried away on page 388 he does actually say, with respect to women, that 'The Great War made a huge difference ...'. Typically, information about women gaining the vote is tucked away in a footnote at the bottom of the page.

'Politics of the body'

Using the wondrous Marie Stopes film, I have already touched on contraception. A mass of evidence indicates that knowledge, and use, of the male sheath greatly increased due to the upheavals of war, and that, in the post war years, whatever anti-contraception policies governments might officially follow, use of contraceptives of various kinds continued to expand. With regard to the question of a woman's right to control her own fertility, it is broadly true that her lot improved most in those countries where the war had contributed to bringing about revolution, and where, as I have put it, revolution entailed a new respect for 'the common woman' as well as 'the common man' (Russia, Austria-Hungary, Germany – see Units 10–11). France was the country in which, partly because of religious and moral ideologies which continued to be very strong everywhere, but mainly because of fears that after the slaughter of the war the French population was going to go on falling behind that of Germany, pro-population policies, supporting the notion that women's most important function was having children, were most vigorously pursued. But they were not in fact very successful. To help you assess for yourself the differences in outcomes in

Germany and France (not so very different, you may think) I am going to quote first from *The Politics of the Body in Weimar Germany: Women's Reproductive Rights and Duties*, by Cornelie Usborne, and then from a general history of France by a male author (perhaps showing that ordinary male historians are more aware of these issues than advocates of gender history would recognize).

At a time when every other country in the world, except Soviet Russia, prescribed severe penalties for women who underwent an abortion, and France and Belgium actually tightened their abortion restrictions, the proposals of the German socialists, to permit abortion on demand, were indeed courageous. On 2 July 1920 the USPD [Independent Socialists] called for a total repeal of the abortion law ... which even the Soviet Union had not effected; there abortion was permitted only if performed in hospitals, and from 1923 it was subject to a strict medical, social, or eugenic indication. [There were further motions from the Social Democrats – SPD – and the Communists – KPD but none were successful in the Reichstag] ... [the Communists] accused the SPD of hypocrisy for 'promising women the earth' in street rallies but failing them in parliament. The most bitter attacks were directed against Radbruch, the Reich justice minister, for failing to proceed on either the SPD or KPD motion.

It is ... naïve to be surprised at the failure of the 1920 motions to win debating-time in the Reichstag which was taken up with other urgent business: six changes of government within the first parliamentary session; the imposition of reparations, which had serious psychological effects on the government and resulted in the hyper-inflation of 1922–3; currency stabilisation, food shortages and widespread malnutrition ...

Radbruch, who was Justice Minister for only fifteen months, not unreasonably channelled his department's energy into a complete revision of the Penal Code rather than into piecemeal reform which had little prospect of success. Reform of the Penal Code of 1871 was long overdue. Work on this had begun as early as 1902 and there had been two preliminary drafts in 1909 and 1913 ... before the war interrupted work. An updated draft by the Criminal Law Commission of 1919 was published only upon Radbruch's personal initiative. In less than one year from taking office, Radbruch succeeded, in September 1922, in presenting the first official draft by the Reich Justice Ministry to the cabinet ... The draft was based upon close co-operation with the Austrian Justice Minister in the hope of a future amalgamation of the legal system of these two German-speaking nations. ...

Although it did not include legalised abortion, Radbruch's draft did propose more lenient sentencing for abortion than the Code of 1871. It recommended that the penalty for women and their accomplices be reduced from penal servitude to imprisonment ... [the issue of abortion was debated in the Reichstag and in the Upper Chamber – the Reichsrat – during 1925].

... The vote in the legal committee [of the Reichstag] had revealed the deep divisions between parties, which it seemed could not be bridged. For any motion to be carried it needed the support not only of the KPD but also of the DDP (democrats) and the moderate Right DVP. Unlike the Center [Catholic party] and the DNVP [Nationalist Right], the DVP was not opposed to reform as long as it was moderate. The DVP also favoured change but had rejected abortion on demand. The alternative proposals were debated without delay by the Reichsrat in January 1926. The Upper Chamber's lukewarm response even to this uncontentious version indicates that more radical demands would have been rejected. When discussed in the Legal Committee of the Reichstag in March 1926, the motion received the qualified approval of the DDP and DVP members, as well as of the Communists, who were in favour of total repeal but ready 'to support any small improvement'.

The SPD's calculations had been right. The motion was adopted by a majority of two, fifteen votes to thirteen. When it was debated on the floor of the house, on 5 and 7 May 1926, it was passed by 213 votes to 173 with a majority of forty. It had been supported by the DDP, DVP and the small Economy party. The debate showed clearly the strength of feeling against the concept of legalised abortion ... Dr Marie- Elizabeth Lüders (DEP), a leading member of the DEF [Federation of German Women's Associations], said that her party supported the motion because 'the severe laws' had failed to 'save the life of even one infant'. But, in keeping with the conservative attitude of the bourgeois women's movement in this matter, she warned that she could not back a more radical motion. The Center spokesman said that, as a matter of 'ideology and national welfare', legalised abortion could never be accepted by his party, 'because it would be a serious attack on the foundation of our people and our beliefs' ...

The amended law of 18 May 1926 was a compromise and a far cry from the reform long fought for by Communists and Social Democrats. Nevertheless, it constituted a significant improvement. It was also one of the few reforms in sexual politics which reached the statute book. The new law condensed articles 218–20 [of the Penal Code] into a single new article 218. This commuted penal servitude to plain gaol sentences both for women who had undergone abortions and for their accomplices. Attempted abortion remained an offence. Commercial abortions or those performed without consent continued to be punishable by penal servitude, which was, furthermore, increased from a maximum of ten to fifteen years. ... Yet the benefit for women offenders and their accomplices was considerable. They no longer faced penal servitude, the serious social stigma entailing the loss of all civil rights. Moreover, suspects could no longer be routinely remanded in custody, which had sometimes lasted over a year. Where as previously the minimum to which a sentence could be reduced, under extenuating circumstances, was six month's imprisonment, the 1926 law set a new minimum of 1 day's imprisonment or a fine of 3 marks, the cost of about 3 pounds of butter. The new regulation was also of great symbolic significance: much to the horror of the denominational parties, who regarded the foetus as a living being at all stages of gestation, after 1926 abortion ceased to be rated as homicide, which had to be tried by jury. It was now a simple misdemeanour tried by a court of lay assessors, who were usually sympathetic towards defendants.

The 1926 Act made Germany's abortion law the most lenient in Western Europe, a fact which enraged conservative politicians ...

The benefits of the new law were noticeable almost immediately. After only six months, the annual total of sentences to penal servitude had dropped to sixty-three, and those to one year and more in prison to 160 ...

(Usborne, *The Politics of the Body*, 1992, pp.166–74)

Conscious that the German population was increasing twice as fast as its own, the French government tried to shorten the odds by encouraging a substantial influx of foreign labour and by instituting a series of penalties and inducements to further the birth-rate. A law of 31 July 1920 prescribed up to six month's imprisonment for even the mere offer of contraception information, and up to three years in prison for attempted abortion – a sentence that was increased to ten years in July 1939. Yet, despite these draconian prescriptions, the law on contraception was very loosely applied. It is true that many of the coyly discreet advertisements for contraceptives disappeared from the newspapers, or became so arcane as to be intelligible only to the initiated; and they likewise disappeared from the safety curtains of theatres, where they had always been something of an embarrassment to parents, parrying the questions of puzzled children during the entr'acte. Yet the sale of sheaths continued largely unmolested, provided it was discreet; they were tacitly recognised as keeping down illegitimacy and helping to prevent the spread of venereal diseases. Indeed, sales increased as sheaths became cheaper and more reliable. ... Even so, all the available evidence indicates that premature withdrawal and various forms of onanism continued to be the most practised form of birth control – and here the State like the Church was powerless. Not surprisingly, the areas with the highest birth-rates were those where Catholic religious observance was most marked. However, the findings of Ogino and Knaus on the 'safe period' in 1930–1 provided a form of birth-control which was acceptable to the Church – and which was cautiously welcomed by the Vatican after the fiasco of earlier ecclesiastical patronage of safe-period methods, in which well-meaning parish clergy had been bitterly blamed for unwanted pregnancies. The State made no attempt to interfere with publications propagating the Ogino-Knaus system – perhaps surmising that it might not prove much more successful than its ill-starred predecessors.

Nor did the fearsome penalties for abortion act as an effective deterrent: a third of French pregnancies were terminated in this fashion during the inter-war period. And with abortions averaging 400,000 per annum, the *faiseuses d'anges* [makers of angels] eliminated more French lives in a year than the German armies did in the worst year of the war ...

(Maurice Larkin, *France Since the Popular Front: Government and People 1936–1996*, p.7)

You may feel, as I do, that there is something unpleasant about Larkin's final phrase. The horrific phenomenon which throughout our period afflicted too many women of the poorer classes was the backstreet abortion – to be fair to Larkin he alludes to this on pp.179–80. The figure he gives there of 20,000 deaths a year from such abortions applies to France (and, in a smaller population, to Italy) throughout our period (see Marwick, *The Sixties*, 1998, chapter 13)). Affluence after World War II brought amelioration, but legislative change did not come till the 1970s. Apart possibly from the examples of Germany and Russia (Catholic ideology was strong in Austria) World War I was of little relevance to this too-long hidden topic.

Concluding remarks

I take the family separately in the section on 'Institutions and values', but it is perhaps worthwhile remembering here the instances already noted of welfare legislation, institution of family allowances, and so on. These on the whole did improve the quality of material life within the family, though it could be argued that all of this legislation served to reinforce the traditional image and role of women. But to keep things fully in perspective, I want you to finish this section by turning to the *Secondary Sources* and reading 'The German nation's obligations to the heroes' widows of World War I' by Karin Hausen, from *Behind the Lines: Gender and the Two World Wars,* edited by Higonnet, Jenson, Michel and Weitz (1987).

High and popular culture

High culture

It would be salutary to start off by re-reading the article by Josipovici in the Course Reader (it was first referred to in Book 1). No historian worth his or her salt would ever dream of denying that the new modes characteristic of modernism which predominate in high culture in the twentieth century were already being practised before World War I. The debate is over whether the war was essentially irrelevant to developments in high culture, or whether it helped to give greater acceptability to the new modes and brought a fairly definite end (I must be careful not to exaggerate, or be absolutist or closed) to the spirit of optimism and belief in rational progress which had still characterized much high culture. For a discussion of these points with regard to the visual arts and music, you will need to turn to your audio-cassettes.

Exercise Listen to part 1 of audio 1, noting down answers to the questions asked on the cassette. ■

Exercise Now listen to part 2 of audio 1 and write down answers to the questions asked there. ■

You will have noted that both of these cassettes are presented by me, and you may wish to be on guard against my views on the consequences of war. More than this, you may have been struck by the fact that when a historian attempts to generalize in a brief space about matters of high culture, he or she runs the risk of sounding like one of the Sunday colour supplements, or possibly even a candidate for 'Pseuds' Corner' in *Private Eye*. You may feel that I have failed to negotiate that risk successfully. Thus, in order to pose the terms of debate over war's effects on literature, I am going to give you a selection of quotations from three other academic authors.

The first quotation is the conclusion to John Cruickshank's *Variations on Catastrophe*, which is a study of war's effects on various French literary figures:

> We noted in the very first chapter of this study that many men in 1914 looked forward to a war as a potential form of moral transformation for society, or as a means of release from the social constrictions of peacetime attitudes and morals. But we also saw that, in the end, technological warfare appeared to

an increasing number of participants as nothing other than a peculiarly dramatic and condensed image of the new industrial society ... The war appeared to dramatize and to intensify social alienation. The hierarchies associated with an increasingly industrial and urban civilization were never quite the same again. After 1918 they were to be increasingly challenged.

At a different though relevant level ... war also seemed to destroy a number of the old moral certainties. The contrast between the home front and the battlefront itself bred scepticism and suspicion. Furthermore, the propagandist exploitation and simplification of government and resounding moral absolutes left them meaningless and generally repellent. Moral indifference and moral relativism followed. The '*années folles*' ['crazy years'] of the 1920s seem an inevitable consequence. We are in the world of E. M. Forster's 'everything exists, nothing has value ...'

It would certainly be wrong to suggest that the Great War was the sole and initiating cause of the trends just mentioned. But it indicated awareness of them and probably accelerated them. Without the Great War there would not have been so rapid a growth in philosophical nihilism, social dissent, ethical relativism, and the contending political ideologies of fascism and communism. These doubts were widely experienced as a crisis within the mind and spirit of twentieth-century man. They were seen as part and parcel of a new emergency of which the war was an external manifestation. George A. Panishas [philosopher and literary critic] implies too direct a causal connection when he describes such things as 'the legacy of the Great War'. But he describes very accurately the postwar state of affairs – and a state of affairs which the Great War helped to dramatize and confirm – when he writes of 'the alienation, the meaninglessness, the cynicism, the hate, the despair, the confusion, the suspicion, the fear, the doubt that possesses modern man even in the midst of his triumphs in science and technology.' It was after 1918 that modern man set out again 'in search of a soul'. The direction which this search was to take was affected in a fundamental way by the catastrophe of 1914–18.

(John Cruickshank, *Variations on Catastrophe*, 1982, pp.190–2)

The notion of the war having destroyed Victorian confidence and optimism is supported by philosopher John Searle who writes: 'My guess is that the greatest single psychological blow to the intellectual optimism of the nineteenth century was not an intellectual development at all but rather the catastrophe of the First World War' (John Searle, *Mind, Language and Society: Doing Philosophy in the Real World*, 1999, p.2). My second quotation is from *German Novels on the First World War and Their Ideological Implications, 1918-1933* by Martin Travers:

Some novels advance explicitly political interpretations of the war. Adam Scharrer, for example, in his *Vaterlandslose Gesellen* [*Young Men Without a Country*], tries to show that the professional and ideological differences that separated the ordinary soldier from his officer reflected the conflict of class interests endemic within 'capitalist' society as a whole and devotes much of his novel to an analysis of the industrial and party-political nature of that conflict. A similar kind of overtly political stance is noticeable in certain writers from the extreme Right, in, for example, Ernst Jünger, Franz Schauwecker or Josef Magnus Wehner. Although such writers were not concerned with the socio-economic determinants of the war, they were nevertheless fully aware of the political heritage left by the First World War, and did all they could to exploit that legacy in their own writings.

It is, in fact, the unique perspective evident in the work of many of these nationalist authors, a strange mixture of historical observation and myth-poetical vision, that points to the second way literary text can engage with political issues. For these exponents of nationalist ideology, the war was not so much a definable historical event as a meeting place for the transcendental values of comradeship, self-sacrifice and leadership: the war, in short, was a *symbol* of that kind of personal and social ethics that the Weimar Republic was felt to negate, both in its theory and practice of parliamentary politics. For a writer of war fiction to deny one or all of these values was, irrespective of his conscious or explicit political goals, tantamount to a counter-offensive against this nationalist interpretation of war.

It is this fact which explains the controversy that surrounded the publication of E. M. Remarque's *Im Westen nichts Neues [All Quiet on the Western Front]* in 1929. If one approaches Remarque's work within the framework of traditional literary criticism or with the dogmatic expectations of the cruder type of Marxist methodology, the political reception of this apparently most 'apolitical' of all war novels must remain a mystery, for, unlike most of the novels referred to above, *Im Westen nichts Neues* contains little overt political sentiment. Nor can we draw upon circumstantial statements to help us in this matter; Remarque, perhaps in the hope of securing its popular reception, continually played down the ideological implications of his novel, emphasizing instead its imputed universal message about the horrors of war (a procedure which, as we shall see, has influenced many of his modern critics).

Once returned to its historical context, however, the critical strategy of Remarque's novel becomes much clearer. For Remarque takes all the components of the nationalist view of war – the insistence upon the ideals of 1914 and the sense of righteous purpose felt by the nation, the suggestion that comradeship and group solidarity survived the final material onslaught, and the final essential assertion that the war left a positive spiritual legacy – and subjects them to poignant and forceful rebuttal. It is, then, the *thematic symbolism* of Remarque's novel that we must look for in our second kind of political implication.

(Martin Travers, *German Novels on the First World War and Their Ideological Implications, 1918-1933*, 1982, pp.10–11)

Finally, I quote from the much acclaimed book, *The Great War and Modern Memory* by Paul Fussell, the distinguished American professor of English (who had first-hand experience of war with the American army in World War II). Fussell's theme here is the 'irony' of war – war is not straightforward, war is a massive cruel deception on mankind, war explodes the myth of progress (the 'Meliorist myth').

The war as ironic action

Every war is ironic because every war is worse than expected. Every war constitutes an irony of situation because its means are so melodramatically disproportionate to its presumed ends. In the Great War eight million people were destroyed because two persons, the Archduke Francis Ferdinand and his Consort, had been shot. The Second World War offers even more preposterous ironies. Ostensibly begun to guarantee the sovereignty of Poland, that war managed to bring about Poland's bondage and humiliation. Air bombardment, which was supposed to shorten the war, prolonged it by inviting those who were its target to cast themselves in the role of victim-heroes and thus stiffen their resolve.

But the Great War was more ironic than any before or since. It was a hideous embarrassment to the prevailing Meliorist myth which had dominated the public consciousness for a century. It reversed the Idea of Progress. The day after the British entered the war Henry James wrote a friend:

> The plunge of civilization into this abyss of blood and darkness ... is a thing that so gives away the whole long age during which we have supposed the world to be, with whatever abatement, gradually bettering, that to have to take it all now for what the treacherous years were all the while really making for and meaning is too tragic for any words.

James's essential point was rendered in rowdier terms by a much smaller writer, Philip Gibbs, as he remembered the popularity during the war of what today would be called Black Humor. 'The more revolting it was,' he says, 'the more [people] shouted with laughter':

> It was ... the laughter of mortals at the trick which had been played on them by an ironical fate. They had been taught to believe that the whole object of life was to reach out to beauty and love, and that mankind, in its progress to perfection, had killed the beast instinct, cruelty, blood-lust, the primitive, savage law of survival by tooth and claw and club and axe. All poetry, all art, all religion had preached this gospel and this promise. Now that ideal was broken like a china vase to the ground. The contrast between That and This was devastating ... The war-time humor of the soul roared with mirth at the sight of all that dignity and elegance despoiled.

The British fought the war for four years and three months. Its potential of ironic meaning, considered not now in relation to the complacencies of the past but in itself alone, emerges when we consider its events chronologically. The five last months of 1914, starting August 4, when the British declared war on the Central Powers, began with free manoeuvre in Belgium and Northern France and ended with both sides locked into the infamous trench system. Before this stalemate, the British engaged in one major retreat and fought two large battles, although *battles* is perhaps not the best word, having been visited upon these events by subsequent historiography in the interest of neatness and the assumption of something like a rational causality. To call these things *battles* is to imply an understandable continuity with earlier British history and to imply that the war makes sense in a traditional way. As

Esmé Wingfield-Stratford [a writer of popular history] points out, 'A vast literature has been produced in the attempt to bring [the Great War] into line with other wars by highlighting its so-called battles by such impressive names as Loos, Verdun, the Somme, and Passchendaele ...' This is to try to suggest that these events parallel Blenheim and Waterloo not only in glory but in structure and meaning ...

Irony and memory

The innocent army fully attained the knowledge of good and evil at the Somme on July 1, 1916. That moment, one of the most interesting in the whole long history of human disillusion, can stand as the type of all the ironic actions of the war. What could remain of confidence in Divine assistance once it was known what Haig wrote his wife just before the attack: 'I feel that every step in my plan has been taken with the Divine help'? 'The wire has never been so well cut,' he confided to his diary, 'nor the artillery preparation so thorough.' His hopes were those of every man. Private E. C. Stanley recalls: 'I was very pleased when I heard that my battalion would be in the attack. I thought this would be the last battle of the war and I didn't want to miss it. I remember writing to my mother, telling her I would be home for August Bank Holiday.' Even the weather cooperated to intensify the irony, just as during the summer of 1914. 'On the first of July,' Sassoon says, 'the weather, after an early morning mist, was of the kind commonly called heavenly.' Thirteen years after that day Henry Williamson recalled it vividly:

> I see men arising and walking forward; and I go forward with them, in a glassy delirium wherein some seem to pause, with bowed heads, and sink carefully to their knees, and roll slowly over, and lie still. Others roll and roll, and scream and grip my legs in uttermost fear, and I have to struggle to break away, while the dust and earth on my tunic changes from grey to red. And I go on with aching feet, up and down across ground like a huge ruined honeycomb, and my wave melts away, and the second wave comes up, and also melts away, and then the third wave merges into the ruins of the first and second, and after a while the fourth blunders into the remnants of the others, and we begin to run forward to catch up with the barrage, gasping and sweating, in bunches, anyhow, every bit of the months of drill and rehearsal forgotten, for who could have imagined that the 'Big Push' was going to be this?

What assists Williamson's recall is precisely the ironic pattern which subsequent vision had laid over the events. In reading memoirs of the war, one notices the same phenomenon over and over. By applying to the past a paradigm of ironic action, a rememberer is enabled to locate, draw forth, and finally shape into significance an event or a moment which otherwise would merge without meaning into the general undifferentiated stream.

I am saying that there seems to be one dominating form of modern understanding: that it is essentially ironic; and that it originates largely in the application of mind and memory to the events of the Great War.
(Paul Fussell, *The Great War and Modern Memory*, 1975, pp.7–9, 29–30, 35; footnotes excluded).

Discussion   My quotations, I think, give you in lucid and self-explanatory form the main points that distinguished authorities have made about the war's effects on literature. What Fussell terms 'the Ironic' might be seen as a key element in Modernism, verging perhaps on what is now often called 'Postmodernism'. ■

The evidence (not all of it, as we need to study writers' letters, diaries, and other contextual matter) is in the works of literature themselves. Again the question arises: should we be studying works during the war, or works written *after*?

Presumably, while we might think a Social Insurance Act passed in 1929 would perhaps only be tenuously linked to the war, a novel published in 1929, but totally preoccupied with the war, would on the contrary be a tribute to the long-lasting, if not permanent effects of the war. Anyway, I want you now to read three texts: one from an English poem written during the war, one from a French novel written during the war, and one from a German novel written in the late 1920s.

Exercise   Now turn to *Primary Sources 1: World War I*, and carefully read the three documents listed below; then in each case note down answers to the following questions:

1   What distinctive formal and stylistic elements do you think can be related to the war and/or modernism?

2   In what way is the content related to the experience of war?

3   Is the document supportive or critical of the waging of the war?

4   With respect to Extract (c), does anything indicate that, unlike *Under Fire*, this novel is the product of reflections ten years later?

Extract (a): Document II.12, 'Strange meeting' by Wilfred Owen.

Extract (b): Document II.13, the final pages of the novel *Under Fire* (1915) by Henri Barbusse. Published quite early in the war, this novel was immensely successful, yet also highly controversial. Though an older man, Barbusse himself served in the trenches before being invalided home.

Extract (c): Document II.14, the final pages of Erich Maria Remarque's novel *All Quiet on the Western Front*. Not published until 1929, this novel was also an immense success, though hated by right-wing German patriots. Remarque was of normal enlistment age, had direct front-line experience, but was also invalided home. ■

Specimen answers and discussion   **Extract (a)**

The most striking formal element in the poem is that it is organized in couplets, but rather strange ones: in each case the 'rhyme' is only a 'half-rhyme' 'groined/ groaned', 'tigress/progress', 'mystery/mastery', etc. This was a mode pioneered by Owen and not widely to be found, I believe, before the war. One could interpret it as a relaxation in formality induced by the upheavals of the war and developed also, perhaps, as the only possible mode for grappling with the appalling horrors and *irony* of war ('pretty' rhymes certainly would not do). Furthermore, Owen coins rather strange words of his own ('groined', 'richlier'). The whole, also, is in a slightly informal, narrative style. Summing this up, one might say that the quite new and awful experiences of war called forth new modes of poetic expression. These modes, of course, are very much in keeping with the innovations of modernism.

The poem is 'about' death on the battlefield of, it transpires, both the British narrator and his German enemy. It is about the terrible loss of war ('undone years', 'the hopelessness'), particularly for young men on the verge, the poem suggests, of great discoveries which might have been of benefit to others. The poem, of course, is 'about' – 'The pity of war, the pity war distilled', the best-remembered line in the whole poem. It is 'about', in effect, the deeper comradeship, the appalling shared experience, of men technically classed as enemies. It is utterly and completely 'about' the experience of war, and not in any way 'about' anything else.

This is not an overt, violent denunciation of war. Yet in its almost understated, but profoundly moving, reflection on the pity and the tragic loss of war, it is, for all that, perhaps a profoundly effective criticism of the waging of the war. Poetry, though it is of fundamental importance to understand exactly what the poet is saying, is open to personal and subjective interpretation, so these responses of mine are offered simply as guidance on the sorts of things one might get from this poem.

Extract (b)

Evidently this is not a conventional ending to a conventional, 'story-telling' novel. There is a declamatory style which is both polemical and poetical. The narrator is making direct statements, rather than letting these emerge, as in the traditional novel, from the events narrated, or from the views expressed by the characters. The passage is 'non-traditional' and therefore 'modern'. Again, it is a matter for your own judgement how far you accept the argument that this 'modern' style was required to cope with the immense issues thrown up by the war.

This is absolutely and exclusively a scene set in the French front line. Every point made is a point about the nature and experience of war.

Almost the whole of the passage seems to be so vigorously critical of the waging of the war, and the governments responsible, that it is surprising to find that the novel was published while the war was still being fought. The sufferings of the soldiers are sympathetically exposed, yet at the same time, in most unheroic mode, they are recognized to be 'murderers'. There is vigorous condemnation of financiers, 'feeble-minded' jingoes, and parsons. The religion of militarism is 'bad and stupid and malignant'. Yet the ultimate conclusion is, to say the least, ambiguous. The chapter itself is entitled 'The Dawn', and it appears that Barbusse is suggesting that from all the horrific slaughter 'a tranquil gloom' will emerge, so that then all the miseries and slaughter will have resulted in at least one step of progress. There is nothing at all reprehensible in this kind of ambiguity. Barbusse, in common with Wilfred Owen, had believed that Germany was a menace to civilization. What they are both saying, perhaps, is that the war, and the way it was fought, was out of all proportion to its objectives, with Barbusse leaving a sufficiently open ending (I am not for a moment saying that this was his reason) for the French government to see it as *not being a direct and comprehensive attack on the French war effort*. But it is an utter mistake to look at these literary artefacts from the point of view of whether they are 'anti-war' or not. It is, as Fussell so brilliantly points out, the horrific irony of the war that they expose.

Extract (c)

If you have any familiarity at all with German literature, you will be struck by the brief, staccato, almost journalistic sentences (the translation, I should say, is absolutely faithful to the original). The contrast in sentence length compared with that of the pre-war (and post-war) novels of Thomas Mann, for example, is quite stunning. This style is very effective for conveying the direct experience of war, and it is indeed a style which characterizes a particular type of twentieth-century novel.

The entire short chapter is a reflection on the war which is known to be nearly over, and how life has been utterly changed by the war.

Again there is no violent denunciation of war. The tone is of resignation and melancholy. Because the tone was not heroic, the novel was read by German nationalists (quite correctly, in fact) as not being an endorsement of the German war effort, of Germany military valour and virtue.

The points about the war generation becoming a forgotten generation are, I think, very much a product of the experience which former soldiers like Remarque actually had in the 1920s. It was possible for Barbusse, perfectly genuinely I think, to perceive a glimmer of hope, to believe in some possible positive results from all the sacrifice; this was less possible for Remarque writing at the end of the 1920s. □

During the war a great deal of literature was produced, glorifying the heroism of the troops and insisting on the rightness of the national cause. It is now somewhat fashionable in historical and cultural studies to argue that since the patriotic, if rather unpretentious, novels sold far more widely than the more intellectual agonizings over, and criticisms of, the war, they are much more 'important'. *(Under Fire* and *All Quiet on the Western Front* were highly successful, but their audience, cumulatively very large over the years, was undoubtedly provided by the educated reading public, that is to say the middle class and upwards, with a leavening of politically aware, or self-improving, working-class readers).

Exercise   Do you agree with the argument that novels in general supporting the values of militarism and patriotism, which sold widely to the lower-middle class and the working class, are historically more significant than the 'élite' novels and poems I have been discussing? Give reasons for your answer. ∎

Specimen answer   First of all, there is the very important point that, in the past, history, and particularly the history of the movement of ideas, has been written entirely on the basis of what relatively small minorities thought. It is important, especially as we go further into 'mass society' to know what the mass of the people were reading and, presumably, thinking. Most people in all countries almost certainly continued to believe in the values of nationalism, and the need for military action under certain circumstances to defend the rights and interests of their own nation. There was much heroism in the First World War, and it was almost certainly the wish of the ordinary family to see that heroism recognized, and certainly not cynically condemned.

I started with some reasons for the significance of 'élite' novels, but arguing on lines like these, you could well say that the 'popular', 'nationalistic' novels are more important. □

Popular culture

Exercise   Turn to Roberts, p.45–6.

1   What reasons does he give for the expansion of popular culture *before* 1914?

2   What does he identify as a major artefact in modern popular culture?

3   What effect do you think World War I had on the history of this artefact? ■

Specimen answers and discussion
1   (a) Rising real wages; (b) cheaper consumer goods, big stores and central markets, and cheaper transport; (c) increased leisure activities; (d) greater wellbeing; (e) new pleasures; (f) popular education and increased literacy.

2   'Monster newspapers'. Of course, earlier centuries had had their own artefacts of popular culture, but modern historians often place great emphasis on the founding of *Le Journal,* the *Daily Mail, Le Petit Parisien,* and (in Russia) *Novoe Vremya.* Note, however, that these are papers aimed more at the lower-middle class than at the working class.

3   (a) There was a general hunger for war news. Familiarity with the notion of the newspaper expanded (particularly in the Balkans, as we saw). (b) At the same time governments everywhere exercised censorship (though note that often newspapers exercised voluntary censorship – they wanted to 'win the war' too). I think the first development had the greater long-term effect. □

Exercise   If censorship makes newspapers an unreliable source for what soldiers really felt about the war, where might we look for more reliable information? ■

Specimen answer and discussion   This is not an easy one: 'soldiers' letters (also subject to censorship) and diaries' would be a good answer. But strictly within the sphere of popular culture the really interesting area, which historians have recently begun to explore fully, is 'the popular culture of the trenches' – 'trench newspapers', the revues, sketches, song-and-dance shows, etc., which soldiers organized for themselves (recall the page from the *Wipers Times* which was reproduced in Unit 5).

Popular war revues, stage shows on the civilian front, etc., do give us a sense of the widespread (and genuine) feelings of patriotism on the home fronts. But if I wanted to make a really clinching argument in favour of the value to the historian of popular culture (in comparison, say, with high culture) I'd give a high place to this 'popular culture of the trenches'. Conclusions must be tentative, but on the whole this culture does seem to reflect the established patterns of pre-war years, showing that soldiers tended to accept their lot in society, treated the awful conditions of war with both resignation and great wit, had little respect for their 'betters' at home, but felt that they had no alternative to fighting on. It could be argued that forms of popular culture already developed before the war (music hall songs, certain stereotyped characters and jokes) and now taken over and adapted to trench life, helped to sustain the fighting men in their horrific tasks. (There is a brief treatment in Marc Ferro, *The Great War,* 1973, pp.155-7; a major work on the British side is John Fuller, *Troop Morale and Popular Culture in the British and Dominion Armies, 1914–1918,* 1990. □

Exercise   In the section on 'Customs and behaviour', I identified some new developments in popular culture. What were these, and how, if at all, do they relate to the war? ∎

Specimen answer and discussion

(a)   Film.

(b)   Gramophone and records.

(c)   Public dance halls.

(d)   Radio.

I have suggested that radio depended upon technological developments fostered, though not originated, by the demands of war. The demands of war, also, I have suggested, gave middle- and upper-class respectability to film. The special experiences of war legitimized public dancing, and encouraged the import of American jazz. The growth and extent of American influences on popular culture is one of the great issues of twentieth-century historical study. Logistically, and geopolitically, World War I brought America into Europe. The connections between the developing modes of popular culture and the war are not direct, but that they exist is beyond question. This book (and indeed much of AA312 as a whole) is about teasing out with as much precision as possible just exactly what these relationships are. Some historians have seen World War I as the great divide marking the beginning of mass society and technology-based popular culture. It depends partly on which developments you emphasize, partly on what you see as the main sources of modern popular culture. Roberts obviously places the origins much further back. Some commentators stress the advent of film, some the arrival of radio (but it is perhaps World War II which makes radio something like a necessity in every household). □

Exercise   There is one form of high cultural practice which perhaps more than any other impinges directly on the majority of the people (particularly in urban areas). What is this art form? How might it have been affected by the war? ∎

Specimen answer and discussion   Architecture. Wartime destruction meant there had to be rebuilding. More important, the end of the war (with the revolutions associated with it) was seen as a time for starting anew, a time for wholeheartedly applying the tenets of modernism to architecture.

Indeed, the 1920s are seen in the realm of architecture as the 'Heroic period of the new architecture' (see Charles Jencks, *Modern Movements in Architecture,* 1982, p.32). Beginning in October 1922, the Swiss architect Le Corbusier began writing a series of articles which were influential throughout Europe. He wrote: 'A great effort has begun ... There is a new spirit: it is a spirit of construction and of synthesis guided by a clear conception' (quoted by Jencks, *Modern Movements).* □

In the new Russia there was the movement known as 'constructivism'. In the new Weimar Germany there was the celebrated architectural school of the Bauhaus, led by two of the most famous of all twentieth-century architects, Mies van der Rohe and Walter Gropius.

Institutions and values

Leaving the family to the end, I first concentrate on political institutions and values. By this point you will have picked up several hints as to what has changed within this sphere. Again, it will help your understanding if you try first of all to work out what sort of changes had taken place between the pre-war and the post-war years. To give you a basis and, as it were, a stimulus, I want you to turn to the exercise chart which I completed for you in Book 1, Unit 4.

Exercise   Look at the exercise chart in Book 1, Unit 4. As you can see, this chart is divided up by countries. I want you to take each country in turn, going each time direct to the final section, 'institutions and values'. In the case of each country, make notes on the main changes that have taken place, as compared with pre-war days. Try to indicate the significance of the war in bringing about these changes. ■

Specimen answer
and discussion
United Kingdom

All men now have the vote, together with women over 30 (provided they fulfil a small property qualification). Votes for all women came, without much fuss, in 1928. It could be argued that participation in the war effort was the key factor in the gaining of votes by both men and women. Events have moved decisively towards independence for the bulk of Ireland, the Irish Free State being declared in 1921. It might be argued that Britain's hold on the major part of Ireland was inherently insecure and that the war tested this. Ideas of collectivism and state enterprise were greatly strengthened during the war, though there was a determined effort to return to the principles of *laissez-faire*. Because of the rise of the Labour Party (perhaps attributable to working-class participation in the war effort) there was now a three-party system rather than the stable two-party one.

France   Adult males continued, of course, to have the vote, but, despite a significant swing of opinion, women did not get the vote at the end of the war. French socialism split (you may well not know this) between socialists and communists, but this can be more directly related to the Bolshevik revolution than to the war as such. French labour had gained something in prestige, but was still not a very strong influence on the policies of the state. France's immense sufferings and losses, despite its being on the winning side, helped to encourage right-wing nationalistic movements.

Italy   Liberal values and democratic principles were not firmly established in pre-war Italy. The exigencies of war undoubtedly had a deeply destabilizing effect, and although there were, as elsewhere, moves towards further liberal democratic reforms, an immense stimulus was also given to extreme right-wing nationalism, helping, it may be argued, to pave the way for the fascist takeover of power (these matters will be discussed much more fully in Book 3).

Germany   Here the major changes were the German Revolution and the establishment of democracy; the gaining of prestige by organized labour; the split in the socialist movement; and the great stimulus, from the bitterness of defeat, to right-wing nationalism. These matters will be taken up in Units 10–12.

Russia   Obviously, the most overwhelming changes in values and institutions took place here, and these too will be the subject matter of Units 10–12.

Austria   Here too we have immense changes, with the Habsburg monarchy disappearing. In appearance, at least, democratic values were established in Austria itself, with democratic socialism a powerful force. This again is a subject area examined in Units 10–12. □

The family

In the introduction to the justly famous collection of essays, edited by Richard Wall and Jay Winter, *The Upheaval of War: Family, Work and Welfare in Europe, 1914–1918*, the two editors declare that the essays in their book:

> ... suggest that the full effect of the war was to restore pre-war social forms rather than to undermine them. Perhaps it was only natural that the catastrophic human losses of the war led to a reinforcement of family life in its aftermath. Perhaps it was understandable that ex-soldiers, many of whom returned home defeated and disillusioned, insisted that their place within the family was preserved or even enhanced. Perhaps some women even welcomed the restoration after 1918; certainly few people were asked for their opinion about an issue central to their welfare and their lives. But the weight of evidence from many quarters seems to point towards the view that, in terms of the social history of the European family, the First World War was more a conservative than a revolutionary force.
>
> (1988, p.4)

Exercise   I wonder if you can remember, from my preliminary discussion of the effects of World War I on the position of women, an extract I quoted from an autobiography which suggested a different view, for Britain at least, of the effects of the war on the family? You probably won't remember the exact details, but try now to see if you can roughly identify the extract and what it said. ∎

Specimen answer   The extract was from Robert Roberts, *The Classic Slum,* 1971, p.174 – this book
and discussion   being the autobiography of someone who was brought up in a shop in a working-class area in Salford, before, during, and after the First World War. You'll find the extract on page 32 of Unit 1. It would be well worth while going back to read it again. □

You could also reflect on what Roberts says in the second paragraph on page 388, to which I have already referred.

We can all agree that the basic framework of the family was not changed by the war. However, I am not sure that the detailed essays published by Wall and Winter fully bear out their conclusions. A good subject for discussion with your tutor!

Previously I have taken religion under this heading, but nothing, I think, needs to be added to Bill Purdue's discussions under the heading 'National cohesion'.

3   FILM AND THE FIRST WORLD WAR

The medium of film had existed for two decades before the outbreak of the First World War. In that time it had grown from being little more than a cottage industry to become a huge international economic undertaking. The war, however, was to have highly significant effects on the film industry. In economic terms, the war brought about a realignment in the international film industry that has lasted ever since. In 1914, film production and distribution was dominated by French, Italian and British companies. By 1918, however, these had given way to the expansionist interests of the American film industry, which came to dominate the world market. In cultural terms, however, it was during the war that the cinema acquired a kudos which it had hitherto lacked. Previously regarded by intellectuals as a low-brow, vulgar form of popular entertainment, the cinema played an important role during the war both in informing the general public about the war's progress and in shaping attitudes towards the war. Ranging from the official British account of the *Battle of the Somme* (1916) to Charlie Chaplin's 'Little Tramp' joining up in the US comedy *Shoulder Arms* (1918), films served the interests of the state in promoting the war effort. In this section, we will be examining the relationship between film and society in Europe during the First World War, first by discussing the consequences of the war for the main European film industries, and then by considering the use of film as a historical source, for which we will be looking at some of the extracts on video-cassette 1.

European national cinemas

As with other aspects of social and cultural change, it would be naive to assume that it was the impact of war alone which brought about transformation in the film industry. Already, before the outbreak of war, the film industry was undergoing important changes. In its first decade or so (*c*.1895–1905), cinema exploited the novelty-value of moving pictures by producing films which relied essentially upon the display of action (stunts, chases, optical tricks, etc.) – a style which is known as 'the cinema of attractions'. In the decade or so before the outbreak of war, however, filmmakers explored ways of telling stories through visual means – a style known as 'the cinema of narrative integration'. The narrative (or story) film was firmly established as the dominant type of film before the outbreak of war. The cinema's first attempts at cultural legitimation can be seen in the primitive Shakespearean and Dickensian adaptations that were a characteristic of both British and American filmmaking in the late 1900s and early 1910s. During this period, filmmakers were also exploring the expressive possibilities of film style, realizing that factors such as framing, lighting and editing were important in creating mood and effect. It was in the midst of these changes that the war broke out.

Exercise   'Before World War I, the cinema was largely an international affair' (K. Thompson and D. Bordwell, *Film History*, 1994, p.56). Consider this statement by film historians Kristin Thompson and David Bordwell, then try to answer the following two questions:

1   Why was the cinema an 'international affair' before the war?

2   How might this have changed as a consequence of the war? ■

Specimen answers   1   The most important factor in the internationalism of cinema is that at this
and discussion   time the medium was silent ('talking pictures' did not arrive until the late 1920s). Silent film was a truly international medium in that it bypassed barriers of language and literacy in a way that other forms of cultural expression (such as novels or poetry) could not. The absence of spoken dialogue meant that films were easily exported, as all that a distributor in another country needed to do was translate the inter-titles (the inserts used to convey dialogue or plot information). Furthermore, as films were easily exported, technical and stylistic discoveries made in one country were quickly seen and adopted elsewhere. Many aspects of film style were used in the same way internationally: for example the practice of 'continuity editing' (matching one shot to another) was more or less standardized before the outbreak of war.

2   The war disrupted the free flow of films across national boundaries. Obviously, British and French films were not shown in Germany, and *vice versa*. A few countries were partially or completely cut off from imports – Germany and Russia were both isolated in this way. For the first time, distinctive national cinemas with their own stylistic practices emerged, rather than the open flow of films and ideas that had previously been the case. □

The effects of war for all European film industries were felt both in the disruption of trade between European countries and in the material losses and physical devastation brought about by the conflict. However, different national film industries responded to the war in different ways, and while most were in a weaker economic condition in 1918 than they had been in 1914, in certain countries, principally Germany and Russia, the war was to transform the cinema, sometimes in quite radical ways. What I'm going to do now is to sketch in the main developments for the film industries of Britain, France, Italy, Germany, Russia and the Scandinavian countries. I'm including Scandinavia for two reasons. First, the Scandinavian countries (especially Denmark and Sweden) provide perhaps the first example of the emergence of culturally distinctive national cinemas in Europe. And second, they provide a means of comparing the effects of war on the belligerent nations with what happened in neutral countries.

Britain

The 'pictures' were extremely popular in Britain before the First World War. The first purpose-built cinemas appeared in 1907–8 (previously most films had been shown in converted music halls) and their numbers increased so rapidly that there were 1,600 by 1910 and 3,500 by 1915. In 1908 there had been only three registered distribution companies, but by the end of 1914 there were 1,833.

Britain was also the centre of the pre-war international export market, due to its dependent colonial and Commonwealth trading partners, its large shipping and trading network, and, until 1915, tariff-free imports. But while these factors all suggest that the British film industry was in a healthy state at the outbreak of war, they do disguise other trends. The majority of films shown in British cinemas were American, and box-office profits were used to rent more American films rather than invest in British production. There was a slight revival in British production in the years immediately before the outbreak of war: in 1910 some 15 per cent of films released in Britain were of British origin, rising to 25 per cent in 1914. This temporary revival was fuelled by a spate of longer 'feature' films, mostly adapted from novels and plays. Although the number of feature films produced in Britain fluctuated during the war (15 in 1914, 73 in 1915, 107 in 1916, 66 in 1917, 76 in 1918), the overall percentage of British films shown on British screens declined as American dominance increased. American films were widely regarded as being technically superior to their British counterparts, by both critics and audiences. The perceived inferiority of British films was due in no small measure to a shortage of capital for investment in production, a direct consequence of the war. In respect of American dominance of the British market, the war accelerated a process that had already started before and which was to continue, and even accelerate, in the 1920s: by 1923, for example, British films accounted for only 10 per cent of those shown.

In certain other respects, however, the war was to have a direct impact on the British film industry. For a country whose film industry was based largely on distribution and re-export, the war proved disastrous: the disruption of continental markets, difficulties in shipping due to the reallocation of cargo space to essential war materials, and an import duty on films all impacted on the industry. These problems were compounded by the rise of an aggressively entrepreneurial studio system in the USA, whereby the major companies set up their own international distribution networks rather than, as before, carrying on most of their overseas trade with Britain, which re-exported the films. In 1917, the leading British trade paper *The Bioscope* observed with much indignation: 'For many years London has enjoyed the distinction of being the acknowledged film centre of the world, but today its position is assailed by America, and we find the principal organ of the cinematograph industry in that country avowedly confessing that now is the time for Americans to corner the world's film markets'. The cumulative effect of all these factors was that the British film industry emerged from the war in a substantially weaker economic condition than it had been when hostilities commenced. Domestic production was in a parlous state, while American films dominated British screens. As an official report on the British film industry ruefully noted some three and a half decades later: 'With the end of the war came an opportunity for British production to reassert itself, but by now it had become a stranger in its own home' (*The British Film Industry*, 1952, p.32).

France

During the early 1910s the French film industry was buoyant, with a high level of demand for new films at home and healthy exports which meant that production was thriving. The leading production company, Pathé Frères, was strong in the American market, and, although American films were already starting to encroach on French screens by 1914, they had not yet achieved the same level of dominance as they had in Britain. At the outbreak of war, however, film production in France came to an abrupt halt. With the expectation of a short but intense conflict, no plans had been made for the continuation of the film industry. Instead, it was expected that general mobilization would account for industry personnel, that the consequently empty film studios would be used as barracks, and that Pathé's film stock factory at Vincennes would be used for the production of war materials. By the end of 1914, when it had become apparent that the war would not be over quickly, some cinemas reopened. Film production resumed early in 1915, though it did not reach its pre-war levels. Pathé remained profitable by distributing films made by independent producers, though as these included American companies the consequence was to help American films gain a greater share of the French market. Pathé's greatest popular success came with the distribution of the serial melodrama *The Perils of Pauline*, starring the original 'serial queen', Pearl White. French writer Philippe Soupault suggests how intensely this escapist fare affected Parisian audiences:

> Then one day we saw hanging on the walls great posters as long as serpents. At every street-corner a man, his face covered with a red handkerchief, leveled [*sic*] a revolver at the peaceful passerby. We imagined that we heard galloping hooves, the roar of motors, explosions, and cries of death. We rushed into the cinema, and realized immediately that everything had changed. On the screen appeared the smile of Pearl White - that almost ferocious smile which announced the revolution, the beginning of a new world.
>
> (Quoted in Richard Abel, *French Cinema: The First Wave, 1915–1929*, 1984, p.10)

Both French intellectuals and the public lapped up the films of American stars such as Douglas Fairbanks, Lillian Gish, William S. Hart and, above all, Charlie Chaplin. The popularity of these stars, whose films were melodramatic and escapist, suggests not only the acceptance of the 'new' culture of America, but also a change in the tastes of French audiences, who before the war had been enamoured of Italian classical spectacles. The result, however, was that, as in Britain, by the end of the war French producers were left trying vainly to stave off American dominance of their home screens.

Italy

The Italian film industry, like the French, had flourished in the early 1910s, with lavish historical feature films such as *Quo Vadis?* (1913), *The Last Days of Pompeii* (1913) and *Cabiria* (1914) enjoying enormous success both at home and abroad. The success of these films not only meant that the Italian domestic market was more resistant to American films before the war, but it also gave the Italian industry a toe-hold in the American market, where these films were popular with audiences and highly influential upon filmmakers such as D.W. Griffith. Italy entered the war later than Britain and France, which initially gave the Italian film industry an advantage in relation to the declining production levels in both those countries. But once involved in the war, Italy faced the same problems as other belligerent nations: the redeployment of the labour force, an inadequate supply of raw film stock, and shipping priorities for essential war materials. Consequently, domestic production declined and exports fell off dramatically. After the war, Italy was unable to regain its former prominence in the international market place, while the attempts of a large new production company, the *Unione Cinematografica Italiana*, formed in 1919, similarly failed to revive domestic production.

Germany

The German film industry had not been especially significant before 1912. German films were not widely exported, while imports dominated the domestic market. From 1912, however, this situation began to be reversed as the film industry started to expand and German films became more popular with domestic audiences. Germany followed the example of the American film industry in developing a star system: the most popular stars were the blonde Henny Porten, who was portrayed as the ideal of German womanhood, and the Danish actress Astrid Nielsen, whose films ranged from comedies to tragic melodramas. Even so, German screens were dominated by imports from France, Italy, Denmark and the USA. Ironically, when war broke out, two pacifist films were showing in Berlin cinemas, one French (*Guerre à la guerre/ War on War*), the other German (*Die Waffen nieder!/ Ground Arms!*) – both films were quickly withdrawn.

The effects of the war for the German film industry, in contrast to those of the Allied powers, were largely beneficial. Germany's industry was able to consolidate its own market, because Germany no longer imported films from France, Britain or Italy. All foreign imports were banned from 1916. There was a boom in German domestic production. Whereas in August 1914 there were only 25 German-owned production or distribution companies, by 1918 there were 130. This boom was due in no small measure to an increase in cinema attendances and a rise in the number of cinemas in Germany, from 2,446 in 1914 to 3,130 in 1917. The war also fostered a greater interest in the medium of film on the part of the state. As early as 1914, industrialists such as Alfred Hugenberg of Krupps realised that film had great potential as a medium of political influence. In 1917, Hugenberg was put in charge of the newly-founded Ufa (*Universum Film Aktiengesellschaft*), which became the largest German film company. The setting up of Ufa was supported by no less a figure than General Erich Ludendorff, who declared:

> The war has demonstrated the paramount power of images and of film as means of enlightenment and influence. Unfortunately our enemies have used the advantages that they enjoy in that area so thoroughly that they have caused us great damage. ... For the war to be concluded successfully, it is absolutely imperative that film be employed with the greatest force in all places where German influence is still possible.
>
> (Quoted in Peter Jelavich, 'German culture in the Great War', 1999, p.42)

Ludendorff clearly recognized the value of film as an instrument of propaganda (we'll be looking at the role of British film propaganda during the war, to which he alludes, later). Ufa, partly financed by the government acting through the Deutsche Bank, was an amalgamation of existing companies which assumed control of film studios, sales networks and chains of cinemas, thus giving it an effective monopoly of film production, distribution and exhibition inside

Germany. The purpose of this officially-backed corporation was to bring together Germany's best directors, scriptwriters and stars to make patriotic films in support of the war effort. In the event, Ufa had relatively little to show before the Western Front collapsed in August 1918, but under the post-war Weimar government it was privatized and became the flagship film production company that it was intended to be.

Russia

Like Germany, Russia developed a distinctive national cinema as a result of its near-isolation during the war. Before the war Russia depended upon imports for 90 per cent of its films, with Pathé of France being its leading provider. The first Russian production company was started in 1907 by photographer A.O. Drankov, followed a year later by a second, Khanzhonkov. While audiences preferred foreign films, by the eve of war Russia had a small but reasonably healthy production industry. At the outbreak of war, however, Russia's borders were closed, and foreign distributors closed their Moscow offices. The combination of war-related transport problems and the decline in production levels among its French, British and Italian allies meant that the Russian film industry had to fend for itself. Despite the problems of production resources in wartime, domestic production actually increased, with new production companies being set up, including the third of the three important Russian producers, Yermoliev. By 1916, domestic production had reached some 500 films. At the same time, a distinctive style of filmmaking emerged in Russia, exemplified by the work of directors Evgeny Bauer and Yakov Protazanov who specialized in brooding melodramas. Whereas production in other countries was dominated by light entertainment, in Russia there was a preference for psychological films with a slow pace, an intense acting style and tragic endings. Russian filmmakers deliberately differentiated their films from those of other countries, which is one of the characteristics of a genuine national cinema. As one trade paper put it: "'All's well that ends well!' This is the guiding principle of foreign cinema. But Russian cinema stubbornly refuses to accept this and goes its own way. Here "All's well that ends badly" – we need tragic endings' (quoted in Thompson and Bordwell, *Film History*, 1994, p.59). However, this national cinema was short-lived. The Bolshevik Revolution in 1917 brought film production almost to a standstill, and by the time filmmaking started again in earnest in the early 1920s the slow, brooding style of wartime Russian cinema was regarded as old-fashioned and backward. (We will be looking at post-Revolutionary Russian/Soviet cinema in Book 3).

Scandinavia

Arguably the most distinctive European national cinema at the outbreak of war was that of Denmark. The Danish film industry was well established and production was healthy. The *Nordisk Films Kompagni* (Nordisk Film Company), set up in 1906 by a Copenhagen cinema owner called Ole Olsen, had within a few years become the second largest film company in Europe (behind Pathé). Nordisk specialized in the production of genre films which were similar to American ones, including melodramas, farces and thrillers, though Danish films were characterized by their realistic and naturalistic scenery. Nordisk's top director in the early 1910s was August Blom, whose most important film was *Atlantis* (1913), a melodrama about the sinking of an ocean liner (inspired by the *Titanic* disaster of the previous year). The immediate pre-war period was something of a 'golden age' for Danish cinema, but with the outbreak of war the situation deteriorated. Nordisk's most important foreign market was Germany, and, while it initially benefited from the exclusion of French films from the German market, the German ban on all imported films in 1916 came as a severe blow to Nordisk, which temporarily discontinued production in 1917. When it resumed after the war it was effectively beginning from nothing, and Nordisk never regained its position in the international film market. The case of Denmark, therefore, provides an example of a country that remained neutral but whose film industry was still severely affected by the war.

In Sweden, by contrast, the process was reversed as the war saw the beginnings of a 'golden age' that was to last into the 1920s. The success of Nordisk in Denmark had been the inspiration for the formation of a small Swedish company, *Svenska Biografteatern* (Swedish Biograph), which soon became the country's leading producer. From 1912, Sweden began producing a string of distinctive films, most of which were made by three directors: Georg af Klerker, Mauritz Stiller and Victor Sjöström. As, from the outbreak of war, Germany was blockading film imports to several northern European countries, relatively few foreign films were shown in Sweden, meaning that demand for the home-made product was greater. Sweden was one of the first countries to create a national cinema by drawing deliberately on its own indigenous culture, with films that were based on Swedish literature and were characterized by their striking visual use of natural scenery and landscapes. Films such as Sjöström's *Terje Vigen* (1916) and *The Outlaw and His Wife* (1917) made a great impact when, belatedly, they were released abroad, and Swedish cinema was generally recognized as the first major alternative to Hollywood to emerge after the war.

Exercise   To what extent do you think participation in the First World War contributed to the emergence of distinctive national cinemas in Europe? Write a short paragraph in answer to this question. ■

Specimen answer   While it was certainly the case that the war helped to foster a new sense of filmic and cultural identity in countries such as Germany and, especially, Russia, it cannot be said that participation in the war was a prerequisite for the emergence of a distinctive national style of filmmaking, as the case of neutral Sweden illustrates. In other countries, such as Britain, France and Italy, the decline in domestic production and the increased popularity of American films suggests that the war may have contributed to the erosion of the sense of a national filmic identity. The case of Denmark illustrates that neutral countries also felt the economic consequences of war, where the loss of a key foreign market meant the end of a healthy national cinema that had existed before the war.

Discussion   There are two key points to emphasize: first, that participation in the war affected different countries in different ways; and second, that the effects of war were also felt in non-belligerent nations. But while the effects of the war for different European film industries were mixed, there are some common factors. Those countries where a national cinema can be seen to have emerged, whether belligerent or neutral, had one thing in common: the number of imported foreign films was drastically reduced due to the war. The dearth of foreign films tended to boost domestic production in order to fulfil demand. In those countries which experienced declining levels of domestic production, and where imports were less restricted, the void tended to be filled by American films. The major factor that cannot be ignored is that the relative weakness of the European film industries as a consequence of war worked to the benefit of the American film industry, by now based largely in Hollywood, California. By 1918 American films were regarded as more modern and technically more sophisticated than their European counterparts, which tended to cling on to old-fashioned ways of doing things. American dominance of the international film market after the war was to lead politicians and cultural commentators in the 1920s to voice their concerns about the 'Americanization' of popular culture. The consequences of the First World War for the international film industry are summed up thus by film historian William Uricchio:

> The war, then, served not only to dismantle Europe's dominant pre-war industries, but, ironically, to construct a tacit consensus regarding the national importance of cinema. The latter point underwent a curious permutation which assisted the US penetration of markets such as England [*sic*], France and Italy, and meanwhile stimulated the distinctive national identities of the German and Russian cinemas. As the specifically 'national' character of the European allies' cinema became increasingly associated with the gruelling war effort and pre-war national identities, the US cinema increasingly appeared as a morale booster and harbinger of a new internationalism. Chaplin's appeal to French children, workers, and intellectuals alike outlined the trajectory which American feature films would follow by the war's end, as US films served the cultural functions of social unification and entertainment while expressing the emphatically modern *Zeitgeist* of the post-war era.
>
> (William Uricchio, 'The First World War and the Crisis in Europe', 1996, p.67) □

Film as a historical source

You'll remember from Unit 1 that one of the aims of this course is to assist students in 'the critical analysis and interpretation of primary source materials, including ... film'. Film can be an exceptionally useful, though at the same time a very problematic, primary source material for the historian. Before we go any further, however, a quick exercise to ensure that we are all entirely sure about what primary film sources are.

Exercise   Consider the following list of five films and identify which are primary sources for the war:

1   *All Quiet on the Western Front* (1930): a Hollywood film, directed by Lewis Milestone, based on the German novel by Erich Maria Remarque (1929).

2   *Battle of the Somme* (1916): the official British film record of the campaign.

3   *Bei unseren Helden an der Somme/With Our Heroes on the Somme* (1917): the official German film record of the battle.

4   *La Grande Illusion* (1937): a French film, directed by Jean Renoir, about French airmen in a German prison camp.

5   *Regeneration* (1997): a British film, directed by Gillies MacKinnon, based on the novel by Pat Barker which charts the real-life relationships between Dr William Rivers, Siegfried Sassoon and Wilfrid Owen. ■

Specimen answer   I hope you got this right! Only (2) and (3) are primary sources for the war, as they were produced during the war itself. (1), (4) and (5) were produced after the war, and, in the case of (5), at a very considerable remove from it. I hope you weren't fooled into thinking that (5) was a primary source because it was based on real people. These later films might be considered primary sources for the periods in which they were made – *All Quiet on the Western Front* perhaps exemplifying pacifist sentiments in the aftermath of the war, *La Grande Illusion* illustrating social attitudes and values in 1930s France – but not for the period in which they are set.

Discussion   You might have thought this exercise was pretty basic, which of course it is, but it does serve a useful purpose. Many of our impressions of what the First World War was like, especially for soldiers on the Western Front, have been derived from films made after the war itself. Anyone who has seen *All Quiet on the Western Front* or *Regeneration* – or other celebrated films about the war such as Stanley Kubrick's *Paths of Glory* (1957) and Joseph Losey's *King and Country* (1964) – cannot help but notice the powerful way in which they present the war as horrific and futile. However, these films represent post-war attitudes towards the war; they could all be described as 'anti-war' films. I think you would agree that you would not expect anti-war sentiments to be expressed in films made during the war itself, especially those which were produced for propaganda purposes. A more practical consideration about film of the First World War concerns the authenticity of film material. On more than one occasion I've seen extracts from *All Quiet on the Western Front* (recognizable through long and technically complicated camera tracking shots) turn up in television documentaries purporting to show trench warfare! □

Having ensured that we are looking at film as a primary source, then, what use can we make of it? Ever since the invention of cinematography it has been claimed that film can be used as a source of historical evidence. In 1895, pioneer British filmmaker W. K. L Dickson suggested that historians would benefit from film records of 'great national scenes' which would be more vital than other 'dry and misleading accounts, tinged with the exaggerations of the chroniclers' minds' (quoted in Anthony Aldgate, *Cinema and History*, 1979, p.2). Dickson had the opportunity to put his idea into practice when he was sent to South Africa during the Boer War as an official cameraman for the Biograph Company. In 1898, the Polish filmmaker Boleslaw Matuszewski described the cinema as '*une nouvelle source de l'histoire*' and went on to declare: 'The cinema may not give a complete history, but what it gives is incontestably and absolutely true' (ibid, p.3).

As historians, of course, we would do well to be extremely cautious about the assumption that a film record of anything is 'incontestably and absolutely true'. As we will see, the old axiom that 'the camera never lies' does not really hold true. Some of the very earliest supposed film records were fakes: a British film of 1900 purporting to show the Boxer Rebellion in China was actually filmed in Wales. As with any other historical source, film needs to be treated with caution: its authenticity needs to be established, the conditions under which it was produced need to be considered, the intentions of the filmmakers need to be discussed, and the possibilities of bias and partiality need to be weighed up. Indeed, as with other sources, we can usefully distinguish between 'witting' and 'unwitting' testimony: while film may have a deliberate intent, a particular point to make, that is not to say that it cannot also be revealing in other ways which were not intended by the filmmaker. As film historian Karsten Fledelius has pointed out:

> Often the most interesting evidence is the 'unwitting testimony' of the cinematographic recordings, all those incidental aspects of reality which have just 'slipped' into the camera without being consciously recorded by the cameraman. The 'evidence by accident' may be extremely valuable to the historian.

(Quoted in Arthur Marwick, *The Nature of History*, 1989, p.218)

Exercise   I want you now to look at items 1–4 on video-cassette 1. These are all extracts from newsreels of 1914 showing troops leaving Britain, France and Turkey for the front. As you watch them, note down what you think is useful to the historian in these extracts, distinguishing between 'witting' and 'unwitting' testimony. ■

Specimen answer   The witting testimony in all the extracts is to show that troops are leaving for the front in good cheer. The two British newsreels, in particular, show the soldiers waving both at the camera and at the crowds. The Turkish newsreel emphasizes that the men are volunteers – note the inter-title stating 'Enlisting volunteers in the villages' – though to my mind the men filing past the camera there do not look anywhere near as keen to be going off to war as the British were. Both the British and the French newsreels show crowds of civilians waving off the troops, with some people marching alongside the parades. This suggests that the soldiers were held in some esteem by the civilian population – which was not necessarily the case, of course, in all European countries at the time. As far as unwitting testimony is concerned, the extracts give us a good idea of the uniforms and equipment of the respective countries. The British and French troops certainly look better equipped than the Turks. Finally, if you were looking closely, you may have noticed in the French newsreel that a good number of the troops had darker complexions than the civilians – they are probably Algerians – but that all the NCOs marching alongside the columns were white. This sort of 'evidence by accident' would be of interest, for example, to a military historian, or even to a French social historian, for what it reveals about the composition of the French army in 1914.

Discussion   Witting and unwitting testimony are useful, and important, categories, though the difference between them is not always clear-cut. Take another look at the first three extracts and ask yourself whether these pieces of film really do provide us with any solid evidence regarding popular attitudes towards war in 1914. Just because we see people waving off the troops does not necessarily mean that they supported the war in principle – they are just as likely to be waving to their friends or families. Like any other source, filmic evidence needs to be compared to other sources to get a full picture. As the French historian Marc Ferro has pointed out, writing about the images of soldiers in 1914: 'They marched off to war, their faces a picture of delight. Film is of course deceptive and a more searching examination would show other images – the anguish of a father, a fiancé, or a husband' (*The Great War 1914–1918*, p.xi). □

The First World War is the first conflict for which a lot of filmic evidence exists. This was due in large measure to the encouragement which governments gave to film cameramen to record the fighting. For the remainder of this section, I'm going to focus on the ways in which the British made use of film in an official capacity during the war.

Filming the war: official British film propaganda

At the outbreak of war there was no official machinery for the filming of the British army at war. Indeed, in September 1914 an outright ban was placed on film cameras and newsmen at the front line by Lord Kitchener, the Secretary of State for War. While British military authorities were antipathetic towards the press, they were merely indifferent towards the cinema. In official eyes, according to a Department of Information report sent to the War Cabinet in 1917, the cinema was 'almost universally regarded as an instrument for the entertainment of the masses; the educated classes thought of "the pictures" as responsible for turning romantic schoolboys into juvenile highwaymen, as a sort of moving edition of the "penny dreadful"' (quoted in S. D. Badsey, *'Battle of the Somme*: British war-propaganda', 1983, p.100). The potential for film as a means of reporting the war effort to the general public was not immediately appreciated. In the absence of newsreels or 'actuality' films, there was a boom in fictional war dramas.

It was not until the summer of 1915 that an arrangement was made between the War Office and the film trade, under the auspices of a body called the British Topical Committee for War Films. There was agreement in official circles that official films should be factual, actuality films: 'real British war films, as distinct from faked war dramas', as Sir George Barclay, the British ambassador in Bucharest, put it (quoted in Nicholas Reeves, *The Power of Film Propaganda*, 1999, p.23). The first cameramen allowed in British sectors of the Western Front arrived in November 1915, and the first short newsreels of the front line were shown publicly in London in January 1916.

As the government was not prepared to fund the production of films, the Topical Committee agreed to provide all the equipment and pay the cameramen's salaries, in return for which it was granted exclusive rights to exploit the films commercially in Britain and throughout the Empire (except in India and Egypt, where the War Office retained control of exhibition). In so far as people at home had been starved of information about the war, it could reasonably be expected that films from the front would prove successful commercially. The film trade was naturally influenced by economic considerations, albeit that it was agreed a proportion of profits should be donated to military and naval charities.

The first films produced under the Topical Committee's agreement with the War Office were heralded by a full-page advertisement in the trade press which declared: 'The British Army in France. The Official Pictures'. Some twenty-seven short films were released during the first six months of 1916, but they met with a lukewarm reaction overall from press and public. Why was this, given that people were eager for news of the war? In the words of Nicholas Reeves, a historian of official British film propaganda during the First World War:

> The nature of the films makes it easy to understand this acute sense of disappointment. The cinema trade's long-standing desire to film at the front derived from an assumption that it would be possible to achieve close, dramatic footage of the fighting itself, and while the advertising never explicitly promised footage of that kind, this was almost certainly what the paying audiences anticipated. In practice, a combination of the technological limitations of the cameras and the deeply cautious approach of the intelligence officers who supervised the cameramen, meant that none of these films included any such footage, concentrating instead on those rather more mundane, less dramatic activities, which were also a crucial part of life at the front. Thus the Western Front films released in the first half of 1916 demonstrate that, even in a strongly favourable climate, propaganda films can fail.

(Reeves, *The Power of Film Propaganda*, 1999, pp.25–6)

The first major official British film of the war, *Battle of the Somme*, came about unintentionally. In June 1916, two British cameramen, Geoffrey Malins and J. B. McDowell, were sent to film the British Fourth Army launching its offensive along the River Somme. They filmed the artillery bombardment and British troops being marched up through villages behind the lines. On the morning of 1 July Malins filmed the explosion of a giant mine under the German strongpoint at Hawthorn Ridge, then followed men of the 1st Lancashire Fusiliers moving up through the approach trenches. He was unable to film the actual assault, in which the Fusiliers were mown down by German machine-gun fire, without putting himself in the firing line. He therefore joined his colleague McDowell at the Minden dressing post, where they filmed the wounded of both sides being brought in. They also filmed captured German trenches and, finally, the survivors of the assault of 1 July coming out of the line to rest.

The first rushes of the material taken by Malins and McDowell were shown to the Topical Committee in London on 12 July. The Committee decided that a full-length film should be made from the material. Entitled *Battle of the Somme*, the film opened in thirty-four cinemas in London on 21 August and in other major cities a week later.

From what evidence we have, it seems that *Battle of the Somme* made an enormous impact on the British public. There were press reports of hundreds of thousands of people flocking to see it. The patriotic appeal of the film was emphasized in its promotion: one cinema exhibitor in Leeds advertised a visit to see it as 'a duty you owe to the Imperial Government'. The film received official endorsement when the King saw it at Windsor and was quoted as saying 'the public should see these pictures that they may have some idea of what the army is doing'. The press reviews of the film were extremely enthusiastic. The *Bioscope* opined that 'no written description by an eyewitness, however graphic his pen; no illustration by any artist, no matter how facile his pencil; no verbal description by the most interested participator in the event, could hope to convey to the man at home the reality of modern warfare with the force and conviction shown in this marvellous series of pictures'. And *The Times* declared: 'If anything were needed to justify the existence of the cinematograph, it is to be found in [this] wonderful series of films'. This latter quotation, in particular, provides useful evidence of how contemporary commentators saw the cinema coming of age through its role in reporting the war.

Yet this reaction was not universal, and there were some voices which were uneasy about the images of warfare presented in the film. The Dean of Durham wrote to *The Times* protesting that 'crowds of Londoners feel no scruple at feasting their eyes on pictures which present the passion and death of British soldiers in the *Battle of the Somme* ... I beg leave respectfully to enter a protest against an entertainment which wounds the hearts and violates the very sanctities of bereavement'. While this reaction was certainly not representative, it does give some indication of the highly charged and emotive atmosphere in which the film was received.

Exercise   I want you now to look at item 5 on video-cassette 1, which is an extract from *Battle of the Somme* showing British troops and German prisoners coming to a dressing station behind the British lines. As with the previous exercise, you should note down what you think there is in this extract that is valuable to the historian. In particular, what impression does it give of the experience of battle? ■

Specimen answer   While the extract tells us nothing about the battle itself, we can see the effects of battle in the faces of soldiers on both sides, many of whom look dazed and confused. While some men look at the camera, there is nothing like the waving and cheering that characterized the newsreels of 1914. The pictures of both British and German wounded gives some indication of the common experience of warfare. There does not appear to be any antagonism between the British and German soldiers: you may have noted one scene in which a British soldier is handing out cigarettes to the prisoners (though the line of men standing in the background watching this act suggests that it may have been staged for the camera). Interestingly, given that so many of our impressions of the Somme are of men falling down in the mud, this extract shows the ground to be hard, and the weather hot and dusty (note the number of men in shirt-sleeves).

Discussion   The most interesting thing about the extract to my mind, however, is the inter-title at the beginning which states: 'British Wounded and Nerve-Shattered German Prisoners Arriving'. We know that the British army long wanted to deny that 'shell shock' was a real medical condition. The implication of this inter-title is that British soldiers do not suffer from shell shock, but that German soldiers do. This is an example of propaganda, intended to create the impression for audiences at home that the Germans' ability and will to fight was being destroyed – which, as we know, was very far from the truth in 1916. In other respects, too, there is cause to doubt some of the 'evidence' presented by *Battle of the Somme*. It has since been proved that some of the scenes in the film, including shots of British soldiers going 'over the top', were faked. If you think about it, this isn't all that surprising, as a cameraman, with a bulky piece of equipment to carry, was unlikely to have stood up in No Man's Land to film an attack. However, according to Roger Smither, Keeper of Film at the Imperial War Museum, 'while *The Battle of the Somme* [sic] does contain some faked film, the proportion of such film to the whole work is actually quite small' ('"A wonderful idea of the fighting": the question of fakes in *The Battle of the Somme*', 1988, p.15). What we don't have any evidence about one way or the other, unfortunately, is whether audiences in 1916 detected the faked, or 'reconstructed', scenes.

Battle of the Somme stands out as the foremost British film record of the war on the Western Front. It was followed by another two 'battle' pictures, both rather ponderously titled: *Battle of the Ancre and the Advance of the Tanks* (1916) and *The German Retreat and the Battle of Arras* (1917). While *Battle of the Ancre* was almost as successful as its predecessor, perhaps because it contained footage of the British army's new 'wonder' weapon, the tank, by the time that *Battle of Arras* was released in June 1917 the public's appetite for this type of film was on the wane. By this time, there was evidence of a change in public opinion as it became clear that the Somme had been very far from the glorious victory expected. When *Battle of Arras* was released, footage of the dead and wounded, which had featured prominently in the two earlier films, was mostly cut out.

In May 1917, Lord Beaverbrook, the press baron who, as Chancellor of the Duchy of Lancaster in the Lloyd George government was involved in various aspects of the war effort, asserted that 'the present style of films is played out. The public is jaded and we have to tickle its palate with something a little more dramatic in the future if we are to maintain our sales'. At Beaverbrook's instigation, the film taken on the Western Front was now to be used for an official newsreel. Newsreels were an established part of the programme in British cinemas, though at this time the market was dominated by two French-owned newsreels, *Gaumont Graphic* and *Pathé Gazette*. The one British newsreel, *Topical Budget*, was taken over by the War Office and relaunched as the *War Office Official Topical Budget*. The creation of an official newsreel was part of a rationalization of all official propaganda activities that resulted, in March 1918, in the creation of a Ministry of Information, under Beaverbrook. *War Office Official Topical Budget* was to be produced twice-weekly until the end of the war, though its name was changed in February 1918 to *Pictorial News (Official)*. By this time there were seven official cameramen in different theatres of war: four on the Western Front, one in Egypt, one in Mesopotamia and one with the Royal Navy. The newsreel was primarily a vehicle for film taken by these cameramen, though it also included some news items about the home front to illustrate the new demands that war was making on British industry. Among the events which *War Office Official Topical Budget/Pictorial News (Official)* covered were the entry of General Allenby into Jerusalem in February 1918 and the signing of the peace treaty between Germany and the Allies in the Hall of Mirrors at the Palace of Versailles on 28 June 1919. After the war, as the official apparatus was wound up, the newsreel reverted to its original name of *Topical Budget*.

In conclusion, how effective was the British government's use of film as a medium of propaganda during the First World War? In order to answer this question, it is necessary to make a distinction between the role of film in recording the war effort and its role in generating support for the war effort. As far as its role in recording the British war effort is concerned, it seems clear that, after a hesitant start, film was put to good use in showing audiences both at home and overseas something of the nature of the war. The mostly enthusiastic reception of *Battle of the Somme* shows just how eager the public were to see film from the front. Having said that, the film benefited from being released at a time when public opinion was still broadly committed to the war. When *Battle of Arras* was released in the summer of 1917, its less successful reception was due in large measure to an increasing sense of war-weariness. In the considered opinion of Nicholas Reeves, 'whatever the propagandists may have thought at the time … public opinion in Britain during the First World War was more influenced by the changing nature of the war and by people's own direct, personal experiences of the war, than it was by the official films, or indeed any other form of wartime propaganda' (Reeves, *The Power of Film Propaganda*, 1999, p.38). □

References

Abel, Richard (1984), *The French Cinema: The First Wave, 1915-1929*, Princeton University Press.

Aldcroft, D. H. (1977) *From Versailles to Wall Street, 1919–1929*, Penguin.

Aldgate, Anthony (1979), *Cinema and History: British Newsreels and the Spanish Civil War*, Scolar Press.

Badsey, S. D. (1983) 'Battle of the Somme: British war-propaganda', *Historical Journal of Film, Radio and Television*, vol.3, no.2, pp.99–115.

Barton, B. and Foy, M. (1999) *The Easter Rising*, Sutton.

The British Film Industry: A report on its history and present organisation with special reference to the economic problems of British feature film production (1952), Political and Economic Planning.

Becker, J-J. (1985) *The Great War and the French People,* trans. A. Pomerans, Berg.

Beckett, J. V. (1988) *The Aristocracy in England 1660–1919*, Blackwell.

Bessell, Richard (1993) *Germany After the War*, Clarendon Press (extract reprinted in Course Reader).

Bessell, Richard (1997) 'State and society in Germany in the aftermath of the First World War' in W. R. Lee and Eve Rosenhaft (eds), *State, Social Policy and Social Change in Germany 1880–1994*, Berg.

Constantine, S., Kirby, M. W., and Rose M. R. (eds) (1995), *The First World War in British History*, Edward Arnold.

Cruickshank, J. (1982) *Variations on Catastrophe: Some French Responses to the Great War*, Oxford University Press.

Danaïllow, G. T. (1932) *Les effets de la guerre en Bulgarie,* Carnegie Endowment for International Peace, Yale University Press.

Davies, Norman (1996) *Europe, A History,* Oxford University Press.

Feldman, G. (1966) *Army, Industry and Labor in Germany 1914–1918,* Princeton University Press.

Fermor, P. Leigh (1977) *A Time of Gifts,* London, John Murray.

Ferro, Marc (1973) *The Great War 1914–18,* trans. Nicole Stone, Routledge and Kegan Paul.

Fisher, H. A. L. (1935) *A History of Europe,* vol. III, Houghton Mifflin.

Fridensen, P. (1992) *The French Home Front 1914–1918,* Berg.

Fuller, J. G. (1990), *Troop Morale and Popular Culture in the British and Dominion Armies, 1914–1918,* Clarendon Press.

Fussell, P. (1975) *The Great War and Modern Memory,* Oxford University Press.

Gagnon, P. (1972) *France since 1789* (revised edn), New York, Harper and Row.

Geyer, M. (1981) 'Professionals and Junkers: German re-armament and politics in the Weimar Republic', in Bessel, R. and Feuchtwanger, E. J. (eds) *Social Change and Political Development in Weimar Germany,* Croom Helm.

Golovin, N. (1931) *The Russian Army in the World War,* Carnegie Endowment for International Peace, Yale University Press.

Hajnal, J. (1965) 'European marriage patterns in perspective', in D. V. C. Glass and D. E. C. Eversley (eds) *Population in History: Essays in Historical Demography,* Edward Arnold.

Higonnet, M. *et al.* (1987) *Behind the Lines: Gender and the Two World Wars,* Yale University Press.

Jelavich, Peter (1999) 'German culture in the Great War', in Roshwald and Stiles (eds) (1999) pp.32–57.

Jencks, C. (1982) *Modern Movements in Architecture,* Penguin (first published 1973).

Kirk, D. (1946) *Europe's Population in the Interwar Years,* League of Nations.

Kosinsky, L. A. (1970) *The Population of Europe,* Longman.

Larkin, Maurice (1977) *France since the Popular Front: Government and People 1936–1996,* Clarendon Press.

Lee, W. R., and Rosenhaft, E. (eds) (1997) *State, Social Policy and Social Change in Germany 1880–1994,* Berg.

Lentin, A. (1985) *Lloyd George, Woodrow Wilson and the Guilt of Germany,* Leicester University Press.

Leslie, R. F. (ed.) (1987) *The History of Poland since 1863,* Cambridge University Press.

Macartney, C. A. and Palmer, A. W. (1962) *Independent Eastern Europe,* Macmillan.

McMillan, J. R. (1981) *Housewife or Harlot,* Harvester Press.

Maier, C. S. (1975) *Recasting Bourgeois Europe: Stabilization in the Decade after World War 1,* Princeton University Press (extracts reprinted in Course Reader).

Martel, G. (ed.) (1986) '*Origins of the Second World War' Reconsidered,* Allen and Unwin.

Marwick, A. (1974) *War and Social Change in the Twentieth Century,* Macmillan.

Marwick, Arthur (1989), *The Nature of History,* 3rd edn, Macmillan.

Marwick, A. (1991) *The Deluge: British Society and the First World War,* (2nd edition), Macmillan.

May, A. J. (1966) *The Passing of the Hapsburg Monarchy 1914–1918,* University of Pennsylvania Press.

Mayer, A. J. (1981) *The Persistence of the Old Regime: Europe to the Great War,* Pantheon.

Medlicott, W. N. (1940) *British Foreign Policy since Versailles,* Methuen.

Middlemas, K. (1979) *Politics in Industrial Society: The Experience of the British System since 1911,* Deutsch.

Mitchell, B. R. (1975) *European Historical Statistics 1750–1970,* Columbia University Press.

Mitrany, D. (1936) *The Effect of the War in South-Eastern Europe,* Oxford University Press.

Mommsen, W. (1988) 'The social consequences of World War I: the case of Germany', in A. Marwick (ed.) *Total War and Social Change,* Macmillan.

Mosse, G. L. (1988) *The Culture of Western Europe,* Westview Press.

Nicolson, H. (1952) *King George V,* Constable.

Nicolson, H. (1944) *Peacemaking 1919,* Constable.

O'Connor, T. P. (1884) *Lord Beaconsfield, a Biography,* Lond.

Polonsky, A. (1983) 'The breakdown of parliamentary government', in R. F. Leslie (ed.) *The History of Poland since 1863,* Cambridge University Press.

Reeves, Nicholas (1999), *The Power of Film Propaganda: Myth or Reality?,* Cassell.

Reid, A. (1988) 'World War I and the working class in Britain', in A. Marwick (ed.) *Total War and Social Change,* Macmillan.

Reinhard, M. R. *et al.* (1968) *Histoire générale de la population mondiale,* Montchrestien.

Riasanovsky, N. V. (1984) *History of Russia,* Oxford University Press.

Roberts, R. (1971) *The Classic Slum: Salford Life in the First Quarter of the Century,* Manchester University Press.

Rogger, H. (1983) *Russia in the Age of Modernisation and Revolution 1881–1917,* Longman.

Rose, K. (1983) *King George V,* Macmillan.

Roshwald, Aviel, and Stites, Richard (eds) (1999) *European Culture in the Great War: The arts, entertainment, and propaganda, 1914–1918*, Cambridge University Press.

Searle, John (1999) *Mind, Language and Society: Doing Philosophy in the Real World*, Weidenfeld and Nicolson.

Sked, Alan (1989) *The Habsburg Monarchy*, Longman.

Smith, Paul (1996) *Feminism and the Third Republic: Women's Political and Civil Rights in France 1918–1945*, Clarendon Press.

Smither, Roger (1988), '"A wonderful idea of the fighting": the question of fakes in *The Battle of the Somme*', *Imperial War Museum Review*, no.3, pp.4–16.

Stone, N. (1983) *Europe Transformed 1878–1919*, London, Fontana.

Taylor, A. J. P. (1961) *The Origins of the Second World War*, Hamish Hamilton.

Thompson, F. M. L. (1963) *English Landed Society in the Nineteenth Century*, Routledge and Kegan Paul.

Thompson, Kristin, and Bordwell, David (1994) *Film History: An Introduction*, McGraw-Hill.

Travers, M. (1982) *German Novels on the First World War and Their Ideological Implications, 1918–1933*, Akademischer Verlag Hans-Dieter Heing.

Uricchio, William (1996), 'The First World War and the Crisis in Europe', in Nowell-Smith, Geoffrey (ed.), *The Oxford History of World Cinema*, Oxford University Press, pp.62–70.

Urlanis, B. C. (1970) in L. A. Kosinsky (ed.) *The Population of Europe: A Geographical Perspective*, Longman.

Usborne, Cornelie (1992) *The Politics of the Body in Weimar Germany: Women's Reproductive Rights and Duties*, Macmillan.

Waites, B. (1976) 'The effect of the First World War on class and status in England 1910-20', *Journal of Contemporary History*, vol. II, no. 1.

Waites, B. (1988) *A Class Society at War: England 1914-18*, Berg.

Wall, R. and Winter, J. (1989) *The Upheaval of War: Family, Work and Welfare in Europe, 1914–1918*, Cambridge University Press.

Weindling, Paul (1997) 'Eugenics and the Welfare State during the Weimar Republic', in W. R. Lee and Eve Rosenshaft (eds) *State, Social Policy and Social Change in Germany 1880–1994*, Berg.

Wilson, T. (1986) *The Myriad Faces of War: Britain and the Great War 1914–18*, Polity Press.

Winter, J. M. (1986) *The Great War and the British People*, Macmillan.

Woytinsky, W. S. and E. S. (1953) *World Population and Production: Trends and Outlook*, Twentieth Century Fund.

Yovanovitch, D. (1929) *Les effets économiques et sociaux de la guerre en Serbie*, Carnegie Endowment.

Further reading

Dibbets, Karel, and Hogenkamp, Bert (eds) (1995), *Film and the First World War*, Amsterdam University Press.

Kelly, Andrew (1997), *Cinema and the Great War*, Routledge.

McKernan, Luke (1992), *Topical Budget: The Great British News Film*, British Film Institute.

Malins, Geoffrey (1920), *How I Filmed the War*, Herbert Jenkens.

Marwick, A. (2000) *A History of the Modern British Isles 1914–99*, Blackwell.

Paris, Michael (ed.) (2000) *The First World War and Popular Cinema*, Edinburgh University Press.

Reeves, Nicholas (1986), *Official British Film Propaganda during the First World War*, Croom Helm.

Reeves, Nicholas (1993), 'The power of film propaganda: myth or reality?', *Historical Journal of Film, Radio and Television*, vol.13, no.2, pp.181–201.

Reeves, Nicholas (1997), 'Cinema, spectatorship and propaganda: *Battle of the Somme* (1916) and its contemporary audience', *Historical Journal of Film, Radio and Television*, vol.17, no.1, pp.5–28.

Townshend, C. (2005) *Easter 1916: the Irish Rebellion*, Allen Lane.

Units 11–13 THE RUSSIAN AND GERMAN REVOLUTIONS AND THE COLLAPSE OF THE HABSBURG EMPIRE: A COMPARATIVE STUDY

CLIVE EMSLEY, DAVID ENGLANDER AND MARK PITTAWAY

(Sections 1–5 by Clive Emsley; sections 6, 7 and 8 by David Englander, revised by Mark Pittaway; section 9 by Mark Pittaway; section 10 by Clive Emsley)

Emsley

Englander

11

12

P. Hanray

Ensley

Units 11–13 are not separated into three discrete units, although they do, of course, represent three weeks' work. For the purposes of your study time, therefore, Unit 11 covers sections 1–5, Unit 12 covers sections 6–8 and Unit 13 covers sections 9 and 10.

Open University students of these units will need to refer to:

Set book: J. M. Roberts, *Europe 1880–1945*, Longman, 2001

Primary Sources 1: World War I, eds Arthur Marwick and Wendy Simpson, Open University, 2000

Maps Booklet

Video 1
Audio 1

Define: "revolution"

social (incl.
ethnicity)

political

military

economic

INTRODUCTION

Many, perhaps most, European governments were concerned about revolution, or at least violent demonstrations by trades unions, socialists and/or peasants. There had been revolution in Russia in 1905; in June 1914 Italy had been shaken by the violence of 'Red Week'. Some German army officers toyed with the idea of *Staatsstreich* (in effect, a coup by the Kaiser's inner circle), by which the repressive power available to the crown would be used to forestall any threat from the *Socialdemokratische Partei Deutschlands* (SPD); in 1913 Bethmann Hollweg expressed concern that the Kaiser was continually talking about abolishing or at least chastising the *Reichstag* and using one of his adjutant generals for the task. But when war came, no one thought that, for several major participants, it would end in the total destruction of their regime.

In 1914 there were four empires in central and eastern Europe: the Austro-Hungarian, German, Russian and Turkish. Eight years later each of these had been defeated and had ceased to exist; furthermore, all have been said to have experienced 'revolution'. The small Balkan states that existed between these empires in 1914 experienced similar political and social upheaval, though their problems have not always been graced with the term 'revolution'. In the following three units we want you to think about the events of war and revolution in central and eastern Europe between *c*.1914 and *c*.1921.

When you have completed these three units you should:

1   appreciate the main semantic problems that arise with the word 'revolution';

2   have a grasp of the basic outline of the events of war and revolution during the period *c*.1914 to *c*.1921 in central and eastern Europe;

3   be able to make your own informed assessment of the interrelationship between war and revolution in these parts of Europe.

1   CONCEPTUALIZATION: REVOLUTION AND WORLD WAR I

'Revolution' is a word much used (perhaps over-used) by academics as well as journalists and politicians. Thus we have references to revolutions in government, to industrial revolutions, intellectual revolutions, managerial revolutions, scientific revolutions, student revolutions, in addition to the kinds of political revolutions which engulfed France during the 1790s and Russia in 1917. Generally speaking, however, all of these uses are in some way referring to change, and "change which is both fundamental and sudden".

Emsley

"political
revolution"

Our concern in this unit is essentially political revolution. This is defined in the *Oxford English Dictionary* as 'a complete overthrow of the established government in any country by those who were previously subject to it; a forcible substitution of a new ruler or form of government'. This definition seems to me to ignore one crucial element, mass participation, without which there is not always a great deal of difference between a *coup d'état* (a 'palace revolution' if you like) and the kind of upheaval which we are discussing. Yet even the notion of the forcible and sudden overthrow of one system of government by a violent upheaval involving mass participation does not take us much further forward in explaining the process of political revolution. A consensus appears to be emerging among historians and political scientists that the process of political revolution involves:

1   a total breakdown of government and particularly of the state's monopoly of armed force; leading to

2   a struggle between different armed power blocs for control of the state; these power blocs might be organized paramilitary formations, improvised groups like the soldiers' and workers' councils in Russia, or spontaneous peasant *jacqueries;*

3   the revolution is brought to an end when one of these blocs emerges as dominant and is able to reconstitute the sovereign power of the state. Often the most violent stage of the revolution occurs when a power bloc (or an amalgam of such blocs) has made itself master in the centre and then sets out to impose its authority on the provinces.

[handwritten margin notes: "What it is: 'political revolution'"; "meant controlling the means of production; ownership"; "didn't happen until October"]

This definition portrays revolution as a specifically political process; it is not concerned to cover the macro-conceptualization of Marxist historiography, which sees revolutions as key events in the process whereby one socio-economic system is replaced by another. In this definition it is not important whether the English Revolution of the 1640s and the French Revolution of the 1790s were crucial moments in the shift from feudalism to capitalism. Nor is it important whether the Russian Revolution, which is central to these units, was a crucial moment in the overthrow of capitalism. However, many of the individual revolutionary activists who participated in the events which we will be discussing did conceive of their action and their revolutions in these Marxist terms.

Exercise   From your basic historical and general knowledge make a list of what might be considered as the general causes of revolution. I would also like you to think carefully about the validity of the causes that you list – just how valid are the kinds of general causes suggested for revolution? ■

Specimen answer   Your list may have looked something like the following:

1   Conflict between classes, with a new and powerful class in society seeking political power commensurate with its economic and/or social prominence.

2   Conspiracy and subversion.

3   A revolutionary ideology.

4   Economic disruption or upheaval causing discontent.

5   A repressive regime causing anger and discontent.

6   Serious divisions and a crisis of confidence within the old regime which renders it powerless to suppress the initial disorders.

7   The collapse of a regime in the face of a serious external threat, e.g. war, which first enables other groups to contend for power and then enables one of those groups ultimately to seize power. □

Discussion   This list is in no particular or significant order, and you probably noted down other, different causes. I hope that I will cover them now as I look at the list in some detail, suggesting where these 'causes' may be useful, and where they may not.

1   'Class', as you will recall from Book 1, Units 1 and 3, is a word which is fraught with problems of definition. For some scholars, notably Marxists, 'class' necessarily entails 'consciousness' and 'conflict'; other scholars, though they recognize that specific tensions or specific grievances at specific times can cause conflict between certain identifiable social groups or classes, attempt to use class in a more neutral way. In phrasing my answer above I was careful not to use the term 'class conflict', though the answer did go on to suggest something of a broad Marxist interpretation. Yet it is insufficient to say that 'class conflict' or 'conflict between classes' is the cause of revolutions, since what has to be explained is why, at a particular moment, that conflict became revolution; even if 'class conflict' is perennial, revolutions are not.

Most of the revolutions that we will be looking at in these units involved clashes between social groups – workers against employers, peasants against wealthy landowners. They also involved clashes between ethnic groups; on some occasions ethnic divisions might be said to have corresponded with social divisions, but this was by no means always the case.

2   The notion of an 'enemy within' ever active in fermenting disorder and conspiring to overthrow a particular government continues to be popular among some politicians, government officials and journalists, even in the twenty-first century; few (if any) serious historians would see revolutionaries as important in *causing* a revolution. What is never satisfactorily explained by those who take such conspiracy theory seriously is precisely how revolutionary activists manage, first, to dupe the masses and bring them on to the streets and, second, to undermine totally the police and soldiers who could normally be expected to suppress the initial disorder. However, this is not to deny that in central and eastern Europe at the beginning of the twentieth century there were groups of revolutionaries, and that they did agitate through deeds and through the printed and spoken word. Moreover, when revolutionary action had begun they sought to take it over and to control it.

But actions, speeches and pamphlets which criticized and perhaps, in consequence, helped to undermine the authoritarian empires of 1914 were not just the work of dedicated revolutionaries. Moderate reformers, some of whom had close links with the ruling élite and/or who were willing to work within the existing system, also called for change and the correction of what they perceived as abuses.

3   The question of a revolutionary ideology as a cause of revolution is linked to my previous comments. Ideological orthodoxy became all-important for many early twentieth-century socialists; it shaped their perceptions and dictated their course of action. Arguments about orthodoxy became internecine: should socialists work within the existing order, or should

[handwritten margin note: transformation of land ownership, peasants garbed]

they stand out against any amelioration of the working class's lot so as to hasten revolution? The war brought another debate: Lenin, most notably, savaged socialists:

> who are helping 'their own' bourgeoisie to rob other countries and enslave other nations. That is the very substance of chauvinism – to defend one's 'own' Fatherland even when its acts are aimed at enslaving other peoples' Fatherlands.
>
> (V. I. Lenin, 'Opportunism and the collapse of the Second International', 1915, pp.109–10)

However, these theoretical debates had little impact when it came to bringing people on to the streets in the initial disorders of the revolutions. The root causes here were generally more immediate bread-and-butter issues (often quite literally, since bread shortages could bring about disorder). The task of the revolutionary activist was then to persuade the crowds of the relevance of his or her party's orthodoxy to the people's needs, and to do this an ideology might need dilution or a rather different focus.

4   Economic disruption and distress brought people on to the streets, yet that in itself did not automatically create a revolution. Food riots were widespread during times of dearth throughout the eighteenth and nineteenth centuries. Leon Trotsky noted that 'the mere existence of privations is not enough to cause an insurrection; if it were the masses would always be in revolt'. Equally, C. Dobrogeanu-Gherea, a leader of the Romanian Social Democrats who made a detailed analysis of the agrarian question in his native country, concluded, with reference to the peasantry, that extreme misery 'dulls the mind, numbs the soul, destroys energy and the spirit of revolt, and leads to resignation and blind submission – a state of mind diametrically opposed to that which leads to revolt' (quoted in Henry L. Roberts, *Rumania: Political Problems of an Agrarian State*, 1951, p.5). But historians still tend to point to a link between the economic situation of a country and revolution. Much of recent debate has concluded that revolutions have followed a period of rising economic expectations and success which has been rudely interrupted by a recession or some kind of acute economic crisis.

5   Of course, repression often can create anger and discontent among those who are being, or have been, repressed. But repression can also be effective. There are two significant things to bear in mind about the impact of repression on the beginning of a revolution: first, some repression possibly can create sufficient discontent among a large enough section of the population to prompt it into vigorous and violent action when the opportunity arises; but secondly, and perhaps more importantly, in the first act of serious revolutionary disorder the forces of repression often fail either because they are given no clear direction, or because they are reluctant to take action.

6   The idea of there being serious divisions and a crisis of confidence within the old regime is, perhaps, the element which you were least likely to have noted in my initial exercise. Most analysts of revolution, however, now seem

agreed that such a crisis of confidence is a significant cause of the phenomenon both at the occasion of the outbreak of disorder (it can contribute to the failure of repression noted above) and over the longer term. I have already touched on this in point 2 above with reference to individuals linked to the élite seeking change. In his classic comparative analysis, *The Anatomy of Revolution*, Crane Brinton suggested that:

> the ruling classes in our [old regime] societies seem, and not simply *a posteriori* because they were overthrown, to have been unsuccessful in fulfilling their functions. The Russians here provide us with a *locus classicus*. To judge from what appears of them in print, Russian aristocrats for decades before 1917 had been in the habit of bemoaning the futility of life, the backwardness of Russia, the Slavic sorrows of their condition. No doubt this is an exaggeration. But clearly many of the Russian ruling classes had an uneasy feeling that their privileges would not last. Many of them, like Tolstoy, went over to the other side. Others turned liberal and began that process of granting concessions here and withdrawing them there ... Even in court circles, it was quite the fashion by 1916 to ridicule the Czar and his intimates.
>
> (Crane Brinton, *The Anatomy of Revolution*, 1965, p.52)

7   The external threat bringing about the collapse of a regime draws together many of the other 'causes', but first let me reiterate that these 'causes' should not be taken either singly or together as 'fundamental laws' governing the causes of revolutions. There remains considerable debate and controversy. The list is simply to provide you with some questions to think about as you explore the upheavals in central and eastern Europe which followed World War I. This brings us to the key question here: <u>what was the interrelationship between war and revolution?</u>

Exercise   How do you suppose the pressures of war might influence most, if not all, of the causes noted above? ∎

Specimen answer   The pressure of war, especially if it was going badly, could exacerbate, or even create, some of these causes. Low morale might worsen a crisis of confidence among a country's rulers, and might also make the police and the army unreliable when it came to internal repression. <u>The economic disruptions of war foster unrest. Working women in Petrograd appear to have been spending 40 hours a week in food queues early in 1917; these queues became forums for debate.</u> In such circumstances revolutionary calls and slogans become more attractive.

It is also worth considering here the notion that <u>participation in war can have a radicalizing effect.</u> In some instances conscription possibly widened some men's horizons; while it provided some with the opportunity for social mobility, it might have made others discontented with their lot in civilian life. Conscription into a wartime army might have given such discontent a rather different and a sharper focus as men asked, first, what they were fighting for, and, second, what they were going to get for their effort and sacrifice.

Pressure of war:

vs

Pressure of peace:

Furthermore, if the high command and the government seemed incompetent, and either lost the war or seemed likely to lose it, the loyalty of such soldiers and sailors could become questionable. □

Exercise Do you suppose that the demand for 'unconditional surrender' which has been common in the total wars of the twentieth century might have any impact on the government of a defeated country? ■

Specimen answer Military defeat followed by unconditional surrender is likely to undermine the legitimacy of any government in the eyes of its people, making it very difficult for such a government to continue, even supposing that the victorious power, or powers, were prepared to permit this.

In her book *On Revolution* (1963), Hannah Arendt draws attention to 'the little noticed but quite noteworthy fact that since the end of the First World War we almost automatically expect that no government, and no state or form of government, will be strong enough to survive a defeat in war' (p.15). She goes on to suggest that 'among the most certain consequences' of defeat in modern war is 'a revolutionary change in government' either brought about by the people of the defeated state or enforced by the victorious powers. □

(p. 5)

As with the 'causes' of revolution, it is not intended that you should take these suggestions about the interrelationship between war and revolution as unproblematic. They are rather in the nature of hypotheses with which we can explore the historical evidence relating to the changes in central and eastern Europe in the aftermath of World War I.

Arendt adds that "even prior to the horror of nuclear warfare, wars had become politically [...] a matter of life and death."

2 RUSSIA: THE REVOLUTION OF 1917

Exercise Read Roberts (set book) pp.336–9 and answer the following questions:

1   How many 'revolutions' does Roberts identify in Russia during 1917?
2   What are the differences between these 'revolutions'? ■ *ROBERTS*

Specimen answers 1   Roberts identifies two Russian 'revolutions' in 1917: the first in February (March according to the western, Gregorian calendar), and the second in October (November).

2   The essential difference is that the February Revolution was 'an extemporization', whereas that of October was a planned coup conducted by the Bolsheviks. □

Discussion Like Roberts, many historians have written of two 'revolutions' in 1917, recognizing that the two events they are describing are very different. Thinking back to the definitions which I suggested at the beginning of the previous section and which described a revolution as a lengthy political process, it is equally possible, and equally common among historians, to regard the whole of 1917, and even the years immediately following, as the Russian Revolution.

(pp. 7-8)

"Twenty years [after the end of WWII] it has become almost a matter of course that the end of war is revolution, and that the only cause which ~~could~~ possibly could justify it is the revolutionary cause of freedom."

Exercise   Documents II.15–II.18 in *Primary Sources 1: World War I* are drawn from the proceedings of the state *Duma* between 1915 and 1916. The first of these is the programme of the Progressives, and there follow extracts from three parliamentary speeches.

Read them now and consider what they suggest to you about the following questions:

1   How is the war going at the time the documents were drafted and the speeches were made?

2   What did different members of the *Duma* consider to be the necessary remedies for Russia's problems?

3   What were the attitudes in the *Duma* towards the Tsar and his governments? ∎

Specimen answers   1   The implication in the documents from both 1915 and 1916 is that the war is going badly, though no one here ever advocates anything other than pursuing the war to a successful conclusion.

2   The majority Progressive Bloc was keen to have some kind of coalition government which pursued liberal and reformist policies and behaved in a strictly legal manner and kept the military out of civilian affairs. On the political right, Markov expressed concern that the Progressive Bloc's language could provoke the masses into revolution, while Purishkevich, a member of the same right-wing party, was critical of the hypocrisy and paralysis of government, the Germanophile tendencies in the organs of government, and the influence of Rasputin.

3   There is much criticism of the Tsar's government in all of these documents, but no direct criticisms of the Tsar himself and no calls for an end to the regime. However, the criticism of the government and of Rasputin's influence, together with the Progressive Bloc's urging of an authority 'supported by the confidence of the people', imply an increasing division between the political groups in the *Duma* and their monarch.

While Miliukov's speech suggests unity in the Progressive Bloc, there was, in fact, a growing split between the Kadets and the Octobrists, who advocated change through legal and parliamentary means, and those on the left who talked about 'action' without specifying clearly what they meant. During the winter of 1916/17 several plots were contemplated by politicians and even by people close to the throne; generally the plans centred on the removal of the Tsar and/ or the Tsarina and the creation of a regency under the Tsar's brother on behalf of the heir, the Tsarevitch Alexis. Sir George Buchanan, the British Ambassador, found himself approached by a grand duchess proposing that the Tsarina be 'annihilated'. In the event the only plot to come to fruition was the murder of Rasputin by a group of right-wingers including Purishkevich. □

Exercise   Turning back to Roberts, pp.336–7, note down what he considers to be the general causes of the February Revolution. ∎

Specimen answer   1   War-weariness brought about by military defeat and starvation, which fostered strikes in the factories and desertion from, and mutiny in, the army.

2   Cracking morale in the army.

3   Scandals involving the autocracy.

4   A collapse of the old order as much as an insurrection by a new order.

Roberts also warns that the adherents of Marxist orthodoxy have tended to exaggerate the contribution of those with the theoretical programmes and the logic of Marxist conceptualization of revolutions as central to the working out of the process of history. □

I want now to expand upon, and in some instances qualify, these causes. I have little to add on the subject of (3) above, however – the principal scandal was that of Rasputin; there were also rumours and suggestions that the Tsarina, who was German by birth, was in league with the enemy.

On the home front, life in general, and the economy in particular, had been seriously disrupted by mobilization. By the end of 1916 over 14 million men had been mobilized. The heaviest burden fell on the peasantry: almost half of the male rural labour force had been called up by the end of 1916, and the census of 1917 revealed that in most of the Russian provinces anything from one-third to two-thirds of the peasant households had lost their male workers. The demands of war drastically reduced the number of draft animals on the land; most factories producing agricultural machinery were turned over to war production, while those that were left were last in line for fuel and metal supplies. Mobilization affected urban workers to a much lesser extent; those working directly for the war effort were generally exempt from military service, and in trades where skills and demands for their product were at a premium, workers used the strike weapon to push up wages. Wartime inflation, however, tended increasingly to cancel out wage increases. In October 1916 the Petrograd Security Police reported that 'While the wages of the masses have risen 50 per cent, and only in certain categories 100 to 200 per cent (metalworkers, machinists, electricians), the prices on all products have increased 100 to 500 per cent.' The report went on to give data based on one plant to demonstrate how wages were affected by wartime inflation (see Table 11–13.1). Table 11–13.2 gives some idea of the impact of wartime inflation on the increasing wages of one group of skilled Moscow workers. Table 11–13.3 shows the impact of inflation on an average worker's daily food basket.

Table 11–13.1   Cost of different items in Petrograd

Item	Cost (pre-war)	Cost (October 1916)
Rent for a corner	2 to 3 rubles monthly	8 to 12 rubles
Dinner (in a tearoom)	15 to 20 kopeks	1 ruble to 1 ruble 20 kopeks (at the same place)
Tea (in a tearoom)	7 kopeks	35 kopeks
Boots	5 to 6 rubles	20 to 30 rubles
Skirt	75 to 90 kopeks	2 rubles 50 kopeks to 3 rubles

(Source: George Vernadsky *et al.* (eds) *A Source Book for Russian History from Early Times to 1917*, 1972, vol. 3, p.868)

Table 11–13.2   Moscow machine-workers' annual wages, 1913–17

Year	Annual wage (in rubles)	Annual wage (at 1913 money rate)
1913	469	469
1916	1,062	516
1917	2,382	308

Source: based on Diane Koenker, 'Moscow workers in 1917', 1976, pp.123–4.

Table 11–13.3   Cost of a Moscow worker's daily food basket[1]

Year	Daily cost (kopeks)	Change (1913 = 100)
1913	24.23	100
1914	26.53	109
1915	31.70	131
1916	49.47	204
1917 (January)	87.51	361

[1] This is based on the experience of textile workers; it does not take account of the change of eating habits brought about by shortages and the increasing prices of meat and potatoes.

(Source: Koenker, 'Moscow workers in 1917', p.125)

Wartime production demands led to an increase in the number of factory workers in the big cities: there were 242,600 workers in Petrograd in 1914 and 391,800 in 1917; in Moscow the factory labour force increased from 153,223 to 205,919. The Tsarist government took extensive powers against organized labour and strike activity, yet after a brief respite during the first five months of the war the number of strikes began to rise (see Table 11–13.4). The authorities saw political agitators behind the strikes but it is difficult to assess the role of union activists and political agitators. The giant Putilov Works in Petrograd had 20,000 workers, but only 150 of them were Bolsheviks in February 1917. Agitators and activists began receiving German financial support in March 1915, though it is unlikely that many knew where the money was coming from, least of all the strikers in Petrograd and in the Nikolayev naval yard, whose strike pay in January 1916 came from this source.

Table 11–13.4   Strikes, 1905–17[1]

Year	Strikes	Strikers (in 000s)	Political strikers
1905	13,995	2,863	6,024
1906	6,114	1,108	2,950
1907	3,573	740	2,558
1908	892	176	464
1909	340	64	50
1910	222	47	8
1911	466	105	24
1912	2,032	725	1,300
1913	2,404	887	1,034
1914 (total)	3,535	1,337	2,401
1914 (Aug.–Dec.)	68	35	–
1915	928	540	213
1916	1,284	952	243
1917 (Jan.–Feb.)	1,330	676	–

[1] Based on the reports of the Factory Inspectorate, which by 1917 supervised 12,392 institutions employing two million workers, respectively 40 per cent of factories and 70 per cent of factory workers.

(Source: Koenker, 'Moscow workers in 1917', p.125)

Russian military losses were enormous. While the statistics are unreliable because of the haphazard way in which they were collected, it seems generally accepted that by the end of October 1916 the Russian army had lost between 1.6 and 1.8 million killed, with another two million as prisoners of war and over one million more 'missing'. Early in 1916 there had been reports of troops fraternizing with the enemy. General Brusilov briefly improved discipline and morale, and his summer offensive met with early success, but some troops disappeared from the front and there were occasional mutinies. The military postal censors reported that letters from the home front were increasingly expressing the desire for peace and that they were having a depressive effect on the troops; the soldiers' letters home were full of complaints. Yet while senior officers at the front expressed alarm about morale and about replacements (some of whom were political exiles or exiled strikers) they also spoke of 'excellent' discipline. In part at least this was very likely bravado and a reluctance to admit discipline problems. The old control within the army was changing; the war, according to Orlando Figes, was acting as a powerful 'democratizer' (Orlando Figes, *A People's Tragedy: The Russian Revolution 1891–1924*, 1996, p.264). Discipline was enforced by NCOs and the enormous losses among these ranks meant promotion for new men. The new NCOs were peasants, generally in their early twenties and with rarely more than four years' education. If high-born senior commanders expected these NCOs to act as a bridge between them and the men, then they were seriously mistaken. The sympathies and loyalties of the NCOs remained with the men. When trouble broke out in Petrograd it was often young NCOs who led the men into mutiny. Sergeant Sergei Kirpichnikov, for example, recalled telling his men:

> that it would be better to die with honour than to obey any further orders to shoot at the crowds: 'Our fathers, mothers, sisters, brothers and brides are begging for bread,' I said. 'Are we going to kill them? Did you see the blood on the streets today? I say we shouldn't take up positions tomorrow. I myself refuse to go.' And, as one, the soldiers cried out: 'We shall stay with you!'

(Quoted in Figes, pp.313–14)

[margin note: mutiny (knew about begging for bread)]

Similarly Sergeant Fedor Lind, a slightly older man, who had also been promoted because of his courage and leadership at the front, led men of the Preobrazhensky Regiment against police and Cossacks attacking a crowd.

The precise number of troops in the Petrograd garrison early in 1917 is unclear; there appear to have been between 322,000 and 466,800 men in the city and its vicinity. After the police (3,500 men) and the Cossacks (3,200 cavalry) they constituted the third line of defence in case of disorder. The morale of the troops in Petrograd was particularly low. They were bored with barrack life and highly resentful of their officers – at least at the front, junior officers shared the privations of their men. A large number of the soldiers in Petrograd were in their forties; younger men were the first choice for the front. There were some men in training, like the conscripts who stuck with Sergeant Kirpichnikov, and others recuperating from wounds or sickness, as well as strikers mobilized as a punishment. When the strikes and food riots began, some troops obeyed orders and acted against the crowds; others, even the usually loyal Cossacks, began to fraternize. Then, on 11 March (26 February 'old style') fraternization turned into a full-scale mutiny as one unit and then another killed their officers and began exchanging fire with those troops who remained loyal.

In addition to soldiers there were large numbers of sailors in the immediate vicinity of Petrograd. The city itself is at the eastern end of the Gulf of Finland, which juts off the Baltic Sea. Some fifteen miles west of Petrograd, in the Gulf, lies Kottin Island with the town of Kronstadt at its eastern tip. Kronstadt was the headquarters of the Russian Baltic fleet (see Map 4 in the *Maps Booklet*). There had been spasmodic fighting between warships in the Baltic, but much of the time the Russian sailors were idle, cooped up below decks on their ships or else idle in barracks. Naval officers enforced a harsh and brutal discipline on their men. The sailors, while conscripts, were generally from a different social background from the largely peasant soldiers. One of their number recalled:

> The Kronstadt sailors were a politically advanced element. The point is that the very conditions of service in the Navy call for persons who possess special technical training, that is they require skilled workers. Every sailor is, in the first place, a specialist: a minelayer, an electrician, a gunner, an engineer, and so on. Every special trade presupposes a certain body of knowledge and a certain technical training obtained through practice. Consequently, those accepted into the Navy were in the main workers who had passed through a trade school and had by practical experience mastered some special skill. The Navy was particularly keen to take in fitters, electricians, engineers, mechanics, blacksmiths, and so on.

(Quoted in F. F. Raskolnikov, *Kronstadt and Petrograd in 1917*, 1982, p.36)

The sailors of Kronstadt were not important in the initial trouble in Petrograd, but they seized the opportunity offered by the army mutinies in the city to execute unpopular officers (including the two principal admirals) and to imprison many more. Later on they were to play a significant role in the revolutionary events.

Against the advice of many advisers who feared that military disaster which could be attributed to the Tsar would compromise the monarchy, Nicholas II had taken personal command of the army in 1915. In March 1917, while at his military headquarters, he received regular reports on the situation in Petrograd from police and garrison commanders. He ordered them to suppress the disorder. On 11 March the chairman of the *Duma*, Mikhail V. Rodzianko, telegraphed the Tsar urging him of the necessity 'that some person enjoying the confidence of the country be entrusted immediately with the formation of a new government'. Nicholas suspended the *Duma*. This, together with the trouble on the streets, prodded the *Duma* into action. It refused to disperse and, following a popular invasion of the Tauride Palace where the *Duma* met, the party leaders decided to establish themselves as a Provisional Committee. On 14 March (1 March 'old style') the committee nominated a Provisional Government; the following day the Tsar abdicated. 2 March (05)

Exercise   Document II.19 in *Primary Sources 1: World War I* is the proclamation issued by a committee of the *Duma* announcing the formation of the Provisional Government. Read it now and answer the following questions:

1   Is the opening paragraph a fair reflection of events?

2   What kinds of reforms are promised in the document?

3   What promises are made about the war and the economic difficulties? ■

Specimen answers   1   The implication here is that the *Duma* was the prime mover in the events which brought down the old regime – hardly a fair representation of what had happened.

2   Essentially the document promises liberal constitutional reforms.

3   There is no mention of either the war or the economic difficulties of the country. □   *Doesn't deliver on 'military' or 'economic' objectives.*

Exercise   Document II.20 in *Primary Sources 1: World War I* is 'Order No 1' issued by the Petrograd Soviet of Workers' and Soldiers' Deputies on the same day that the *Duma* announced the Provisional Government. Read it now and answer the following questions:

1   What is created by this document?

2   Does the document suggest any potential for friction between the Petrograd Soviet and the *Duma*? ■

Specimen answers   1   Committees of elected representatives of the lower military ranks who, in turn, are to send representatives to the Soviet.

2   In some instances Order No 1 appears to be authorizing some of the same things as the Proclamation of the Provisional Government (see in particular principle 8 of the latter and resolutions 6 and 7 of the former). But,

obviously, two organizations, even if in agreement on some things, have the potential for friction, and resolution 4 of Order No 1 states clearly that the Soviet will not adhere to orders with which it disagrees. □

The existence of the Petrograd Soviet and the Provisional Government responsible to the *Duma* created the problem of what was subsequently referred to as 'dual power'. Initially the Soviet was not as suspicious of, or hostile towards, the *Duma* and the Provisional Government as these latter were of the Soviet. The Soviet was predominantly Menshevik with a sprinkling of Socialist Revolutionaries, rather than Bolshevik (if you are unsure of, or have forgotten, the different political groupings on the Russian left see Roberts pp.337–8). The Mensheviks wanted to use their influence in the Soviet to keep the Provisional Government from veering off on the path of old regime reaction; under Lenin the Bolsheviks were later to use their growing influence in the Soviet to undermine the Provisional Government. Other towns and cities followed up the example of Petrograd and established soviets of their own; seventy-seven were in communication with Petrograd within a month of the March uprising; in addition there were other elected committees in factories and in the army. Order No 1 was significant in inspiring those in the army. Most of these other soviets had, initially, Menshevik majorities; generally speaking, however, they sought to establish local coalition governments drawn from all parties and classes.

*excitement.
hope, aspirations*

The weeks following the Tsar's abdication were a period of tremendous hope and excitement. Peasants, workers and soldiers meeting in different committees and soviets passed resolutions outlining their aspirations under the new order. These broad aspirations are shown in Tables 11–13.5 to 11–13.7

Exercise   Study the demands outlined in Tables 11–13.5 to 11–13.7.

1   Are the most common demands of workers and peasants economic or political?

2   What do these demands suggest in general about attitudes towards:

(a) the old order;

(b) the war?

3   While there are no percentages given for the soldiers' demands, what seem to be the similarities and the differences between them and the workers and peasants? ■

Table 11–13.5   The aspirations of the working class: table of statistics (based on 100 motions voted in March 1917)[1]

General policies		Percentage of motions in support of policy
A	Measures against the Tsar	2
B	Measure against the old administration	3
C	Formation of a democratic republic	14
D	Universal suffrage	5
E	Confidence in government	3
F	Distrust of government	11
G	Decentralization	0
H	Hasten meeting of Constituent Assembly	12
I	Free education	3
J	Graduated tax	0
K	Defence proclamations	3
L	In favour of peace without annexations or revolutionary contributions	3
M	Elimination of professional army	1
Problems pertaining to the workers		
N	Eight-hour day	51
O	No overtime (7 times formally, 7 times with the addition 'unless better paid')	14
P	Guaranteed wages and social security	11
Q	Pay rise	18
R	Hiring question	7
S	Foremen and choice of foremen	2
T	Sanitary conditions	15
U	Factory committee role	12
V	Worker administration	4
W	International slogans	7
X	Land for the peasants	9
Y	To learn to wait for pay rises and various advantages, to be patient	1

[1] These first hundred motions are valid for the period March 3 to March 28. They concern factory workers. The regional breakdown is as follows: Petrograd 40 per cent, Moscow 25 per cent, other cities 35 per cent.

(Source: Marc Ferro, *The Russian Revolution of February 1917*, 1972, p.115)

Table 11–13.6 The aspirations of the peasantry: table of statistics[1]

General policies		Percentage of motions in support of policy
A	Measures against the Tsar	4
B	Measure against the old administration	16
C	Formation of a democratic republic	24
D	Universal suffrage	9
E	Confidence in government	10 (7 in March)
F	Distrust of government	10 (in April)
G	Decentralization	12
H	Hasten meeting of Constituent [Assembly]	17
I	Free public education	10
J	Graduated income tax and no other	6
K	Defence proclamation	4
L	In favour of a quick, just peace	23
M	Abolition of professional army	3
N	Measures of safeguards against large landowners	11
	Agricultural questions	
O	Lowering of land rents	17
P	Forbidding of sale of land until [discussion in] Constituent	13
Q	No squatting	4
R	The Constituent will settle the questions of lands and agrarian questions	15
S	Seizure of state lands, crown lands (fiefs)	20
T	Seizure of state lands, crown lands, and large estates	31
U	Seizure of land without compensation	15
V	Abolition of private property	7
W	Socialization of land, nationalization	12
X	Give land back to the *obschchina*	2
Y	The land to those who work it, in accordance with their strength (no pay)	18
Z	Egalitarian status (norm)	8
AA	Administration and distribution of the lands by the municipalities, soviets, etc.	15

[1] This table has been compiled from the first one hundred resolutions found among the three hundred documents assembled by the Soviet historians on the agrarian question for the months of March and April. This sample is as good as any other, since there is a correlation between the selection made here and the breakdown of the agrarian troubles between February and October. It should be noted that in the gathering of documents there is an over-representation of the Moscow and Valdimir regions (near Moscow) which is due to the greater development of historical research in the capital. Aside from this distortion, the governments of Tula (9 resolutions), Ryazan (6 resolutions), Kaluga, Pskov and Smolensk are represented in this table by five or more resolutions. These are the regions where the agrarian troubles were the most numerous. Half of these hundred resolutions bear on the regions which saw the most intense agrarian troubles. The rest bear on the most diversified provinces – thirty-three governments are represented out of about fifty for European Russia. It can be estimated that this sample gives an indication of the aspirations of the Russian peasantry.

(Source: Ferro, *The Russian Revolution of February 1917*, pp.124–5)

Table 11–13.7   The aspirations of the soldiers

1   A soldiers' organization to fight attempts to restore the old régime.

2   The organization of the army in such a way that Socialists will be elected to the Constituent.

3   While maintaining an active defence, we demand that steps be taken for peace negotiations between all belligerents.

4   That soldiers' committees control the operations decided on by the general staff.

5   An immediate meeting of the Constituent Assembly, which by equal and secret vote, will immediately decide on the form of government. We will give our full support to the formation of a democratic republic.

6   Recognition of the freedom of assembly, press, and speech, of the right to form unions and to strike; the extension of political rights to the armed forces.

7   The end of discrimination on account of religion or nationality.

8   Formation of militia, with elected commanders, for the maintenance of local governments.

9   Election of local authorities.

10   Graduated income tax.

11   Separation of Church and state.

12   Confiscation of lands from owners, the state, the Church, etc.; the land to belong to those who work it.

13   The eight-hour day.

14   Social security for workers, providing for old age, disability, sickness, pregnancy.

15   Pension for disabled war veterans.

16   Compulsory education to sixteen years of age.

17   Formation of a League of Nations for Disarmament.

18   The Petrograd Soviet, Defender of the People, will be defended with all our might.

(Source: Ferro, *The Russian Revolution of February 1917*, p.134)

Specimen answers

1   The most common demands are economic rather than political: 51 per cent of the workers' motions included demands for the eight-hour day; 50 per cent of the peasants' motions included demands for the seizure of land.

2   (a) There were few demands for action against the Tsar and the old administration; the peasants were much keener on the latter than the workers. (b) The war, too, was not central to the aspirations of the workers but, possibly because of the impact of the war in rural areas, between one-fifth and one-quarter of the peasant resolutions called for a speedy but just peace.

3   As might be expected, the soldiers' demands reflect those of the workers and peasants – the confiscation of land, the eight-hour day, a Constituent Assembly. There are demands for peace negotiation between all belligerents, but not the demands for an immediate peace. Some of the soldiers' resolutions were much broader than those on the home front – a League of Nations for Disarmament, compulsory education to the age of 16; others, like war pensions and soldiers' committees, related directly to their current experience. □

Discussion   It is worth emphasizing here that immediately after the February Revolution the troops were not calling for peace at any price. It seems that the troops at the front believed they should continue fighting for the honour of Russia and their revolution; if fighting the Germans was to be considered as a mark of patriotism, they did not want their officers to have a monopoly on patriotism. Bolshevik militants who urged a stand for peace in front-line soldiers' meetings found the troops reluctant to embrace the idea. When they were engaged in combat in the spring and summer of 1917, most Russian troops continued to fight in a courageous and disciplined manner. The troops who did participate in calls for peace appear, most commonly, to have been those in reserve regiments and especially those billeted in large cities.

Exercise   Remembering the ethnic diversity of the Russian Empire discussed in Book 1, Unit 2, what other aspirations do you suppose could have been encouraged by the fall of the old order? ■

Specimen answer   National aspirations among the minority peoples. The fall of the Tsar fostered
and discussion   the hopes of the Finns for a restoration of their autonomy. Poles demanded autonomy, as well as a separate Polish army serving within the Russian army. (Similar demands for their own national army were later taken up by other ethnic groups.) The situation with regard to Poland was complicated by the fact that Russian Poland was occupied by German and Austro-Hungarian troops, which had recognized Polish independence in November 1916. Demands for autonomy were also heard from other Baltic peoples in the provinces of Estonia, Latvia and Lithuania. In Kiev, Ukrainian nationalists formed a Central Ukrainian Council, the *Rada*, and called for autonomy. The Cossacks had special privileges in return for the obligation of all men to serve in the army for twenty years from the age of 18. The Cossack village held its land in common and the villages were run by elected assemblies. Cossack landholdings were larger than those of ordinary peasants in the empire; during the summer of 1917 many Cossacks were concerned that the peasants would seize their land while they were away serving in the army – Cossack units were less prone to the general disintegration, being more cohesive and having fewer grievances. In September 1917 a Cossack *Rada* was formed. Russian Jews tended to act rather differently from other ethnic groups. The end of the old order promised an end to discrimination and periodic pogroms. While extreme Zionists campaigned eagerly for a Jewish homeland in Palestine, many more Russian Jews discarded their separate identity and sought to merge with the mass of new Russian citizens. □

The Provisional Government was worried by the demands of minority peoples, but it made some concessions: Finnish autonomy was restored; Polish independence was recognized in principle; the use of national languages was permitted, and some of the restrictions imposed by the Tsarist regime were lifted. A series of other reforms was introduced, many of which were promised in the Provisional Government's manifesto – freedom of the press, of worship and of association; local militias to replace Tsarist police; the abolition of the death penalty; the disestablishment of the Church; and the independence of the judiciary. But problems mounted. The overthrow of the old regime did not suddenly change the unfavourable war situation. The Provisional Government

didn't solve the military problem. Or deliver on the 'war' front

was determined to continue the war, partly to win international recognition (Britain and France had recognized the government provided Russia remained their ally), and partly in the hope that the war would unify people behind the new regime (Miliukov, now Foreign Minister, was a historian, and both he and others looked back to the way in which the French people appeared to have been united during the French revolutionary wars). Perhaps most important to the Provisional Government, however, was the way they perceived Russia as a liberal democracy, in league with other liberal democracies against reactionary monarchies.

If the fall of the old order did not immediately change the situation on the battle fronts, nor did it immediately achieve the aspirations of workers and peasants. Both groups began taking action on their own behalf. In 47 out of 73 Moscow factories for which we have information, the workers implemented the eight-hour day themselves; only afterwards did the city's soviet order all Moscow enterprises to institute the eight-hour day with no reduction in salary and overtime for extra hours, and pass a resolution calling on the Provisional Government to legislate nationally. In the countryside the peasants began seizing land, sometimes clashing with the new militia as they did so. As the internal disorder increased, so the army began to melt away. Initially it seems to have been the troops furthest from the front who deserted, but as troops at the front became infected with radical propaganda, as they heard of land seizures (and they wanted their 'share'), as negotiations for peace failed to materialize, and as fears increased that many officers wanted to reimpose the old system of discipline, so the front-line soldiers also began to go home. In February there were reported to be about 1,700 desertions a week; this rose to 8,600 in May and 12,000 in July. Deserters, soldiers on leave, and delegates from soldiers' committees were alleged to be radicalizing the peasantry and were commonly identified as being involved in peasant action; but it was also known for peasants to turn on deserters whom they did not know and send them back to the front or kill them. Separate localities began following policies which most appealed to those running them; they had little idea of what was going on in Petrograd, while the Provisional Government had little idea of, and virtually no control over, events in the provinces.

It was in this increasing anarchy that Lenin, returning from exile in April 1917, introduced his slogans 'All power to the soviets' and, probably of much more importance given the situation in Russia and at the battle front, 'Peace, bread, land'. As noted above, the Bolsheviks were not a majority in the soviets, but Lenin saw these bodies as instruments with which to undermine the Provisional Government and within which he could develop a power base. He was the only political leader to oppose the new regime, and this brought him and his party increasing popularity as the Provisional Government was regarded with mounting frustration and suspicion for its inability to alleviate continuing shortages and inflation. Furthermore, the government repeatedly postponed the election which would have given the new regime some semblance of legitimacy. These postponements were partly due to the difficulty of compiling the necessary electoral registers and organizing elections in wartime; but it is also probable that the ministers, aware of their diminishing standing in the country, feared defeat. Twice the Provisional Government reconstituted itself, the first time in May, the second time in August. On each occasion there was a shift to the left, but insufficient to satisfy the militants like the Kronstadt sailors, who took to the streets of Petrograd in July; yet such shifts were too far for others, like General Kornilov, the new supreme commander, who attempted an abortive coup in August.

The 'revolution' of October/November was not the end of violence and upheaval in Russia; nor, arguably, was it the end of the process of political revolution. But before moving on to post-1917 events I want you to think again about the interrelationship of war and revolution. Some Soviet historians maintained that the revolution would have occurred even without the war, since the conflict of classes made it inevitable. Indeed, they argued that the war actually retarded the revolution by bringing about an initial degree of false national solidarity. The strike figures in Table 11–13.4 might be said to support their argument, though a Bolshevik call for a general strike in the summer of 1914 (and before the war) met with very little support outside Petrograd. In other quarters it has been argued that the revolution was the result of structural problems within the old regime (particularly the repressive, reactionary nature of the autocracy) which were exacerbated by the war; this view was popular among both Soviet and western historians during the interwar years. However, since World War II some western historians, including Alexander Gerschenkron (whose theories concerning economic backwardness were discussed in Book 1, Unit 2), have asserted that the reforms following the revolution of 1905 promised, albeit gradually and haltingly, to put Russia on the road to political and social stability. Stolypin's economic reforms, moreover, seem to have started the process of modernizing the economy. In the opinion of these historians it was the war which brought about revolution by imposing intolerable strain on government and people.

3   RUSSIA: PEACE, CIVIL WAR AND INTERVENTION

(You will find it helpful to refer to the map of the Russian Revolution in your *Maps Booklet* while studying this section.)

Exercise   Read Roberts, pp.242–5 and 339–40; then study Map 5 on p.xviii of Roberts and answer the following questions:

1   Why did the Russians agree to the Treaty of Brest-Litovsk?

2   What were the results of the treaty? ■

Specimen answers   1   While opinion, even among the Bolsheviks, was divided over signing the treaty when it was initially drafted, once the Germans resumed their offensive the Russians had very little choice but to agree.

2   Russia lost vast tracts of territory by the treaty, principally lands in which there were ethnic groups calling for independence. By accentuating some of the divisions between the Bolsheviks and others, the treaty also accelerated civil war. □

Hopes that the peace treaty would offer the chance of some internal stability were quickly dashed. During the four years following Brest-Litovsk, foreign powers intervened in Russia's affairs, while civil war aggravated economic problems which, in turn, provoked still more unrest.

The initial intervention was made by German and Austro-Hungarian troops. After forcing the issue of the peace treaty the Germans occupied the Ukraine briefly, and a small Austrian force established itself in Odessa. The Germans were also active in the Baltic, notably assisting the Finnish 'Whites' in defeating the 'Reds' and in disarming the Russian troops remaining in what became a new, independent, liberal, democratic Finnish state. Article 12 of the armistice signed between Germany and the Allies towards the end of 1918 revealed the latter's fears of Bolshevism and insisted that German troops maintain their presence in the Baltic. In fact the German army entrusted with this task melted away much as Russian troops had melted away from the fronts in 1917, but this was not the end of German involvement. Early in 1919 the largest of the *Freikorps* units – the Baltic *Landeswehr* and the Iron Division – marched into the Baltic lands to 'defend the Fatherland from Russian Bolshevism'. They also had plans for German *Lebensraum* (living space), with the promise of land and Latvian citizenship being held out to the *Freikorps* volunteers. Eventually, their supply lines were cut by a Franco-British naval squadron and they were defeated by combined Latvian and Estonian armies.

British, French, United States and Japanese troops were also deployed at different extremities of Russia during 1918 and 1919. Fearful of a German and Turkish push on the oilfields around Baku as the Russian armies dissolved, small British units were ordered into Transcaspia. A few British troops were landed at Murmansk in March 1918; these were not unwelcome to the Bolsheviks, who were then concerned about a German advance. In August many more troops from Britain and other Allied powers began disembarking at Archangel and Vladivostok. Most of the Allied intervention in Russian affairs, however, was in sending military equipment and supplies; initially, it was maintained that the supplies were for those troops continuing the war against the Germans, although, as time went on, the supplies were clearly meant for those fighting the Bolsheviks. Only towards the end of their stay were the Allied troops themselves fully committed to action against the Bolsheviks. Most of the intervention forces were withdrawn in September and October 1919; only the Japanese continued to keep troops in Siberia until 1922.

The White armies did not call for a return of the Tsar. They claimed to want a restoration of military discipline but, above all, an end to both the Bolshevik regime and the anarchy which was sweeping through Russia. As something of an afterthought their leaders also spoke of reconvening the Constituent Assembly so that the people could decide on their form of government. But the problem with the White leaders was that their mentality remained rooted in the old regime and they never produced a convincing ideological alternative. A large White army was originally established in the Don region towards the end of 1917; it later named itself the Armed Forces of South Russia. The Don was a Cossack region: some Cossacks joined the army; others were wary, not wishing to bring Bolshevik troops into their lands to fight the Whites; other Cossacks, accepting a Bolshevik promise that their lands were now safe in their own hands, were Red. A second, large White army was organized in central Russia;

towards the end of 1918 it was put under the command of Admiral Kolchak with its headquarters in Omsk. The civil war ebbed and flowed, but 1919 was the high point for the Whites: Kolchak's forces moved west in the spring, meeting with early successes; later in the year General Deniken, in command of the southern army, advanced on Moscow, while a third White army, under General Yudenich, pushed along the Baltic coast into the outskirts of Petrograd. But the Whites were weakened by their failure to win peasant support. The peasants seem to have seen little difference between the Reds and the Whites: both factions wanted the peasants' young men for their armies; both requisitioned their produce – and Deniken's army developed an appalling reputation for its corruption and anti-semitism. If anything, the peasants seem marginally to have preferred the Bolsheviks, who were, after all, clearly opposed to the old order, and had sanctioned land seizure by the peasants. Nor were the Whites prepared to make any promises to insurgent nationalities about the future; this was one reason why Estonians and Finns did not help Yudenich in his drive on Petrograd. Although all of the White advances were driven back in 1919, it was not until the defeat of General Wrangel (who replaced Deniken in the south) in the Caucasus and the Crimea towards the end of 1920 that the civil war was effectively over.

If Estonians and Finns felt that it was against their interests to embroil themselves in conflict with the Bolsheviks, this was not the case with every national army. The Czech Legion was the inspiration of Thomas Masaryk, a former philosophy professor at the University of Prague who had become a leading spokesman for the Bohemian people before the war. <u>Masaryk believed that an army recruited from Czechs and Slovaks and fighting beside the Allies was a means of securing Czech nationhood.</u> The first legionnaires were recruited from Czechs and Slovaks living outside the Austro-Hungarian Empire, or from deserters (especially on the Italian front) who had no desire to fight for a German victory. In the summer of 1917 the Russian Provisional Government agreed to the formation of a legion from among Czech and Slovak prisoners of war. Following the events of November and the opening of peace talks with the Germans, it became clear that the Russian Czech Legion was not going to be able to fight on the eastern front. In February 1918 agreement was reached with the Bolsheviks for the legion to travel by train to Vladivostok, where it would embark for Europe and the western front; by now the legion was technically a part of the French army. Clashes with local Bolsheviks as the Czechs travelled east resulted in the legion, some 30,000 strong, seizing all but one of the principal towns and cities along 2,500 miles of the Trans-Siberian Railway; as an additional means of ensuring their passage to France, the Czechs linked with the White armies of Kolchak. In the end the legionnaires finished their war service in Russia, continuing technically as part of the French intervention force.

A few months after the last Czechs left Vladivostok bound for their new nation state, the armies of another nation state created (or rather, in this instance recreated) by the Treaty of Versailles marched across Russia's western border. Josef Pilsudski, leader of the new Poland, dreamed of restoring the vast Greater Poland of the eighteenth century. In June 1919 Pilsudski's army occupied Kiev, the capital of the Ukraine. A Red Army counter-attack pushed the Poles to within fifteen miles of Warsaw. For Bolshevik leaders the speed and success of their advance seemed to presage the success of a world-wide Communist advance;

similar thoughts crossed the minds of the British and French governments. Inspired and guided by the French General Weygand, the Poles counter-attacked in their turn and drove the Russians back across their frontiers, seizing a chunk of Lithuania while they were about it. The ensuing peace also secured the Polish frontier much further to the east than originally planned.

Baltic peoples, Czechs and Poles all ended World War I with their own nation states. But not all of the ethnic minorities who became involved against the Bolsheviks were as successful. The army of the Ukrainian *Rada* is an obvious example; it was fairly rapidly overwhelmed by the forces of the Bolsheviks, yet this did not prevent the Ukraine from becoming a battleground throughout the period 1918 to 1920. Deniken and Wrangel fought the Bolsheviks there, as did the Poles of Pilsudski; and the partisan army of Nestor Ivanovich Makhno fought them all. Makhno was a peasant born in the Ukraine; imprisoned by the Tsarist regime in 1908 for his anarchist associations, he was released by the revolutionary crowds in Moscow in March 1917. The Makhnovschchina were, generally speaking, peasants of the southern Ukraine whose main influence lay in a semi-circle with a 150-mile radius drawn from the northern shore of the Sea of Azov. They had seized the land when the opportunity presented itself in 1917. They were opposed to the idea of the state, and suspicious of towns and cities. They envisaged a society of self-governing, largely self-sufficient communes. 'Every commune', recalled Makhno,

> comprised ten families of peasants and workers, i.e. a total of 100, 200 or 300 members. By decision of the regional Congress of agrarian communes every commune received a normal amount of land, i.e. as much as its members could cultivate, situated in the immediate vicinity of the commune and composed of land formerly belonging to .the *pomeschiki* [aristocrats and landowning gentry]. They also received cattle and farm-equipment from
> . these former estates.
>
> (Quoted in E. J. Hobsbawm, *Primitive Rebels*, 1971, p.184)

Makhno was an extremely capable guerrilla commander who first led his men against the forces of the Ukrainian *Rada*, then against German and Austro-Hungarian occupation units. The Makhnovschchina were prepared to ally with the Bolsheviks against the Whites, but there was little common ground between them. The Bolsheviks labelled the Makhnovschchina as 'bandits', a charge in which there was probably an element of truth. Makhnovist theorists (and these were very few in number) condemned the Bolsheviks for subordinating everything to the state:

> The State is everything, the individual worker – nothing. This is the main precept of Bolshevism. For the State is personified by functionaries, and in fact it is they who are everything; the working class is nothing.
>
> (Peter Arshinov, *History of the Makhnovist Movement*, 1974, p.70)

The Makhnovschchina were finally beaten by the Reds in 1921, and Makhno himself was forced into exile.

Other peasants also rose against the Bolsheviks. In the central province of Tambov, some 50,000 insurgents led by A. S. Antonov were active during 1920 and 1921. Like Makhno, Antonov proved to be a very capable partisan leader. He was a former member of the Socialist Revolutionary Party which had developed a large following among the peasantry. Hostility to the excesses of

war communism was the spark which prompted insurrection in Tambov. But
here, as elsewhere, the peasants were essentially seeking a restoration of the
self-rule which they had enjoyed in 1917–18. The slogan 'Soviet Power without
the Communists' is illustrative of this, as was the peasants' confused thinking
about Lenin and the Bolsheviks as friends and heroes for bringing them peace,
land and community control through their own soviets, while Trotsky and the
Communists were enemies for bringing civil war, collectivization and
requisitioning, and for abolishing the soviets.

The Bolsheviks' ultimate military success in the civil war was achieved by the
new Red Army. During 1917 the Bolsheviks had relied on their cadres within the
old army and navy and on Red Guards for their military shock troops. The Red
Guards were not affiliated to the Bolsheviks; they were militias generally
organized at individual factories. As might be expected, the Guards were
overwhelmingly young working-class men and, like most of Russia's urban
workers, a high proportion of them (perhaps just over half) had been born in
rural districts. Along with much of the urban working class, the Red Guards were
Bolshevized between March and November, but the Bolsheviks still preferred to
rely on cadres within the existing armed forces, and notably on the Kronstadt
sailors, in the crucial events of November. When the Germans renewed their
offensive in January 1918, some hoped to see the Red Guard extended and
transformed into a new proletarian army; the general staff of the Petrograd Red
Guard, for example, had a plan which would have authorized the committees in
each factory to mobilize 20 per cent of their workforce, thus producing 80,000
fighting men.

> Of this, 12.5 per cent or 10,000 men must be on active service for a whole
> week, after which they will return to the factory as a reserve. In this way, in
> two months, the 80,000 men will have carried out their service.
>   The 10,000 Red Guards on active service will be split into two parts: one
> half (5,000) for defence of the town, which will pay the Guards; the other will
> be the factory reserve, the Red Guards receiving their pay from factory
> managements or the government.

(Quoted in Marc Ferro, *October 1917*, 1980, p.283)

The Bolsheviks did not follow up such proposals and sought to halt the German
advance with volunteers. But volunteers proved to be insufficient to stop the
Germans; then, as the civil war developed, there was an even greater need for
men. In the early summer of 1918, universal, compulsory military service was
introduced and social groups and professions such as former lawyers (the
Bolsheviks had abolished the bar), priests, monks and bourgeois (i.e. non-
Communist) journalists, were no longer exempt. At the same time strict military
discipline was reintroduced and the election of officers, which had begun in
March 1917 and had been legally sanctioned the following December, was
abolished. More than two-thirds of the officers in this new army were former
Tsarist officers. Trotsky, the People's Commissar for War reasoned thus to Lenin:

> Many of them commit acts of treachery. But on the railways, too, instances of
> sabotage are in evidence in the routing of troop trains. Yet nobody suggests
> replacing railway engineers by Communists ... It is essential to make the
> entire military hierarchy more compact and get rid of the ballast by extracting

those general staff officers that are efficient and loyal to us and not on any account by replacing them by party ignoramuses.

(Quoted in John Ellis, *Armies in Revolution*, 1973, p.192)

These military 'specialists' from the old army were supervised by political commissars. Also, military party members were shifted when and where possible to weak areas, since it appeared that the presence of committed Communists in a unit considerably improved effectiveness in combat (though the best troops were not always card-carrying Bolsheviks – the 40,000 sailors who provided Trotsky with some of his finest shock troops were unquestionably revolutionary militants, but not necessarily Bolsheviks). Desertion was a constant problem. Nevertheless at the beginning of 1919 the Red Army numbered just under 400,000; by the close of the following year it had reached more than three million and it was still growing.

An army of such size needed feeding, and so too did the urban workers. A blockade imposed by the capitalist powers, together with their military intervention, shut off the possibility of purchasing food abroad. These problems coalesced with Bolshevik ideology to produce the system known as 'war communism'. The centralized Bolshevik state nationalized major industry and sought to control both production and distribution. The intention was that the peasants would supply the towns and cities in return for industrial products. However, the shortage of raw materials and fuel meant that very little was produced in the factories; furthermore there were major problems of organizing distribution in a country as vast as Russia when the men responsible had little experience and when war and civil war had disrupted, and continued to disrupt and destroy, the transport system (see Table 11–13.8). The peasants understandably objected to parting with produce for nothing. They began sowing fewer crops and reverting to subsistence agriculture; in 1920 the sown acreage of Russia was three-fifths of what it had been in 1913. The Red Army began requisitioning to feed itself; the *Cheka*, the Red security police, began requisitioning to feed the towns and cities. This, together with conscription, provoked many of the peasant risings. The Tambov insurgents sang:

Oh, sorrow, oh, sorrow, the soldier tortures the peasant and still takes, oh, sorrow, three poods [a pood is thirty-six pounds] for each eater.

They also sang:

Deserter I was born, deserter shall I die. Shoot me on the spot; I don't go into the Red Army. To us came a commissar and two Red Army soldiers. All the same we won't go. Don't hope for us.

(Both quotations from W. H. Chamberlain, *The Russian Revolution*, 1965, vol. 2, p.438)

Table 11–13.8 Russian railways, 1917–19

Date	No. of locomotives	Percentage fit for use	No. of freight wagons	Percentage fit for use
Jan. 1917	20,394	83.5	537,328	95.8
Dec. 1918	8,955	52.2		
Dec. 1919			244,443	83.4

(Source: based on Chamberlain, *The Russian Revolution*, vol. 2, p.108)

Table 11–13.9   Paper rubles in circulation, 1914–21

Date	No. of paper rubles
1 July 1914	1,630,400,000
1 March 1917	10,044,000,000
1 Nov. 1917	19,477,900,000
1 Jan. 1918	27,650,000,000
1 Jan. 1919	61,326,000,000
1 Jan. 1920	225,015,000,000
1 Jan. 1921	1,168,596,000,000

(Source: based on Chamberlain, *The Russian Revolution*, vol. 2, p.103)

The economic problems of 1918 to 1921 aggravated the inflation created during the war; both the Tsarist and the Provisional Government had sought, in part, to finance the war by printing money (see Table 11–13.9). Moreover, as the number of paper rubles grew, there was a decline in the value of gold rubles; the gold ruble of January 1921 was worth just over 5 per cent of that of January 1918. Urban workers were paid in food, clothing and shoes, but peasant recalcitrance, distribution problems and rationing reduced thousands to the brink of starvation. The population of the large cities of northern Russia declined by over a half between 1916 and 1920. People returned to the villages where they were born, either for good or to get and take back food for their starving families in the cities. In the latter case they ran the risk of being branded as 'speculators' and losing their goods to the armed road-block detachments; these squads were regularly condemned for arbitrariness, brutality, and for keeping the goods which they confiscated for their own use. Workers who stayed in the cities periodically absented themselves from their factories to steal or to make small household articles which could then be exchanged on the black market for food. The decline in standards of nutrition and the lack of fuel to heat homes in the bitter winters weakened people's resistance to disease; between January 1918 and January 1920 an estimated seven million died from malnutrition and epidemic.

The question might be asked: why did the urban industrial workers who had contributed so significantly to the downfall of the Tsar not rise up against the rigours of war communism? Several reasons might be advanced. The few benefits which workers had secured may have blunted the militancy of a few: some workers moved from their poor quarters into the homes of the well-to-do which had been either abandoned or confiscated; also, Bolshevik labour and welfare legislation, while often violated, did promise, and sometimes deliver, new benefits. Possibly the day-to-day struggle against starvation sapped the energies of many. The number of active young workers in the cities declined with mobilization for the Red Army and with the exodus into the countryside. The activity of the *Cheka* probably reduced the potential anti-Bolshevik shop-floor leadership; certainly many Mensheviks and Socialist Revolutionaries (SRs) were arrested. However, it would be wrong to assume that the urban workers remained quiescent. While evidence is fragmentary, there were strikes in 1918, rather fewer in 1919 and 1920, but an upsurge in the winter of 1920/21 when the civil war was over; the capitalist states' blockade ended but conditions did not improve; and the Red Army was not demobilized – flushed with the army's military success Trotsky was keen to employ it as forced labour in rebuilding the country. The most serious protest against the Bolsheviks came from a group of what might be called sympathetic workers early in 1921, with the Kronstadt Mutiny.

Exercise   Turn to *Primary Sources 1: World War I* and read the declarations of the Kronstadt mutineers in Documents II.21 and II.22; then answer the following questions:

1   What were the principal objects of the sailors' complaints?

2   What did the sailors want? ■

Specimen answers   1   The sailors condemned the Bolsheviks/Communist Party for being unrepresentative and in some ways worse than the Tsarist regime. They objected to the imprisonment of other left-wingers, to war communism and the way in which the Communists were endeavouring to enforce their ideas on the Russian people.

2   They wanted a 'third revolution' to overthrow the Bolshevik/Communist dictatorship and to establish a system of free associations which truly represented peasants and workers. They wanted peasants to be able to work their own land and workers to be able to produce their own handicrafts if they so wished. □

In essence the Kronstadt sailors wanted a decentralized state with local elected soviets running society. Kronstadt itself had been run on similar lines since early 1917. The local soviet, with a mixture of Bolsheviks, anarchists, left-wing SRs and other radicals, had stood out against the Provisional Government and declared itself to be the sole power in the city. General meetings were held, almost daily, at the city's focal point, Anchor Square, which was capable of holding 25,000 or more people. During the period 1917 to 1920 local committees organized everything: there were committees to run houses, ships and factories. Neighbourhoods established agricultural communes of about fifty persons each which cultivated every piece of arable land on the island; these collective vegetable gardens helped the city through the worst of the food shortages during the civil war. While the sailors were not, as a body, anarchists, the spirit of anarchism (which we met earlier among the Makhnovschchina) was clearly present, as was the desire for the autonomy of locally elected bodies; this was reflected in such slogans as 'All power to the soviets but not the parties'.

There was no widespread planning and organization behind the Kronstadt rising. In some respects the sailors chose a bad time; the strikes in Petrograd were collapsing, and since the civil war and the Russo-Polish war were over, the best units of the Red Army were available. Also, since the spring thaw had yet to come, the Reds could attack the city over the ice. Kronstadt held out for just over two weeks; the ferocious fighting resulted in probably 10,000 Red Army casualties, 1,600 Kronstadters killed and wounded, 2,500 of them taken prisoner and over 8,000 fleeing to Finland.

The rising was in full swing when the 10th Party Congress of the Bolsheviks assembled in Moscow. It would be wrong to say that the sailors' action led to the abolition of war communism; Lenin was already considering the end of food requisitioning in December 1920, together with the idea of introducing taxation in kind and allowing peasants to dispose of any surplus as they wished, once they had met their obligation to the state. Nevertheless, events at Kronstadt did focus the delegates' minds, and the Congress took the first steps in dismantling war communism and permitting the development of a mixed economy. The tax in kind and the peasants' right to dispose of their surplus were agreed; Trotsky's labour armies were disbanded, and trades unions were granted new freedoms, notably the election of officials and free debate on issues affecting their members.

4   GERMANY: WAR AND REVOLUTION

Exercise

Read Roberts, pp.227–8 and 236–42, concentrating on his discussion of the internal politics of wartime Germany; read also Document II.23 in *Primary Sources 1: World War I*, 'The Reichstag Resolution of 19 July 1917', and then answer the following questions:

1   How did the government of Germany change during the war?

2   What happened to the SPD during the war?

3   What is the essential demand voiced in Document II.23? ■

Specimen answers and discussion

1   The military became dominant in government, pushing civilian politicians and even Wilhelm II even further into the background.

Before the war the military were able to bypass civilian ministers and communicate directly with the Kaiser; the *Reichstag* had no say in the selection of ministers and virtually no influence in government. The war accentuated these traits. People living in wartime Germany began to speak of a growing military 'dictatorship', an idea taken up by subsequent historians. The driving force behind this military government was Ludendorff. Under Ludendorff, in the last two years of war, the *Oberste Heeresleitung* (the Supreme Command) became involved in labour policy and the problems of food supply and raw materials; Ludendorff also had an influence on the resignations of Bethmann Hollweg as Chancellor and Richard von Kühlmann as Foreign Minister. However, in spite of Ludendorff's ability and efficiency in organizing armies in the field, his organization of the home front was less successful. In his analysis of the military role in internal politics Gerald Feldman concludes:

(1865 - 1937)

> Unlike the later totalitarian dictatorship of Hitler, whose mad imperialist adventure was preceded by a ruthless 'coordination' (*Gleichschaltung*) of German society, the dictatorship of Ludendorff was dependent upon the acquiescence of an independent labor movement and of a military and civilian bureaucracy whose traditional modes of operation were unsuitable for the conduct of a total war ... [Also] like Bethmann Hollweg, Ludendorff tended to vacillate.
>
> (Feldman, *Army, Industry and Labor in Germany 1914–1918*, 1966, p.407)

2   The SPD split between those still prepared to support the government in the prosecution of the war and a new Independent Socialist Party, which demanded peace.

The war created new difficulties for the SPD and for the Imperial Government in its relations with the SPD. Patriotic political and trades union leaders of the party were keen to develop a new relationship with the government, even to the extent of accepting the monarchical system. However, they recognized that such a policy would need explaining to the rank and file, which had been given pre-war instruction in a party line of revolution and republicanism. The government, eager for labour's support in the war, recognized the need to promise some concessions. A memorandum emanating from the Imperial Chancellory on 27 October 1914 noted:

> There is no doubt that the common danger has won the German <u>workers for the nation.</u> It offers perhaps the last opportunity to win them not only for the nation, but also for the state. The workers who return home as soldiers crowned with victory will not be disposed to follow a Social Democracy that is an enemy of the Fatherland and revolutionary. But they will remain workers. The state must seek to avoid treating the labor movement as an enemy. It must call upon the unions and avoid giving the anti-state dogmatists of the old Social Democracy slogans under which they can again lead the workers against the state.
>
> (Quoted in Feldman, p.119)

But the promises were vague, and the SPD had to deliver something to convince its membership of the validity of its new policy. The length of the war helped the SPD and convinced the government that it must make some concessions; most notably, in 1916, there was a relaxation in the trades union legislation in order to allow the recruitment of workers under 18. The SPD's attempts to secure a reform of the Prussian suffrage, however, came to nothing. After the 'Peace Resolution' of 1917, the SPD were taken rather more into the government's confidence, and its leaders appear to have believed that the party was now recognized and accepted as a significant force in the state. The new party programme, announced in May 1918, made little reference to socialism, no reference to the collective ownership of the means of production, and could, in many ways, be described as liberal democratic.

As Roberts notes, the split in the socialists crossed the old divisions in the party. The incident which separated the Independent Socialists (*Unabhängige Social-demokratische Partei Deutschlands* – USPD) was the demand for a prompt end to the war. The USPD included Eduard Bernstein, the theorist of revisionism who might, in normal times, have been expected to go along with some improvement in relations with the government. It also included some of Bernstein's fiercest critics on the subject of revisionism, notably Karl Liebknecht and Rosa Luxemburg. Liebknecht and Luxemburg, both imprisoned during the second half of the war, were also recognized as leaders of the Spartacists. Though not a separate party during the war, on 30 December 1918 the Spartacists became the core of the new *Kommunistische Partei Deutschlands* (KPD).

3   The wording of the document is imprecise. In the resolution the *Reichstag* essentially expresses a desire for peace without forced acquisitions and without economic, financial or political oppression.

This, in spite of its woolly phrasing, is the document know as the 'Peace Resolution'. It marked the end of the *Burgfrieden* (fortress truce) which had existed since August 1914 and which had united all parties in the *Reichstag* behind the government in the prosecution of the war. While the military still spoke confidently in terms of total victory over the enemy, more and more deputies began voicing doubts about the conduct of the war, the dominance of the military, and the need for negotiated peace. □

Exercise   Read Roberts, pp.252 and 367–8, and then answer the following questions:

1   What events constitute the German Revolution in Roberts's account?

2   What were the causes of this revolution? ∎

Specimen answers   1   Roberts's account is not really very clear about what constituted the revolution, but a succession of events in October and November 1918 brought about the collapse of the old order: the army's call for an armistice; naval mutiny; the abdication of Wilhelm II; bringing the socialists into government; uprising in Bavaria spreading to Berlin. Then, early in 1919, there was a 'minor civil war' with a Spartacist uprising in Berlin and the destruction of the Soviet Republic in Bavaria.

2   The collapse of Germany's allies and the army announcing the need for an armistice; the beginning of cracks in morale. □

Exercise   Read Document II.24 in *Primary Sources 1: World War I*, the extract from Hans Peter Hanssen's diary. What elements does this extract suggest contributed to the revolution? ∎

Specimen answer   Starvation; dissatisfaction even in the army; hostility to the Kaiser; the inability of the police to act against at least some critics. □

The traditional view is that the German Revolution of November 1918 was brought about largely by war-weariness. During the war the German people had suffered severely from food shortages and inflation. General rationing was introduced in 1916, but the allowance of food was below subsistence level in some instances, and it was considerably below that which even some of the most unfortunate had experienced in peacetime (see Tables 11–13.10 and 11–13.11). The problems were aggravated by the fact that the stipulated ration allowances were not always available; imports from overseas were shut off by the Allied blockade, and little could be expected from Germany's own allies. The winter of 1916/17 became known as 'the turnip winter', as that root vegetable became a staple food; the cereal harvest had been poor and there were extreme difficulties of supply transport. A black market flourished and substitute (*ersatz*) foods were developed, some of which had no nutritional value. In March 1918 a system of compulsory regulation and licensing was introduced when there were more than 11,000 such products on the market.

Table 11–13.10 Wartime rations of basic food in Germany as a percentage of peacetime consumption

	1 July 1916 to 30 June 1917	1 July 1917 to 30 June 1918	1 July 1918 to 28 December 1918
Meat	31.2	19.8	11.8
Fish	51.0	–	4.7
Eggs	18.3	12.5	13.3
Butter	22.0	21.3	28.0
Cheese	2.5	3.8	14.8
Pulses	14.2	0.9	6.6
Sugar	48.5	55.5–66.7	82.1
Vegetable fats	39.0	40.5	16.6
Potatoes	70.8	94.2	94.2
Flour	52.5	47.1	48.1

(Source: Richard Bessel, *Germany After the First World War*, 1993, p.36)

Table 11–13.11 Weekly diets for one adult

Hamburg poorhouse, 1900	Düsseldorf rations, January 1917	Düsseldorf rations, April 1918
Potatoes 8.3lb	Potatoes 3lb	Potatoes 7lb
Rye bread 9.6lb	'War bread'[1] 3.5lb	
Meat 600g	Meat, sausage 200g	Meat, sausage 200g
Sausage 60g	–	–
Whole milk 1,400g	Whole milk 100g	Whole milk 90g
Skim milk 1,000g	–	Canned milk 126g
Flour 185g	Milling product 120g	Milling product 170g
		Soup flour 50g
Sugar 90g	Sugar 200g	Sugar 200g
Butter 260g	Butter, fats 62.5g	Butter, fats 62.5g
Pork lard 110g	–	–
Eggs 1	–	Eggs 1
Cheese 60g	–	Cheese 12.5g
Quark [like cream cheese] 100g	Spread 60g	Spread 200g
Herring 350g	–	Bouillon cube 1
Dried fruit 280g	–	Pudding powder 57g
Honey 350g	–	–
Rice 160g	–	–
Lentils 460g	–	–
Barley 80g	–	–
Beer 350g	–	–
Syrup 55g	–	–
Cabbage 750g	Vegetables?	Vegetables?
Nutritional value of above		
Calories 26,500	7,900	11,200
Protein (g) 1,000	260	350

[1] *'K-brot'*, K for *Krieg* (war), or *Kartoffel* (potato). The variety manufactured in Düsseldorf was 85 per cent rye flour and 15 per cent potato flour.

(Source: Elizabeth H. Tobin, 'War and the working class: the case of Düsseldorf 1914–1918', 1985, pp.282 and 284)

Before the war the peasantry had been inclined to find a variety of scapegoats for their problems – American farmers, commercial capitalists, middlemen. Management of the economy by the government during wartime, however, provided a different scapegoat. The government's management of the agricultural sector was often ill-conceived and clumsy. In October 1914, for example, it set maximum prices for bread grain but not for feed grain; when the latter rose rapidly, peasants fed their livestock on potatoes and, in consequence, potatoes virtually disappeared from the market in early 1915. Wartime controls became tougher, more rational and rather better enforced in the second half of the war, but no more popular with the peasants; searches for hidden farm produce early in 1918 embittered the peasantry still more. The peasants resisted and circumvented the regulations where possible; they also profited from the black market as both sellers and, in the case of chemical fertilizers which were in short supply because of the war, as buyers. But agricultural wages lagged far behind industrial wages and this, together with conscription, helped to denude farming of labour. In spite of the interrelationship which developed between the peasantry and the urban dwellers through the black market, a profound hostility began to emerge in the way that rural producer and urban consumer regarded each other. The peasants, especially the farmers and smallholders of the west and south, saw the war economy as working solely for the benefit of the urban consumer; the latter, discontented by rationing and shortages, believed that there was always plenty of food available in the countryside.

The experience of urban dwellers varied greatly during the war. The shortage of male workers encouraged the use of new flow production techniques, especially in the important war industries of optics and metallurgy. These changes, in turn, levelled some traditional wage differentials. But the war economy also fostered the growth of differentials between pay in war industries and civilian industries. In the former, between 1914 and 1918 the daily earnings of male workers increased by 152 per cent and those of female workers by 186 per cent; in the latter the increases were 81 per cent and 102 per cent respectively. (It is important to note that, on average, women continued to earn about half the wages of men.) Those in the war industries were also better off because they received most of the food premiums given to 'hard working' and 'hardest working' members of the workforce. With pay increases, some working-class families managed to approach the living standards of some of the middle class. This was due equally to an overall decline in the position of many members of the middle class, especially those on fixed incomes who suffered acutely from the wartime inflation. Nor were white-collar workers and independent artisans entitled to the extra food rations given to munitions workers, or able to benefit from the illegal bonuses provided by some industrial employers. The decline in their living standards fuelled discontent among sections of the middle class and made them rather more sympathetic to demands for reform and even socialist ideas. The corresponding rise in the living standards of sections of the working class, however, did not end discontent in that quarter. The problems of inflation, rationing and shortages appeared large in working-class family budgets, prompting disorder and increasing participation in strikes (see Table 11–13.12).

Table 11–13.12   Average number of people participating in strikes per month, August 1914–18

1914 (August)	0
1915	1,000
1916	10,000
1917	50,000
1918	100,000

(Source: Gerd Hardach, *The First World War 1914–1918*, 1977, pp.183–4)

Most of these strikes were organized at shop-floor level, not by the trades union leadership, and they were indicative of a growing split between the rank and file and the leadership. Like the political chiefs of the majority SPD, trades union leaders increasingly allied with the military authorities to support the war effort; this was particularly the case with the announcement of the Hindenburg programme for war production and the Patriotic Auxiliary Service Law (*Vaterländischer Hilfsdienst*) of December 1916. This law effectively militarized both the economy and the workforce: all males between 16 and 60 who were not in the army were henceforth regarded as members of the auxiliary services under the authority of the Minister for War; compulsory arbitration was established for labour disputes; local workers' committees were to be elected in factories employing fifty or more workers. The trades union leaders were generally satisfied with this system in as much as it gave them the recognition they had long sought from both employers and the state; at the same time they were alarmed by the way in which the elected factory committees tended to go their own ways against the national leadership. The declining authority of the leadership at shop-floor level was exposed by the massive strike in Berlin in January 1918, which eventually involved perhaps as many as half a million workers whose elected council demanded:

1   a prompt peace without annexations or reparations;

2   workers' participation in the negotiations for peace;

3   the democratization of the Prussian franchise;

4   the democratization of the *Reich*;

5   the abolition of the Patriotic Auxiliary Service Law and of the *Belagerungszustand* (siege law) which had been in operation since 1914 and which gave the army wide powers to curtail civil liberties and political activity;

6   an amnesty for all political prisoners;

7   improvements in the supply and quality of food.

The leaders of the socialist trades unions refused to back the strike; the majority SPD hierarchy dared not condemn it and sought to negotiate; the military authorities used force. While the actual figures are unreliable, it is possible that as many as 50,000 strikers were subsequently conscripted.

The conscription of strikers brought men into the army who were as likely to undermine morale and discipline as to yield to the latter. The German military did not fall apart in 1918 as dramatically as the Russians had done a year earlier, but there were increasing problems. The postal censors who read and reported on the letters sent home by the troops were describing alarming trends in the summer of 1917; troops were describing the war as a swindle, criticizing their officers, condemning capitalists for profiteering from the conflict, and urging relatives not to subscribe to war loans. When, following the Russian collapse, German soldiers began to be transferred from the east to the western front, up to 10 per cent of them used the move as an opportunity to desert. The problems became more serious when the spring offensive of 1918 came to a halt and the allies counter-attacked. Men found a variety of means to avoid or 'miss' the trains taking them back to the front after leave or convalescence; they got minor prison sentences; they 'lost' equipment. The Army Command introduced stiffer penalties, but to little effect. One officer estimated that, in the closing months of the war, there were between 750,000 and a million 'shirkers' (*Drückeberger*), and on 1 November 1918 an adjutant in the Prussian War Ministry reckoned that there were some 20,000 'deserters and similar riff-raff' in Berlin alone (quoted in Bessel, pp.47–8).

Ludendorff is reported to have told his staff on 1 October that the army was 'unfortunately, heavily infected with the poison of Spartacist-Socialist ideas' (quoted in Feldman, p.515). Desertion, or at best men going absent without leave, began to be a serious problem in the closing months of the war. Soldiers' councils (*Soldatenräte*) appeared in the army; obviously there was some inspiration from Russia, but there was also encouragement and guidance from those conscripted as a punishment for strike activity. As in Russia, the navy, with its large numbers of skilled workmen, was especially radical. The naval mutiny at Kiel in October 1918 (and there had been a similar, unsuccessful mutiny among sailors during the previous year) sparked off much revolutionary activity. Mobile flying squads of sailors spread revolutionary ideas throughout Germany, and the People's Naval Division (*Volksmarine*) provided dedicated shock troops for the revolution in Berlin.

'Soviets' were not confined to the military. The first had appeared briefly in Leipzig in 1917, directing a strike against a reduction in the bread ration. In November 1918 they were established in every major town and city. Concern about an Allied invasion after the collapse of Austria-Hungary, together with a resurgence of separatist feeling, gave the Workers' and Soldiers' Council in Munich the opportunity to declare an independent Bavarian Republic on 8 November. These councils were not Bolshevik; that in Munich was led by Kurt Eisner, a member of the USPD, but most of the councils were prepared to go along with the majority socialist leaders who found themselves running Germany. The congress of the councils which met in Berlin in December co-operated with the majority SPD leaders in setting National Assembly elections for the following January; the USPD did not and, outmanoeuvred, its leaders resigned from the Provisional Government and withdrew its co-operation with the majority party. However, whether or not they worked with the SPD leaders, the councils were tainted by the Russian example and were eyed with suspicion. Philipp Scheidemann, the SPD leader who had proclaimed the new German Republic on 9 November, expressed concern that:

> They come in from the street and hold placards under our noses saying: All Power to the Workers' and Soldiers' Councils! At the same time, however, they let you understand: If you do not do what we want, we will kick you out ... They can only represent a force as long as they are in possession of the majority of machine guns. What is Russia's present would then become a

certain future for Germany ... We need bread, peace and work ... The Councils can bring us neither bread nor peace. They will create civil war for us.

(Quoted in Koppel S. Pinson, *Modern Germany: Its History and Civilization*, 1966, pp.370–1)

Exercise To whom could the majority SPD turn for 'machine guns' to combat any threat from the councils or the left? ■

Specimen answer Those sections of the army which were not disintegrating. □

Discussion In return for promises that the new government would support the officer corps in maintaining army discipline, endeavour to keep the army supplied and oppose 'Bolshevism', General Wilhelm Groener, who had replaced Ludendorff, assured the SPD leader Friedrich Ebert of the army's support.

Exercise Given the events of the war years, do you think it surprising that the SPD leaders and the army's officer corps should have become allies in 1918? ■

Specimen answer While the majority SPD remained Marxist in theory, in practice it had become much more like a liberal democratic party. Furthermore, during the war years its leaders and the army command had got to know each other and had, to some extent, worked together in the war effort. In 1918, since both saw a threat from the left, it was logical that, whether they liked each other or not, they should decide to work together to stabilize the changes that had been made. □

Discussion The army was not alone in accepting, at least temporarily, the collapse of the old order and the need to make some links with moderates so as to check Bolshevism. On 15 November 1918 the Association of Employers, representing industrialists throughout Germany, agreed to many of the demands that had been pressed by the socialist trades unions before 1914: the recognition of unions as the official representatives of the labour force and of the worker's rights to join a union; collective bargaining; and the eight-hour day. In return the industrialists received the implicit acceptance of their right to own and run their factories.

5 GERMANY: UPRISING AND PUTSCH

For most historians, as for most contemporaries who lived through the events, the collapse of the old order and the sporadic fighting of November and December 1918, as reactionary groups were mopped up and elements of the left clashed for the first time, constitute the 'German Revolution'. However, disorder continued over a much longer period as the Weimar regime sought to establish itself as the sole recognized sovereign authority. Given the definition of the political process of revolution in section 1, there is some justification in looking at the uprisings and putsches of the period 1918–23 as the working out of the German Revolution.

The initial trouble was at the centre of political power in Berlin as, during January 1919, the SPD government confronted a left coalition of revolutionary shop stewards, the radical Berlin USPD and the new KPD. Liebknecht and other leaders of the KPD did not consider the time opportune for an armed insurrection, but they were swept along by the enthusiasm of others, notably the shop stewards. The Spartacist uprising of January was a disaster and was brutally crushed; Liebknecht and Luxemburg were murdered after their capture. However, Spartacist and left-wing USPD activity continued: a general strike in Berlin in March led to the imposition of martial law and to more fighting, and throughout the industrial districts of Germany there were strikes and risings in the first half of 1919. The Kapp Putsch of March 1920 provoked insurrectionary strikes in central Germany and particularly in the Ruhr. There were abortive KPD risings in 1921 and again in 1923.

The Spartacists, the KPD and the left USPD drew support from the unemployed, of whom there were thousands in Germany during the early months of peace as demobilized soldiers and sailors looked for work and as the economy had to reorganize for peace. Throughout the Weimar period the Communists continued to recruit from the unemployed, but they also found strong support among certain trades and in certain cities. It can be argued that disillusion with the SPD leadership in wartime, coupled with that leadership's hostility to workers' militancy early in 1919, fostered support for the left. But it is also true that some of the most militant centres during the Weimar Republic (such as Brunswick, Düsseldorf and Wuppertal) and some of the most militant trade groups (such as metalworkers and the miners of the Ruhr) were also noted for their militancy before 1914. The Ruhr miners were not to be bought off with the shorter hours and better pay granted at the end of the war; they wanted, as they had when their union was established in 1890, control of their workplace; in 1919 and 1920 they took up arms to achieve this end.

The SPD government had also to contend with the problem of Bavaria. Local elections at the beginning of 1919 had resulted in a major defeat for Kurt Eisner and the USPD. There was doubt as to how Eisner and the Workers' and Soldiers' Council would respond, but before he could make his intentions known, Eisner was shot dead by a reactionary student. Out of the developing shambles three rival governments emerged; a coalition under Johannes Hoffman of the SPD established itself eventually in Nuremberg; a Soviet government led by a group of young romantic intellectuals, largely members of the USPD, was established in Munich; and a second Soviet government, also in Munich, was set up by an altogether tougher and more down-to-earth Spartacist group. Hoffmann, like the SPD in Berlin, looked for assistance from the old army in Bavaria, but an early defeat sent him begging for troops from the federal government in Berlin. After a week of savage fighting at the end of April and the beginning of May 1919, the soviets in Munich were destroyed; the soviets' leaders who were not killed in the fighting were either murdered after capture, or sentenced to death or to long prison terms.

Eisner's Bavarian Republic was the only radical uprising to receive peasant support, and even this was limited and short-lived. Eisner cultivated his ties with local peasant leaders and built on long-standing progressive interest groups established among the Bavarian peasantry and their antipathy towards a central government dominated by Prussians.

Exercise   In what ways do you suppose that the war may have made the peasantry disinclined to support the urban uprisings? ■

Specimen answer   The war economy, generally speaking, made the peasants suspicious of, and hostile towards, urban consumers. □

Discussion   In fact this hostility worsened in the first months of peace when undernourished urban workers, who had suffered most from wartime rationing and extortionate black market food prices, set out, often in gangs, to take food in the countryside. The peasants responded to these expeditions with violence. These gangs confirmed the peasants' prejudices about dangerous and essentially idle urban workers and convinced them that the government was either powerless or siding with the predators.

[handwritten margin note: proletariat + peasants fighting each other.]

The peasant councils that appeared at the end of the war tended to be dominated by the same people who had taken charge of agrarian interest groups before 1914, namely estate owners, often aristocrats. During the war this élite had been patriotic, often ultranationalist, but they had also condemned the injustices of the war economy. Furthermore, while they criticized the controls on agricultural production, they were not slow to point out to the peasantry that the individuals calling most vociferously for such controls were invariably those who also called for political reform. Until the publication of recent research on the countryside and rural dwellers, historians tended to argue that the peasantry was unthinkingly conservative or that it allowed itself to be manipulated by the agrarian élite in the latter's conservative interest. It is now clear, however, that the criticism levelled at the economic policies of the wartime government and the immediate post-war regime genuinely reflected the interests of peasants. In both the east and the more advanced west of Germany, it is at least arguable that while the leadership remained largely unchanged, the radical tone of agricultural interest groups and particularly the open criticism of government policy were in keeping with grassroots feeling.

> Claims of the unity of all agricultural producers had a firm basis in the common experience of all peasants under the war economy, a system which all peasants saw as making impossible demands and intervening at will into their economic lives. Protest against state intervention into agricultural production was not orchestrated from above but originated in the daily experience of the individual agricultural producer ... Even where new and independent agricultural organizations, outside the traditional interest-groups framework, emerged in the months following the end of the war, they showed no sympathy to the new order, and shared the common demand for an immediate end to state intervention into the agricultural sector.
>
> (Robert G. Moeller, 'Dimensions of social conflict in the Great War', 1981, pp.167–8)

As noted in the preceding section, in order to maintain their position and deal with threats from the left, the SPD leadership entered into an agreement with the officer corps, as troops were needed to do the fighting. The gradual disintegration of the army before the armistice gathered pace rapidly as troops left the front lines and crossed back into Germany. A few units maintained a modicum of order, but the answer to the immediate military need was found not in the surviving remnants of the Imperial army but in the *Freikorps*. The idea of the *Freikorps* appears to have originated with General Georg von Maercker. Early in December 1918, concerned by the military collapse all around him, Maercker requested, and received, authorization from his military superiors to form a volunteer rifle corps. The force was to be selected from the best men who volunteered out of the old army. It was to be organized along the lines of the élite storm troops (*Sturmbataillone*) which had proved so effective in the later stages of the war. Although the corps was to be disciplined, the discipline was to be based on consent, as in the *Sturmbataillone*, rather than on the rigid, unthinking discipline of much of the old army. The privates of each company were to elect *Vertrauensleute* (trusted men) who were to be the channel for any complaints and who were to be consulted by the officers on questions of food and leave. Maercker found no shortage of volunteers; some were professional soldiers with nothing to return to in civilian life, and among many of these the notion that a weak home front had stabbed the army in the back in 1918 seems already to have been present; others were motivated primarily by patriotism and/or a fear and loathing of Bolshevism. By 4 January, when Maercker paraded his men before Chancellor Ebert and the Defence Minister, Gustav Noske, the volunteer rifles numbered 4,000 men and were equipped with machine guns and even artillery. By the same date similar *Freikorps* were being organized elsewhere. These were the units which brutally smashed the Spartacist risings, but as the demands for them increased, there was a change in the character of the volunteers. By April, when the *Freikorps* approached 400,000 men, many of the new recruits were not drawn from the old army or from former front-line soldiers. The new volunteers were often conservative, middle-class young men who had missed the war but who were motivated by fanatical anti-socialism, sometimes also by monarchism, German '*Volk*-ish-ness' and overt anti-semitism; it was not lost on these volunteers that many of the left's theorists and leaders (for example Eisner, Liebknecht, Luxemburg and, of course, Marx) were Jews. Some of the later *Freikorps* consisted of only a few hundred men and were set up by junior officers; they were able to maintain a degree of independence by accepting finance not from the government but from the Anti-Bolshevik League established by a group of wealthy industrialists. The suppression of the Spartacist rising in Berlin in January had been savage; the terror unleashed on Munich by the *Freikorps* in May 1919 terrified even the respectable middle-class burghers who had hailed them as liberators.

When the *Freikorps'* tasks were completed (at least in the eyes of the government) a new and major problem developed: how to get them to disband? Major General Count Rüdiger von der Goltz had been sent with the *Freikorps* units to defend the north-east against Bolshevism, and proceeded to take over Latvia. The Allies protested but the SPD leaders had no way of making von der Goltz and his men come home; indeed, they were concerned that the Baltic *Freikorps* might decide to march on Berlin. The government's powerlessness was exposed in November 1919, when a new *Freikorps* was openly recruited in Berlin to assist von der Goltz in Latvia. In March 1920 some of the Baltic *Freikorps* joined with Ehrhardt's *Freikorps* when it refused to disband, and set in motion the Kapp Putsch. The government fled before the disgruntled troops as they entered Berlin to be greeted, 'by chance', by Ludendorff; Wolfgang Kapp, an obscure civil servant and previously an organizer of the *Vaterlandspartei*, was proclaimed Chancellor. Kapp's administration lasted five days. He was ineffectual, his supporters were divided, the civil service in general (largely left over from the old regime) remained loyal to the Weimar government, but perhaps most important, Berlin was completely paralysed by a general strike called against the putsch. Significantly the *Reichswehr*, the small army of 100,000 men authorized by the Versailles Treaty, took no action against the putsch.

Government financial support of the *Freikorps* finished early in 1920. Officially the units were disbanded, but some continued as units of the Black *Reichswehr*, a clandestine reserve army maintained in defiance of the Versailles Treaty and which virtually doubled the size of the authorized *Reichswehr*. In October 1923 groups of the Black *Reichswehr* were involved in the Küstin Putsch. On this occasion the regular army did act against them; generals in the regular army were responsible for organizing and equipping the Black *Reichswehr* and they were not prepared to have their authority and discipline challenged. Some *Freikorps* continued as military clubs; a few followed their leaders as a body into the paramilitary *Sturmabteilung* of the infant Nazi Party, which, in alliance with Ludendorff, staged its own putsch in Munich in 1923. Some involved themselves in right-wing political murder gangs: members of the Ehrhardt *Freikorps*, for example, formed 'Organization Consul' which, in August 1921, carried out the assassination of Matthias Erzberger, the leader of the Catholic Centre Party who was hated by the extreme right because he had led the German armistice delegation of November 1918.

6 AUSTRIA-HUNGARY AT WAR

Introduction

If you had been around in the summer of 1914 and were asked to bet on the victor of the First World War, would you have put money on Austria-Hungary? Of course not! To the intelligent punter the ramshackle multinational empire, which sprawled across east-central Europe, must have looked less like a winner than any of the other combatants. The Austro-Hungarian Empire in 1914 possessed neither political nor economic unity. The Dual Monarchy represented the negation of nationalism and the denial of political independence at a time when these forces were burning with unprecedented intensity. Its brittle stability rested on the skilful application of the age-old principle of divide and rule, so that loyalty to the Emperor was, for its oppressed nationalities, the best safeguard against local domination by a bigger minority. This precarious balance was not only difficult to sustain; it was also costly.

Far from proceeding towards an integrated economy, therefore, the Habsburg Empire in 1914 was in the process of recession, moving rapidly towards a set of self-sufficient units, each concerned to escape the pull of the industrially more advanced provinces of the north and west. For the fear that it would bring Dalmatia into the Austrian economic sphere, Hungary opposed the construction of an inter-connecting railroad; it also obstructed the development of closer economic ties between Serbia and the monarchy for fear that this would disadvantage its own agricultural exports. The empire's relatively poor inland waterway facilities underscored the economic importance of railways, for the Danube, by comparison with the Rhine, is inferior in terms of both its location and its navigability. The politico-economic particularism of Austria and Hungary nevertheless conspired to limit the development of an extensive and efficient railway system. Magyar nationalism prevented the centralized administration of the network, which remained under separate control from Austria, Hungary and Bosnia-Herzegovina. The system – or more accurately the want of a system – provoked a good deal of chaos and conflict. Goods shipped by train were loaded on ships at Trieste and reloaded on a train at a Dalmatian seaport simply because Hungarian intransigence prevented the construction of a railway across Croatia. Equally, the Austrians refused to permit the Hungarians to ship goods directly to Prussian Silesia or Berlin. By comparison with Germany, the Austro-Hungarian network was stunted. Pre-war Austro-Hungarian mileage totalled 277,036 miles in a 264,204 square mile area. German railway lines, by contrast, were three times as long in a 208,830 square mile area.

The effect of these antagonistic relationships on the monarchy's war-making capacities were almost totally negative. In an old but useful study of the process of disintegration, _The Dissolution of the Habsburg Monarchy_ (1929), Oscar Jaszi argued that attempts to mobilize the Austro-Hungarian economy were destined to fail because the economy remained unbalanced, being dominated by primary production and with an industrial base that was insufficient to meet the requirements of mass industrialized warfare. The imbalance between agriculture and industry was certainly striking. Industrial development was highly localized; most of it was confined to the areas around Vienna, Gras-Loeben, northern Bohemia and Silesia. Agricultural products accounted for an average 75 per cent of the monarchy's exports before the war. Industrial employment in 1900 absorbed a mere 13.4 per cent of the active population in Hungary and only 23.3 per cent in Austria, compared with 37.5 per cent in Germany.

Though small, the industrial sector was dynamic. Growth rates in the Dual Monarchy rose sharply in the generation before 1914 and bore comparison with the more advanced European powers. Not so absolute quantities. Mineral resources, in particular, remained insufficient and underdeveloped. Austro-Hungarian raw material production reached 359 million German marks in 1913 compared to a production value of 1,845 million marks in Germany. The monarchy wanted for everything except wood, lignite and petroleum. Although a world leader in iron production, the total output from Austro-Hungarian furnaces was easily dwarfed by that of its rivals. Indeed, by comparison with the output of the leading iron-producing states, Austria-Hungary's iron production was puny. The United States, Germany, Great Britain, France and Russia with 33, 18.8, 11, 5.4 and 4.9 million tons output respectively were all far in advance of Austria-Hungary's 2.5 million tons. Although the empire was a producer of high-grade steel, Austria-Hungary was well behind other belligerents in terms of output. Even before the war brought unprecedented demands for consumption, pig-iron producers within the Dual Monarchy were suffering from a massive shortage of capacity and could not meet the growth in demand. Its machine industry, too, was undersized and inadequate for the requirements of modern warfare.

Additional burdens shouldered by industry included capital shortages, penal taxation and extensive cartelization. The Austro-Hungarian economy was dominated by industrial monopolies which sought, through restricted competition, low wages and high prices, to secure profits rather than production. These conditions, taken together, were sufficient to convince some that the Danube monarchy had lost the war even before the first shot was fired. Oscar Jaszi, who was so minded, wrote that, 'in 1913, the Austro-Hungarian Monarchy was already a defeated empire from the economic point of view and as such went into the world war in 1914'. Jaszi's views, echoed by A. J. P. Taylor in a more amusing study published in 1948 (*The Habsburg Monarchy*), have not been seriously challenged by more recent scholarship. General monographs and textbook accounts are in the main dismissive of the Austro-Hungarian war economy. Roberts, for example, does not bother to mention it at all!

The Habsburg army has been equally neglected. On the eve of war the army was certainly in a parlous condition. In structure and composition it mirrored the complexities of the empire it claimed to defend. The joint Austro-Hungarian army (the Imperial and Royal army) was supplemented by the Austrian defence army, the *Landwehr*, and its Hungarian variant, the *Honvéd*. Beneath them the *Landsturm*, the ultimate reserve, sought recruits from able-bodied men who were not required by the other three formations. Responsibility for these various forces was equally diffuse. The Austro-Hungarian army was administered by the War Ministry under the direction of the Austrian and Hungarian parliamentary delegations who controlled the purse strings; the *Landwehr* was controlled by the Austrian Ministry of Defence, and the *Honvéd* by its Hungarian analogue.

It was not an impressive force. One the eve of war the Habsburg armed forces were under-powered and under-strength. There was, in fact, a marked disparity between the growth of the population of the empire and the size of its armed forces. Between 1870 and 1914 the former rose 40 per cent, while the increase in the military establishment was only 12 per cent. Trained manpower was insufficient because spending was insufficient. Austria-Hungary, writes A. J. P. Taylor in *The Habsburg Monarchy*, 'though ranking only after Russia and Germany in population ... spent less than any Great Power – a quarter of Russian or German expenditure, a third of British or French, and even less that Italian'. In 1914 Austria-Hungary could mobilize a mere forty-eight infantry divisions – and that was only attained through the inclusion of the second-line units of the *Landwehr* and the *Honvéd* – compared with ninety-three for Russia, eighty-eight for France and eleven for Serbia. 'The truth is', suggests Holger Herwig, 'that Habsburg military forces were designed not to fight a major war but rather to maintain the delicate political balance in the Empire' (Holger H. Herwig, *The First World War*, 1997, p.13).

The Habsburg army was short on equipment as well as manpower. In both weight and quality it was wanting. Its firepower was farcical: about 66 per cent of the rifles supplied to the troops in 1914/15 were antiquated 1888 models. Austro-Hungarian divisions were also woefully deficient in artillery: a German, a Russian and a Serbian division possessed eighty, fifty-nine and forty guns respectively in comparison to thirty-two in the Balkans and forty-two in the north for an Austro-Hungarian division. Habsburg artillery was, in fact, relatively weaker in 1914 than it had been in 1866, since in the move to rapid-firing guns with six rather than eight guns per battery, the monarchy had not raised the number of batteries as other states had done.

The joint Austro-Hungarian army was more than a military formation, however. Apart from the monarchy, it was the main focus of supranationality. Its role as a nursery of dynastic feeling was taken seriously. Measures were introduced to prevent the over-representation of the empire's numerous nationalities, so that for every 1,000 men in the ranks of the Imperial and Royal army, there were 267 Germans, 223 Magyars, 135 Czechs, 85 Poles, 81 Ruthenes, 67 Croats and Serbs, 64 Romanians, 38 Slovaks, 26 Slovenes and 14 Italians. Command of this multilingual and multicultural force posed problems which were formidable but not without precedent. The British had managed to weld the disparate elements of the Indian sub-continent into a cohesive and effective fighting formation; and the Habsburg generals were no less skilful. Polish, Czech, South Slav and Ruthene regiments received their orders in the limited vocabulary of the *Kommandosprache*, the sixty-odd words of German that constituted the language of command; for the rest, instruction was in the *Regimentssprache*, given in their own tongue. Officers were drawn from the middle class: one-third were Magyars and Slavs, the remainder Germans, a reflection of their numerical weight within the educated and better-off elements. Whatever their origin, officers were expected to master the language of the regiment to which they had been posted and familiarize themselves with the customs of the men under their command. Those who failed to establish such rapport were transferred or dismissed from the service.

The military value of the Habsburg army, though, was not immediately apparent. Contemporary analysts, distracted by its diversity, underestimated the stamina of its soldiery, their corporate spirit and dedication to duty. The Austro-Hungarian high command was equally sceptical; fears of nationalist subversion prompted its demand for a pre-emptive war before the morale and fighting efficiency of the troops were fatally impaired. German commanders were contemptuous of an ally whom they regarded as inefficient, slovenly and degenerate. The experience of the eastern front confirmed these prejudices; their post-war writings are peppered with caustic comments on the third-rate fighting qualities of 'the Austrians', their incompetence and lack of moral fibre. Historians, taking their cue from the generals, have tended to present the Austro-Hungarian army as a shambles – less an example of lions led by donkeys, as with the British, and more a case of *schmucks* led by even greater *schmucks*. In recent years the clearest statement of this sort comes from the pen of Norman Stone. His book, *The Eastern Front 1914–1917* (1975), is a stylish study, which supplies an English audience with a panoramic survey of a neglected but crucial theatre of war. In his prize-winning account – it won the Wolfson Prize for the best historical work of the year – Stone identifies the lack of aggression as one of the principal defects of the military forces of the monarchy. The problem, he tells us, was that 'the army was not ruthlessly tyrannical, in the Prussian style. The Austrians did not have the Prussian knack of making anybody and everybody fight for Prussia, by virtue of a ruthless authoritarianism.' The Austrian war effort, we are led to believe, was directed by duds and *dummkopfs*.

Stone is an authority on east-central Europe and so we must treat his views with respect. In the sections that follow we shall consider the adequacy of the Prussian perspective in relation to the military effort of the Habsburg Empire. Specifically, we shall examine the organization of the war economy, its effect upon the performance of the armed forces, and the social and political consequences arising therefrom. I shall suggest that the war effort of the Austro-Hungarian Empire, as presented by Stone and others, is in need of revision. The empire's military effort wasn't good, but neither was it the unholy mess portrayed by the critics.

War economy

Austria-Hungary was no worse prepared for war than any other belligerent. Its statesmen and soldiers, like their compeers in Paris, Berlin and St Petersburg, anticipated a short, sharp encounter on the field of glory and had made no comprehensive plans for the mobilization of the monarchy's human and productive resources. Partial measures, however, were better than none. The War Service Law of 1912, a piece of legislation prompted by fear of fall-out from the Balkan Wars, provided for the militarization of the economy in the event of an emergency. Baldly summarized, the Act placed the entire population of the empire and its industrial and agricultural resources at the disposal of the military. The War Ministry was empowered to requisition and direct factories, to bypass market mechanisms and commandeer essential military supplies, and to draft labour for industry. Provision was included for the industrial conscription of all able-bodied adult males; freedom of movement was abolished and workers were placed under military discipline and law. Loss of production due to industrial unrest was to be minimal until the second half of the war.

Loss of production due to error and inefficiency in the organization of the monarchy's resources was another matter. At the close of September 1916, von Tschirschky, the knowledgeable German Ambassador in Vienna, reported on the internal situation of the monarchy. His pessimistic prognosis identified seven major areas in which Austrian economic mobilization was deficient.

Exercise   Turn now to Document II.25 in *Primary Sources 1: World War I*. Read the report carefully and then list the principal sources of ambassadorial concern. ■

Specimen answer   Manpower shortages, a lack of co-ordination in the management of the war economy, consumer shortages, a crisis of distribution, currency depreciation, a resurgent nationalism, and internal unrest – these, Berlin was informed, raised doubts about the monarchy's ability to prolong the struggle. □

It is, of course, a biased document, full of national prejudice: the Austrians advance under German tutelage; their faults are of their own making. Nevertheless, von Tschirschky's comments are not without insight. His report emphasizes the fact that mass industrialized warfare is largely a matter of real resources – labour, raw materials and productive capacity; that fighting power is determined by the manner in which resources are allocated among the armed forces, the armament industry, producers of capital goods, and the suppliers of the civilian population. In short, defeat or victory depends upon the optimal allocation of resources.

The resource-led character of the ambassador's report might seem surprising; it shouldn't. It was the Germans under Rathenau's leadership who formulated the concept of a special 'war economy' (*Kriegswirtschaft*) characterized by the control and co-ordination of raw material supplies and the elimination of wasteful competition. His strictures upon the monarchy's fragmented war effort, the evils of protectionism and nationalism, were unquestionably major sources of weakness. So was the collapse of the currency. But it was the imbalance between military-industrial needs and civilian consumption which ultimately proved fatal. Notwithstanding von Tschirschky's belief in German superiority, it was the same defect which proved to be the undoing of the German war economy.

In Austria-Hungary, as in Germany, the authorities were slow to realize that in total war civilians as well as soldiers must march on their stomachs. Failure to maintain a proper relationship between agriculture and industry brought famine, civil unrest and growing demands for 'bread and peace'. Had the Central Powers (Germany and Austria-Hungary) adopted measures to sustain civilian consumption comparable with those of the British, the outcome of the war might well have been different. In 1916, however, the emphasis was on maximizing the output of armaments and ammunition; in this sphere, as von Tschirschky readily agreed, the Austro-Hungarians had made 'surprising progress'.

Industrial mobilization

German industrial mobilization provided a model for the organization and development of the Austrian war economy. The Austrians were persuaded to establish a whole range of trusts, boards, combines and commissions to procure and distribute raw materials and labour. As in Germany – indeed, as everywhere else – experiments in state control were accompanied by a good deal of waste and inefficiency. There were many mistakes. Indiscriminate recruitment for the armed forces meant that precious skilled labour was lost to vital war industries. Large numbers of miners and metalworkers, inducted into the army at the opening and bloodiest phase of the fighting, never returned; as one authority put it, 'the best qualified workers were left lying in the Carpathian mountains'. Conflict and chaos emerged from the competing claims of the War Ministry and the Trade Ministry to organize production. There was much muddle, unnecessary duplication of effort, and overlapping jurisdictions. Agencies proliferated: five were required to process a single ox – one for leather, one for meat, one for bone, one for fat, and one for procurement. No governmental body with control over the entire economy existed until the formation of the Commission for War and Transitional Economy in 1917.

For all that, there were a lot of positive achievements, some of which were remarkable. The military authorities, in particular, displayed energy and enterprise in organizing heavy industry and mining. In the monarchy, as elsewhere, changes in the composition of the workforce followed as production processes were restructured to alleviate labour shortages and increase output. Replacements for men called to the colours were found from women, juveniles and prisoners of war. The feminization of the armament and metal manufacturing industries was particularly pronounced, as Table 11–13.13

shows. In some factories women made up more than half the labour force, and until 1917, when their numbers were halved by the substitution of prisoners of war, women comprised 15 per cent of the workforce engaged in the manufacture of coke. The overall increase in the female labour force has been put at about 40 per cent; in all, about one million women entered the labour force in Austria during World War I.

Table 11–13.13   Proportion of female workers in Viennese metal industries

Year	Total workforce	Female workers	% female
1913	65,789	12,180	18.51
1914	69,065	15,407	22.31
1915	78,068	20,767	26.60
1916	70,124	24,401	34.80
1917	86,807	31,401	36.17

(Source: R. Wall and J. M. Winter (eds) *The Upheaval of War,* 1988, p.119)

The restructuring of the labour force and the standardization of production worked wonders. So too did the battery of measures brought forward by the War Ministry to mobilize heavy industry. Through the use of direct grants and subsidies, extensive substitution, careful husbandry and close regulation of minerals and metals, output was massively increased; new factories were built, old mines re-opened and new mines sunk. Less than three weeks before the armistice, there were still fifty-seven Austro-Hungarian divisions engaged on the southern front against a formidable Entente force, while another six divisions were fighting alongside the Germans on the western front. The presence of the Austro-Hungarian army in the field in late 1918 confirms the substantial achievements of the war economy. Some measure of those achievements can be gauged from the production statistics shown in Table 11–13.14. It will be seen that, once the industrial dislocation of the opening phase of the war had been overcome, output rose spectacularly. The production of iron ore, pig iron and steel increased by 11, 5 and 25 per cent respectively in 1915 and attained new heights thereafter. In 1916 the production of ferrous metals soared above the record year of 1913: iron ore and pig iron production rose 15 per cent and steel output leapt 33 per cent over the record 1913 output; high productivity in the iron and steel industry was in fact sufficient to satisfy most of the ferrous metal requirements of the armaments industry during the first half of the fighting. It could not be sustained beyond 1917, but it was impressive while it lasted.

From the non-ferrous metals there came a similar story. Of strategic importance in the manufacture of armaments, these were even more scarce than iron and steel. Pre-war production satisfied the demand for aluminium, but was unable to supply any of the tin and nickel demand from internal sources. In 1913 domestic production accounted for only 4,052 tons of pure copper, and 36,500 tons were imported to meet industrial requirements. After 1914 imports from Germany made good some of the deficit; intensive recycling provided the rest. Industry was progressively stripped of its non-ferrous metals; householders, too, were compelled to contribute. Ultimately every copper-containing item was taken. Household goods and fittings were surrendered; copper was removed from roofs and lightning rods; and chandeliers, bathtubs, brass crucifixes, even church bells, were mobilized in defence of the empire.

Table 11–13.14   Ferrous metal production (tons) 1913–18

Year	Iron ore	Pig iron	Steel
1913	3,343,356	1,632,874	1,840,000
1914	2,509,365	1,487,822	1,539,000
1915	2,901,599	1,572,325	1,979,000
1916	3,900,000	1,900,000	2,750,000
1917	2,829,000	1,595,000	2,424,000
1918	n.a.	n.a.	1,461,000

(Source: J. Robert Wegs, 'Austrian economic mobilization during World War I, with particular emphasis on heavy industry', 1970, p.89)

Exercise   Examine Table 11–13.15 and briefly summarize the effect of these measures. ■

Table 11–13.15   Copper production and acquisition (tons) during World War I

	1915	1916	1917	1918 (until Sept.)
(a) *Domestic copper*				
Foundry production	6,528	7,774	5,279	3,330
Commandeered copper	2,298	5,727	1,715	641
Direct purchase by the Central Metal Authority:				
Scrap metal	1,148	1,268	2,537	1,343
Metal equipment	434	3,480	72	46
Industrial metal	4,272	4,392	2,741	756
Total	14,680	22,641	12,344	6,116
(b) *Domestic copper alloy*				
Commandeered:				
Church bells	–	3,703	9,771	1,119
Other	2,597	1,621	137	6
Purchased by the Central Metal Authority:				
Scrap metal	817	1,650 ·	1,282	703
Metal equipment	625	1,969	59	91
Industrial metal	1,613	2,887	1,008	458
Total	5,652	11,830	12,257	2,377
(c) *Foreign purchases*				
Central Metal Authority Purchases:				
Copper	4,829	6,904	2,585	
Copper alloy	754	28	–	
Consignments from Germany:				
Copper	9,493	3,095	2,695	
Copper alloy	825	–	–	
Total	15,901	10,027	5,280	

(Source: J. Robert Wegs, 'The marshalling of copper: an index of Austro-Hungarian economic mobilization during World War I', 1976/7, p.193)

Specimen answer   It will be seen that record production increases in 1916 exceeded the 1913 production by 48 per cent. The importance of the state procurement agency, the Central Metal Authority, is clearly shown. In 1916, its interventions accounted for 45 per cent of the 34,471 tons that were available before imports; the inclusion of copper purchases from Germany brought its contribution to more than half the total supply. Its unremitting efforts also helped mitigate the effects of the fall-off in production in 1917. However, the church bells, which played so signal a part in offsetting the reduction in output in that year, could only be commandeered once. As production plummeted, ever more desperate measures were required. In 1918 the military authorities, following the example set by Germany, confiscated brass door-latches; shop windows, too, were dismantled and stripped of their copper content.

The same drive and initiative characterized the procurement and substitution of zinc, tin and lead, but to no avail. By the close of 1917 the non-ferrous metal industry had reached its limits, and much the same was true of other sectors of heavy industry. Output had attained record levels, and there might have been still greater production triumphs had the Central Powers been able to co-ordinate their war effort. □

The Central Powers: conflict and co-operation

Apart from foodstuffs, allied co-operation in the economic sphere was limited in range and effectiveness. Co-operation between the two powers took the form of bilateral trade deals whereby the monarchy received supplies for its metal and armament industries and in exchange provided the Germans with petroleum, bauxite and other scarce commodities. Beyond that, however, there was little unity. On the exploitation of the occupied territories, for example, neither side could agree. Austrian attempts to secure a fixed share of captured material in France and the Low Countries were curtly brushed aside; German demands for dominion in Poland likewise received short shrift from a once great power that had come to fear its ally more than the enemy. These fears were justified. German ambitions, if realized, entailed the demise of the Danube Monarchy; as these ambitions unfolded, Habsburg hackles rose appreciably. *Mitteleuropa*, the organizing concept of the war aims of the Central Powers, was increasingly viewed as a source of coercion rather than co-ordination. The Austro-Hungarians, however, would not willingly comply; absorption into a central European confederation under German tutelage was steadfastly resisted. To the end, the monarchy retained its political and economic independence.

Its status as a military power, though, was compromised by the poor performance of its generals. Until the summer of 1916 the Habsburg armed forces had held their own on all fronts, being neither more nor less successful than either their allies or their opponents. The Brusilov offensive, however, dealt the Austro-Hungarian forces a shattering blow from which they never quite recovered. Thereafter the military was unable to resist pressure for the establishment of a unified command under the direction of German generals. The formation of a Supreme War Command, in September 1916, signalled the end of Austria-Hungary as an independent military power. Still, the economies which might have followed were not realized, and there was no standardization of weapons systems.

Friction, moreover, was not eliminated. As casualties spiralled and victory receded, and as shortages became ever more acute, the Central Powers grew peevish and recriminatory: the Germans were accused of arrogance, the Austrians of ineptitude; each blamed the other for their own failings. Habsburg soldiers were convinced that their blood was being shed needlessly to reduce German losses, while the Germans were aggrieved at being 'shackled to a corpse'. Faced with these contentious parties, the historian is inclined to act as a policeman called to a domestic quarrel. Wherever the fault lies, it is clear that the Central Powers failed to achieve a degree of co-operation and co-ordination comparable with that of their enemies (see Roberts, pp.226–7).

Transport

By the close of 1917 industrial mobilization had passed its peak. The exhaustion of resources, human and physical, made it impossible to sustain output, let alone increase it further. In the armaments industry, for example, a critical shortage of horses for moving artillery pieces meant that field cannon lay idle when horses were required for newly created howitzer batteries. Transportation, or the want thereof, was without doubt the principal impediment to the smooth functioning of the war economy. Quite simply, the railway network did not possess sufficient carrying capacity to service the exceptional demands of the state at war. Of the 12,000 locomotives available at the beginning of the war, anything from two-fifths to one-half were constantly in repair, while the enemy captures and depredations depleted the stock of railway cars – in 1914 alone the monarchy lost 15,000 to the Russians in the retreat from Galicia. Furthermore, the loss of qualified personnel to the military reduced the productivity of labour at a time of greater need. Efficiency inevitably suffered: load limits fell, speeds were reduced, freight deteriorated in unattended cars, and locomotives became unserviceable. Some of this was avoidable. Indiscriminate military recruitment made the crisis worse than it need have been. In 1914, for example, the assumption that the war would be over by Christmas led to the call-up of 35,500 skilled railway workers (12 per cent of the total) and their supposed temporary replacement with 31,500 women. Other difficulties arose from the activities of those politicians who, in order to protect domestic industry from foreign competition, opposed purchases of additional locomotives and rolling stock from abroad. In consequence there was a growing discrepancy between production and consumption. Producers, inadequately supplied with railway cars, could not get food to the cities, iron to the foundries, oil to the refineries, or coal to the factories. In July 1918 vast quantities of coal were stockpiled at the pithead: the Ostrau-Karwiner coal district had 73,600 tons of coal and 35,300 tons of coke awaiting transport, while the north-west Bohemian lignite district had 37,400 tons of coal and the Carlsbad district 7,160 tons. Ironically, it was the slump in industrial activity in 1918 that created the additional capacity which enabled the defeated Habsburg armies to be returned home within one month of the conclusion of hostilities. The railways lost the empire the war but saved the new republic.

Currency depreciation

How was the massive increase in public expenditure to be paid for? The principles of Austrian war finance were fairly straightforward: loans were preferred to taxation on the assumption that the enemy would foot the bill on the morrow of victory; in the meantime outstanding differences between income and expenditure were settled by printing more money. War loans were obtained in the capital market and supplied a further opportunity for public participation and legitimation of the war effort; bank credits, by contrast, were secret and obtained principally by printing new paper currency of the Austro-Hungarian Bank. From July 1914 to October 1918 the amount of money in circulation rose from 2.19 milliard to 35.53 milliard kronen. No comparable increase in the quantity of goods and services available accompanied this extraordinary expansion of the money supply, and prices soared. Between 1914 and 1918 the official cost of living index in Austria registered an increase of 1,226 per cent. Against such a background, 'the amazing patience and self-abnegation of the people', to quote Redilich, the historian of Austrian war government, was truly remarkable (*Austrian War Government*, 1932). By the end of the war the real income of industrial workers had fallen to less than half of the pre-war level. Inflation, however, struck with even greater severity at civil servants, salaried workers, pensioners and others on fixed incomes.

Industrial unrest

The end of the war saw professors wandering the streets of Vienna without a shirt on their back, and white-collar workers taking handouts from communal kitchens set up to sustain the starving. Shortages were such that scientists turned in vain to chestnuts, even to rats, in pursuit of substitutes for scarce fats! Although the Austro-Hungarian Monarchy before the war was more self-sufficient in food production than Germany, France or Britain, the reduction in deliveries from Hungary and the reduction in the peasant population as a result of conscription created a crisis of subsistence. Grain production fell from 9.2 million tons in 1914 to 6.2 million tons in 1917 and 5.3 million tons in 1918. Inevitably, the lack of food, fuel and clothing took its toll on civilian health. In the three years up to 1917, said Vienna's Chief Health Officer, the incidence of tuberculosis had more than doubled. 'The physical strength of the great part of the population', he added, 'is so undermined with insufficient nourishment that they are unable to withstand sickness, and unless food conditions speedily improve the death rate from tuberculosis will run much higher.' The political repercussions were equally grave.

As early as 1915 miners had gone on strike in protest against unsatisfactory and uncertain food supplies; the same shortage of comestibles provoked further stoppages in January and March the following year. Thereafter, notwithstanding military repression, strikes grew in frequency and intensity. In January 1918 when meat and potato consumption in Austria was down to 23 grams and 70 grams per person per day, the reduction of the flour ration from 200 grams to 165 grams set off a strike wave which engulfed the whole of industrial Austria and brought Budapest to a standstill. Workers' councils were elected, and demonstrations for bread and peace and against the militarization of the factories were held.

But for the restraining hand of social democracy, the Habsburgs might have gone the same way as the Romanovs there and then. Convinced that a socialist seizure of power would convert the monarchy into a battlefield on which the German and Entente forces would meet, the Social Democratic Party acted as an intermediary between government and workers, performing a critical role in the restoration of order. Its tribunal function, performed with great gusto, was sufficient to marginalize the Austrian Communist Party, which had emerged out of the crisis, and retain leadership of a radicalized labour movement that was itself in process of transformation.

As in Britain, military participation was accompanied by increased participation from unskilled elements who were previously excluded from the labour movement. In the year 1913, the Social Democratic Party had 91,000 members in the German districts of Inner Austria; in 1919, the number was 332,391. In 1913 the trades unions in the same area enrolled 253,137 members; in 1919 the number was 772,146. Two-thirds of the party and trades union membership were new recruits. These untrained and inexperienced workers were welcomed by the Social Democrats as a master receives an apprentice. The masses were to be taken in hand so that they were not seduced by the growing consciousness of their own power into dangerous and ill-considered assaults upon the polity.

The May mutinies

Until the closing stages of the war, the combat effectiveness of the Austro-Hungarian army remained unimpaired. At the beginning of 1918 it was a confident, conquering force occupying vast tracts of the Ukraine, the Balkans and Upper Italy. Support for the monarchy held firm. The disposition of the Romanian, Ruthenian and Bosnian troops summoned to crush the January strikes in Vienna, for example, was not in question. 'There was no doubt', wrote a leader of the Social Democrats, 'that these troops were strong and reliable enough to put down any attempt among the masses to transform the strike into an act of revolution.' The armed forces, however, could not indefinitely withstand the process of decay and disintegration within the supranational empire. The violent mutiny at Boeche di Cattaro, in February 1918, signified the extent of disaffection within the navy. From the fleet to the army, sedition spread fast. Beginning in the spring, the military was convulsed by a rash of desertions, depredations, mutinies and other disturbances. Slovene troops mutinied in Judenberg; Serbian troops in Fünfkirchen; Czech troops in Ljubljana; and Magyar troops in Budapest. In Croatia, Slavonia and Bosnia-Herzegovina armed bands of deserters, the self-styled 'Green Cadres', plundered the countryside in defiance of both the civil and military authorities; others volunteered for service with the various 'legions' that began to proliferate among the oppressed national minorities. Military service, far from promoting supranational sentiment, was fast destroying it. Combat, it seemed, had transformed peasants into politicians; conscripts with no previous political experience had become an insurgent force that threatened the safety of the realm. Is such an interpretation accurate or are appearances deceiving? To help us form a judgement we shall examine the first of these incidents a little more closely.

During the night of 12/13 May 1918 the small German town of Judenberg in Upper Styria was at the mercy of mutinous troops of the reserve battalion of the 17th Infantry Regiment. Soldiers, many the worse for drink, roamed the streets abusing civilians, pillaging shops, shouting slogans and shooting up the railway station. In all, 1,181 men participated in the mutiny; almost half were convicted by courts-martial and seven were executed. The Judenberg mutiny, the first serious outbreak, exemplified the radicalizing process within the military. In the course of their peregrinations through the town the rebels shouted:

> Let us go home comrades, this is not for us but also for our friends in the fronts. The war must be ended now, whoever is a Slovene, join us. We are going home; they should give us more bread to eat and end the war; up with the Bolsheviks, long live bread, down with the war.
>
> (Quoted in Z. A. B. Zeman, *The Break-up of the Habsburg Empire 1914–1918*, 1961, p.143)

Exercise   What do these slogans tell you about the outlook of the mutineers? Re-read them carefully and then itemize the sources of unrest. Now see how your list compares with mine. ■

Specimen answer   The appeal to Slovene troops suggests elements of nationalism; support for Bolshevism would seem to indicate a political perspective – Roberts certainly thinks so (see p.247); and there are signs, too, of war-weariness, possibly pacifism, homesickness and hunger. The precise balance, though, is difficult to determine; just how difficult will become clear as we examine each element separately. Since the last item is both easiest to deal with and the most significant, we shall take it first. □

Hunger

Exercise   Table 11–13.16 shows the state of the daily military bread ration (in grams) during the war. Does it tell you anything of significance about the timing and character of unrest in the military? ■

Table 11–13.16   Austro-Hungarian army's daily bread rations, 1917–18

	Up to 15 April 1917	*After 15 April 1917*	*After 11 Aug. 1917*
Field army:	500	478	480
Ersatz [reserve] and rear:	400	240	240

	September 1917	December 1917	April 1918	August 1918
Field army:	470	470	283	300
Ersatz and rear:	263	320	180	200

(Source: Richard B. Spence, 'Yugoslavs, the Austro-Hungarian army and the First World War', 1981, p.249)

Specimen answer   Two aspects are outstanding. Note, first, the striking difference between the rations supplied to combatants and those supplied to others. The explanation is straightforward: fighting being more arduous than training, those at the sharp end were deemed to be more deserving than reserve formations in the rear. It will also be seen that, with respect to the reduction and reallocation of rations, those in the rear received less but lost more than soldiers at the front. It should be added that the figures shown in the table are nominal quantities; as a rule the difference between allocation and consumption was considerable.

Note, too, the course of the cuts; the drastic reduction of April 1918 – in the rear the bread ration was more than halved – directly preceded the outbreak of the major mutinies. 'I went hungry in Russia long enough, and I won't go hungry here too', exclaimed one of the Judenberg mutineers to a terrified resident. 'Why do you Germans have enough to eat and we so little?' The fact that such troops were eating less than the surrounding population also had a disastrous effect on discipline; the prospect of a square meal prompted many a deserter.

But while food was in short supply, wine was readily available and consumed in vast quantities. Hungry soldiers in the reserve units were often drunk and disorderly, and in all the mutinies listed above, such soldiers were prominent. □

Political awareness

Protest against deprivation and the failure to satisfy material wants was one thing; unrest due to political subversion was something else. The latter was an undoubted feature of the May mutinies; pro-Bolshevik slogans were adopted by disaffected soldiers in all the units involved. The Austro-Hungarian high command found the source of subversion easy to identify. The fault, the generals concluded, lay neither with themselves nor in their stars but in the revolutionary agitation spread by repatriated prisoners of war who had been indoctrinated in the course of their captivity. Their numbers were considerable. By the close of 1917 there were an estimated two million Austro-Hungarian soldiers imprisoned in Russia whom the Bolsheviks sought to influence. The methods of mass psychological warfare were applied to persuade captive soldiers to take up arms in defence of socialism, peace and brotherhood. The compliant were rewarded, whereas intransigents were punished and the indifferent neglected. To the Soviet regime the potential of the prisoners of war was twofold; on the one hand they represented a trained reserve on which the Red Army might draw; on the other, properly educated, they might form politically conscious cadres to promote permanent revolution. 'The proletariat', they were reminded, 'has no homeland'. Those awaiting repatriation were enjoined to 'Inflame the country you are returning to, but inflame it not with hatred, but with true fire. Put an end to the state of the capitalists, priests and robber barons. Returning prisoners of war: REVOLT.'

Following the peace of Brest-Litovsk, hundreds of thousands of Austro-Hungarian soldiers were returned from Russian prisoner-of-war camps. The generals, though keen to restore them to active service, were concerned to exclude Communist infiltrators from the army. A network of ideological decontamination units was created through which the returned prisoners were passed in order to separate suspect and unreliable elements. Those considered sound – and they constituted the vast majority – were posted to army retraining centres for reconditioning in tactics, discipline and army life. Having completed the four-week course, the ex-prisoners were given a month's leave and then required to report to their reserve units in preparation for the resumption of front-line service.

The screening process was not foolproof, however, and subversives slipped through, although their influence should not be unduly magnified. Bolshevik attempts to undermine the loyalties of prisoners of war and mobilize them in defence of world revolution met with a muted response from the captive masses; the turncoats who fought with the Reds were a tiny minority who were driven by instrumental rather than ideological considerations. The length of service of the estimated 85,000 to 100,000 Hungarian prisoners who took arms on the Bolshevik side, for example, was limited to days and weeks; as the opportunity arose they deserted and made for home. One in three, possibly more, never arrived. Still, conditions in the camps were such that death *en route* seemed worth the gamble. Pro-Bolshevik sentiment among Austrian and Magyar prisoners was more a matter of personal protection than political commitment. By the spring of 1917, at least 600,000 prisoners of war had died in captivity. To inmates suffering and starving in disease-ridden camps the appeal of Bolshevism was like the alternative to old age; in short, Habsburg soldiers were better Red than dead.

Unrest among returned prisoners of war was not, therefore, political in provenance. The vast majority, though unaffected by Bolshevism, were reluctant to rejoin their units at the front. Having been captured and imprisoned they felt that they had 'done their bit'. 'First and foremost we want to know why we are fighting this war without sense or purpose now for four years', one angry ex-PoW demanded of General Anton Lipoščák, 'then we want to know why we prisoners of war cannot finally go home.' The general's own angry response led to shooting. Not only were the ex-prisoners unprepared for the resumption of active service, they were infuriated by the brevity of their leave and disturbed by the hunger, privations and distress encountered during their four weeks *en famille*. The Bolshevik slogans expressed by such men during the May mutinies were a vehicle for the dramatic registration of protest, not the prelude to an armed uprising and seizure of power. In this their conduct was comparable with the British soldiers at Shoreham who in 1917 broke camp, shouting in similar terms in order to ventilate their grievances. Hoisting the Red flag was a signal to the authorities, not a statement of political commitment.

Homesickness, war-weariness and pacifism

Of these, the last is of least importance. There is little evidence that the mutineers were animated by a coherent body of anti-war thought. War-weariness, by contrast, was a form of non-doctrinal pacifism which was not unrelated to the enormous number of casualties sustained in the previous three years. Slovene losses were particularly heavy; by the close of 1917 there were on average 28 dead for every 1,000 of their number, a casualty rate exceeded only by the Austro-Germans. Croat casualties, too, were heavy and bore comparison with those of the Slovenes; Bosnia-Herzegovina had a casualty rate of 19.1 and Dalmatia 18.1. All in all, something like 2,500,000 Austro-Hungarian soldiers had been killed or permanently disabled by the end of 1917. Among the warring nations, the Austro-Hungarian Empire had the highest ratio of casualties. Of the 8,300,000 men called to the colours during the war, at least 6,200,000 became casualties. 'It is no exaggeration to say', writes Istvan Deak, 'that, towards the end of the war, the Austro-Hungarian army was made up of men who had been wounded earlier, who had been seriously ill or frostbitten, or who had returned from Russian POW camps' ('Shades of 1848: war, revolution and nationality conflict in Austria-Hungary 1914–20', 1977).

Death and injury on such a scale affected the composure and cohesion of the armed forces. War losses were unevenly distributed. Among Bosnian regiments, for example, it was the higher level of casualties among Muslims and Croats which made the Serbs unmanageable. In short, the most effective troops were the most vulnerable; replacements were often less fit and invariably less committed.

The *Ersatz* Reserve, the principal source of supply, was a receptacle for troops deemed to be unsuitable for combat duties. Students, teachers and priests, who were exempted from active service, were assigned to support roles along with those conscripts who for some reason were best kept out of the front line. Exposed to agitation from the native population among whom they were stationed, these troops gave constant trouble. 'Throughout the war', writes Richard B. Spence, 'the vast majority of disciplinary problems, and outright criminal activity, would occur in the Ersatz and rear service units which became the dumping grounds for troops and officers considered unfit for service at the front.' Significantly, the May mutineers were all drawn from the *Ersatz* battalions.

The increase in disaffection among Yugoslav soldiers was also related to the deterioration of political and economic conditions in the territories from which they were drawn. Professor Stone's conviction that the Austrian military were insufficiently tough, and wanting in the animality of their ally, was not shared by the oppressed nationalities of the empire, particularly the Slav and Latin elements who, in the words of Redilich, were subjected to 'the unrestricted, unlimited and quite ruthless use of the power of command and punishment'. Note, too, von Tschirschky's observations (Document II.25). The application of unlimited dictatorial authority to secure the submission of a suspect population was accompanied by summary executions and a good deal of brutality on the part of the military, which did nothing for the fighting spirit of loyal Slavic soldiers at the front.

Conditions at home and the high level of casualties affected the spirit as well as the structure of the army. The carnage dampened the conscript's resolve to enter or remain with his unit. This was so in all armies, but the peasant character of the Habsburg army made the problem more acute.

Peasant armies are particularly susceptible to a form of homesickness which limits the field of their operations. Although World War I provides nothing comparable with the *nostalgie* which so devastated the French revolutionary armies, the peasant character of the continental powers meant that such influences were still present. The collapse of the Russian armies pinpoints the potent effect of peasant localism. During the course of the October Revolution peasant recruits, taken far from home, often arrived at the front subdued, bewildered and depressed. Desertion to the enemy was much less of a problem than desertion to go home; the Green Cadres drew much of their strength from this appeal.

Nationalism

It had long been assumed that the bitter national antagonism between Magyars and Germans, and practically all the other peoples of the empire, would be the undoing of the armed forces and the state they served. These fears were exaggerated: mobilization proceeded without hindrance, Slavic troops did not desert *en masse*, and the army did not fall apart. True, there were some local difficulties: anti-war riots among reserve formations in Bohemia in September 1914 were followed by the wholesale defection of the 29th Infantry from Prague in April 1915. In the main, however, loyalty to the dynasty was stronger than expected. This is not to say that within the Habsburg army nationalism was negligible. Nor was it a negative force. Whether separatist sentiment acted as a source of cohesion or disintegration depended on local circumstances. There was in fact a good deal of variation between national groups and the particular fronts on which they were engaged. Roman Catholic Croat and Slovene troops and Bosnian Muslims were generally more reliable than the Orthodox Serbs; Slavs pitted against Italians fought with great enthusiasm; Croats against Serbs were savage; Bosnian Muslims were brutal. Against Russians, however, Slavic solders were markedly less effective, though here, too, variations were pronounced. Serbs excepted, South Slavs were more steadfast than Czech, Ukrainian or Romanians, who were more prone to surrender or desert. But whereas their Russophile propensities made the latter more or less useless on the eastern front, the deep ethnic, religious and cultural differences that separated Catholic Croats from Orthodox Serbs encouraged excess and the barbarization of warfare in the Balkans. Italy's cultural and territorial pretensions in the Adriatic served likewise to sustain the offensive spirit of the Yugoslav troops, who until the close of 1918 remained firmly entrenched on Italian soil.

It was the lack of homogeneity which prevented the recurrence of large-scale mutinies such as those that had immobilized the French and destroyed the Russian armies in the spring and summer of 1917. The same bitter divisions frustrated attempts to recruit volunteers from among the large number of Austro-Hungarian prisoners of war in Russia. Although the Slavs received preferential treatment from their fraternal captors, ethnic antagonisms and inter-communal conflict made them reluctant to renounce their allegiance to the Emperor. Mistrust of Serbian supremacy on the part of the Croats and Slovenes, for example, was sufficient to ensure that the projected Adriatic Legion was still-born. Indeed, only 10 per cent of South Slavs joined the volunteers, and these were largely Serbs. Even the Czech Legion, the largest and most famous of these volunteer formations, enrolled between one-fourth and one-fifth of the estimated 2000,000 Czech and Slovak prisoners of war. Imperial troops were not, then, anxious to tear off their rosettes and eagles in support of Greater Serbia, or take up arms in the name of multinational entities like Yugoslavia and Czechoslovakia. Among the dissidents who did respond to Russian propaganda, committed nationalists, like the socialists, were a minority; more often than not the volunteers were motivated by personal rather than political considerations.

The Green Cadres, who combined nationalist and revolutionary goals with the more traditional occupation of banditry, underscore the diverse sources of unrest in the army. The Green Cadre phenomenon was first identified in July 1916. A report from the Karlovac area noted that troops from the *Ersatz* battalion of the 96th Infantry Regiment, assisted by friends and relatives, were deserting their units, hiding their arms, and taking to the forests. By the spring of 1918 bands of armed deserters, ten to forty in number, roamed the hills and woods of Croatia, Slavonia, Bosnia-Herzegovina, Dalmatia and Istria; and by the autumn an estimated 50,000 were operating throughout the region. Turnover was rapid. Bosnian bands rarely stayed together for more than a few weeks; in Croatia and Slavonia, by contrast, the bands were more orderly, with elected officers and considerable quantities of guns, booty and false documents. In some districts groups of armed deserters became the magnet for disaffected elements, civilian and military. In the Srem, where formations sometimes operated at battalion strength, the deserter bands were reported to have included 'homeless people, day-labourers, and Gypsies ... all armed to the teeth', while the village of Davidovici was said to have been pillaged by an armed group wearing Russian, Serbian and Austrian uniforms. In other parts of Bosnia-Herzegovina the Green Cadre bands consisted of deserters and troops absent without leave, who lived by plunder during the autumn and summer but returned to their units in winter when food was scarce and the climate inhospitable.

What are we to make of these people? Should they be characterized as brigands, freedom fighters, revolutionaries, or what? One authority concludes that in most cases they were probably something of each. 'The relative degree of criminality, nationalism or radicalism', writes Richard Spence, 'undoubtedly depended on the mixture of individuals within each group.' The Greens were in certain respects primitive rebels – peasant protesters operating out of a remote rural setting, often with local assistance, and without a general political orientation beyond resistance to oppression and poverty. To propertied and privileged sorts they were nothing more than common criminals; historians know better. The substantial criminal component of the Greens is not denied, nor is the criminality of their conduct disputed. It is the meaning and significance of their actions that remain problematic.

For remote peasant communities without understanding of the characteristic forms of modern social movements – organization and policy, programme and ideology – social banditry represented an available and acceptable response to the disruptive effects of industrialized warfare. Historically the connection between brigands and freedom fighters was strong: Balkan bandits who engaged the Turkish oppressor were cast as national heroes; those who took to the hills in defiance of authority were likewise lionized. In these parts Robin Hood spoke a Serbo-Croatian dialect. The Green Cadres were clearly an outgrowth of this tradition; insurrectionary rather than revolutionary, anti-German or anti-Magyar rather than pro-nationalist, they represented a pre-political phenomenon which perhaps anticipated the Communist partisans of World War II but remained rooted in the past.

October 1918: the collapse of the Austro-Hungarian Empire

After the May mutinies the diffusion of discontent rapidly reached a critical mass. On 21 October 1918, the deputies of German Austria constituted themselves a Provisional National Assembly and proclaimed the formation of the Austrian state. A Political Council, chosen from the Provisional National Assembly and representative of all parties, assumed the role of government. Just as the Political

Council was made up of all parties in the Provisional National Assembly, so the state secretaries it appointed were drawn from all parties; and for the first time Austrian socialists obtained a share in government. Events moved quickly (for the chronology of collapse see Roberts, pp.251–2). By the close of the month the Italian front had collapsed and Czechoslovakia and Croatia, like Poland before them, had declared independence; in Laibach, Trieste and Bosnia-Herzegovina, power fell from Habsburg hands; the dissolution of the Austro-Hungarian Empire was complete.

7 THE NEW AUSTRIA

Revolution? What revolution?

An Austrian national state was the first and most obvious successor to the Habsburg Monarchy. How far the creation of the new Austrian Republic was the product of, or for that matter was accompanied by, revolution is an open question. Poles, Czechs, Hungarians, Serbs, Slovenes, Croatians – all experienced national and political revolutions at the end of World War I. Historians, while they differ in interpretation, are agreed about the far-reaching character of the changes that took place. However, about the status of post-war Austria there is no such unanimity. Was there a revolution in 1918/19 or merely a military collapse? For some the replacement of an absolute or quasi-constitutional monarchy by a democratic republic is taken as sufficient proof. From a comparative study of central Europe at the end of World War I, F. L. Carsten concludes unequivocally that a revolution had occurred in Austria. The sudden and dramatic circumstances that brought six hundred years of Habsburg rule to a close transformed the political structure of the country. Carsten writes:

> The German deputies of the *Reichsrat* had no authority to appoint a provisional government, the emperor was forced to renounce the exercise of his constitutional powers, and the Habsburg state disappeared for good. It was replaced by something entirely new: a state of the German-speaking provinces which also claimed authority over German-speaking Bohemia and Moravia. This in itself was a revolutionary act, as these provinces had never formed a state ... 'German Austria' was the product of a constitutional and political revolution.
>
> (F. L. Carsten, *Revolution in Central Europe*, 1972)

Some scholars go even further. C. A. Macartney, for example, wrote a pioneering study of the infant republic with the revealing title *The Social Revolution in Austria* (1929).

Others are adamant that no such revolution occurred: the monarchy quit but was not overthrown; the state apparatus was modified but not transformed; social inequality persisted; and private property remained fundamentally unchanged. Martin Kitchen, in his study *The Coming of Austrian Fascism* (1980), thus places the term in quotation marks. 'It is extremely doubtful', he writes, 'whether it is permissible to use the term "revolution" to describe the events in Austria at the end of the war'; he is 'certain that the collapse of the monarchy and the establishment of the republic were not the work of the Social Democrats, but rather the result of a process of internal decay'. In short, the monarchy had disappeared by disintegration and dismemberment. How far does the Austrian case fit into Clive Emsley's discussion of revolution in section 1? If Kitchen is right and there was no revolution, how can we characterize the changes that did take place in Austria at the end of the war? Does the emergence of the Austrian Republic provide evidence of unguided political change, or does it represent a revolution that failed?

The Austrian Republic and the revolutionary challenge

Within the Political Council of the Provisional National Assembly – as we saw in section 6 above – all political parties were represented: German nationalists and liberals, the Catholic Christian Socials and the Social Democrats. The monarchy was abolished on 12 November and a republic was declared. This was, however, the result not of revolutionary action but of a political accommodation born out of defeat in war. The Emperor voluntarily renounced his role in state affairs while the more conservative parties represented in the Political Council recognized that there was little alternative to the abolition of the monarchy. Austria remained independent for the time being but the Provisional National Assembly expressed the desire to form 'a constituent part of the German Republic'. This, however, was not to be, for reasons that will be discussed below. In February 1919 a National Assembly was elected to frame the constitution and to conclude a peace treaty: the Social Democrats and Christian Socials emerged as the largest parties in the new assembly and formed a coalition government. This excluded the significant number of German nationalist and liberal deputies elected from government.

In addition to the challenge of the peace treaty the new state was confronted with serious economic problems that fed political discontent. Karl Renner, the Austrian Republic's first Chancellor, commented that 'the new state had taken over a field of ruins'. By comparison with the Austro-Hungarian Empire the young republic was much reduced in territory, population and mineral resources. The food situation was critical. Agricultural production, disrupted by war, had fallen by 53 per cent since 1913. Austria's peasant population – less than 1 per cent of farms were above 500 acres in size – could not provide sufficient to feed the population.

Starvation exacerbated deep and growing divisions between town and country. On the eve of war Cisleithan Austria had only seven cities of 100,000 inhabitants in a country of 28 million; Hungary, with 20 million people, had only two. Vienna, like Budapest, dwarfed all rivals. The former was more than the seat of government and a centre of conspicuous consumption; for all its *Kultur* and *fin de siècle* romance, Vienna was also a great industrial district. Under dualism its population rose from just over half a million to 1,675,000 in 1900, and to more than two million in 1914. The dismemberment of the Habsburg Empire after the war made its proletarian and 'wen-like' character seem even more pronounced; in February 1919 there were 113,905 unemployed in Vienna, 161,803 in Austria. Likewise, Budapest, was more than Hungary's cultural and economic capital; it, too, occupied a top-heavy position in relation to the provinces; for while accounting for approximately one-tenth of the total population of post 1919 Hungary, the city contained 28 per cent of its workforce and two-thirds of its principal industries.

In both Austria and Hungary war had intensified antagonisms between town and country, and set producers and consumers at each other's throats. Moreover, the conditions which made wartime requisitioning a necessity did not disappear with the termination of hostilities. Peasants who still found themselves compelled to sell their produce below the market price were prone to withhold supplies; landowners were equally resistant, particularly in Hungary, where uncertainty as to agrarian policy led them to refuse to cultivate their fields. The downward spiral was accelerated by the collapse in industrial production, which meant that, in any case, neither Vienna nor Budapest had much to offer the countryside in exchange for the food they required.

Apart from food, it was the coal supply which rapidly became the most pressing of problems. The new state had acquired about 12 per cent of the population of the empire, 30 per cent of its industrial workers, but less than 1 per cent of its coal supplies. Austrian industry ground to a standstill: iron and steel production practically ceased; metal and machine manufacturers closed down; brick, lime and cement works put out their furnaces; building operations were abandoned. Transport, too, seized up; streetcar traffic in Vienna declined dramatically; the railway passenger disappeared.

In addition to its starving population and crumbling industries, the Austrian Republic was confronted with a huge deficit in the national budget, with rocketing inflation and with failing banks whose assets and dealings were located in areas of the empire now separated from Austria. Apart from foreign loans, the authorities sought to print their way out of the crisis. The complete collapse of the currency was narrowly averted through the intervention of the League of Nations, but only four years after the end of the war. By then the average real income of workers and employees was 25 per cent below the level of 1914; the savings of the middle classes had been wiped out.

In this environment Austria's Social Democrats – a key partner in the republic's new coalition government – did not fuel the embers of discontent. They were mindful of the conservatism of the peasantry and indeed of much of provincial Austrian society, as well as of the desperate economic situation. They therefore sought stability and to contain the revolutionary elements whose uncontrolled actions seemed certain to provoke civil war and foreign intervention.

Principal among these elements were demobilized soldiers and the war disabled. 'The social revolution which arose out of the war', leading Social Democrat ideologist Otto Bauer wrote, 'proceeded from the barracks rather than from the factories' (*The Austrian Revolution*, 1925). Bauer presented the Austrian soldiery as a disorderly and dangerous force, given to violence and excess, brutalized by war, and capable of untold mischief: 'Where blind obedience had hitherto reigned, an elemental, instinctive, anarchical revolutionary movement now set in.' Of course, not all demobilized servicemen were so susceptible. The 'overwhelming majority', he readily conceded, 'were dominated by an irresistible desire to return home to wives and children'. By sheer good fortune these were helped on their way by the last great service the railways performed. The creation of a system of labour exchanges and provision of unemployment benefit, introduced with unseemly haste between 4 and 6 November, further served to reduce the number of disorderly men roaming the streets of Vienna on the look-out for trouble.

The residue supplied Communist extremism with a convenient constituency. Unemployed and disabled veterans, particularly those who had seen service on the eastern front, coupled with romantic revolutionaries from among the reserve officers, marched about the town displaying the menacing manners of a Red Guard. In April 1919 the 'more unstable among the unemployed and the demobilized and disabled soldiers' were persuaded to participate in an armed attack on the parliament buildings. Bauer's analysis leaves no doubt that the creation of the *Volkswehr* – a professional army of left-wing activists under the supervision of the Social Democrat controlled Defence Ministry – was designed to arrest the disorder and chaos consequent upon defeat and demobilization.

Soldiers were perceived by the Social Democrats less as a positive revolutionary force in need of encouragement and more as a wild beast in need of domestication. Like the British labour movement, the Social Democratic Party acted primarily to prevent aggrieved servicemen falling into the hands of extremists. But whereas British socialists were concerned about the activities of the right, their Austrian compeers feared the revolutionary left; for 'with the returned soldier', wrote Bauer, 'the revolutionary opportunists [the Austrian Communist] allied himself, hoping for power, place, dignity and income from the subversion of the existing order.'

The Social Democrats potentially faced a challenge not only from the revolutionary left, from within the ranks of the demobilized and the unemployed, but from within the factories themselves. Workers' councils had been formed as early as January 1918 during anti-war strikes across the Austrian part of the monarchy, in which as many as 550,000 workers are believed to have participated. These workers' councils were swiftly taken over by the Social Democratic Party. It ended the strike by securing concessions from the Imperial Government. It then integrated the strikers into its organization and marginalized the more radical activists. By October 1918, when the workers' councils spread across industry, they were firmly under the control of the Social Democrats. From November onwards the workers' councils acted as little more than cheerleaders for social democracy. 'Our activities in the workers' and soldiers' councils', Bauer boasted, 'kept the masses away from the Communists.'

As with the soldiers, the war brought about a fundamental change in the outlook of the proletariat. Although the Social Democrats' 'activities in the workers' ... councils' had helped defuse the strikes of January 1918, they had not quelled the radicalism among workers that had sparked them. Austrian workers were by no means immune to the revolution in the factories in Russia, Germany and Hungary, where the socialization of industry was the number one priority. On 7 April 1919, for example, the managers of the giant Donawitz Works of the Alpine *Montangesellschaft* were deposed by workers demanding the right of self-determination in industry. The Works' Committees Law, enacted the following month, was more concerned, however, with the extension of trades union power and the restoration of labour discipline than with self-government in industry. Employers, once they had recovered their composure, were by no means uniformly hostile. 'In many large undertakings', wrote a Vienna factory inspector in his annual report for 1920, 'the works' committees maintain strict discipline among the staff, and in this respect assist the management of the enterprise.' 'In many factories', he concluded, 'the works' committees have introduced a system of fines for breach of discipline.' Bauer was equally enraptured. 'The more the employers recognized that only the influence of the works' committees made the restoration of discipline possible', he wrote, 'the stronger was the influence which they were obliged to concede to the works' committees.'

These concessions, though, were small. Austrian social democracy, for all its protestations to the contrary, recoiled from any move towards the destruction of the capitalist domination of production. Iron and wood, the two most important raw materials, and coal and water, the two key sources of energy, were thus found to be unsuited to public control for the fear that any attempt at forcible appropriation might offend foreign stockholders.

Exercise   Return to the discussion of the concept of revolution in section 1 and then consider how far events in Austria in 1918–19 can be seen as a revolution. ■

Specimen answer   You might have said that although the government of the Habsburg state collapsed in defeat there was no 'total' breakdown of government. The parties that formed the Political Council of the Provisional National Assembly ensured a transfer of power that, given the circumstances, was relatively peaceful.

You might also have said that the radicalization of demobilized soldiers, the unemployed and factory workers in the face of economic collapse threatened to create a struggle between different armed power blocs. The participation of the Social Democrats in the government, and their policy of actively containing the revolutionary left, helped avert social revolution. □

Discussion   You will have noted, however, that there were many factors present in the Austrian situation that contributed to revolution elsewhere. Economic collapse, industrial protest, and the radicalism of demobilized soldiers might be listed among these. All were consequences of Austria's wartime experience and above all of its experience of defeat. They contributed to post-war radicalism in Austria that was largely sidelined by the policies pursued by the Social Democrats; by 1918 they sought a reformist road to socialism as part of a larger German state.

The Treaty of St Germain and the First Republic

Post-war conditions did not allow Austria to become 'a constituent part of the German Republic' as the Provisional National Assembly had wished. Peace with the Allies was formally reached when the Treaty of St Germain was signed on 10 September 1919. The treaty defined the borders of the new Austrian Republic. These borders left a territory much smaller than that of Cisleithan Austria. The Czech Lands of Bohemia and Moravia, as well as the German-inhabited Sudetenländer, were transferred to the new state of Czechoslovakia. These were the most economically developed parts of Austria-Hungary on the eve of World War I. Of all industry located in the Austrian part of the monarchy in 1910, 56 per cent could be found in Bohemia and Moravia. The western territory of Tirol was partitioned – the Allies accepted the occupation of the south of the province by Italy. In addition the Allies forced the new Austria to accept a war guilt clause, thus treating the First Republic as the direct successor to the Habsburg

Monarchy. Lastly, it was banned from becoming a part of Germany and was forced to change its official name from German-Austria to plain Austria.

It is difficult to disagree with Barbara Jelavich that 'the Treaty shaped the history of the First Austrian Republic' even if we might disagree with her statement that the treaty 'laid the basis of its subsequent downfall' (Jelavich, *Modern Austria*, 1987, p.156). The creation of new states destroyed the links that had bound markets together within the monarchy. With the loss of the Czech Lands, the new Austria was a predominantly agrarian state – most industry was concentrated in Vienna and in certain regions such as the southern industrial province of Styria. This fed poor economic performance – Austrian gross national product failed to reach its 1913 level for much of the 1920s, surpassing it only in 1929 on the eve of the Great Depression. The industrial and mining sectors stagnated, causing high unemployment for much of the 1920s. The years between 1918 and 1922 were ones of high inflation, and 1922 saw hyper-inflation.

The circumstances of the First Republic were not even to allow space for the reformist strategy advocated by the country's Social Democrats. Although they participated in a coalition with the Catholic Christian Socials in its first years, this was far from a happy partnership. Christian Socials distrusted the Social Democrats. Suspicious of the left's anti-clerical rhetoric and of its ideological hostility to private property, many Christian Socials displayed open hostility towards their partners in government. Social Democrats hoped to form a left-wing government in order to pursue their own distinctive left-wing strategy. The coalition gradually disintegrated during 1920, and governments down to 1934 were formed by coalitions of right-of-centre parties dominated by the Christian Socials.

Ideological division was reinforced by the social divide between town and country described earlier in this section. The peasantry remained fiercely loyal to the Christian Socials and openly hostile to the Social Democrats, as did much of the provincial middle class. The Social Democrats formed a strong opposition at national level. They were able to attempt their reformist strategy on a more limited scale than they had once hoped in Vienna, where they pursued an ambitious programme of social reform.

War and defeat in Austria created a new republican state, but they did not bring about a social revolution of the kind that occurred in Russia. The forces that drove revolution elsewhere were contained during the early years of the First Republic. In the smaller Austria recognized by the Allies in the Treaty of St Germain there was little prospect even for modest social reform. The country's rural majority backed a clerical conservative party that dominated politics at national level, and that defined itself in part by opposition to what many of its members regarded as 'godless Marxism'. The Social Democrats remained strong among the working class in the capital. This alone ensured that the republic was characterized by sharp political conflict throughout the interwar years.

8   DEFEAT, REVOLUTION AND COUNTER-REVOLUTION IN HUNGARY

Events in Hungary were more dramatic than those in Austria. Military defeat led directly to political revolution, and the threat of territorial dismemberment to social revolution. The Hungarian Soviet Republic lasted for 133 days. During its short life it faced the challenge of internal revolt, as well as direct military intervention against it by Romania and Czechoslovakia. Then, on 1 August 1919, with the Romanian army poised to enter Budapest, the government of Béla Kun collapsed; he and his Communist coadjutors fled the country. The revolution was over; the counter-revolution had begun. There followed an orgy of blood-letting and political violence as Hungary succumbed to a 'White Terror', directed against Communists and Jews, directed by a régime that combined authoritarian conservatism with the politics of the radical right fronted by Admiral Miklós Horthy. We might ask: why was the revolution so short-lived? Why was the political reaction to it so violent? Roberts, who encapsulates the rise and fall of the revolutionary regime in four sentences (p.259), offers an account which may reasonably be considered too schematic to provide a satisfactory answer. We shall, therefore, pause to examine war, defeat, revolution and their aftermath in Hungary to see how they compare with events in Austria. This will prepare us for a discussion on the impact of war on the political order in east-central Europe in section 9, and then for a closer engagement with the general issues of war and revolution in section 10.

Hungary and the war

The outbreak of war in Hungary, as in other parts of the empire, was received with enthusiasm. Hungarian Social Democrats, like their Austrian counterparts, were well to the fore in their resistance to 'Russian barbarism' and support of the Central Powers. But as casualties mounted and the fighting continued, death and disruption became less and less tolerable. In Transleithania, as elsewhere, the defective war economy proved decisive. The failure to preserve a just equilibrium between military requirements and civilian consumption led to shortages of consumer goods and a sharp deterioration in the living standards of the population. The widespread development of black-market profiteering pinpointed the inadequacies of requisitioning and rationing and the attendant problems of state control. From 1916 onwards the labour movement revived; industrial unrest grew apace. The foundation of the Independence Party under Count Mihály Károlyi, with its demands for peace without annexation and far-reaching internal reforms, signified a serious lack of confidence among the monarchy's generals and politicians.

The Russian Revolution changed everything. In the words of the Social Democratic Party, 'it struck a mortal blow at every despotic power in the world'. Hungarian workers were elated and encouraged to press their claims with renewed vigour. In the spring of 1917 vital war production industries were brought to a standstill as war-weary and distressed workers downed tools in defiance of military discipline; May Day once more became the occasion for mass demonstrations; class solidarity and class awareness found organized expression in the growth of trades unions, whose membership soared in excess of 200,000. The intelligentsia, too, found wartime radicalism irresistible; new socialist groups proliferated; demands for peace and progress gathered momentum.

On 25 November 1917 at the Hall of Industry in Budapest there took place a mass demonstration in support of the socialist revolution. Several hundred thousand workers cheered demands for a general strike and the formation of workers' councils. Hungarian social democracy was unable to contain the rising groundswell. Dissatisfaction with the reformist leadership of the party and its trades unions found expression in the formation of a breakaway Revolutionary Socialist group, which pressed for the creation of a Soviet-style republic. The climax came shortly after; the three-day strike that began on 18 January 1918 spread across the country, involved more than half a million workers and led, in some places, to the formation of workers' councils. The government, recovering from an initial fright, turned to repression; arrests followed, bans were imposed, and a special security headquarters was set up for the defence of 'internal order'.

Repression was no longer sufficient to stem the tide of revolution. By the summer of 1918 the crisis on the home front was so acute that nothing short of a miracle could resolve it. Hungary, once the bread-basket of the empire, was on the verge of starvation, without fuel and desperate for raw materials. The real wages of workers fell to 53 per cent of their pre-war level, that of day-labourers in agriculture to 46 per cent, and that of employees to 33 per cent. In these circumstances, troops firing upon strikers at the MÁVAG plant in Budapest provoked a nine-day general strike and mass demonstrations against the war and the government. Significantly, it was the intervention of the Social Democrats rather than the action of the army which brought the issue to a close.

The Bourgeois-democratic Revolution, November 1918 to March 1919

With its armies disintegrating, its peoples starving, and the enemy at the gates, a socialist seizure of power within the Austro-Hungarian Empire seemed a distinct possibility. However, Hungarian social democracy, like its Austrian counterpart, showed no inclination to lead the working class towards the socialist commonwealth. Instead it preferred to play a second fiddle to non-socialist political forces in Károlyi's National Council, a broad-based grouping of middle-class democrats and radicals which came into being in the dying stages of the conflict to maintain public order, supervise the transition from empire to republic, and preserve Hungary's territorial integrity.

The National Council was formed on 25 October 1918; within seven days the Bourgeois-democratic Revolution was victorious. On the morning of 31 October soldiers and workers occupied the public buildings of Budapest (including the city commandant's headquarters), bringing to a climax several days of demonstrations in favour of a Károlyi government. By now the authorities could do no more than roll with the punches. On the same day the new coalition government took office, pledged to Hungarian independence, universal suffrage, civil rights, social reform and land reform. On 16 November 1918 the formal and the real caught up with one another: Hungary became a democratic republic.

It was a bloodless business. For the government and its supporters the events of 31 October marked the end of the revolution; reconstruction was to be a gradual and peaceable process conducted within a framework of law and order. Workers, soldiers and landless peasants thought otherwise. In the countryside, news of the revolution touched off a series of arbitrary seizures of food and property; expropriators were expropriated, the gendarmerie disarmed, and local bureaucrats dismissed. Elsewhere, workers' and soldiers' councils erupted with equal spontaneity. The labour movement grew with celerity. Trades union membership rose from 215,000 in January 1918 to 721,000 in December 1918, and above one million by February 1919.

The creation of the Party of Communists in Hungary – the first of several Communist parties that have existed during the country's recent history – in November 1918 gave organization and direction to the elemental passions of the peasantry and the revolutionary unrest of the workers' councils. Its convenors were former Social Democrats who had been taken prisoner of war in Russia and subsequently fought with the Bolsheviks during the October Revolution. Béla Kun, their leader, had worked with Lenin, and derived great prestige from that association. The party, which also gained the support of the left-wing opposition within the Social Democratic Party and the Revolutionary Socialists, promptly set about organizing the factories and the fields as well as the armed forces. Its programme called for the replacement of the bourgeois polity by a socialist formation run by the workers' councils and for the crushing of the counter-revolution. This last point is significant. Disaffected landowners, uprooted by war and revolution, and fearful for their person, position and property, were already massing in the various radical right-wing military detachments. From the beginning of the Bourgeois-democratic Revolution the radical right was joined not only by landowners but by a significant number of army officers, senior gendarmes, civil servants and other public officials.

The success or failure of the Bourgeois-democratic Revolution, however, depended less upon internal reforms undertaken by the Károlyi government and more upon the actions and policies pursued by the victorious allies. Károlyi was known for his Wilsonian sympathies and this, it was hoped, would secure more favourable treatment from the Entente powers. Indeed, one of the cornerstones of the regime was its national minorities policy. The creation of an 'Eastern Switzerland', a new form of coexistence based on autonomous rights for Hungary's oppressed peoples, would, it was hoped, enable democratic Hungary to distance itself from the foreign, domestic and national minority policies of the Dual Monarchy and in so doing preserve the lands of historic Hungary. But it was too late: the Transylvanian Romanians wished for nothing but to join with Romania; the Slovaks of northern Hungary preferred to join the Czechoslovak Republic; and the South Slavs sought to join the Serb-Croat-Slovene state. The victorious great powers, who had secretly agreed during the war to transfer two-thirds of Hungary's territory to Romania, Yugoslavia and Czechoslovakia, persisted in treating the republic as a defeated country; it was their insistence upon the violation of its territorial integrity that led directly to the collapse of Hungarian democracy. On 20 March 1919 Lieutenant-Colonel Vix, the French representative in Budapest, presented the Károlyi government with a demand for a substantial slice of the nation's south-eastern districts. Acceptance was out of the question. Károlyi warned the Allies that if these claims were conceded, Bolshevism in Hungary would be triumphant. His protestations were ignored and he resigned.

Proclamation of the Hungarian Soviet Republic

The Party of Communists was by now a force to be reckoned with; its support was particularly strong among war invalids, demobilized soldiers and the workless who had been drawn by Kun's promises of jobs and high wages for everyone and large indemnities for returned servicemen. By March, Communist agitation had made inroads into the trades unions as bread queues lengthened and problems, for which the collaborationist Social Democrats were held responsible, mounted. The Social Democrats were themselves unsure as to whether they should crush the Communists, outbid them, or join them. The Vix note resolved their difficulties. The choice now lay between a Communist dictatorship and counter-revolution. The Social Democrats could not govern alone and the Communists would not govern without them; there was no alternative to a joint revolutionary government.

The new government, called the Revolutionary Governing Council, was formed on 21 March 1919. Ministerial portfolios (commissariats) were divided equally between Communists and Social Democrats. Béla Kun, who headed the Commissariat of Foreign Affairs, was acknowledged as its head; both domestic and foreign policy rested in his hands. Its programme, announced the following day, included the establishment of the dictatorship of the proletariat and the construction of a socialist society in alliance with the Soviet Union. The new Hungarian Soviet Republic renounced all annexationist claims, desiring peaceful co-existence with the western powers and their allies.

The revolutionary dictatorship

To create socialism in a predominantly agrarian country like Hungary posed problems of exceptional complexity; to do so in the aftermath of the bloodiest war in history and against a background of material exhaustion and military defeat suggested the impossible. Kun and his associates recognized these constraints but refused to be bound by them. The Hungarian Soviet Republic, in their eyes, represented the beginning of a revolutionary transformation, not the end. In a backward society, lacking a self-confident and dynamic middle class, and with a proletariat of uncertain judgement, democratic politics could only be vested in the hands of a dedicated few who supplied the vanguard of the proletariat. The revolutionary regime, Kun declared, was 'a dictatorship of an active minority on behalf of the large and passive proletariat' which must of necessity 'act in a strong and merciless fashion ... At least until such time as the revolution spread to the European countries'.

On the first day of office, the Revolutionary Governing Council declared a state of martial law and banned the sale of alcohol as a public order measure. A number of far-reaching reforms in the machinery of the state were promptly instituted. The old professional army was replaced by a new and politically aware Red Army; the police and gendarmerie, reorganized into a unified Red Guard, were likewise presented as defenders of revolutionary virtue. The system of justice was reorganized: the courts were replaced by revolutionary tribunals, and justice was administered by workers advised by trained lawyers.

In industry the state expropriated all establishments employing more than twenty workers. The newly socialized enterprises were placed under the administration of state-appointed trustees supervised by small workers' councils. The state began to integrate industry into a comprehensive system of economic planning that would serve as the basis of a fully socialist economy. At the same time flats were confiscated and distributed to working-class families, and rents were cut by 20 per cent. In the factories an eight-hour day was introduced, and some workers' wages were increased by as much as 80 per cent. Although the commercial and retail sectors were not nationalized they were placed under state supervision. Prices were fixed in order to ensure that working-class families enjoyed an adequate diet. Despite these measures the state was powerless to prevent galloping hidden inflation as many sellers transferred their goods to the black market.

On the critical issue of land reform, the Revolutionary Governing Council was equally uncompromising. It announced that 'whoever does not work, cannot retain any land'. It therefore collectivized medium-sized and large estates. It disappointed many agricultural labourers by refusing to distribute to them land that could be farmed individually, and instead sought to transform the estates into either agricultural co-operatives or state farms. In practice there was little difference between the two forms of ownership.

State ownership was also extended to all primary and secondary schools which, previously, had been largely Church-controlled. Plans for the introduction of a uniform eight-grade school were drawn up, new textbooks commissioned and a new curriculum proposed. Priests, friars and nuns were allowed to remain in their teaching posts on condition that they quit their orders and entered the service of the state. The cultural and scientific life of the country was revitalized: Bártok joined the Directory of Music, Lukács the Directory of Writers.

The Social Democrats and Communists fused into a single party: the Socialist Party of Hungary. The Revolutionary Governing Council remade the institutions of government and public administration, stripping away the old counties that had formed the basis of local government in the monarchy and replacing them with the soviets that gave the republic its name. The franchise was expanded to cover about half the total population. When single list elections were held for the new bodies in April 1919 half of those eligible to vote turned out. Participation in these elections gave a good, if imperfect, indicator of public support for the revolutionary regime; industrial workers turned out to vote enthusiastically; in the villages and the agrarian towns on the Great Plain the population stayed at home. Urban industrial workers rallied to the Red Army when the Soviet Republic was threatened by the armies of neighbouring countries in mid-May. This demonstrated the enthusiasm of sections of the population for the revolution. It was not to be enough, however. Hungary's small proletariat, centred on Budapest, on provincial industrial cities like Miskolc and Sálgótarján, and in isolated mining towns, supported the Soviet Republic to the end.

The revolutionary regime failed to mobilize society beyond its immediate working-class base. Behind this failure there was a certain high-handedness and contempt for the masses which cost the regime dearly. Too often Kun and his associates seemed determined to thrust Communist internationalism down

Magyar throats in a manner calculated to give maximum offence. Kun, who condemned all 'petty-bourgeois overtures ... to social patriotism and bourgeois nationalism' and spoke frequently about feeling 'no more akin to the Hungarian proletariat than, let us say, the American, Czech or Russian', derided all appeals to Magyar sentiment. Upon the proclamation of the Soviet Republic, there took place an officially sanctioned iconoclasm reminiscent of that of the sixteenth century: statues of national kings and heroes were dismantled, the national anthem was banned, and the display of national colours prohibited. Suggestions that the national flag be hoisted alongside the red flag and national emblems be attached to the caps of Red Army soldiers were rejected out of hand, even though officers and men desired nothing else.

In the countryside, too, the Communist dictatorship showed scant respect for peasant sensibilities. Lenin's advice on the primacy of land redistribution and the pressing need to satisfy the requirements of the landless peasant was disregarded; instead the agrarian proletariat was harangued by urban agitators and rural life was held up to ridicule. All that such people held dear – family, Church and community – were mocked, derided and condemned as mindless, superstitious and retrograde. Criticism from the countryside was treated with equal contempt. Provincial delegates at the National Congress of Soviets, who met on 14 June 1919, were uncompromisingly hostile to the 'Soviet bureaucracy' and 'the dictatorship of the proletariat'. Kun, impatient with this 'counter-revolutionary prattle', promptly had the proceedings adjourned.

The rough handling of the countryside was more than an expression of the personal pique of the peoples' commissars. The resort to revolutionary violence and excess was symptomatic of the sharp deterioration in relations between town and country, aggravated by disruption due to war and the continued Allied economic blockade. This led Kun and the commissars to adopt a variant of 'war communism' so as to feed Budapest and its proletariat. Supplies from peasants accused of hoarding were subject to confiscation and requisition; those who resisted were condemned as enemies of the revolution and punished, as were villagers who declined to accept the paper currency of the revolutionary republic. Coercion was also required to maintain discipline and production on unpopular agricultural collectives. The Red Terror unleashed against a recalcitrant countryside claimed between 370 and 587 lives.

There were, also, structural weaknesses that undermined the ability of the regime to operate. The state apparatus, though reorganized, had not been transformed. The non-availability of recruits from the proletariat compelled dependence upon those of uncertain loyalties. The Red Army, for example, relied on political commissars attached to army corps and individual units to work alongside commanders who were in the main professional soldiers; the Red Guard, too, was staffed with servants of the old regime. Nowhere was the shortage of cadres more apparent than in the management of collectivization. Commissars of production, appointed to head the new state-run collectives, were drawn overwhelmingly from the former owners or stewards of the large estates; there was no other source of expertise available. The rapidity with which the collectives were dismantled and the old owners restored on the appearance of the Romanian invader indicated the fair-weather character of the state apparatus.

The nationalization of economic life and the shortage of personnel, which led to the delegation of authority to bourgeois experts and the re-employment of the old bureaucracy, had a negative effect on the masses. The civil service was detested before the war for its corruption and rude response to those with no special claim to its favours.

By the end of June the Red Army, which had repulsed the Romanians and Czechs, thus reconquering the whole of Slovakia, was so diminished as to be well nigh useless. The regime was simply unable to sustain a war on two fronts: against the foreign armies in the field and the counter-revolutionaries at home. It was this, plus the promise of a Romanian withdrawal from the food-rich areas east of the Tisza, which led Kun to concede Allied demands for the military evacuation of the northern regions. The decision to pull out of Slovakia without any guarantees that the Romanians would fulfil their part of the bargain led to the resignation of the army high command, desertions, and a collapse in the morale of the population which saw its hard-won victories squandered and its nationalist aspirations trampled upon by a regime that seemed both incompetent and insensitive.

The fall of the Hungarian Soviet Republic

On 30 July 1919 the Romanian army broke through the Hungarian lines of defence, crossed the Tisza and stood within one hundred kilometres of Budapest. The Revolutionary Governing Council promptly resigned. Kun and his commissars fled the country. On 1 August the Romanians entered Budapest. Private property and the old state apparatus were restored forthwith. On 2 August the revolutionary tribunals were abolished and the courts restored; the following day saw the dissolution of the Red Guard and its replacement by police with their previous commanders. On 4 August the nationalized tenements were returned to their former owners and rent control was abolished; two days later industrial and commercial enterprises which had been taken into the public domain were restored to private ownership. The White Terror was to begin shortly afterwards.

Counter-revolutionary Hungary

The new government headed by Gyula Peidl initially attempted to send out an olive branch to the non-socialist parties who had also formed part of the opposition in the days of the monarchy. Peidl was not to last long. Faced with Romanian troops and the existence of a large number of armed right-wing groups intent on radically reversing the policies of the Bourgeois-democratic Revolution, he resigned on 6 August. Peidl was replaced by a government headed by István Friedrich, a manufacturer who claimed the support of the Habsburgs. Friedrich was not in charge of the country. He had to negotiate with two other centres of power: the Romanian army who remained in the country until April 1920, anxious to gain control of Transylvania, and the rival self-proclaimed 'government' in the provincial city of Szeged.

The counter-revolutionary government had been formed during the period of the Soviet Republic out of all those groups who opposed both the bourgeois-democratic and Soviet revolutions. As such it rested on an alliance between ultra-conservatives from among the aristocratic élite, the civil service and the military, and the radical right. Though the 'government' accepted the authority of Friedrich, some of its members did not. They were led by the Minister of Defence in the Szeged 'government', Admiral Miklós Horthy, who assembled a 30,000 strong military force with himself at its head. During the autumn of 1919 this force was to gain a fearsome reputation. It sought to sweep away the remnants of the Soviet Republic from rural Hungary. This it did with considerable brutality. It murdered many who had served the revolutionary regime. Together with members of radical right-wing paramilitaries, some of its detachments participated in several pogroms in the country, thus seeking to link anti-communism with anti-semitism. Horthy entered Budapest on 16 November riding a white horse at the head of his army. He made his intentions clear, condemning the population of the city for 'attacking a thousand years of history' and describing the Hungarian capital as a 'city of sin'.

Even before Horthy's arrival in late August, the Friedrich government had begun with retribution against those who had supported the Kun regime. The law was changed to prosecute for theft those who had participated in the socialization of the economy. Large numbers of workers, but also significant numbers of poor peasants and left-wing intellectuals, were imprisoned. Those held responsible for serious political offences during the revolutionary regime were executed; seventy-four people were put to death between August 1919 and December 1920. In addition to legal repression, the arrival of the counter-revolutionary army represented a new stage in the suppression of the revolution. During the last half of 1919 and the first half of 1920 the counter-revolutionary army was joined by radical right-wing paramilitary organizations in its search for those deemed responsible for the Soviet Republic. It has been estimated that around 5,000 people died as a result of the White Terror and that as many as 70,000 suffered imprisonment. Even key figures in cultural life were not left untouched – composers Bártok and Kodály were prosecuted. Many more among them, for example Lukács, Jászi and Polányi, left Hungary. The labour movement suffered severe harassment; in the coal mines military discipline was imposed immediately following the White Terror. This came to an end only as a result of a pact signed between Prime Minister István Bethlen and the Social Democrat leader Károly Peyer in December 1921 in which the labour movement gained political freedom in exchange for agreeing to relinquish organization of both the agricultural proletariat and public officials.

When relatively democratic elections were held under pressure from the Allies in January 1920 non-socialist parties emerged as the country's dominant political force. The peasant-based Smallholders' Party, which supported land reform, emerged as the largest political force thanks to the introduction of a secret ballot. Close behind came the Christian National Unity Party, the political organization of Hungary's aristocratic class. This election did not mark the beginning of a process of liberalization, however. The new National Assembly, unable to restore the monarchy, instead sought to elect a Regent to act as head of state in the monarch's place. On 1 March 1920 they elected Horthy to this position, under considerable pressure from the country's military who occupied the square in front of the National Assembly building in order to exert their influence on the legislators assembled inside.

The aristocratic élite in the Christian National Unity Party formed the fulcrum of the new political system. The more conservative members of the generally reformist Smallholders' Party were co-opted with the promise of a modest land reform that was enacted in autumn 1920. István Bethlen, Prime Minister from April 1921, further restricted democratic elements within the political system. Whereas in most of Europe, World War I and its aftermath led to a permanent widening of the franchise, in Hungary the political élite sought a return to the pre-war situation as soon as possible. In 1922 the franchise was restricted, based on, among other things, stringent citizenship tests. The proportion of Hungarian citizens eligible to vote fell from 40 per cent in 1919 to a mere 28 per cent in 1922.

The issues of territorial revision and widespread anti-semitism played a decisive role in shaping the politics of interwar Hungary. The Treaty of Trianon, signed in 1920, stripped Hungary of two-thirds of its pre-war territory. Romania gained Transylvania, Czechoslovakia gained Slovakia, Yugoslavia took Croatia and Vojvodina, and Austria all of Burgenland with the exception of Sopron. The treaty was bitterly opposed within Hungary, to no avail, and the counter-revolutionary government in Budapest set its revision as a goal of foreign policy almost as soon as the ink on the treaty was dry. The unemployed public officials and dispossessed landlords who flooded into the reduced Hungary from the lost lands provided an eager constituency for movements of the radical right that promised the overthrow of the post-war order, and the re-creation of greater Hungary.

The counter-revolution had seen the explosive growth of political anti-semitism. The radical right blamed Hungary's Jewish population for defeat in war, for spreading 'internationalist' ideas that had led to revolution and to Bolshevism, and indeed for the harsh terms of the peace treaty. The far right within the counter-revolutionary movement argued for national renewal based on the creation of what they described as a 'national-Christian intelligentsia' in order to combat the forces of 'internationalism'. Such programmes were explicitly directed against the Jewish population; the White Terror had been marked as much by anti-semitic as anti-communist violence. Furthermore, in the climate that followed the collapse of the Soviet Republic, aristocratic ultra-conservatives came to accept much of the analysis of the far right. The National Assembly indeed passed the so-called *numerus clausus* law in 1920 which placed obstacles in front of Jewish students seeking to enter the country's universities. The law was the first of many anti-semitic measures to be passed in interwar Hungary.

The nature of Hungary's counter-revolutionary regime has been the subject of much debate among historians in Hungary itself in recent years. Many have argued that the Horthy regime was of the radical right, fascist, or at least quasi-fascist. Others – some of whom have sought to rehabilitate Horthy's political reputation – have described the regime as conservative, ultra-conservative, reactionary or nationalist. In some respects it represented an aristocratic ultra-conservatism: the counter-revolutionary regime, though authoritarian, was never a dictatorship; parliamentary institutions continued to function, the rule of law was never entirely abandoned. Furthermore it was based on aristocratic rule, bolstered by a restrictive franchise and the abandonment of the secret ballot in much of the countryside. In other respects it looked forward to fascism: the political representatives of radical right-wing paramilitary groups active in the White Terror represented one pillar of the counter-revolutionary regime;

anti-semitism formed an integral part of the ideology of the governing class. It justified its rule on the basis of securing revision of the Treaty of Trianon and guarding against Bolshevism.

Conclusion

Exercise

This is a convenient point to pause and consider, by way of conclusion, how the post-war situation in Hungary compares with that of Austria. From what you have read so far in these units you should be able to identify, in general terms, certain similarities and differences between the revolutionary republics. In a paragraph or two try to list their salient characteristics. ■

Specimen answer

Perhaps the most obvious conclusion you might have reached is that revolutionary situations do not necessarily produce revolutionary outcomes. In neither Austria nor Hungary was there a successful socialist revolution. In the former it was the initiative of the three major political parties – the Social Democrats, the Christian Social Party and the German Nationals – that produced the Provisional National Assembly and coalition government that supervised the transition from empire to republic. In this drama the Social Democrats performed a supporting role; both script and direction were supplied by the bourgeois parties. In Hungary, however, the collapse of the monarchy produced a weak democratic government sandwiched between the forces of socialist revolution and counter-revolution. Socialist revolution failed because communism could not extend its support beyond its immediate working-class constituency. Its collapse resulted in victory for a violent counter-revolutionary movement that constrained even modest democratization and closed the door on social change.

Indeed not only in Hungary but also in Austria the balance of forces was against socialist revolution. In a part of the world that was still agrarian in character, the attitude of the peasants was decisive; without their co-operation the revolution could be starved into submission. In both countries the urban working class supplied too narrow a social base for socialism. The fate of the revolution depended upon the countryside. Austrian social democracy recognized as much; Hungarian communism was more adventurous. Inspired by the prospect of world revolution, it cast caution to the winds. Never knowing what Stalin knew, it plunged into collectivization without cadres. The revolution was doomed from the start. □

Peasants and workers, however, were not the sole source of revolutionary enthusiasm. In both countries returning soldiers performed a permanent part in the radicalizing process. Indeed, at the outset the Party of Communists in Hungary was little more than an ex-servicemen's association. 'In its early stages', wrote Franz Borkenau in 1939, 'the communist movement in Hungary was not proletarian in character. Its mainstay was the soldiers in demobilization, of which at least a considerable part were peasants' (*World Communism*, 1971 edition). However, neither Austrian social democracy nor Hungarian communism sought to load ex-servicemen with special rewards in order to create a privileged and loyal following. The former, relying upon the combined effects of unemployment benefit and a still functioning train service, sought to rid itself of them as fast as possible. The *Volkswehr* and the soldiers' councils were, likewise, thought of as instruments of order. The Hungarian Communists, whose need to arm the revolution was even greater, also failed to exploit the full potential inherent in the available supply of nationalist-minded land-hungry soldiers. The Communists were almost as keen as the Austrian Social Democrats to marginalize the ex-service element. Kun, who for months had encouraged radical veterans to press for back pay of 5,400 kronen, subsequently told representatives who arrived at his commissariat 'to get out ... or otherwise you'll get 5,400 machine-gun bullets in your head'.

Neither the *Volkswehr* nor the Red Army could, in any case, absorb the socially uprooted and *déclassé* elements created by the victories of the Entente, who quickly found fellowship among the opponents of the left. In both countries defeat and demobilization produced a massive dislocation in the bourgeois class and status order; inflation and insecurity, the rise of organized labour, national territorial losses, and the loss of place and position, radicalized the middle classes. In dualist Hungary, for example, there developed a vociferous anti-semitism comparable with that of pre-war Vienna, where Jews had long been perceived as competitors by businessmen as well as by the professional middle classes. Antagonisms of this sort narrowed further support for socialism and in post-war Hungary formed one of the bedrocks of counter-revolutionary ideology. The Jews found themselves blamed for Bolshevism and for the dismemberment of historic Hungary. Consequently Hungary's Jews were actively discriminated against from the very beginning of the Horthy regime. In both countries, however, middle-class anti-semitism was to form the background to the political success of radical right-wing movements in the interwar years.

The international situation was not propitious. From the outset the success of the Hungarian Revolution hinged upon support from Soviet Russia and the spread of revolution in central Europe. It was soon clear that the hinge had stuck fast. For Austrian social democracy the Entente's embargo on Austrian-German unification closed the democratic route to socialism without making Bolshevism seem a more viable or attractive option. Quite simply, the precariousness of Vienna's food supply precluded any move towards a Soviet-style regime. Soviet Russia, furthermore, was not in a position to help anyone. The socialist revolution, declared the *Arbeiter Zeitung*, waited upon the rising of industrial workers in Britain and France. The editorial of 23 March 1919, two days after the proclamation of the Hungarian Soviet Republic, ran:

> True, we could dethrone the bourgeoisie of our country ... a few battalions would suffice. But in regard to the Entente bourgeoisie, we are chained in a manner quite different from that of the Hungarian proletariat. Dictatorship of the proletariat here would be equivalent to a provocation and a declaration of war. The Hungarians advise us ... to link up with Moscow; but Moscow is far away, the Soviet armies are still more than 1000km from us ... Today we are powerless; but when the proletariat of the Entente countries rise against their bourgeoisie, then, in alliance with it, we too shall break our chains.

As you will see in Book 3, Unit 14, historians are increasingly impressed by the strength and continuity of power and the resistance of the social order in modern societies to revolutionary political change. Now, it is unquestionably the case that the Austrian Revolution failed to transform the state apparatus. For example, the *Volkswehr* and the soldiers' councils, the most significant attempt to socialize the military, were quickly undermined by the bourgeois parties in the coalition government. Indeed, this was one of the issues that precipitated the break-up of the government, and the departure of the Social Democrats into permanent opposition. As to the ephemeral achievements of the Hungarian Soviet Republic, comment is superfluous.

The collapse of the monarchy produced two new states stripped of territory that were economically handicapped. Both states struggled during the interwar years with the consequences of the treaties that had settled their borders – consequences that were both economic and political. In both states socialism of either the revolutionary or reformist variety was firmly off the agenda by 1921. Defeat and revolution shaped the political settlements in both countries though in different ways. The insistence of Austria's Social Democrats on a reformist strategy and their success in marginalizing revolutionary alternatives on the left bought a degree of political stability that allowed a democracy, albeit a flawed democracy, to develop in post-war Austria. In Hungary the weakness of the Social Democrats and of the Bourgeois-democratic Revolution in the face of the revolutionary left led to the establishment of a short-lived Soviet Republic. This, in turn was succeeded by violent counter-revolution. In Austria the events that followed the collapse of the monarchy led to improvements in wages and working conditions and in welfare provision, which, if they fell short of socialism, were not negligible to those concerned. In Hungary the labour movement was marginalized during the interwar years and largely impotent in the face of an ultra-conservative regime that increasingly looked to the radical right.

9   EASTERN EUROPE'S NEW NATION STATES

Introduction

Among the most obvious of the political consequences of World War I was the reshaping of the map of central and eastern Europe. In the lands between Germany and Russia multinational empires were swept away and replaced with a variety of new nation states. In sections 7 and 8 we saw how the destruction of Austria-Hungary in the aftermath of its defeat led to the creation of two small states: an Austria shorn of territory, polarized by political conflict, deeply uncertain of its own identity and a Hungary swept by the forces of revolution and counter-revolution, governed throughout the interwar years by an aristocratic élite that sought the return of the old state that had existed before 1914.

The Austrian Republic and rump Hungary were not the only new nation states to arise out of the collapse of the multinational empires that had dominated the region during the pre-war years. Out of the ruins of the Russian Empire Finland gained its independence, Poland overcame its partition and the Baltic states – Estonia, Latvia and Lithuania – acquired statehood. Out of Austria-Hungary two entirely new multinational states were born. Czechoslovakia emerged, unifying the north Slavs of the vanished monarchy in a new state governed from Prague. The South Slavs of the monarchy – Croats, Slovenes and Bosnians – were unified with the Serbs in the Kingdom of Yugoslavia.

The Slavs of Austria-Hungary, long denied real national self-determination under the monarchy, were not the only ones to gain from its break-up. Multinational Transylvania, with its mixed population of Romanians, Hungarians and Germans, was transferred from Hungary to Romania. This allowed Romanian political élites to realize their dream of a Greater Romania, at the cost of considerable antagonism with their Hungarian neighbours.

In this section we will examine the creation of the most important of these nation states: Poland in the north, and Czechoslovakia and Yugoslavia in the centre and the south. We will pay particular attention to notions of war, nationalism and revolution and ask how far these factors shaped the creation of these states and the internal political settlements within their borders. We will also consider some of the debates about these states and their origins and look at how they have been shaped by subsequent political changes in east-central Europe.

Exercise   By way of an introduction think carefully about all you have read in sections 1–8 concerning revolution and the collapse of the Russian Empire and Austria-Hungary. Think about how the creation of the new nation states relates to the themes of war and revolution. ■

Specimen answer   Your conclusions will be provisional, of course. You might have noted that the very collapse of multinational empires and their replacement by entirely new nation states was a revolutionary change in itself. The political authority of the imperial states collapsed as the result of defeat in war, and they were replaced by new institutions created by insurgent groups with their own political programmes. You will remember that in section 7 we drew attention to the fact that 'Poles, Czechs, Hungarians, Serbs, Slovenes, Croatians – all experienced national and political revolution at the end of World War I'. You may have noticed that some of the states were not entirely new. Independent Serbia formed the basis for Yugoslavia, though the extent to which Yugoslavia was, or should have been, simply an extension of Serbia has provoked conflict right up until the present day. □

For now I want to turn back to the notion of national and political revolutions. The creation of these states has been seen as the product of national awakening. Self-aware nations were trapped in the rigid political framework of multinational empires; World War I and its aftermath generated the political conditions that allowed these nations to achieve statehood. Commentators like R. W. Seton-Watson, who wrote on the region during the interwar period and World War II, adopted this perspective. His *A History of the Czechs and Slovaks* (1943) is an example of these kinds of argument: tracing the history of the Czechoslovak nation deep into the pre-modern period, he portrayed the state – dismembered by Hitler in 1938 – as the product of centuries of North Slav history.

These views were attacked during the interwar years by historians and commentators who supported territorial revision and believed that the new states were merely the product of cynical diplomacy. They argued that the new states created at the end of World War I were based on ignorance, on the part of peacemakers, of the tiers of history that bound territories together. Often such arguments were marshalled to support the goals of states whose leaders believed they had been wronged by the post-war peace treaties. Pro-Hungarian historian C. A. Macartney in *Hungary and her Successors: The Treaty of Trianon and its Consequences* (1937) assembled an impressive amount of statistical and other evidence to support his claim that Hungary's post World War I borders, and by implication the creation and extension of the states around it, were merely the product of cynical diplomacy conducted without regard to history or to the aspirations of the populations concerned.

The debate, though now sixty years old, is one with contemporary relevance. With the interventions of Hitler between 1938 and 1941, those of Stalin between 1939 and 1945, and the upheaval in 1991–3 with the collapse of communism, the borders established in the region at the end of World War I crumbled and shifted, bringing dire consequences for many of those affected. It is important to ask how far the creation of new states was supported by genuine national feeling among their populations, and how far they were the result of skilful diplomacy by nationalist politicians and intellectuals.

With the collapse of communism in 1989, the break-up of Czechoslovakia in 1993, and the bloody Yugoslav Civil War that has rumbled since 1991, there has been renewed interest in the relationship between state and nation in the countries created at the end of World War I. Historians have increasingly sought to examine the problems faced by the new nation states in governing the multi-ethnic patchwork that is eastern Europe. Iván T. Berend in his *Decades of Crisis: Central and Eastern Europe before World War II* (1998) argues that the new nation states of the post World War I period were the product of 'belated national revolutions' that were not only belated but incomplete. Others have gone further, arguing that the consequences of World War I and the creation of new nation states have caused much of the region's subsequent instability. As historian Charles Ingrao has commented:

> Given the region's complex ethnic demography, the decision to replace a multinational entity with nation states actually worsened what had been reasonably tolerable interethnic tension ... it was simply impossible to create a system of geographically contiguous, ethnically homogeneous political entities.
>
> (Ingrao, *Ten Untaught Lessons about Central Europe*, 1996, pp.8–9)

The debate about the degree to which the creation of new nation states was the product of national revolution or national awakening is one with contemporary relevance. Some of the following cases explore these themes more completely than do others. I will start by looking at Poland, and then shift my attention to Czechoslovakia and Yugoslavia.

Poland

Poland had not enjoyed statehood since the late eighteenth century. It was partitioned three times, in 1772, 1793 and 1795. The south of the country – Galicia – was part of Austria-Hungary; the west, stretching from Danzig (Gdansk) to Poznan, was part of the German Empire; the east of the country, stretching from west of Warsaw almost to Kiev, know as Congress Poland, was part of the Russian Empire. The outbreak of war in 1914 represented both considerable danger and an opportunity for Poland; it was partitioned by combatant powers who faced each other across its territory. While the war threatened to draw Polish civilians directly into conflict, the instability it created raised the possibility of Polish statehood. Pan-Polish parties had become active in the decades immediately before World War I. They had organized themselves around the twin poles of nationalism and socialism. The right-of-centre National Democrats under Roman Dmowski represented one of these tendencies. A nationalist party, it supported an independent Polish state and assimilation for minorities within its borders. The party was profoundly anti-semitic; it regarded the country's substantial Jewish population as an element that had hindered the development of national consciousness. The other important tendency was represented by the left and particularly by the Polish Socialist Party. The Socialists were themselves divided into those who gave precedence to national, Polish goals, and those who stressed the internationalist goals of socialism and revolution. Both groupings were to play a central role in the making of the new Poland.

Polish politicians sought almost immediately to exploit the situation created by the outbreak of war. Józef Piłsudski, a central figure on the national wing of the Socialist Party, organized a group of pro-Polish fighters who, with tacit support from Austria-Hungary, entered Congress Poland with the intention of provoking an uprising against Russian rule. The venture failed because of suspicion of Pilsudski's socialism among the Poles living in Congress Poland, and distrust of a figure supported, if only tacitly, by the Central Powers. The National Democrats – though they distrusted Piłsudski – sought a promise from Germany and Austria-Hungary of an independent Poland, if only in Congress Poland, in exchange for the creation of Polish units that would fight with the central powers. Only vague statements of support were forthcoming from Austria and little change of policy was visible in German Poland. A Polish National Committee was formed in Austrian Galicia, though without the support of the National Democrats, and Polish legions were created that operated within the Austro-Hungarian army.

At the outbreak of war, faced with the early expeditions of Piłsudski, the Russians attempted to head off rebellion in Congress Poland by issuing a manifesto for the Poles. They expressed support for a united Poland which, though ruled by the Russian Tsar, would enjoy substantial linguistic, cultural and political autonomy. The National Democrats and Dmowski regarded an alliance with the Russians as the best route to full independence; indeed Dmowski saw the unification of Poland under Russian rule as a necessary first step to independence. Consequently the National Democrats and their allies founded a rival Polish National Committee in Warsaw that explicitly rejected the vague promises made to the Poles by Austria-Hungary.

This political balance was totally transformed by the German offensive against Russia in 1915. Around two-thirds of Poland was occupied by Germany, the other third by Austria-Hungary. In German-occupied Poland industry was subordinated to the demands of the German war economy, living standards fell, and discontent grew. The occupation by Austria-Hungary was more benign as the Austro-Hungarian authorities introduced to their newly occupied territories the institutions of government that had already existed in Galicia. Plans were drawn up and discussed in both Berlin and Vienna to create pan-Polish political institutions. They agreed to establish a Provisional Council of State, yet they went no further. The plans of the occupying powers foundered on conflict between Germany and Austria-Hungary over which of the two states would enjoy hegemony over any new Polish kingdom.

By the end of 1916 war had achieved little for the Poles. The Russians had promised the unification of Polish territories but not their independence, while the Central Powers promised nothing. In any case, the Russians no longer controlled any Polish territory and their promises were contingent on their victory in war. The prospects for Polish independence were decisively transformed by revolution in Russia in February 1917. The Provisional Government in St Petersburg called for 'the creation of an independent Polish state, comprised of all the lands in which the Polish people constitute a majority of the population', because this 'would be a reliable guarantee for a lasting peace in the new Europe of the future' (quoted in Piotr S. Wandycz *The Lands of Partitioned Poland*, 1974, p.355). Many Polish leaders were suspicious of Russian intentions, realizing, as Lenin did, that a small, newly independent Poland and the Russian state would be far from equal partners. All were aware that at this stage in the war Russia was in no position to deliver on its promise. Events in Russia shifted the attitude of Piłsudski and his allies and led to a radicalization of Polish opinion within the German-occupied territories. The issue came to a head when in late spring 1917 most of the membership of two brigades of the German-directed Polish army refused to take an oath of allegiance to anything other than the Polish nation. Repression followed, the Provisional Council of State collapsed, and Piłsudski was imprisoned. Fearing the outbreak of widespread political unrest, the occupation authorities established a Polish national kingdom headed in the interim by three Regents and a Council of State. This regency was supported by conservative forces and the Socialists were forced to the margins of political life in occupied Poland.

Radicalized national sentiment in occupied Poland was far from pacified, however, though it had to wait until the end of the war to find expression. This sentiment was fuelled by anger at concessions made to the Ukrainians during the negotiation of the Treaty of Brest-Litovsk in 1918, when they were awarded much of Eastern Galicia. The fact that the Poles were not even represented at the negotiation of the treaty fuelled national sentiment in Poland itself. By the summer of 1918 the Socialists had resorted to armed, underground resistance to German rule in Poland.

Rebellion in the German-occupied territories came in October 1918. The regency asserted its independence from Berlin, dissolving the Council of State and declaring a free, independent Poland. Despite initial Socialist opposition Piłsudski, still imprisoned in Germany, was named Minister of War, and the Polish army was transferred to the control of a new Polish government. In Austrian-occupied Poland the collapse of the central powers was met with a similar revolt. A Liquidation Commission was set up in Cracow, capital of Austrian Galicia, to break ties with Austria-Hungary and prepare for incorporation into a new Polish state. By November the movement had become more radical. Left-wing parties led by the Socialists refused to accept the regency and instead proclaimed a Polish Peoples' Republic in Lublin on 7 November. The assertiveness of the Polish left was accompanied by a wave of strikes and the formation of workers' councils across much of the country. National revolution threatened to turn to social revolution.

Social revolution was averted with the return of Piłsudski from prison in Germany on 10 November. Faced with mounting chaos, the three competing political authorities in Poland – the Lublin government, the Liquidation Committee in Cracow, and the regency government in Warsaw – all decided to recognize Piłsudski. A considerable amount of power and of hope was concentrated in one man in November 1918. Roman Dmowski, who had been in the United States, returned to Poland on 19 November, insisting on his right to form a government. Piłsudski, who saw himself only as a temporary head of state, brokered an agreement on the formation of a government, which took office in January 1919.

Exercise   Going back to the definitions of revolution advanced in earlier sections, how far do you think that the creation of an independent Poland represented a national revolution? ■

Specimen answer   Political forces advocating an independent state were able actively to seize power after occupying forces were defeated in war. If we go back to the definition of revolution advanced in section 1, then events in Poland during autumn 1918 clearly match parts 1 and 2 of that definition. However, it remains to be seen whether the sovereign power of the state was successfully reconstituted – that conclusion can only be reached after a discussion of the building of the Polish state. It is important, however, not to confuse national revolution with social revolution. Though the actions of the Lublin government threatened social revolution, this clearly did not occur in the Polish case. □

The achievement of independence was far from the end of the story, however. The new Polish state was left with no clearly defined borders, no meaningful apparatus of government and no real monopoly of violence. The question of the boundaries of the new Poland went to the heart of what the new state should be. Historic Poland was a multi-ethnic patchwork, and the new Poland that would emerge from treaty and war between 1918 and 1922 would not be entirely ethnically Polish. Indeed, in 1921 only 69.2 per cent of the population of the new state declared themselves to be ethnically Polish. Of the country's 27.2 million inhabitants, there were reckoned to be almost 6 million ethnic Ukrainians and 1.1 million ethnic Germans. This is not to mention the nearly 3 million Jews that lived in interwar Poland – excluded from mainstream Polish culture by a mixture of Polish anti-semitism and a desire to preserve their own Yiddish culture.

Poland's national revolution uneasily confronted the multinational reality of the lands it claimed as its own. Its national project was itself built on the notion of an ethnically defined nation inhabiting an historically defined state. Because of the multi-ethnic population of historic Poland, the claims of ethnic Poles placed them in potential conflict with other ethnic groups. As we will see when Czechoslovakia and Yugoslavia are discussed, below, this was far from unique to Poland. In an echo of positions that were adopted elsewhere in post World War I in eastern Europe, Poland's own politicians had thought of their own solutions to the problem.

For Roman Dmowski and the National Democrats the solution was that the new Poland should be based on its eighteenth-century frontiers – in other words, it should restore historic Poland before partition. Yet Poland remained hostile to the aspirations of the national minorities within its boundaries. Dmowski's Poland would be a Poland for Poles. The duty of this new state would be to strengthen ethnic Poles within it through the creation of a Polish middle class, and to invite ethnic minorities to assimilate and thus join a united Polish nation. Others, particularly on the left, argued that the solution to the problems lay in the creation of an association of free and equal nations based on tight, ethnically defined borders. This had been implicit in the programme of the Lublin government – that the national self-determination of Poles, Ukrainians and Lithuanians be achieved and that the bases of peaceful co-existence be laid. The tensions between the historic claims of nationalist politicians and the rights of ethnic minorities to self-determination affected to some degree all the states under discussion. Many of the peacemakers at Paris envisaged a small, ethnically homogeneous Poland.

With Dmowski appointed as Poland's representative to the Paris Peace Conference, the new Polish state had decided that it wished its borders to be based on historic, rather than ethnic, principles. The Paris Peace Conference left the question of Poland's eastern borders unsettled, and as we have seen in section 1 of Units 7–10 the settlement of the country's western borders transferred areas populated by ethnic Germans to Poland. The Treaty of Versailles settled the country's western frontiers. Poznania was transferred to Poland. Danzig was to be made a free city, though the new state was to be given access to sea through the transfer of the lands around it.

The Versailles Treaty left much unresolved, however. Territorial disputes between Germany and the new Poland still existed in parts of East Prussia and Upper Silesia – under the terms of the treaty the future of these territories was to be settled by plebiscite. In July the population in East Prussia voted overwhelmingly to remain part of Germany. In Upper Silesia the requirement that the dispute be settled by plebiscite provoked a violent uprising among the Poles in August 1919. A second rising occurred in 1920, and the plebiscite went ahead in May 1921. Upper Silesia voted by 59.6 per cent to 40.4 per cent to remain with Germany, provoking a third uprising in the industrialized areas where Poles were in the majority. Silesia in the end was partitioned – Polish Upper Silesia, where a quarter of the population were ethnic Germans, was given autonomy within the new Polish state.

Though a smaller dispute with Czechoslovakia over Austrian Silesia was settled in 1920 to the advantage of Prague, the disputes over the western boundaries did not prove as difficult for the new states as did those over its eastern border. As the German Empire collapsed the Poles attempted to expand eastwards, driving into Eastern Galicia, Byelorussia, Lithuania and the Ukraine. This was motivated not only by the desire of nationalists like Dmowski to restore the boundaries of historic Poland but also by Piłsudski's intention to secure Polish independence by weakening Russia. As German power collapsed the Bolsheviks also sought to recover territory to their west, and this sowed the seeds of conflict.

The Poles and the Bolshevik forces clashed first as early as February 1919. The Poles quickly advanced deep in to Byelorussia, taking Minsk in August; they took Eastern Galicia in July 1919. The Bolsheviks, weakened by the civil war, were driven back and sought accommodation with the insurgent Polish forces, though Piłsudski's price for an agreement was too high for the Bolsheviks to accept. Polish troops attacked the Ukraine in May 1920 and swiftly took Kiev, but they were repulsed by the Soviets. The Poles quickly retreated and the Soviets sought to drive them back into Poland and use military victory to establish a Soviet Polish Republic. The Poles retreated as far as Warsaw, where they secured a dramatic victory over the Red Army in August 1920. The Soviets sued for peace, which resulted in the transfer of Eastern Galicia and the west of Byelorussia to Poland. In October 1920, despite Lithuanian protests, Vilnius was also seized and was incorporated into Poland in February 1922.

The new Polish state presided over a multi-ethnic society. In 1921, as we saw above, only 69.2 per cent of Poland's inhabitants were Polish, 14.3 per cent were ethnic Ukrainians, 7.8 per cent were Jewish, 3.9 per cent Byelorussian and another 3.9 per cent were ethnic Germans. The state was also populated by smaller numbers of ethnic Czechs, Lithuanians, Russians and Slovaks. National revolution in the Polish case was not the same as the achievement of national self-determination and, as we shall see, this was the case elsewhere in eastern Europe.

Czechoslovakia

Czechoslovakia was formed in 1918 out of several distinct territories. The first and most important were the industrially developed Czech Lands of Bohemia, Moravia and southern Silesia that formed part of Austria prior to World War I. Slovakia and Ruthenia were poorer, less industrially developed, more agricultural, and were ruled by Hungary prior to the outbreak of war in 1914.

The late nineteenth century had seen the development of a Czech national movement in the industrially developed Czech Lands, asserting Slav demands for greater participation in the Austro-Hungarian Monarchy. At its heart was the Sokol movement, a gymnastics society founded in 1862 that played the explicitly political role of spreading national awareness among Czech youth. This was paralleled by the foundation of *Národni Listý* in 1861 – a national newspaper for the Czechs that played a crucial role in promoting middle-class Czech nationalism. Among the various movements to spring out of the Czech national revival was the Czechoslovakist movement, that argued all the North Slavs in the monarchy – Slovaks and Ruthenes as well as Czechs – should be unified in one independent nation state. For much of the later nineteenth-century Czechoslovakism was a movement confined to a small group of intellectuals – only one wing of the broader Czech national movement. At this time the mainstream sought equal political and cultural rights within the framework of Austria-Hungary. Czechoslovakism was catapulted from obscurity during the early twentieth century by its leader, Tomás Masaryk. Masaryk had become Professor of Philosophy at the newly founded Czech university in Prague in 1882. In 1891 he was elected to the Austrian *Reichsrat* as an advocate of democratic Czech nationalism. During World War I he was successfully to promote his dream of an independent Czechoslovak nation state.

In 1914 public opinion in the Czech Lands was distinctly uneasy about the outbreak of war. Pan-Slav sentiment among the Czechs was strong. Czech nationalists lobbied Russian Tsar Nicholas II in the hope that an independent Kingdom of Bohemia might be brought into being by a Russian victory over Austria-Hungary. Czech soldiers deserted in significant numbers to the Russians during the first months of the war. Masaryk, however, was sceptical about the desirability of a Czech state established as a result of Russian intervention largely because he – as a democrat – was sharply critical of Tsarist autocracy. Instead, he looked to Austria-Hungary's defeat at the hands of the western powers as the source of independence. From autumn 1914 onwards he began to travel abroad to lobby the western powers to secure their support for the creation of a unified Czechoslovak state.

As a result of his activities Masaryk was forced into exile where his political collaborator, Edvard Beneš – a Prague-based Professor of Sociology – was to join him in early 1915. Masaryk and Beneš established contacts with the British and French governments to lobby for a Czechoslovak state, strengthening their position in September 1915 by creating the Czech Foreign Committee. This body gained the support of the majority of Czech emigré groups. Masaryk was able to win many of the supporters of the Foreign Committee for his more Czechoslovakist position. As a result in February 1916 it was renamed the Czechoslovak National Council and its membership was expanded to include Slovak emigré groups. Masaryk's diplomacy in western capitals paid significant dividends. By January 1917 the Allied governments' war aims included the 'liberation of Italians, of Slavs, of Romanians and of Czechoslovaks from foreign domination' (quoted in Mamatey and Luza, *A History of the Czechoslovak Republic*, p.15).

As the emigrés enjoyed diplomatic success in the west they built a military presence. From the Czech soldiers that had deserted to the Russians, Masaryk was able to form a Czech division in 1915. The Russians, however, distrusted Masaryk because of his hostility towards Tsarism, and preferred to work instead with more conservative elements in the Czech nationalist opposition. The events of 1917 were to transform the outlook for the Czechoslovak national cause. First, the Allied powers openly began to threaten the dissolution of Austria-Hungary in the event of victory. The second major shift was brought about by the fall of Tsarism in Russia. This in turn had two effects on the cause of the Czechoslovakist emigrés. The first was to remove the source of Russian hostility to Masaryk. This allowed him to organize a larger Czechoslovak division to be recruited from among prisoners of war in Russia. Secondly it allowed Czech socialists enthusiastically to support the cause of national independence. They had previously been reluctant to do so for fear of strengthening the Tsarist state and its influence in central Europe. In the summer of 1917 they submitted a resolution to the conference of the Socialist International supporting demands for the establishment of an independent Czechoslovakia. Yet the Bolshevik Revolution dashed hopes that the establishment of a Czechoslovak state could be brought about by Russian military victory. Masaryk changed tack by seeking to win President Wilson to the cause of Czechoslovak independence. In this he was aided by a conflict between the Czechoslovak army and the Bolsheviks in Siberia in May 1918. The success of the Czechoslovak army against Bolshevik forces brought the Czechoslovak cause to the attention of western governments nervous about and hostile towards the new Soviet regime. As a by-product of western preparations to intervene in Russia, the Czechoslovak National Council was recognized by France, Britain and the United States during the summer of 1918. By the summer of 1918, therefore, Masaryk had laid the diplomatic groundwork for the foundation of the Czechoslovak state.

It was not only the patient diplomacy of Beneš and Masaryk abroad that drove forward the cause of a Czechoslovak state but the growing radicalization of Slav opinion within the monarchy itself. In May 1917 Czech deputies in the Austrian *Reichsrat* called for all components of what they referred to as 'the Czechoslovak nation' to be incorporated into a Bohemian state. Within Hungary Slovak nationalists began to call for national self-determination.

As the Austro-Hungarian Monarchy collapsed during 1918 national revolution in both the Czech Lands and Slovakia accelerated. The radicalization of opinion in the Czech Lands led to the formation of a new Czechoslovak National Council in Prague in July 1918. This consisted of all the Czech political parties with the exception of the Social Democrats and the Socialists, who together founded a Socialist Council that co-operated with the National Committee. The Slovaks were unable to participate in the body because of Hungarian repression. Although there were growing signs of pro-Czechoslovakist sentiment in Slovakia the Hungarians were able to prevent the formation of a Slovak National Council during the summer, ensuring that the nationalist movement in the territory only came into being in Austria-Hungary with the collapse of the monarchy in October–November.

As Austria-Hungary fell apart the Czechoslovak National Council in Prague declared independence on 28 October. Attempts by the Austrian army to intervene to disband the council were prevented by the refusal of the Austrian troops to obey orders on 30 October. On the same day a Slovak National Council was formed and demanded the right of self-determination for the Slovaks. On the following day an agreement was concluded in Geneva between delegations of the Czechoslovak National Council in Prague and Masaryk's Paris-based emigré national council that paved the way for the establishment of Czechoslovakia. The new state would be an independent, democratic republic with Masaryk as President, Karel Kramár – head of the Prague-based Czechoslovak National Council – as Prime Minister and Edvard Beneš as Foreign Minister. It was not until the final collapse of Austria-Hungary on 12 November that the building of the new Czechoslovak state could begin. A provisional constitution was adopted on 13 November and Masaryk was elected President of the new republic on 14 November.

As in the case of Poland, the new state claimed a territory inhabited by many who were neither Czech nor Slovak. It was inhabited by 6.8 million Czechs, 3.1 million Germans, 1.9 million Slovaks, 750,000 Hungarians and 450,000 Ruthenes. Consequently, as Derek Sayer has pointed out, 'interwar Czechoslovakia was riven by fault lines of ethnicity' (Sayer, *The Coasts of Bohemia*, 1998, p.168). Masaryk was no Dmowski, however. His nationalism was a civic nationalism very much in the Wilsonian mould that stressed the democratic aspects of the philosophy of national self-determination and that accepted the rights of ethnic minorities within the borders of the state. The liberal nationalist philosophy of compromise, combined with the pursuit of social democratic policies by interwar Czechoslovak governments, undoubtedly smoothed over the 'fault lines of ethnicity' and of class identified by Derek Sayer.

That did not mean, however, that the establishment of the new state went unchallenged by some of the ethnic minorities who found themselves incorporated within it. Indeed the limits of Masaryk's politics of compromise were revealed by the fact that two ethnic groups – Germans in the Sudetenland and Hungarians in Slovakia – never truly accepted their incorporation into Czechoslovakia.

Almost as soon as Czechoslovakia was created in 1918 the state was threatened by its 3.1 million strong ethnic German minority. *Die Sudetenländer* (the Sudeten Lands) was the term used by Germans in Austria to refer to Bohemia, Moravia and Silesia. When the deputies of German-Austria constituted themselves as a Provisional National Assembly on 21 October 1918 (see sections 6 and 7) they claimed 'jurisdiction over the whole German ethnic area, particularly the Sudeten territories' (quoted in Bruegel, *Czechoslovakia Before Munich*, 1973, p.22). When the Czechoslovak National Council proclaimed Czechoslovakia on 28 October this placed the two bodies on a direct collision course. On 29 October the ethnic German Deputies in the *Reichsrat* elected from Bohemia proclaimed German Bohemia to be a province of the new German Austrian state. Local governments in German areas of southern Bohemia declared themselves part of the province of Upper Austria, while on 30 October Germans in Silesia and Moravia declared the province of Sudetenland. On 3 November ethnic Germans in southern Moravia declared themselves part of Lower Austria.

The decision of the Provisional National Assembly of Austria on 12 November to seek union with Germany increased the stakes in the growing ethnic conflict as it raised the spectre of the incorporation of a substantial part of the Czech Lands into Germany. The Czechoslovak government intervened militarily, using Czech volunteers from the ranks of the demobilizing army of Austria-Hungary. The German regions were unable to mobilize sufficient support to resist the Czechoslovaks. Austria and Germany – largely as a result of their own internal crises – refused to intervene, and the German regions were occupied by the end of November. The Austrian government protested at the occupation, though the Czechoslovak government – as a result of the skilful diplomacy of Beneš – was able to secure the support of France and the other Allied powers for the continued Czechoslovak occupation.

The Treaty of St Germain, signed in September 1919 with Austria, awarded the German-inhabited Sudeten territories to Czechoslovakia. Czechoslovakia was obliged to sign a separate treaty with the Allies in which she agreed to safeguard the rights of her 'racial, religious and linguistic minorities'. All of the major ethnic German parties who reluctantly accepted incorporation into Czechoslovakia demanded some form of regional autonomy for the German-speaking areas. The Czech parties and the leaders of the republic, including Masaryk, bluntly refused to consider German demands for any kind of political autonomy, insisting instead on a unitary state. This refusal closed the door to any kind of compromise between the ethnic Germans and the Prague-based Czechoslovak political élite.

The second threat came from the Hungarians over Slovakia. Not only was the Hungarian minority in the south of Slovakia worried at being incorporated into a new Slav state, but the revolutionary governments of Mihály Károlyi and later of Béla Kun in Hungary were themselves set on preventing this happening. As the

Slovak National Council was formed on 30 October the forces of revolution in Hungary were gathering strength. Hungarian authority collapsed in the territory over the following days, though the politically inexperienced Slovak national movement was insufficiently organized to fill the vacuum they left behind. On 4 November the Czechoslovak National Committee appointed a four-man Slovak government and sent it – with a small band of gendarmes and volunteers – to establish Czechoslovak authority in Slovakia. The new Károlyi government in Budapest viewed the loss of Slovakia with alarm, and on 11 November sent troops to drive out the Czech forces. Czechoslovak forces were driven back to the Moravian border and the Slovak National Council was disbanded by Hungarian troops. Beneš secured French support to use Allied pressure to persuade the Hungarians to withdraw and allow the Czechoslovaks to occupy Slovakia until the conclusion of the peace treaty. The situation, however, was complicated by bilateral negotiations between Milan Hodza, Czechoslovakia's representative in Budapest, and the Károlyi government. Acting without the support of Prague, Hodza concluded an agreement with the Hungarians that left the whole of southern and eastern Slovakia under the rule of Budapest. Beneš once again turned to France for diplomatic support, and Hungary was instructed to withdraw from Slovakia north of the Danube at the end of November.

During the first months of 1919 Czechoslovakia consolidated its hold over Slovakia. Large numbers of Czech gendarmes and army officials were mobilized to defend Czechoslovak rule over the territory. Public administration was reorganized, but with the appointment of only a small number of Slovaks it came to be dominated by Czechs. Attempts by Hungarian railwaymen to strike against Czechoslovak rule shook Prague's hold on Slovakia, as essential services were maintained only through the use of Czech volunteers. In March the Czechoslovak Commission of the Paris Peace Conference recommended that all of Slovakia down to the Danube be given to Czechoslovakia. In May the army of the Hungarian Soviet Republic invaded Slovakia, overrunning it and driving Czechoslovak forces out of all but a western enclave. On 25 May the short-lived Slovak Soviet Republic was established, but it collapsed when Hungarian troops withdrew in response to an Allied ultimatum on 12 June. Slovakia's status as a constituent part of Czechoslovakia was secured with the signature of the Treaty of Trianon in June 1920.

The substantial Hungarian minority in southern Slovakia, numbering some 750,000, had been incorporated into Czechoslovakia against their will. The majority were concentrated in southern Slovakia and bitterly resented the fixing of the southern border along the Danube. They represented a source of tension in the new state.

The way in which Slovakia had been incorporated into Czechoslovakia also created future problems for the republic. The Slovaks became deeply ambivalent about the Czech dominance of the state. They also opposed Masaryk's unitary conception of the state, preferring some form of autonomy for Slovakia. Though Slovaks regarded rule from Prague as infinitely preferable to rule from Budapest, these resentments were to feed movements supporting Slovak independence and autonomy during the interwar years.

Exercise   Compare the cases of Czechoslovakia and Poland. What similarities and differences do you see between the two states and their genesis? ■

Specimen answer   There are a number of obvious similarities. Both were created as the result of national revolutions that were generated by the defeat of powers in war. Both also claimed governance over territories that were inhabited by multi-ethnic populations. The incorporation of new ethnic minorities was characterized by profound conflict.

There is one obvious difference. The Polish state claimed jurisdiction over only one nation, where Czechoslovakia unified two nations – the Czechs and the Slovaks – politically. The creation of a unitary form of government in a multinational state brought problems for the future. □

The interwar years in Czechoslovakia were to be happier than those in Poland. The ethnic and class divisions in the state were smoothed over. The interwar political élite in Czechoslovakia showed an instinct for political consensus not found elsewhere in eastern Europe. Governments were formed of coalitions of either the moderate left or the moderate right. Social reforms were introduced that benefited both the Czech industrial proletariat and the agrarian poor in Slovakia and Ruthenia, thus binding them to the new state. Land was redistributed from landowners to the peasantry. In industry an eight-hour day was introduced, and comprehensive sickness and unemployment insurance formed the foundations of a welfare state. Social reform stabilized the state – this was much in evidence during industrial unrest in the Czech Lands in 1920. Educational and land reform benefited the peasantry in the poorer parts of the republic. Yet the problem of the aspirations of ethnic Germans and to some extent the Hungarians remained unsolved, leaving difficulties for the future.

Poland was much less happy. The political system was more unstable, parliament filled with a multitude of parties, and a series of fractious coalitions governed the country until 1926. Land reform was introduced but the systematic social reform of Czechoslovakia was absent. The economy was strained by the burden of post-war reconstruction, severe inflation and a German boycott of Polish goods. By April 1926 one-third of the industrial labour force was unemployed. In these circumstances, in May, Pilsudski seized power, though he did not introduce a single-party dictatorship of the kind seen in Italy or, later, in Germany. Despite this he ruled in an authoritarian fashion for the rest of the interwar period.

Yugoslavia: the Kingdom of Serbs, Croats and Slovenes

Yugoslavia was born in 1918 out of the Kingdom of Serbia and the South Slav territories of Austria-Hungary. For much of its history it has been seen as either the product of Serb victory in war, or the achievement of nationhood by the South Slavs. Due to the tragic events of the 1990s that followed the collapse of Yugoslavia in its communist incarnation, attention has focused on the divisions that plagued the new state at its very birth. If these divisions are to be understood it is nevertheless important to understand how Yugoslavs were unified into one state.

Yugoslavia was the product of the Yugoslav ideal – that is the notion that all the South Slav peoples from the Slovenes in the Alpine north to the

Macedonians and Montenegrans in the south were related and should attain statehood as part of one South Slav national state. Yugoslavia itself means land of the South Slavs. In the pre-war South Slav Lands Yugoslavism had considerable appeal, though it often meant different things to different peoples. As far as the Serbian Prime Minister at the outbreak of World War I, Nikola Pašič, was concerned it meant Serbian expansionism; all South Slavs should live under the leadership of a Serbian state. In Croatia, a constituent part of the Austro-Hungarian Monarchy and the Kingdom of Hungary, it meant something quite different. Croatia, despite the limited autonomy it had been granted by Hungary in 1868, desired union with Istria, Dalmatia and Slavonia. It sought to escape the straightjacket of Hungarian rule, believing initially that its route to freedom lay in self-government for all Slavs within the Austro-Hungarian Monarchy; later its intellectuals envisaged a union of South Slav peoples outside of the monarchy. In Bosnia-Herzegovina, under Austrian occupation from 1878, Yugoslavism made headway. Because of its delicate ethnic balance – 40 per cent were Serb, 32 per cent were Muslim Slavs, and another 20 per cent Croat – Yugoslavism provided a unifying force among a population discontented with Austrian rule. Slovenes were less enthusiastic about the incorporation into the South Slav state and instead pressed at the outbreak of war for autonomy within Austria.

The tensions in the region in which the Kingdom of Serbia sought to expand into territories, where discontented Slav populations lived under Austro-Hungarian rule, acted as the spark that ignited world war in 1914. Defeat for the Central Powers could only advance the Yugoslav idea. As it became clear that the war was not going to be over by Christmas 1914, the Serbian government began to formulate a series of positive war aims. The Serbs recognized that if they lost the war their independence was also likely to be lost, together with that of the other independent Serbian kingdom of Montenegro. However, if Serbia were to finish on the winning side, the Serbian government saw the possibility of acting in a role similar to that of the King of Piedmont in the unification of Italy; Serbia could unite the Yugoslav peoples. The Niš Declaration of 7 December 1914, approved by a recently formed coalition government, stated Serbia's aims as the 'liberation' of all Serbs, Croats and Slovenes. Nikola Pašič, the Serbian Prime Minister, began organizing propaganda in the principal Allied nations. In November he sent two Serbs to Rome to establish the 'Yugoslav Committee', which was set up to argue the case for the new state. The committee itself, however, was drawn largely from exiles from the Austro-Hungarian Empire who, while dreaming of a Yugoslav state, were suspicious of possible attempts by Serbia to dominate them. As a consequence, the relations between Pašič's government and the Yugoslav Committee became strained. It ought to be noted here that Serbia's allies were not keen on a Serbian-dominated Yugoslavia. Britain regarded Serbia as a client state of Russia and disliked the prospect of greater Russian influence in the Balkans. Russia, on the other hand, was reluctant to see the Austro-Hungarian Empire dismembered for the example it might set, and it feared that the Orthodox Church in Serbia would suffer because Croats and Slovenes were Catholics, and consequently a Yugoslav state could possibly come under Vatican and Italian influence. To complicate matters further, the Entente powers were keen to persuade Bulgaria and Italy to join the war on their side, and this meant promising both Bulgaria and Italy some of the territory coveted by 'Yugoslavia'.

The Serbian army performed creditably in the early months of the war, driving back invading forces on three occasions. The last invasion force, however, left typhus in its wake, and this immobilized the Serbs in the spring of 1915, causing an estimated 300,000 deaths in the country. The close of the year witnessed an even greater disaster. A combined Austrian and German invasion was launched, Bulgaria entered the war against Serbia, Greece reneged on treaty obligations to assist Serbia if attacked, and British and French troops at Salonika were far too few to be committed to any meaningful action on Serbia's behalf. Avoiding a pincer movement between the Austro-German and Bulgarian armies during the winter of 1915/16, the Serbian army, with thousands of refugees, retreated through the mountains of Macedonia and Albania. The survivors gathered around the government in exile in Corfu.

Occupied Serbia was divided between Austro-Hungarian and Bulgarian rule. The actions of the former were restrained, though the Austrians were determined to reap such economic benefits as they could from the occupied lands. Bulgarian rule was ferocious. The Bulgarians declared that the Serbian state had ceased to exist. They introduced their language into schools, courts, and on inscriptions. They exiled or executed Serbian clergy. They made men of military age liable to conscription in the Bulgarian army. The response was predictable: there was a massive insurrection against the Bulgarians, which was savagely suppressed.

Defeat and exile did not produce unity among the Serbs on Corfu, nor did it resolve the division between the Serbian government and the Yugoslav Committee. The Prince Regent, Alexander, was unhappy with Pašič, and both of them were concerned about the continuance of the secret society in the army that called itself 'Union or Death'. The latter problem was resolved with the arrest and execution of the society's leaders in 1917 for allegedly attempting to kill Alexander on a visit to the Salonika front. Before being shot by firing squad, Colonel Dimitrivec-Apis allegedly shouted, 'Long Live Greater Serbia! Long live Yugoslavia!' The friction between the Serbian government and the Yugoslav Committee was highlighted by the attempt to recruit volunteer units for the Serbian army from Serbs, Croats and Slovenes who had been captured by the Russians while fighting in the Austro-Hungarian army. Serbian officers sent by the Corfu government to command the volunteers appear to have alienated non-Serbs. The February/March Revolution in Russia exacerbated the problem when some of the volunteers and their officers demanded a committee to participate in the command of the corps. Some of the volunteers also demanded that they be known as the Yugoslav Volunteer Corps, that they carry Yugoslav rather than Serbian flags, and that Croats and Slovenes serve in different units from the Serbs. The squabbling led to a departure from the volunteers of about 10,000 of the 30,0000 who had been recruited. In spite of requests from Pašič's government, the Yugoslav Committee was not inclined to intervene to restore order. Difficulties flared again when, in June 1918, the Allies recognized the right to independence of the Poles and the Czechs; the Yugoslav Committee demanded similar recognition, much to Pašič's annoyance.

During the war pro-Yugoslav feeling grew in those territories that formed part of Austria-Hungary. In Croatia the political establishment fell behind the

Yugoslav political project in 1917. The *Ban*, or Governor, of Croatia, Anton Mihailovic, and the leader of the Croatian Peasants' Party, Stjepan Radic, swung behind the Yugoslav idea. Even in Slovenia, which had hitherto been lukewarm about a union of South Slavs, there was a groundswell of opinion in favour of unity. Behind the radicalization of Slav political forces in Austria-Hungary lay the radicalization of society. In 1917 peasants in these territories had begun to avoid army service, or to desert, taking refuge in the woods in large numbers. As the war drew to its close more deserters, returned prisoners of war, and returning soldiers joined the *zeleni kader* (Green Cadres), described by David Englander in section 6 above. As far as these were concerned, the collapse of the old order meant an opportunity of land redistribution; it also meant an opportunity for retribution against rich merchants and big landowners. A very high percentage of the landowners employing Orthodox Serbs and Catholic Croats were Muslims, which gave the uprisings of the Green Cadres a religious character. Some of the cadres also claimed affinity with the Bolsheviks, though as David Englander points out, it is difficult to be sure exactly what this may have meant. As the Habsburg Monarchy crumbled in October 1918 the Green Cadres remained active in the countryside, worker and peasant protest grew and the Italian armies advanced. In the South Slav Lands of the Austro-Hungarian Monarchy an atmosphere of near social revolution reigned.

In the hope of establishing a new and stable kingdom out of the wreckage, a National Council was established in Zagreb in October 1918. When the Imperial Government asked for an armistice it handed the local authority over to the council, which, in turn, proclaimed a new state of Croats, Serbs and Slovenes. It also organized a national guard and proclaimed martial law, neither of which could stop the activities of the Green Cadres. Indeed, the national guard itself often perpetrated crimes against the unfortunate Muslim landowners. Units of ex-prisoners of war were also hastily organized to oppose Italian troops marching into Dalmatia. In the midst of the internal chaos the National Council opened negotiations with the Serbian government and the Yugoslav Committee in Geneva. At the same time Serbian units, fighting their way into their native country, began taking Yugoslav names. On 1 December 1918, following an invitation from the National Council in Zagreb, Prince Alexander proclaimed an Act of Union and assumed the position of Regent of the Kingdom of Serbs, Croats and Slovenes (the title Kingdom of Yugoslavia was not finally adopted until 1929).

For the first year of its existence the new kingdom was run by a Provisional Government and provisional legislature based on a union of the old Serbian parliament, the National Council and regional representatives. No party had an overall majority; indeed, there was a plethora of political groupings, most of them with a strong base in one of the constituent territories. The first truly Yugoslav party was the Democratic Party, established by the merging of several groups from Serbia and the Habsburg Lands; essentially it was liberal and progressive. To the right of the Democrats was Pašič's Serbian Radical Party, which had a firm power-base in Serbia, notably among the peasants, but which also drew support from some in the old Habsburg Lands. Squabbling among different groups on the left led to the creation of the Socialist Workers' Party of Yugoslavia (Communist) in April 1919 and ultimately to the Communist Party of Yugoslavia in June the following year. Large numbers of Yugoslav Communists had experience of revolution in Russia (20,000 of the 50,000 foreign troops in the Red Army were ex-Austro-Hungarian prisoners of war of Croat, Slovene or Serbian origin) and in Hungary; these formed a notably radical element within the party. Most notable among the remaining groups was the Croatian Peasant Party, which was suspicious of what it considered to be Serbian centralization and which hoped for a degree of dualism within the new state.

Exercise Take a little while to think about how the formation of Yugoslavia compares to that of Poland and Czechoslovakia. Jot down some similarities and differences between Yugoslavia and the other two cases. ∎

Specimen answer The most obvious similarity is with Czechoslovakia. United in one state were several different Slav peoples who did not necessarily share the same historical background or culture.

The most obvious difference between Yugoslavia and the other two countries is that Yugoslavia was created as a result of the union of former territories of Austria-Hungary and Serbia. Prior to 1914 Serbia had been an independent state. It had an army and a government bureaucracy, and as such it was well placed to demand a leading role in the new Yugoslavia, something that could only cause tensions in the future. □

Tensions around perceived Serbian centralization proved to be the Achilles' heel of the new state. The Serbs conceived of Yugoslavia as a unitary state. In the absence of real alternatives it was Serb models of public administration that were developed across its territory. Many Serbs and Serb politicians in particular saw the new Yugoslavia as essentially a greater Serbia – they justified this by stating that they had freed other South Slav peoples through war. The Yugoslav army was constituted as a Serb-dominated political force; Croat officers had to apply for their position in the new army, while Serb officers did not. Serb centralism provoked considerable resentment in Muslim regions such as Bosnia-Herzegovina and in non-Slav regions which bore the brunt of policies of Serbianization, such as Kosovo, with its substantial population of ethnic Albanians. In Croatia resentment contributed to the growth of political forces that eventually destroyed democracy in the new Yugoslavia in 1929. From that date on, Yugoslavia was ruled by royal dictatorship. Increasingly the Croats came to feel that they had exchanged limited autonomy within Hungary for subjection in a greater Serb state. Such sentiment was to fuel considerable political instability during the 1920s and 1930s.

10 SOME BROAD CONCLUSIONS

Now comes the problem of trying to draw together some threads and suggest some conclusions. Ignoring the Balkan countries for the moment, World War I began with four empires in east and central Europe, and when the fighting finally ended there were more than twice as many republics covering the same territory – Austria, Czechoslovakia, Estonia, Finland, Germany, Hungary, Latvia, Lithuania, Poland, Turkey and the USSR. In addition, a few small republics like Armenia and the Ukraine had come and gone. In the Balkans the tradition of the victors seizing tracts of land from the vanquished was continued. The scale of the changes in central and eastern Europe can be grasped if you compare maps of Europe in 1914 with the Europe that emerged from the war.

Initially these new republics prided themselves on their liberal constitutions. Hindsight, in the shape of our knowledge of subsequent developments in Germany and the USSR, easily obscures what in 1919 must have looked like the triumph of nineteenth-century liberalism over the old authoritarianism, and this, in itself, might be considered a 'revolution'. '[The] Paris peace settlement saw parliamentary democracy enthroned across Europe', writes Mark Mazower:

> A belt of democracies – stretching from the Baltic Sea down through Germany and Poland to the Balkans – was equipped with new constitutions drawn up according to the most up-to-date liberal principles. British scholar James Bryce, in his 1921 classic *Modern Democracies*, talked about the 'universal acceptance of democracy as the normal and natural form of government'.

> (Mazower, *Dark Continent: Europe's Twentieth Century*, 1998, p.2)

As we now know, however, the triumph was short-lived and a new kind of authoritarianism came to dominate central and southern Europe when, arguably, liberal democracy failed to deliver prosperity. The conflict between constitutional liberalism and populist authoritarianism is an undercurrent in much of what follows in this course, but here it rather deflects us from the events and processes which were most apparent as revolutions in the aftermath of World War I.

The revolutions which swept away the empires in the aftermath of World War I were, in many ways, very different from each other. No one doubts that there was a revolution in Russia, thought the word is used very loosely, so that we can read of the February Revolution followed by the October Revolution, but also have the two events conflated in *the* Russian Revolution in 1917. Whether the revolution in Germany was the sailors' uprising in Kiel, the abdication of the Kaiser and the declaration of the republic, the Spartacist uprising, or a mixture of all of these events (and more) is not always clear in some history books. As you have seen from section 7 above, some historians deny that the term revolution is applicable to any events in the Austrian part of the Habsburg Empire.

The definition of revolution with which these units began does enable us to use the term to describe similar political processes in all of the states we have examined here. As a result of the war each of the four empires witnessed:

1   a breakdown of government and particularly of the state's monopoly of armed forces; leading to

2   a struggle between different armed power blocs for control of the state;

3   finally, the new republics emerged when one of these power blocs had emerged as dominant and was able to reconstitute the sovereign power of the state. In Russia, Germany and Hungary the fiercest stage of the conflict came as a power bloc, having achieved dominance at the centre, sought to reconstitute the state at a time when its frontiers were extremely fluid.

History, of course, is not about proving our definitions and assumptions to be right, but if we can agree on this very broad pattern of political process as 'revolution' within the state were are focusing on, then we can move on to the question of the precise role of World War I in bringing about collapse in these states and in creating the committed rank and file for the subsequent 'revolutionary' conflict.

Each of the four empires suffered serious internal problems because of the war; at different times they also faced varying degrees of desertion and mutinous behaviour by their troops at, or more likely just behind, the front. But the Entente powers experienced similar problems at home – there were food shortages and industrial troubles in Britain, France and Italy both during and immediately after the war —and among their troops and seamen. The French army mutinies of 1917 were the most dramatic of the Entente's problems in this respect, but British and Italian troops also, on occasions, proved difficult and mutinous. From 1917 the general staffs and politicians of the Entente powers were expressing the same kinds of fears about Bolshevism in their armies and about anti-militarism, pacifism and socialism at home, as their counterparts in the Central Powers.

Exercise   Think back very carefully over what you have read in these units and then note down whether you believe that the troops of the Central Powers were radicalized politically by the war. ■

Specimen answer and discussion   There is little evidence to suggest that many troops became committed to revolutionary or radical party politics as a direct result of experience in the trenches. In both Russia and Austria-Hungary it appears to have been second-line or reserve troops who took a more radical stance than the front-line soldiers. These men had longer periods of idleness and, if billeted in large towns at home, they had a greater awareness of the problems and privations of civilians. The sailors of Kronstadt and Kiel were similar; they spent most of the war cooped up below decks in ports, subject to rigid discipline, without the release of going to sea or the emotional experience of enemy action. Where mutinies, the shooting of officers and desertions occurred, they appear generally to have been the product of low morale, hunger, battle fatigue and general war-weariness. □

Exercise   The German Revolution saw the creation of *Freikorps* as well as Spartacist revolutionaries. Out of about 8.5 million German soldiers demobilized in 1918–19, about 400,000 were recruited into different *Freikorps*. The following quotation is from a fairly typical historical analysis. Do you find it convincing?

> The most disastrous effect of World War I, finally, consisted of the miseducation of a whole generation toward solving its problems in a military, authoritarian manner. The war generation fought in volunteer military units (Freecorps) against Polish irregulars and domestic revolutionaries right after the war. In the 1930s they flocked to the Nazi Party, and other rightwing organisations, bringing along a whole ideology of what it meant to be a front-line soldier fighting in the trenches.

(Peter H. Merkl, *The Making of a Stormtrooper*, 1980, p.15) ■

Discussion   So the war produced a generation which was both Bolshevik and fascist? If one in twenty of the demobilized German troops went into *Freikorps*, how many of these went into the Nazi Party? And can we really start making simply causal connections between front-line soldiers and political activists? Perhaps some historians (as well as politicians and journalists) have been rather too willing to blame unpleasant post-war political behaviour on the 'war generation'. Thus all kinds of Red Guards, German *Freikorps* and Nazis, and Italian fascist *squadristi* have been labelled as somehow the products of the trenches. If Nazis and fascists made much of the supposed brotherhood of the front-line soldier, this does not mean that such a brotherhood actually forged their parties. Current research into the political attitudes of soldiers during the war, based largely on the reports of the military postal censors, does not suggest that the war politicized, let alone radicalized, front-line combatants. Rather the men who were conscripted or who volunteered to fight for their countries regarded the war as an interruption to their normal lives in which politics was significant for only a few. The French troops who mutinied in 1917 sang the *Internationale* and threatened to march on Paris; French generals and politicians feared for the state, but as one of the mutineers put it: 'If we have refused orders this is not to lead to the revolution which will be inevitable if we should continue, but to bring peace to the attention of the rulers of the state.' The generals feared that the Russians' example would infect their troops, but the French military postal censors found front-line troops writing home and abusing the Russians, since their revolution meant that there would be more German divisions available for the western front.

If problems on the home front and on the battle front were similar for both the Entente powers and the Central Powers, then the reason for the escalation of these problems into revolution may, perhaps, be found in military defeat. In the introduction to these units I quoted Hannah Arendt's 'noteworthy fact' that we do not expect states or forms of government to survive defeat in modern war. Defeat worsened the problems created by the war: it undermined the authorities' faith in themselves; it undermined the military, the last line of defence of the established order; and significantly it undermined the military in home garrisons first. None of the old regimes were physically overthrown by a massive popular insurrection directed specifically to this end. Rather the old regimes could no longer cope with serious internal emergencies, and it was this which provided the opportunity for groups and individuals, who believed in their own abilities to provide policy and leadership, to struggle for control. Yet here too we must be aware of taking a too mechanistic view of events. In Turkey, for example, on the fringe of Europe and an empire which we have not considered in these units, the military government of Enver Pasha did not survive the war, but the sultanate did, and looked like continuing. It was a new war, against the Greeks, which initiated the revolutionary changes in Turkish politics and society – and this was a war in which the Turks were victorious.

Much of the analysis of revolution has concentrated on 'forces' and 'movements' rather than on leading individual actors. Of course, popular aspirations expressed through demonstrations and 'movements' are important, and I am no advocate of a return to the 'great men of history' school, but individuals too can be important in shaping events. Alexander Kerensky was unable to establish and maintain control in Russia in the spring and summer of 1917 arguably because of his determination to continue the war in the teeth of popular hostility, and because of his inability to provide land for the peasants and food for the population as a whole. Lenin and the Bolshevik leaders rejected theory and historical inevitability when they set out to capture mass support with the slogan 'Peace, Land, Bread'. In Turkey Mustafa Kemal was cautious not to alienate supporters of the Sultan until he and the nationalists were secure and victorious; he then acted swiftly and decisively to establish a republic. It is a truism to conclude that the political system emerging from a revolution will be shaped by the leader and the group who are the most determined and totally ruthless, but who are also politically astute enough to know when to compromise. □

These units began with a discussion of the concept of revolution and the importance given to class conflict within that concept. In recent years 'gender' has become at least as important as 'class' in social history, and while no one could suggest that gender conflict/divisions/perceptions were the driving force of the revolutions studied here, the different roles of gender groups and the impact of the revolutions on gender divisions have increasingly become a focus of research.

As in Britain and France, when the men of the central and eastern European empires went to war in 1914, so women filled the gaps which they left in different industries and services. Nor was it only in factories and transport systems that women worked for the war effort, for they could also do so from their homes. In Germany, for example, there was an enormous growth in female out-work as women, working from home, produced covers for gun parts, baskets to move ammunition in the trenches, belts, gas-masks, uniforms, sandbags; membership of the Women Homeworkers' Union increased from 8,385 in 1913 to 19,644 at the beginning of 1919. A traditional workplace for women, which was also acceptable to the notion of separate spheres, was thus harnessed for the war effort. And this traditional workplace was probably also more acceptable than the factory or transport systems to women who had young children or other dependants. Yet these same women could still be militant in bread queues or over rent rises. In Russia the anger and militancy of women – some of whom were factory workers – in the Petrograd bread queues contributed to the revolutionary events at the beginning of 1917.

In Russia in the summer of 1917 the Women's Battalion of Death was formed and spearheaded an initially successful assault. The battalion was the brainchild of Maria Bochkareva, a former supervisor on factory building sites, who had successfully petitioned the Tsar for permission to fight on the outbreak of war, and who had risen to the rank of sergeant. Bochkareva envisaged her battalion as providing a model of military heroism, and insisted on the honesty and morality of her volunteers. Brusilov himself was keen to see an army based entirely on volunteers who, like these women volunteers, fought only out of patriotic duty; and he also believed that such an army would erode some of the old social division. But when the battalion marched through Petrograd it was the target for abuse and suggestive remarks; many of the troops in Brusilov's command saw the recruitment and deployment of the battalion as illustrative of the Provisional Government's desperation and some, notably Cossack units, refused to serve alongside it. Some feminists in Russia and elsewhere applauded the formation of the battalion. The Bolsheviks considered Bochkareva an enemy because of her support for the war, yet they sanctioned women in the Red Guards, as well as in the more traditional army hospital units. At the opposite extreme, a few women served with the Cheka, and were involved with its torture and sadistic killings.

Women were enfranchised, though often in limited ways, in the USSR in 1917, in Germany and Poland in 1918, in Austria and Czechoslovakia in 1919, in Hungary in 1925, in Turkey in 1930. How far this was because of a pre-war shift in attitudes, because of wartime and/or revolutionary participation, and how far because of a determination to be seen to be breaking with the past to develop self-consciously modern legislative structures is something that can be argued about. Similar developments do not have to have the same cause, and the explanations provided by those responsible for the developments in the different countries can emerge from quite different ideological bases. The constitution of the USSR, for example, declared that the franchise was only for persons living by productive labour and general utility, or for those who worked in the domestic economy and thus enabled others to engage in productive labour. In effect this meant virtually universal suffrage, though the rights of citizenship had nothing to do with a natural birthright but with relationship to the means of production.

The Bolsheviks saw themselves as creating a new society and sexual equality was an important element within this. No other country had written into its constitution or legislated for the far-reaching changes which the Bolsheviks claimed to want to effect. Yet the theorists of equality within the party, like Alexandra Kollontai, were often not understood by other members. The Women's Department of the Central Committee Secretariat (*zhenotdel*), established in 1919, was disparagingly referred to by many male Bolsheviks as the *babotdel* (from the word *baba*, a peasant wife). Many women objected to the liberal divorce laws introduced in 1918 on the grounds that these served primarily as an aid for men to shirk their responsibilities. There were fears that communal nurseries, designed to liberate women from child care, were actually intended to take their children away from them. After almost a decade of war and revolution one Russian woman worker complained that: 'Our position in many respects remains difficult and unenviable. The kitchen, children, washtubs with laundry, work in the factory – this is our world from which few have leapt to freedom' (quoted in Jane McDermid and Anna Hillyar, *Women and Work in Russia 1880–1930*, 1998, p.182).

References

Arendt, H. (1963) *On Revolution*, Penguin.

Arshinov, P. (1974) *History of the Makhnovist Movement (1918–1921)*, Black and Red (first pubd 1932 in Berlin by Russian Anarchists).

Bauer, O. (1925) *The Austrian Revolution*, trans. H. J. Stenning, Leonard Parsons.

Berend, Iván T. (1998) *Decades of Crisis: Central and Eastern Europe before World War II*, University of California Press.

Bessel, R. (1993) *Germany After the First World War*, Clarendon Press.

Borkeneau, F. (1971) *World Communism*, University of Michigan Press (first pubd 1939).

Brinton, C. (1965) *The Anatomy of Revolution*, Vintage Books (revised and expanded edn).

Bruegel, J. W. (1973) *Czechoslovakia before Munich: The German Minority Problem and British Appeasement Policy*, Cambridge University Press.

Carsten, F. L. (1972) *Revolution in Central Europe 1914–18*, Temple.

Chamberlain, W. H. (1965) *The Russian Revolution*, 2 vols, Grosset and Dunlop (revised edn).

Deak, I. (1977) 'Shades of 1848: war, revolution and nationality conflict in Austria-Hungary 1914–1920', in C. L. Bertkely (ed.) *Revolutionary Situations in Europe 1917–1922*, Interuniversity Centre for European Studies, Quebec, pp.87–94.

Ellis, J. (1973) *Armies in Revolution*, Croom Helm.

Feldman, G. D. (1966) *Army, Industry and Labor in Germany 1914–1918*, Princeton University Press.

Ferro, M. (1972) *The Russian Revolution of February 1917*, Routledge and Kegan Paul.

Ferro, M. (1980) *October 1917*, Routledge and Kegan Paul.

Figes, O. (1996) *A People's Tragedy: The Russian Revolution 1891–1924*, Jonathan Cape.

Hardach, G. (1977) *The First World War 1914–1918*, Penguin.

Herwig, H. H. (1997) *The First World War: Austria and Germany*, Arnold.

Hobsbawm, E. J. (1971) *Primitive Rebels*, Manchester University Press.

Ingrao, Charles (1996) *Ten Untaught Lessons about Central Europe – An Historical Perspective*, Centre for Austrian Studies occasional paper, Minneapolis.

Jaszi, O. (1929) *The Dissolution of the Habsburg Monarchy*, Chicago University Press.

Jelavich, Barbara (1987) *Modern Austria: Empire and Republic 1815–1986*, Cambridge University Press.

Kitchen, M. (1980) *The Coming of Austrian Fascism*, Croom Helm.

Koenker, D. (1976) 'Moscow workers in 1917', unpublished PhD thesis, University of Michigan.

Lenin, V. I. (1964) 'Opportunism and the collapse of the Second International', in *Collected Works*, vol. 22, Lawrence and Wishart (first pubd 1915).

Macartney, C. A. (1929) *The Social Revolution in Austria*, Cambridge University Press.

Macartney, C. A. (1937) *Hungary and her Successors: The Treaty of Trianon and its Consequences, 1919–1937*, Oxford University Press.

Mamatey, Victor S. and Luža, Radomír (1973) *A History of the Czechoslovak Republic 1918–1948*, Princeton University Press.

Mazower, M. (1998) *Dark Continent: Europe's Twentieth Century*, Allen Lane.

McDermid, J. and Hillyer, A. (1998) *Women and Work in Russia 1880–1930: A Study in Continuity through Change*, Longman.

Merkl, P. H. (1980) *The Making of a Stormtrooper*, Princeton University Press.

Moeller, R. G. (1981) 'Dimensions of social conflict in the Great War: the view from the German countryside', *Central European History*, vol. 14.

Pinson, K. S. (1966) *Modern Germany: Its History and Civilization*, Macmillan (revised edn).

Raskolnikov, F. F. (1982) *Kronstadt and Petrograd in 1917*, New Park Publications, London (first pubd in the USSR 1925).

Redilich, J. (1932) *Austrian War Government*, Yale University Press.

Roberts, H. L. (1951) *Rumania: Political Problems of an Agrarian State*, Yale University Press.

Romsics, Ignác (1999) *Magyarország Története a XX. Században*, Osiris Kiadó, Budapest.

Sayer, Derek (1998) *The Coasts of Bohemia: A Czech History*, Princeton University Press.

Seton-Watson, R. W. (1943) *A History of the Czechs and Slovaks,* Hutchinson.

Spence, R. B. (1981) 'Yugoslavia, the Austro-Hungarian army and the First World War', unpublished PhD thesis, University of Michigan.

Stone, N. (1975) *The Eastern Front 1914–1917*, Hodder and Stoughton.

Taylor, A. J. P. (1984) *The Habsburg Monarchy*, Hamish Hamilton.

Tobin, E. H. (1985) 'War and the working class: the case of Düsseldorf 1914–18', *Central European History*, vol. 18.

Vernadsky, G. *et al.* (eds) (1972) *A Source Book for Russian History from Early Times to 1917*, Yale University Press.

Wall, R. and Winter, J. M. (eds) (1988) *The Upheaval of War*, Cambridge University Press.

Wandycz, Piotr S. (1974) *The Lands of Partitioned Poland, 1795–1918: A History of East Central Europe*, vol. 7, University of Washington Press.

Wegs, J. R. (1970) 'Austrian economic mobilization during World War I, with particular emphasis on heavy industry', unpublished PhD thesis, University of Illinois.

Wegs, J. R. (1976/7) 'The marshalling of copper: an index of Austro-Hungarian economic mobilization during World War I', *Austrian History Yearbook*, vol. 12–13.

Zeman, Z. A. B. (1961) *The Break-up of the Habsburg Empire 1914–1918: A Study in National and Social Revolution*, Oxford University Press.

Further reading

Berend, Iván T. (1998) *Decades of Crisis: Central and Eastern Europe before World War II*, University of California Press.

Bessel, R. (1993) *Germany After the First World War*, Clarendon Press.

Carsten, F. L. (1972) *Revolution in Central Europe 1914–18*, Temple.

Crampton, R. J. (1994) *Eastern Europe in the Twentieth Century*, Routledge.

Davies, Norman (1981) *God's Playground. A History of Poland: 1795 to the Present*, vol. 2, Clarendon Press.

Feldman, G. D. (1966) *Army, Industry and Labor in Germany 1914–1918*, Princeton University Press.

Figes, O. (1996) *A People's Tragedy: The Russian Revolution 1891–1924*, Jonathan Cape.

Herwig, H. H. (1997) *The First World War: Austria and Germany*, Arnold.

Jelavich, Barbara (1987) *Modern Austria: Empire and Republic 1815–1986*, Cambridge University Press.

Mazower, M. (1998) *Dark Continent: Europe's Twentieth Century*, Allen Lane.

Raleigh, D.J. (2002) *Experiencing Russia's Civil War: Politics, Society and Revolutionary Culture in Saratov, 1917–1922*, Princeton University Press.

Stone, N. (1975) *The Eastern Front 1914–1917*, Hodder and Stoughton.

Taylor, A. J. P. (1984) *The Habsburg Monarchy*, Hamish Hamilton.

Index